Recycling of Industrial Effluents

AF795600

NIPA® GENX ELECTRONIC RESOURCES & SOLUTIONS P. LTD.
New Delhi-110 034

www.nipaers.com
Browse, Search, Read & Buy...
Print Books eChapters
eBooks Publishers
Forthcoming Subject Catalogues
New Titles
Online Resources on:
✓ Current Affairs
✓ Reasoning, Logic & Aptitude
✓ Competitive Examinations
✓ English Language Lab
✓ Writing & Pronunciation Tools
✓ Personality Development
✓ Online Programmes for Professionals
✓ Interview Preparation
Pay Using
PhonePe
Google Pay
paytm
PayPal
UPI
CC Avenue

Recycling of Industrial Effluents

Dr. R. Manivanan
Assistant Research Officer
Central Water and Power Research Station
PUNE

NIPA® GENX ELECTRONIC RESOURCES & SOLUTIONS P. LTD.
New Delhi-110 034

NIPA® GENX ELECTRONIC RESOURCES & SOLUTIONS P. LTD.

101,103, Vikas Surya Plaza, CU Block
L.S.C. Market, Pitam Pura, New Delhi-110 034
Ph : +91 11 27341616, 27341717, 27341718
E-mail: newindiapublishingagency@gmail.com
web: www.nipabooks.com

For customer assistance, please contact
Phone: + 91-11-27 34 17 17
Fax: + 91-11- 27 34 16 16
E-Mail: feedbacks@nipabooks.com

ISBN: 978-81-19254-10-1

Composed and Designed by NIPA®.

Dedicated

To

My beloved Parents

(S. Ramasamy & R. Pancholai),

Wife (S. Mekala)

&

Children

(M. Swathimithran & M. Kanisumithra)

Preface

Water is an important element for life in the earth. It is an essential recurrent natural resource for environmental sustenance, agricultural productivity, industrial growth, power production and enrichment and renewal of land and air. For easy assess to the water, the first human settlements occurred along the banks of rivers and ensuing civilizations flourished in river valleys. For example, the Indian civilization of Mohanjodaro and Harappa developed in the Indus valley, the Egyptian civilization in the Nile valley, the Chinese civilization in the Yangtze valley, the Babylonian civilization between the Tigris and the Euphrates rivers, Aztec Maya and Incas civilizations in the basin of an Amazon river.

The supply of water at any given location is limited and the limits vary considerably. The unprecedented economic development, social transformation, industrial flourishment and technological improvement that have occurred in the world have been in part due to human ingenuity in providing water to various designated uses, often through well scientific and engineered strategies for usage, storing of water and transporting it. There is a direct correlation between the development of these strategies and national development, as exemplified by the grouping of nations of the world into developed countries for example USA, Britain, Japan *etc.*, developing countries like India, Sri Lanka, Pakistan etc., and under developed countries such as Kenya, Lozetho *etc.* From the middle of the nineteenth century to the beginning of twenty first century, hundreds of thousands of water resources projects, water harvesting projects, water conservation projects, water recycling projects, river linking projects, desalination projects for fresh water from sea and treatment of industrial effluents projects were developed and built throughout the world including India, primarily for the purposes of supplying water for drinking water, agricultural irrigation, hydropower generation as well as for energy production, drought amelioration, recreation, flood control, erosion, industrial uses and navigation for water resources and treatment of industrial effluents projects to control water pollution of rivers, lakes, reservoirs, coastal as well as oceans in the world. In India, combined effluent treatment plants were built in the last century. These projects were entirely funded or heavily subsidized by national governments in recognition of the crucial role that water plays in an important role in the human life.

The book contains twenty one chapters reflecting objectives on various aspects of water and forest resources, water pollutions, forest degradation, industrial pollution from them, recycling technology, bio statistics, case studies, treatment technology for industrial effluent, primary, secondary and tertiary treatment with bio reactors, trickling filters, aerators. *Chapter 2* deals with environment, sustainable environment, and carrying capacity. *Chapter 3* deals with environment verses development in India. *Chapter 4* deals with water resources in India like major river basins, fresh water resources, ground water resources, and water resource development. *Chapter 5* provides for water pollution such as surface water pollution, coastal and ocean pollution in India. *Chapter 6* elaborates forest resources like Himalayan forests, Western Ghats and Eastern Ghats. *Chapter 7* deals with forest degradation by physical, chemical, biological, Himalayan, Western and Eastern Ghats forest degradations. *Chapter 8* describes about the various industries, regions of industries and industrial effluents discharged from them with toxic materials. *Chapter 9* deals with effects of industrial pollution. *Chapter 10* includes analysis of industrial effluents with physical-chemical and biological parameters. *Chapter 11* deals with treatment of industrial effluents by primary, secondary and tertiary treatments. *Chapter 12* describes about volatile organic compounds and their treatment. *Chapter 13* deals about World Bank and Indian standards for industrial effluents. *Chapter 14* provides observation of phytosociology of biometric traits. *15th Chapter* elaborates biostatistics and its application in the field of above ground height, basal diameter and biomass of the tree species. *Chapter 16* deals with definition of recycling technology such as conservative, alternate and recent trends in the recycling technology and comparison of these technologies for the best application in respect of industrial effluents. *Chapter 17* and *18* include methods of recycling technology and its applications. *19th Chapter* deals with evopotranspiration of effluents by forest tree species. *Chapter 20* describes applications of recycling technology in the industrial process. *Chapter 21* elaborates about specific case studies for different tree species.

The book will be of great interest to research scientists, NGOs, conservators, foresters, environmental activists, industrialists, research scholars and practitioners in the field of environmental science and engineering, forest resources, water resources, hydrology, bioremediation studies of effluent treatment plant, range sciences, non-renewable energy studies and silviculture. The book will also be interest of management of industrial effluent, minimization programme of liquid waste management. Graduate and Postgraduate students as well as those wishing to conduct further research in environmental science and engineering, hydrology and water resource planning, development and management will find the book to be of value.

September, 2005 **Dr. R. Manivanan**

Acknowledgement

I wish to thank Mrs. V.M. Bendre, Director, Central Water and Power Research Station, Khadakwasla, Pune, India, Shri. C. N. Kanetkar, Joint Director, CWPRS, Pune for their permission and encouragement throughout the preparation of manuscript.

Many colleagues were good enough to send me their research publications and their contribution to this work is highly acknowledged. A good deal of tiresome labour involved in putting together the MS was shared by many friends, too numerous to be named individually, and I thank each one of them for cheerfully giving me their time. To my wife who complied the data and index, spell check, reference checks and also helped in many ways, I wish to record my grateful thanks.

I am thankful to Dr. B. M. Patil, Senior Research Officer, CWPRS, Pune. Shri. A. Yoganath, Shri. K. H. Barve and Shri. Sanjay Nath Jha, CWPRS, Pune for their help and encouragement during the period.

I also wish to take this opportunity to express my sincere appreciation to all the staff members of Mathematical Modelling Centre, CWPRS, Khadakwasla, Pune. I like to express my deep gratitude to his friend Shri. Prafull S.Barathe, for his help and assistance in providing computer facilities.

Dr. R. Manivanan

CONTENTS

1

Introduction

Water is an important element for life on the earth. It is an essential recurrent natural resource for environmental sustenance, agricultural productivity, industrial growth, power production, enrichment and renewal of land and air. For easy assess to the water, the first human settlements occurred along the banks of rivers and ensuing civilizations flourished in river valleys. For example, the Indian civilization of Mohanjodaro and Harappa developed in the Indus valley, the Egyptian civilization in the Nile valley, the Chinese civilization in the Yangtze valley, the Babylonian civilization between the Tigris and the Euphrates rivers, Aztec, Maya and Incas civilization in the basin of Amazon river.

The industrial revolution, which, began in the early 18th century in some European and Asian countries, set in the motion for new forces in the society and greatly changed the pattern of social life on the earth. Rapid industrialization and urbanization subsequently brought many changes in the environment and ecosystems in the world. India also witnessed a phenomenon of industrial development in the post independent era. The last four to five decades have witnessed population explosion and increase in the per capita consumption of food, consumer goods and utilization of natural resources. These have lead to the proportionate increase in the domestic and industrial effluent generation in India. The water pollution is continuously increasing at an alarming rate in Europe and Asia. By the end of this century. India's Population is projected to double itself from its present level. Similarly the per capita consumption of food has been estimated to increase by 40% resulting in 50 % production of industrial and domestic effluents in near future.

Apart from the quantity, there will be qualitative changes in the effluent generation which are likely to contain greater amount of oil, toxic chemicals, detergents and dyes. A large number of these compounds are non-biodegradable and are cumulative, thus rendering toxic product. Certain group of animals and plants are selective in their functions and can executive certain toxic chemicals and heavy metals. These biomes are helping more effectively on recycling of industrial effluent as well as domestic effluent management system.

In nature, there exists a balance between abiotic and biotic communities like animals and plants population, raw materials and total biomass present at any time. This balance ensures natural recycling and optimum production in naturally balanced ecosystems. The plant growth is slow, but it ensures optimum utilization of waste products and a healthy environment. The increased population and its human desire to possess all comforts and pleasures had lead to over exploitation of natural resources. The high demand of natural resources lead to the beginning of waste accumulation due to the creation of man made imbalances in the environment. The environment is to provide up to date information about important concepts in surrounding. Information is presented from an analytical, observational and multidisciplinary perspective from which we must view environmental issues in order to the study successfully.

Ministry of Environment and Forest, Government of India, NGOs, private firms, even few dwellers in the villages and towns are taking serious steps to control and minimize hazardous waste from the production centers such as industries, municipalities, urban centers, public places. It carefully controls the outfalls for deterioration to our ecosystems. The majority of our population residing in rural areas is prone to excessive use of polluted environment due to non-availability of best treatment plants which has led to health problems in the rural ecosystem. The pollutant is drained from the production centers into the natural resources such as lakes, ponds, rivers, coastal, oceans and terrestrial ecosystem lead to natural cycle and enter into the human beings. The following figure (Fig.1.1) shows cyclic processes of toxicants in the ecosystem.

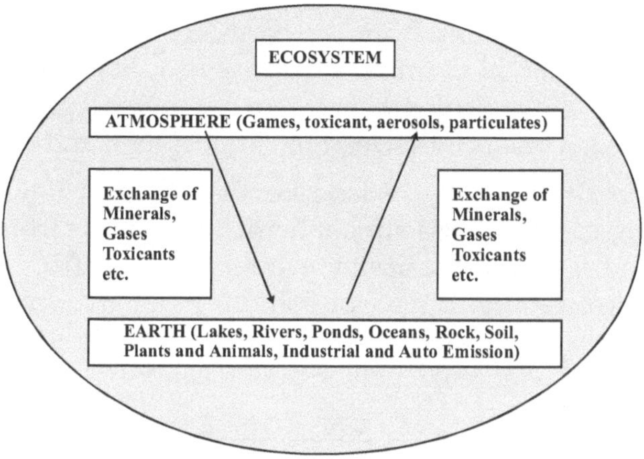

Figure 1.1: Cyclic Processes of Natural Resources in Ecosystem

1.1 General Facts About Water

World oceans cover about three fourth of our earth's surface. According to the UN estimates, the total amount of water on earth is about 1400 million cubic kilometer (m.cu.km.), which is enough to cover the earth with a layer of 3000 meter depth. However the fresh water constitutes a very small proportion of this enormous quantity. About 2.7 % of the total water available on the earth is fresh water of which about 75.2 % lies frozen in Polar regions and another 22.6 % is present as groundwater. The rest is available in ponds, lakes, rivers, atmosphere, moisture, soil and vegetation. It is effectively available for consumption while for other uses a small proportion of the quantity is available in ponds, rivers, lakes and ground water. The crisis about water resources development and management thus arises because most of the water is not available for designated use and secondly it is characterised by its highly uneven spatial distribution. Accordingly, the importance of water has been recognized and greater emphasis is being laid on its economic use and better management resulting in various river linking projects water treatment , bioremediation projects.

Water on the earth is in continous movement through the hydrological cycle. The different water sources of the earth get their water supply from precipitation, while this precipitation in itself is the evaporation from these sources. Water is lost to the atmosphere as vapour from the earth; it condenses and then precipitates back in the form of rain, snow, hail, dew, frost or sleet. This is the hydrologic cycle that continues forever thereby maintaining a balance between the atmosphere and biosphere.

The hydrological cycle describes the transport of water from ice cabs to earth and the atmosphere. It transports from ponds, rivers, lakes, seas, estuaries by evaporation and from plant by evapotranspiration form a cloud and the water droplet storing in the cloud and forming rain. The rainwater comes to the earth forming fresh water lakes, rivers, ponds and seas. This is called as water cycle (Fig.1.2).

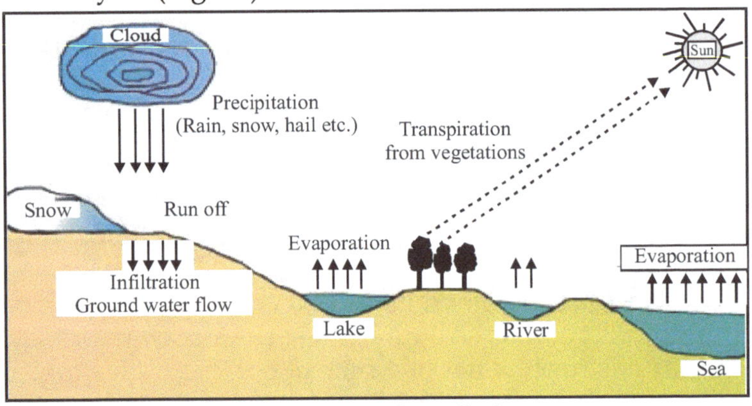

Figure 1.2: Water Cycle

The utilization of water for most of the users such as human, animal or plant involves movement of water. The dynamic and renewable nature of the water resources and the recurrent need for its utilization requires that water resources are measured in terms of its flow rates. Thus water resources have two facets. The dynamic resource, measured, as flow is more relevant for most of developmental needs. The static or fixed nature of the reserve, involving the quantity of water, the length of area of the water bodies is also relevant for some activities like irrigation, pisciculture, navigation, domestic and industrial uses.

Carbon makes up for about half of the biomass on the earth. Carbon is the dominant element in salmon, sheep, douglas fir trees, and blue bunch wheat grass. Carbon cycles exits between the atmosphere mainly in the form of carbon dioxide—and the plants and soil. Photosynthesis fixes carbon from atmospheric carbon dioxide in the form of standing plant matter. Respiration and decay at all levels releases carbon dioxide back into the atmosphere.

In brittle, seasonal-moisture environments, rapid and effective carbon cycling is often blocked. The symptoms are fuel buildup in grass, shrubs, or timber, desertification, lack of humus, organic matter, and water-holding capacity in soils, repeated hot fire and landileitis.

Carbon, and other biologically important elements such as oxygen, nitrogen, hydrogen, potassium, calcium, phosphorus, sulphur, and the trace elements, as well as water, is bank accounts for the diversity and mass of life. These elements and their combination cycles between living organisms, the soil, and sometimes the atmosphere. These cycles, like the earth's atmosphere and soil, were created by earth's biodiversity out of the earth's elements. Even some iron-ore deposits are thought to have been the result of the oxygen produced by Precambrian cyanobacteria reacting with dissolved iron in seawater. Not only the gasoline you burn, but also your pickup truck itself may owe its existence to those pioneers of photosynthesis.

Human activity greatly influences the mineral or element cycles not only on cropland but on range and forestland as well. As with the other ecosystem processes, the water cycle, solar energy flow, and community dynamics—the soil surface is the crucial interface. Where the soil surface is capped, bare, eroding, or where plant and animal residues are not being incorporated back into the soil, mineral cycling is blocked and ineffective

Conversely, concentrations of elements or their combinations, where they are not being effectively cycled, constitutes pollution. Nitrate leaching, eutrophication of lakes and streams, smoke, and massive concentrations of waste from agriculture and urban living are examples. Elements and compounds that are toxic to the life forms that cycle them—such as some heavy metals are another type of pollution.

In this century humans have engaged in large-scale systematic contributions to carbon and nitrogen cycling. With carbon, we are burning fossil carbon and adding it to the atmosphere. Worldwide desertification caused by conventional decision-making has reduced the ability of the biosphere to fix and balance atmospheric carbon.

Nitrogen is the key component of proteins which constitute much to the biological tissue. Crop yields are often limited by the lack of biologically available nitrogen. Ecologist Vaclav Smil concludes that the enormous human population increase in the industrial era was made possible by the development of nitrogen-fixing crop rotations prior to the Industrial Revolution and then by "breaking the nitrogen barrier" *via* the Haber-Bosch ammonia synthesis pioneered in Germany in 1913.

Now, Smil estimates, we are one-third synthetic. A third of the nitrogen that is such an important component of the proteins in our bodies comes from ammonia manufacturing, where inert atmospheric nitrogen is made into biologically reactive ammonia fertilizer with the help of fossil or electric energy. Often, much of this fertilizer is not cycled. Widespread leaching of fertilizer-derived nitrates down into the water table is a problem in many agricultural areas.

Effective mineral cycling requires plants and soils full of life. Plant roots recycle enormous masses of material that otherwise would leach into the water table. Deep rooted plants bring elements and combinations to the surface for subsequent use by shallower-rooted plants. Microorganisms—the bacteria, fungi, algae, protozoa, arthropods, and worms that outweigh the earth's mammals and birds by 50 to 1 break down plant and animal residues into reactive compounds (such as ammonia and urea) that growing plants use.

At the soil surface, air and water are required. Large animals help break down plant residue so that it will cover the ground, feed the microorganisms, and become part of the soil again. Animals of all types—salmon, coyotes, elephants, beetles, geese, and earthworms move and redistribute these elements and combinations, creating chaos of possibilities.

The problems that conventional management focuses on are leaching, waste pollution and toxicity, nutrient loading, erosion, sedimentation, scarcity and maldistribution of nutrients, chemical dependence, biofuel buildup, and atmospheric change. These are insoluble problems until we can see them as symptoms—of impaired mineral cycles, and of thinking that regards pollution, competition, and scarcity as fact, rather than as possible results of a process that we can guide and for which we are responsible.

Analysing the country-wise geographical area, arable land and irrigated area in the world, it is found that among the continents largest geographical area lies in the Africa which is about 23% of the world geographic area. However, Asia with only 21% of world geographical area has about 32% of world's arable land followed by North Central America having about 20% of world's arable land. Africa has only 12% of world's arable land. It has been seen that irrigated area in the world as about 18.5% of the arable land in 1994. In 1989, 63% of world's irrigated area was in Asia, whereas in 1994 this percentage has gone upto 64%. Also 37 % of arable land of Asia was irrigated in 1994. Among Asian countries, India has the largest arable land, which is close to 39% of Asia's arable land. Only United States of America has more arable land than India.

The supply of water at any given location is limited and the limits vary considerably. The unprecedented economic growth, social transformation, industrial growth and technological developments that have occurred in the world have been in due to human ingenuity in providing water to various designated users, often through well- scientific and engineered strategies for usage storing water and transporting it. There is a direct correlation between the development of these strategies and national development, as exemplified by the grouping of nations of the world into developed countries, developing countries and under developed countries. From the middle of the nineteenth century to the beginning of twenty first century, hundreds of thousands of water resources projects, water harvesting projects, water conservation projects, water recycling projects, river linking projects, desalination projects for fresh water from sea and treatment of industrial effluents projects were developed and built throughout the world, primarily for the purposes of supplying water for agricultural irrigation, hydropower generation as well as for energy production, drought amelioration, recreation, flood control, and navigation for water resources and treatment of industrial effluents projects to control water pollution of rivers, lakes, reservoirs, coastal as well as oceans in the world. In India, combined effluent treatment plants were built in the last century. These projects were entirely funded or heavily subsidized by national governments in recognition of the crucial role that water plays in an important role in the human life.

1.2 Why use wastewater for forest irrigation?

When decomposable wastes are recycled through a plantation ecosystem, the principal advantage consists of recycling exclusively outside the food chain. However, several traits of such an operation, are given below :

Ecosystem characteristics

In terms of recycling efficiency, irrigating trees are more efficient than irrigating agricultural crops or grass, because larger areas of foliage are involved in transpiration and greater amounts of perennial biomass can act as the sink for nutrients. Each year, the agricultural crops must build new foliage while growing, thus being effective processors for only part of the growing season. A hardwood forest, on the other hand, needs water continuously, as long as the main species are live. A conifer forest can recycle even longer. In addition, these forests have much greater nutrient requirements, than agricultural crops. Finally, since the root systems of forest species usually penetrates deeper than those of agricultural plants, there is less risk that either the moisture or the nutrients will escape through the root zone.

Low cost treatment

In some countries which can afford it, the cost of secondary treatment of effluent is high and increasing in both monetary and energy terms. For other countries, these costs are simply prohibitive. Thus, many countries are seeking alternative forms of treatment, such as land application methods. If applied correctly, over certain soils and crops, irrigation can be a low-cost, simple and effective means to recycle (primary treated or raw) effluent. Moreover, the sludge recycling can be organized between the rows of planted trees better than spreading it over an agricultural crop. In the forest ecosystem, sludge converts to humus very efficiently, owing to the typical conditions found at the interface forest soil-litter. In turn, the increase in humus content improves soil water relations and prevents fast infiltration of effluent, which can be a hindrance on marginal quality soils.

Safe destruction of germs

When industrial waste is recycled in the environment, pathogens can spread. Typically, the pathogen vectors can multiply only in a restricted set of favourable conditions, usually found in the digestive tract of humans and mammals groups. Thus, irrigating pasture with effluent is very risky, since thereafter parasites eggs can be ingested together with grass grazed by primary consumers. If these vectors are instead sprinkled in the atmosphere and then absorbed in the soil, they won't meet such conditions and will die and decompose. As a result, the irrigation of trees with effluent poses fewer health risks than does the irrigation of agricultural crops, golf courses and lawns.

Water conservation

Wherever a permanent or seasonal water deficit exists, water conservation is a determinant issue. Many communities, generally, capture their drinking water from large rivers, although this source can be affected by climate variations or made less desirable through contamination, especially by agricultural runoff containing fertilizers and pesticides. Almost the same restrictions apply to irrigation water for irrigation of crops. Communities must seriously consider the health hazards before they replace it with treated effluents. If tertiary treatment is not a local alternative, they will be far better off recycling the effluent through forestry irrigation. In dry and warm environments, that are densely populated and usually have few trees, irrigation with effluents may have the added value of making silviculture possible and economical. The recycling unit can even be shaped as a shelterbelt, concurrently protecting the fields against deflation or excessive evapotranspiration.

Nutrient management

The industrial effluent is a protein decomposition product and thus contains many nutrients in inorganic combinations, readily available for plant use. Secondary treated effluents are likewise loaded. Among the most important contaminants of effluents are nitrates, phosphates, sulphates which are tolerated in forest trees only up to a concentration up take capabilities. Once the effluent is land treated, they can go three places:

i. plants can strip them from soil water at rates depending on their need, and store most of them in leaves,
ii. they can be bound chemically to soil humus, and
iii. they can trickle down to groundwater.

While nitrates are mobile, the rest of the nutrients, especially phosphorus and potassium, accumulate in soil without resulting in a pollution risk.

When recycling effluents, only the first alternative is acceptable. In addition, apart of their larger leaf area, species such as poplars and willows can greatly increase their foliar nitrogen content, thus greatly enhancing the efficiency of the recycling system. More important, where land is expensive, irrigating trees can process the same amount of effluent in a smaller area than can irrigating grass, for instance. Existing research data allows for precise balances of nutrients in cropped systems, thus preventing contamination risks.

Greening

Especially in arid zones, green spaces play an important role in people's psychological health and comfort. Green spaces are also important sites in which children can learn and play. Trees represent one of the most dramatic elements of landscapes, appreciated for their differing shape and colour. However, particularly where natural vegetation is sparse, trees need appropriate water supply and protection from desiccating winds. Where fresh water is rare or is prohibitively expensive, effluents can fill this need. In addition, plantations, such as stands of fast-growing trees, greenbelts and various shelterbelts, can be established based on existing wastewater supplies.

1.3 Operational aspects

Establishment of a recycling system based on a fast growing plantation requires the following:

Recycling plantation

Poplars and willows are well-adapted tree species to climatic conditions in the temperate zone. What's more important is that, they grow quickly, produce good quality timber and tolerate floods, longer floods in the case of willows. Their timber can be used as sawlogs and pulpwood, for poplars, and as particleboards, for willows. In addition, both these species develop large foliage and have a great consumptive use, which is essential for this recycling system. Moreover, fertilization studies indicate that their foliar nitrogen content can increase from about 1.5% to up to over 7%, thus being able to recycle large amounts of nitrogen. Through its ability to stand long periods of waterlogging and heavy soils with anaerobic conditions, willow opens the possibility to establish storage ponds that are completely masked.

Irrigation scheduling

Since the daily atmospheric demand for evapotranspiration varies, under this system, irrigation with a fixed rate is not considered ecologically acceptable, especially where it rains often. The irrigation rate, equivalent to poplar consumptive use of water, is added to plantation several times during the day, in a number of waterings corresponding to the potential evapotranspiration of the day. Since the local soil was quite heavy, with low soil hydraulic conductivity, there was no risk of contaminating the groundwater through fast percolation. However, in such conditions, administering the whole rate could result in runoff, which could reduce the uniformity of application.

In other situations, however, the site may be more permeable, with the ensuing risk that only part of the effluent will be consumed and the rest will percolate to groundwater. To avoid such a situation one has to examine the variation of air temperature, rainfall, net radiation, saturation deficit of atmosphere and the result is evopotranspiration resulting evopotranspiration. It is obvious that the Evopotranspiration is driven mainly by the net solar radiation. Also, temperature and saturation deficit have a variation strongly related to net radiation, except when a rain event occurs, cooling the atmosphere and moistening the air, thus depressing the saturation deficit. All these variations are integrated by the daily evopotranspiration figure. To ensure that moisture variations occur only in the half of root zone (1 to 1.5 m), on a permeable site, the daily irrigation rate has to be fragmented in several watering, following the course of the evopotranspiration. Since we could expect that the land allocated to this use might not be of prime agricultural quality (for instance, too permeable), in order to avoid either the overloading or the under usage of the plantation, for a large recycling system. Thus, application rates will be locally adapted, depending on the short time information about the atmospheric demand.

Stand structure and recycling

Over time, a stand of trees tends to close its canopy, which prevents the wind - a factor in the calculation of evopotranspiration from penetrating the plantation to correct this problem, the plantation must be uniformly thinned and then the trees must be pruned of up to 1/3 - 1/2 of their height. These interventions allow the wind to penetrate into the canopy again, thus bringing less humid air into the canopy and enhancing the evopotranspiration. Over time, the pruning improves also the stem quality.

During the lifetime of such a plantation, which depend upon the latitude and desired sort of timber it can be 10 to 25 years, it may need to be pruned at least three times and thinned at least twice. The cost of these cultural operations will be offset by increases in timber value and in the efficiency of recycling.

The stand of trees and sprinkling uniformity

In contrast with agricultural crops, trees impede sprinkler irrigation. Where no special restrictions apply, high-pressure sprinklers can be used very effectively and with good-to-high uniformity, except during windy episodes. Depending on plantation spacing, these sprinklers may harm or destroy the foliage of a few adjacent trees. Around every sprinkler the jet creates a clear space in the shape of a reversed funnel; since the jet moistens the tree crowns from above, the wind might cause some effluent aerosols to drift. However, from both physiological and operational viewpoint this moistening is ideal, since a part of the effluent is intercepted by the crown and evaporates directly from there.

In the special cases where the wind drift must be prevented (for instance, close to a highway or a locality), the irrigation should be designed for medium pressure. After the age of 3 in a poplar plantation, medium pressure sprinklers will operate under the canopy, thus prohibiting the wind drift.

Irrigation with effluent in desert environments

In the case of effluents recycling over desert areas it is still possible to employ plantations for recycling, however in a different manner. Here, under intense solar radiation, high air temperature, low relative humidity, active air circulation and with a long potential growing season, all of which stimulate direct evaporation from leaves, the irrigation has to be different. The frequency of waterings has to be increased while reducing their amount in bursts of only 2 - 4 minutes, so that only the foliage is moistened, followed by intervals of 5 - 7 minutes, necessary for evaporation. Application of such a regime, implying the direct use of evaporation, instead of evapotranspiration, can increase greatly the efficiency of effluents recycling. At the same time, this procedure exposes more effectively the effluent to the sterilizing action of solar radiation.

The book contains twenty one chapters reflecting objectives on various aspects of water and forest resources, water pollutions, forest degradation, industrial pollution from them, recycling technology, bio-statistics, case studies, treatment technologies for industrial effluent, primary, secondary and tertiary treatment with bio-reactors, trickling filters, aerators. *Chapter 2* deals with environment, sustainable environment, and carrying capacity. *Chapter 3* explains the effect of development on environment. *Chapter 4* deals with water resources in India like major river basins, fresh water resources, ground water resources, and water resource development. *Chapter 5* provides for water pollution such as surface water pollution, coastal and ocean pollution in India. *Chapter 6* elaborates forest resources like Himalayan forests, Western Ghats and Eastern Ghats. *Chapter 7* deals with forest degradation by physical, chemical, biological, Himalayan, Western and Eastern Ghats forest degradations. *Chapter 8* describes about the various industries, regions of industries and industrial effluents discharged from them with toxic materials. *Chapter 9* deals with effects of industrial effluents on aquatic ecosystems, effects on humans, effects on animals, effects on plants and effects on materials. *Chapter 10* includes analysis of industrial effluents with physical-chemical and biological parameters. *Chapter 11* deals with treatment of industrial effluents by primary, secondary and tertiary treatments. *Chapter 12* describes about volatile organic compounds and their treatment. *Chapter 13* deals about World and Indian Quality Standards for industrial effluents. *Chapter 14* provides observation of phytosociology of biometric traits. *15th chapter* elaborates biostatistics and its application in the filed of above ground height, basal diameter and biomass of the tree species. *Chapter 16* deals with definition of recycling technology such as conservative, alternate and recent trends in the recycling technology and comparison of these technologies for the best application in respect of industrial effluents. *Chapter 17* and *18* include methods of recycling technology and its applications. whereas *Chapter 19* deals with evopotranspiration of effluents by forest tree species. *Chapter 20* describes applications of recycling technology in the industrial process. *Chapter 21* elaborates about specific case studies for different tree species.

Hence, this book describes water resources, water pollution, industrial water pollution, treatment facilities, forest resources, causes of forest degradation, method of recycling, reuse and some case studies for the forest tree species. These chapters are very essential to discuss for the recycling of industrial effluent by tree species (Manivanan & Das, 2002). It will be interest of graduates, postgraduates, and research scholars in the field environmental sciences and engineering.

— — —

2

Environment

The science is a process of refining our understanding of nature by continual questioning and active investigation on questions. Students can approach science in this manner, rather than as a collection of facts to be memorized. The Environment is to provide up-to-date information to the important concepts in the study of environment. Information is presented from an analytical, observation and multidisciplinary perspective from which we must view environmental issues in order to deal successfully with them. The environment may be defined as response of a human being influenced by various factors such as abiotic and biotic, which are present in the ecosystems.

2.1 Multidisciplinary Approach

The approach of environment science is multi-disciplinary in nature like botany, zoology, physics, hydrology, hydraulics, chemistry, biophysics, biochemistry and biology. It integrates various subjects and includes few of the most important topics of modern civilization as well as oldest philosophical concerns. Applied and basic aspects of environment requires a solid function in the nature of our relationship with nature, in addition to fields like economics, anthropology, history, sociology and philosophy of the environment.

2.2 Sustainabale Environment

Sustainability is a term that has gained much popularity in recent past. It means that a resource is used in such a way that it is available continously, hence, the term is used vaguely and it is some thing we are struggling to study. It means ensuring that the future generations have equal opportunities to utilize the natural resources. In India, it should be understood as sustainable development. It means that the industrial development and environmental conservation should be directly proportional together to go upwards for the rise in economic growth. In recent times, the industrial growth and sustainable development have co-up with conservation of natural resources.

2.3 Carrying Capacity

One of the central environmental questions we must ask is, what is the maximum number of people that the earth can sustain? This maximum amount is known as the carrying capacity, which is usually defined as the maximum number of individuals of a species that can be sustained by an environment without decreasing the capacity of the environment to sustain that same amount in the future. An extreme estimate of the human carrying capacity of the earth would consider only enough land and resources per person to provide basic necessities-like food, water, clothing and air and would not allow for amenities-like wilderness, wildlife, scenery, recreational space. We can also imagine an optimal carrying capacity, which would provide a high standard of living for each individual and an environment that would enable the persistence of all other species present on the earth. An optimal carrying capacity would include ample areas for recreation, wilderness, wildlife and other features that people enjoy.

The world already has example of overexploitation of natural resources such as The African Famine. Starvation in African nations that continues even today first gained worldwide attention in the mid 1980's. Drought and political unrest in Africa have led to major episodes of famine. In one year, as many as 22 African nations suffered catastrophic food shortages and 150 million Africans faced starvation. Four million tones of emergency food was needed. Five million refugees sought food and shelter. Ten years earlier, a similar situation developed following the 1973-74 drought in the Sahel in Africa. At the time

5 lakes Africans starved to death and several million more were permanently affected by malnutrition. By these reasons, the study of environmental sciences is essential for the human life on earth. It included many subjects such as botany, zoology, physics, chemistry, biophysics, biochemistry, ecology, communities, niches, economics, environmental law, planning and architect for conservation of natural resources and sustainable development in the world including India (World Resources Institute, 1995).

— — —

3

Environment *Vs* Development

3.1 Introduction

India, when gained independence in 1947, was predominantly an agrarian economy, with a stagnant national income. The country inherited a weak industrial base, restricted to only a few industries. Agricultural growth was virtually negligible, the country had a stagnant cropped area where by only a very small proportion of agricultural land was irrigated. On the eve of the country's independence, on 15th August 1947, Jawaharlal Nehru, India's Prime Minister, reminded the country that the task ahead included ending poverty, ignorance, and disease and inequality of opportunity. India began the process of planning with the launching of the 1st five-year plan in April 1951. The central purpose of planning was to 'initiate a process of development which would raise living standards and open out to the people new opportunities for a richer and more varied life'. Afterwards, the five-year plans were formulated seeking development in a sustainable manner.

The country, over the past has travelled a long way indeed in its drive towards economic growth, modernization of the economy, feudal economy at the time of independence has been transformed into one based on a fairly developed and diversified industrial structure and a sound agricultural base with a large potential for further industrialization and development. The income and consumption levels of people, on an average, have increased and the consumption basket has diversified. A noteworthy achievement indeed has been the elimination of famines with which the country continued to be afflicted right until independence. That achievement is far from negligible since many other countries in Asia and Africa are yet to free themselves of this malady. There is also other achievement, varying from the successful functioning of a democratic system to the emergence of a strong and large scientific community (Dreze Sen, 1995). The figure 3.1 shows the per capita income during 1997-1998. It shows that the maximum income from Northern India compared to Southern India. However, having adapted the pattern of economic development that brought prosperity to the Western, India has also seen widespread environmental damage and degradation in the pursuit of economic growth. The concern for preserving the environment against the onslaught of industrial expansion, intensification of agricultural, and adoption of a resource-intensive lifestyle has not been given the attention it deserved, and the costs of environmental degradation have not been internalized in the

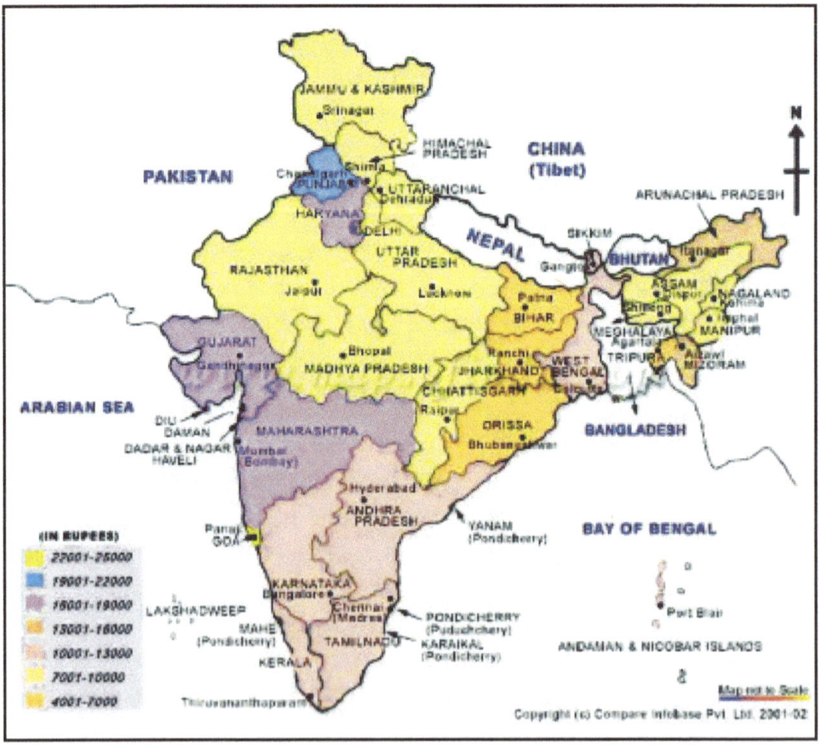

Figure 3.1: Per capita Income of Various States During 1997-1998

development process. While the Indian economy study made by two World Bank staffers shows that the country is paying an enormous price for this onward march, which has brought in its wake ecological devastation and numerous health problems.

One of our aims to assess the economic and social costs associated with environmental degradation with particular reference to its impacts on health and productivity (fig 3.1). We need to ask how far such growth can be considered economically viable, so have also tried to project the state of India's environment and suggest strategies for the sustainable management of India's resources over the next future years.

3.2 Five Year Plans

Next to the agricultural sector, the manufacturing sector has occupied an increasing crucial position in the development of the economy. The country's ability to grow fast, to reduce the pressure of population on agricultural land, to enhance exports, to be competitive, and to create an expanding base for direct and indirect growth of productive employment and income has come to depend upon the growth and efficiency of the manufacturing sector. The 1st Five Year Plan (1951-1956) was a period of stabilization of the economy in agricultural and allied activities (Planning Commission, 1951). After a good start in the second and third Five Year Plans (1956-1961) from a very small industrial base, the growth of the manufacturing sector declined during the late 1960s and the 1970s before it picked up again in the 1980s, since then, with a few brief setbacks, this sector has shown an average annual compound growth rate of about 7per cent (Planning Commission, 1992).

The other critical achievement has been the diversification and expansion of India's industrial capabilities in respect of both capital and consumer goods. The growth of capital goods has been particularly impressive and India can now sustain most of its industries such as textile, food grains, cement chemicals, metallurgy, engineering, power, and transport by domestic production of the required capital goods and only small imports.

The sharp rise in industrial performance after initiating measures to liberalize the import and industrial policies supported during 1980/81 and a better performance by the infrastructure and energy sectors. Due to the foreign exchange crises, curbs in imports and a general resource crunch that constrained demand, the manufacturing sector did experience a recession during 1990/91 and 1991/92. Since then, however, this sector has been growing an annual average growth rate of around 7 %.

We have never had an organized debate on what development is about and what it should achieve. Sustainable development requires thinking and action by several disciplines and by many agencies and departments. There has to be a synergy between health, environment, energy and the development process, a concern which has also now been explicitly recognized even in the approach to the 10th Five Year Plan (Planning Commission, 1997).

Since independence we have still not lost the opportunity, what we need is a re-orientation of our development paradigm to emphasize growth with re-distributive justice and environmental sustainability. For growth to be participating, there must be growth in the first place, and such growth must be sustainable. The present book elaborates to look at how the future years can be made a period which we do not grow, but grow qualitatively consistent with sustainability. Sustainable growth in itself should lay the foundation of a better India.

The Indian economy grew at approximately 1.2%during the first half of the present century. The growth rate in GDP during the first three decades of planning (1950-1980) was higher than that during 1900 to 1946 and hovered around 3.6% a year (Table 3.1) [CMIE, 1995].

The industrial growth and environment conservation shall be directly proportional instead of being indirectly proportionate towards the economic development of the country. So the sustainable development should be followed by each and every industrial development.

Table 3.1: Targeted and Actual Growth Rates During the Five Year Plans

Sr. No.	Plan and years	Target	Actual	Growth in
1.	First Plan 1951/52 to 1955/56	2.1	3.6	National Income
2.	Second Plan 1956/57 to 1960/61	4.5	4.0	National income
3.	Third Plan 1960/61 to 1965/66	5.6	2.2	National income
4.	Fourth Plan 19669/70 to 1973/74	5.7	3.3	Net Domestic Product
5.	Fifth Plan 1974/75 to 1978/79	5.5	3.5	Gross Domestic Product
6.	Sixth Plan 1979/80 to 1984/85	5.2	5.8	Gross Domestic Product
7.	Seventh Plan 1985/86 to 1989/90	5.0	6.0	Gross Domestic Product
8.	Two Annual Plans 1990/91 to 1991/92	-	3.0	Gross Domestic Product
9.	Eighth Plan 1992/93 to 1996/1996/97	5.6	6.5	Gross Domestic Product
10.	Ninth Plan 1998/99	6.3	6.6	Gross Domestic Product
11.	Tenth Plan 2004/2005	7.1	7.6	Gross Domestic Product

Based on advance estimates for 2004/05 made by Central Statistical Organisation.
Source: The Five Year Plans, Published by the Planning Commission, New Delhi

— — —

4

Water Resources

4.1 Introduction

India is a land of many rivers, lakes, ponds, coastal, marines and mountains. Its geographical area of about 329 million hectare is crises crossed by a large number of small and medium, large rivers, some of them figuring amongst the mighty rivers of the world. The rivers and mountains have a greater significance in the history of Indian civilizations, development, religious and spiritual life. It may not be an exaggeration to say that the rivers are the heart and soul of the Indian civilizations

India is a union of States with a federal set up. Politically, the country is divided into 26 States and 7 Union Territories. A major part of India's population of 869 millions (1991 census) is rural and agriculturally oriented for whom the rivers are the source of their life. India is a land of many religions, diversity of cultures and languages. The different regions of the country have different cultural, linguistic and other ethnic groups. The land and people present a vast panorama of diversity in unity. Physiographically, India may be divided into seven well-defined regions. These are: -

a. The Northern Mountains, comprising the mighty Himalayan ranges
b. The Great Plains traversed by the Indus and Ganga, Brahmaputra river systems. As much as one third of this lies in the arid zone of western Rajasthan. The remaining area is mostly fertile plain
c. The Central Highlands, consisting of a wide belt of hills running east-west starting from Aravalli ranges in the west

and terminating in a steep slope in the east. The area lies between the Great Plains and the Deccan Plateau

d. The Peninsular Plateaus comprising the Western Ghats, Eastern Ghats, North Deccan Plateau, South Deccan Plateau and Eastern Plateau
e. The East Coast, a belt of land of about 100-130 km wide, bordering the Bay of Bengal land lying to the east of the Eastern Ghats
f. The West Coast, a narrow belt of land of about 10-25 km wide, bordering the Arabian Sea and lying to the west of the Western Ghats, and
g. The islands, comprising the coral islands of Lakshadeep in Arabian Sea and Andaman and Nicobar Islands of the Bay of Bengal.

The (Fig.4.1) shows the major river basins in India. There are 12 major river basins in India including Indus in the north region to Cauvery in the south region. Medium river basins are west flowing rivers and east flowing rivers consists of 48 basins.

The presence of the great mountain mass formed by the Himalayas in Jammu and Kashmir, Arunachal Pradesh and its spurs on the North and of the ocean on the South are the two major influences operating on the climate of India. The first poses an impenetrable barrier to the influence of cold winds from central Asia, and gives the sub-continent the elements of tropical type of climate. The second, which is the source of cool moisture-laden winds reaching India, gives it the elements of the oceanic type of climate.

India has a very great diversity and variety of climate and an even greater variety of weather conditions. The climate ranges from continental to oceanic, from extremes of heat to extremes of cold, from extreme aridity and negligible rainfall to excessive humidity and torrential rainfall. It is, therefore, necessary to avoid any generalisation as to the prevalence of any particular kind of climate, not only over the country as a whole but over major areas in it. The climatic condition influences the water

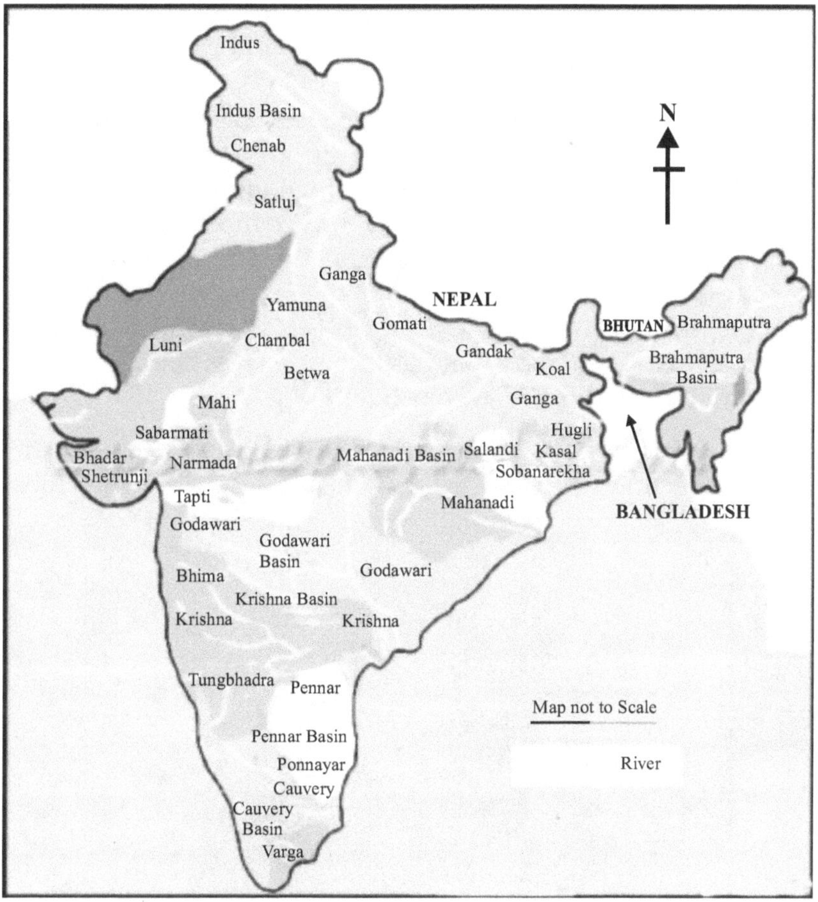

Figure 4.1: Major River Basins of India

resources utilisation of the country to a great extent. There are four main seasons in India summer, winter, rainy and spring season.

Rainfall in India is dependent in differing degrees on the South-West and North-East monsoons, on shallow cyclonic depressions and disturbances and on violent local storms which form regions where cool humid winds of the sea meets hot dry winds from the land and occasionally reach cyclonic dimension. Most of the rainfall in India takes place under the great influence of South West monsoon between June to September except in

Tamil Nadu where it is under the influence of North-East monsoon during October to November. The rainfall shows great variations, unequal seasonal distribution, still more unequal geographical distribution and the frequent departures from the normal. It generally exceeds 1000 mm in areas to the east of Longitude 78 E. It extends to 2500 mm along almost the entire West Coast and Western Ghats and over most of Assam and Sub-Himalayan West Bengal. On the West of the line joining Porbandar to Delhi and thence to Ferozpur the rainfall diminishes rapidly from 500 mm to less than 150 mm in the extreme west. The Peninsular has large areas of rainfall less than 600 mm with pockets of even 500 mm (Fig. 4.2).

The variations in temperature are also marked over the Indian sub-continent. During the winter seasons from November

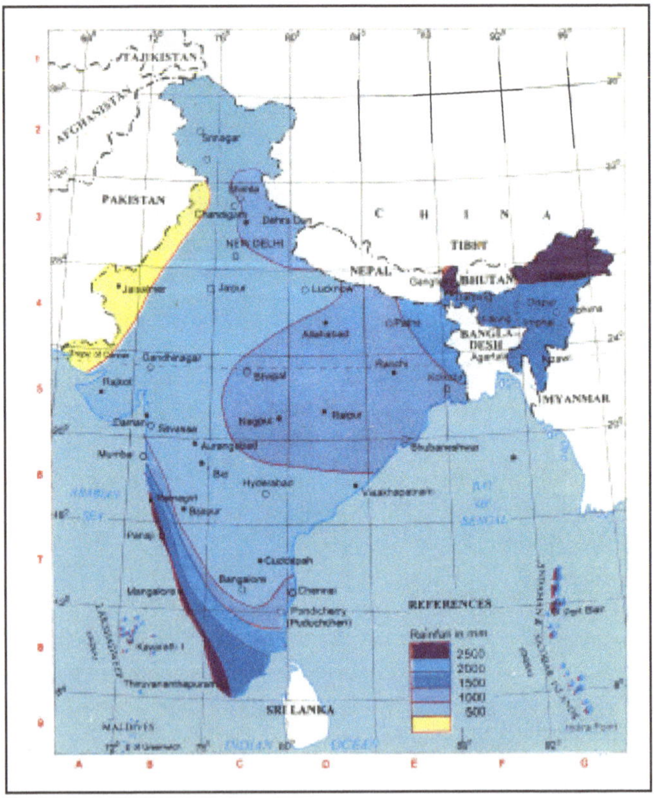

Figure 4.2: Rainfall In India

to February, due to the effect of continental winds over most of the country, the temperature decreases from South to North. The mean maximum temperature during the coldest months of December and January varies from 29°C in some part of the peninsula to about 18°C in the North, whereas the mean minimum varies from about 24 °C in the extreme South to below 5°C in the North. From March to May is usually a period of continuous and rapid rise of temperature. The highest temperature occurs in North India, particularly in the desert regions of the North-West where the maximum may exceed 48°C with the advent of South West Monsoon in June, there is a rapid fall in the maximum temperature in the central portions of the country. The temperature is almost uniform over the area covering two thirds of the country, which gets good rain. In August, there is a marked fall in temperature when the monsoon retreats from North India in September. In Northwest India, in the month of November, the mean maximum temperature is below 38°C and the mean minimum below 10°C. In the extreme North, temperature drops below freezing point.

Evaporation rates closely follows the climatic seasons, and reach their peak in the summer months of April and May and the central areas of the country display the highest evaporation rates during this period. With the onset of monsoon, there is a marked fall in the rate of evaporation. The annual potential evaporation ranges between 150 to 250 cm over most parts of the country. Monthly potential evaporation over the Peninsula increases from 15 cm in December to 40 cm in May. In the North-East, it varies from 6 cm in December to 20 cm in May. It rises to 40 cm in June in West Rajasthan. After the onset of monsoon potential evaporation decreases generally all over the country.

The Planning Commission after examining the earlier studies at the regionalisation of the agricultural economy has recommended that agricultural planning be done on the basis of agroclimatic regions. For resource development, the country has been broadly divided into fifteen agricultural regions based on agro-climatic features, particularly soil type, climate including temperature and rainfall and its variation and water resources availability as follows:

i. Western Himalayan division
ii. Eastern Himalayan region
iii. Lower Gangetic palin region
iv. Middle Gangetic plain region
v. Upper Gangetic plain region
vi. Trans-Gangetic plain region
vii. Eastern plateau and hill region
viii. Central plateau and hill region
ix. Western plateau and hill region
x. Southern plateau and hill region
xi. East coast plain and hill region
xii. West coast plain and hill region
xiii. Gujarat plain and hill region
xiv. Western plain and hill region
xv. Island region

India has many rivers and their basins with nature's blessed. As many as 12 of them are classifled as major rivers whose total catchment area is (252.8 m.ha). Of the major rivers, The Ganga - Brahmaputra Meghana system is the biggest with catchment area of about 110 m.ha, which is more than 43% of the catchment area of all the major rivers in the country. The other major rivers with catchment area more than 10 m.ha are Indus (32.1 m.ha.), Godavari (31.3 m.ha.), Krishna, (25.9 m.ha.) and Mahanadi (14.2 m.ha). The catchment area of medium rivers is about 25 m.ha and Subernarekha with 1.9 m.ha. catchment area is the largest river among the medium rivers in the country (MWR 2003).

Inland water resources of the country are classified as rivers and canals; reservoirs; tanks and ponds; beels, oxbow lakes, derelict water; and brackish water. Other than rivers and canals, total water bodies cover all area of about 7 m.ha. Of these rivers and canals, Uttar Pradesh occupies the first place with the total length of rivers and canals as 31.2 thousand km, which is about 17% of the total length of rivers and canals in the country. Other states following Uttar Pradesh are Jammu and Kashmir and Madhya Pradesh. Among the remaining forms of the inland water resources, tanks and ponds have maximum area (2.9 m.ha.) followed by reservoirs (2.1 m.ha.).

Most of the area under tanks and ponds lies in Southern states of Andhra Pradesh, Karnataka and Tamil Nadu. These states along with West Bengal, Rajasthan and Uttar Pradesh, account for 62% of total area under tanks and ponds in the country. As far as reservoirs are concerned, major states like Andhra Pradesh, Gujarat, Karnataka, Madhya Pradesh, Maharashtra, Orissa, Rajasthan and Uttar Pradesh account for larger portion of area under reservoirs. More than 77% of area under beels, oxbow, lakes and derelict water lies in the states of Orissa, Uttar Pradesh and Assam. Orissa ranks first as regards the total area of brackish water and is followed by Gujarat, Kerala and West Bengal. The total area of inland water resources is, thus, unevenly distributed over the country with five states namely Orissa, Andhra Pradesh, Gujarat, Karnataka and West Bengal accounting for more than half of the country's inland water bodies. The following tables (Table 4.1,4.2,4.3) shows national water resources at a glance.

Table 4.1: National Water Resources at a Glance

S.No.	Items	Quantity (Cu.Km)
1.	Annual Precipitation Volume (Including snowfall)	4000
2.	Average Annual Potential flow in Rivers	1869
3.	Per Capita Water Availability (1997)	1967
4.	Estimated Utilizable Water Resources	1122
	(i) Surface Water Resources	690
	(ii) Ground Water Resources	432

Table 4.2: Major River Basins In India

S. No.	Name of the River	Origin	Length (Km.)	Catchment Area (Sq. Km.)
1.	Indus	Mansarovar (Tibet)	1114 +	321289 +
2.	a) Ganga	Gangotri (Uttar Kashi)	2525 +	861452 +
	b) Brahmaputra	Kailash Range (Tibet)	916 +	194413 +
	c) Barak & other rivers flowing into Meghna, like Gomti, Muhari, Fenny etc.			41723 +
3.	Sabarmati	Aravalli Hills (Rajasthan)	371	21674
4.	Mahi	Dhar (Madhya Pradesh)	583	34842
5.	Narmada	Amarkantak (Madhya Pradesh)	1312	98796
6.	Tapi	Betul (Madhya Pradesh)	724	65145
7.	Brahmani	Ranchi (Bihar)	799	39033
8.	Mahanadi	Nazri Town (Madhya Pradesh)	851	141589
9.	Godavari	Nasik (Maharashtra)	1465	312812
10.	Krishna	Mahabaleshwar (Maharashtra)	1401	258948
11.	Pennar	Kolar (Karnataka)	597	55213
12.	Cauvery	Coorg (Karnataka)	800	81155
			Total	**2528084**

Table 4.3: Medium River Basins

S.No.	Name of the River	Village/Distt. (Origin)	State	Length (Km.)	Catchment Area (Sq. Km)
West Flowing Rivers					
1.	Ozat	Kathiawar	Gujarat	128	3189
2.	Shetrunji	Dalkania	Gujarat	182	5514
3.	Bhadar	Rajkot	Gujarat	198	7094
4.	Aji	Rajkot	Gujarat	106	2139
5.	Dhadhar	Panchmahal	Gujarat	135	2770
6.	Purna	Dhosa	Maharashtra	142	2431
7.	Ambika	Dangs	Maharashtra	142	2715
8.	Vaitarna	Nasik	Maharashtra	171	3637

S.No.	Name of the River	Village/Distt. (Origin)	State	Length (Km.)	Catchment Area (Sq. Km)
9.	Damman-ganga	Nasik	Maharashtra	143	2357
10.	Ulhas	Raigarh	Maharashtra	145	3864
11.	Savitri	Pune	Maharashtra	99	2899
12.	Sastri	Ratnagiri	Maharashtra	64	2174
13.	Washishthi	Ratnagiri	Maharashtra	48	2239
14.	Mandvi	Belgaum	Karnataka	87	2032
15.	Kalinadi	Belgaum	Karnataka	153	5179
16.	Gangavati or Bedti (in upper reaches)	Dharwar	Karnataka	152	3902
17.	Sharavati	Shimoga	Karnataka	122	2209
18.	Netravati	Dakshina	Karnataka Kannada	103	3657
19.	Chaliar or Baypore	Elamtalvi Hills	Kerala	169	2788
20.	Bharatha-puzha (known as Ponnani)	Annamalai Hills	Tamil Nadu	209	6186
21.	Periyar	Sivajini Hills	Kerala	244	5398
22.	Pamba	Devarmalai	Kerala	176	2235
East Flowing Rivers					
23.	Burhabalang	Mayurbahanj	Orissa	164	4837
24.	Baitarni	Keonjhar	Orissa	365	12789
25.	Rushikulya	Phulbani	Orissa	146	7753
26.	Bahuda	Ramgirivillage	Orissa	73	1248
27.	Vamsadhara	Kalahandi	Orissa	221	10830
28.	Nagavali	Kalahandi	Orissa	217	9410
29.	Sarda	Vishakha-patnam	Andhra Pradesh	104	2725
30.	Eleru	Vishakha-patnam	Andhra Pradesh	125	3809
31.	Vogarivagu	Guntur	Andhra Pradesh	102	1348
32.	Gundla-kamma	Kurnool	Andhra Pradesh	220	8494
33.	Musi	Nellore	Andhra Pradesh	112	2219
34.	Paleru	Nellore	Andhra Pradesh	104	2483

S.No.	Name of the River	Village/Distt. (Origin)	State	Length (Km.)	Catchment Area (Sq. Km)
35.	Muneru	Nellore	Andhra Pradesh	122	3734
36.	Swarna-mukhi	Koraput	Orissa	130	3225
37.	Kandleru	Vinukonda	Andhra Pradesh	73	3534
38.	Kortalaiyar	Chinglepet	Tamil Nadu	131	3521
39.	Palar (including tributary Cheyyar)	Kolar	Karnataka	348	17871
40.	Varahandi	North Arcot	Tamil Nadu	94	3044
41.	Ponnaiyar	Kolar	Karnataka	396	14130
42.	Vellar	Chithri Hills	Tamil Nadu	193	8558
43.	Vaigai	Madurai	Tamil Nadu	258	7031
44.	Pambar	Madurai	Tamil Nadu	125	3104
45.	Gundar	Madurai	Tamil Nadu	146	5647
46.	Vaippar	Tirunolvolli	Tamil Nadu	130	5288
47.	Tambraparni	Tirunolvolli	Tamil Nadu	130	5969
48.	Subarnare-kha Nagri/	Ranchi	Bihar	395	19296
				Total	**248505**

The annual per capita availability of renewable fresh water in the country fell from around 5277 cubic metres in 1955 to 2464 cubic metres in 1990. Per capita water availability in 1947 was estimated to have been 6008 cubic metres a year, which has fallen to 2266 cubic meters in 1997. This gives a broad indication of the growing scarcity of water in the country in the fifty years since independence. The following figure (Fig. 4.2) shows the prediction of water resources in India up to 2047. It shows that during 1947 the quantity is about 6000 cubic meters which will comedown to 1000 cubic meters on 2047.

4.2 Fresh Water Resources

Fresh water as a commodity generates concern being an exhaustible resource and due to the environmental issues related to its degradation. With a phenomenal development of water

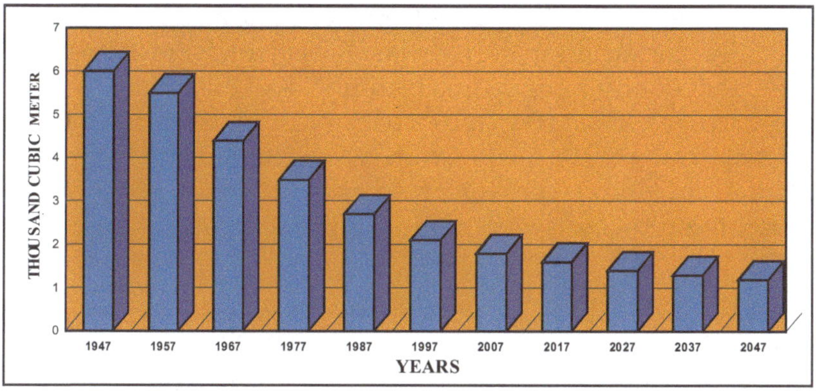

Figure 4.2: Status of Water Resources in India

resources since independence, India has successfully met water requirements for different designated usages. Preserving both the quality and quantity of freshwater resources however, is becoming the most pressing of many environmental challenges on the national horizon. Perhaps, because water is considered as a cheap and readily available resource, people fail to understand that, just how much stress the human demand for water is placing on the natural ecosystems.

India receives an average annual rainfall equivalent of about 4,000 billion cubic metres (BCM). This is the only source of water which is unevenly distributed both spatially as well as temporally. Most of the rainfall is confined to the monsoon season, from June to September, and levels of precipitation vary from 100 mm a year in western Rajasthan to over 9,000 mm a year in the north-eastern state of Meghalaya. With 3,000 BCM of rainfall concentrated over the four monsoon months and the other 1,000 BCM spread over the remaining eight months, our rivers carry 90% of the water during the period from June-November every year. Thus, only 10% of the river flow is available during the other six months in a year. National level statistics for water availability masks for huge disparities from basin-to-basin and region to region. Spatially, the utilizable resource availability in the country varies from 18,417 cubic meters in the Brahmaputra valley to as low as 180 cubic metres in the Sabarmati basin (Chitale 1992). Even within the Ganga basin, water availability varies from 740 cubic meters in Yamuna to 3,379 cubic meters in the Gandak. Rajasthan, for instance, with 8% of the country's population has only 1% of the country's water resources while Bihar with 10% of population has just 5% of the water resources. Thus, while India is considered rich in terms of annual rainfall and total water resources, its uneven geographical distribution causes severe regional and temporal shortages of water resources.

Of 4,000 BCM of water available from rainfall, the mean flow in the country's rivers is about 1,900 BCM. Out of this, only 690 BCM is utilizable. With 177 BCM of live storage created by the existing major and medium dam projects and another 75 BCM of storage from projects under construction, there is still a gap of 440 BCM of water, which is utilized (CWC 1997). The latest assessment of replenishable groundwater resources has been made at 431.9 BCM by the Central Ground Water Board through a large volume of hydrologic and related data. This is the total of potential due to natural recharge from rainfall and due to recharge contributions from canal irrigation. The utilizable groundwater resources have been assessed at 395.6 BCM (70.0 BCM for domestic and industrial uses and 325.6 BCM for irrigation). The CGWB has also assessed the quantum of static ground water resources at 10,812 BCM.

Water availability from other sources and through desalinisation of sea is considered negligible in view of the high cost. The assessed gross available and utilizable water resources of the country, based on conventional technology, are therefore 2,384 BCM and 1,086 BCM, respectively. With an estimated population of one billion in 2001, the available and utilizable water resources per capita per year are 2,384 cubic meter and 1,086 cubic meter respectively against an estimated availability of 6008 cubic meter in 1947. This itself, gives a broad indication of the growing resource scarcity in India in the fifty eight years since independence.

Since independence, India has witnessed an unprecedented increase in population. From a population of about 343 million in 1947, the population has grown at a rate of 2.04% to cross the

1,000 million mark in 2001. With an increasing number of mouths to feed, there has been an additional pressure on agriculture resulting in an increase in net sown area from 119 million hectares in 1951 to 142 million hectares in 1997; high cropping intensity has also resulted in an increased demand for water resources. Domestic water need in the urban areas has also grown notably with the current urban population at 4.5 times the population level in 1950s. The water requirement of the manufacturing sector has increased in proportion to the increase in the sector's share in GDP from about 12% in 1950s to 20% in 1990s. Further, there is a substantial variance in the different user sectors—agriculture, domestic and industry, *vis-à-vis* their share of water demand, resource pricing structure and usage efficiencies, which creates inter-sectoral competitions and conflicts. The agriculture sector, for instance, accounts for about 95% of the total water demand with the subsidised and free regime of supply of power and water resulting in the over-exploitation and inefficient usage of water. The high resource cost for industries, on the other hand, cross- subsidises the water consumed by the other sectors (TERI 2001).

The demand for fresh water has been identified, as the quantity of water required to be supplied for specific use and includes consumptive as well as necessary non-consumptive water requirements for the user sector. The total water withdrawal/utilization for all uses in 1990 was about 518 BCM or 609 m 3 /capita/year. Estimates for total national level water requirements, through an iterative and building block approach, have been made for the years 2010, 2025 and 2050 based on a 4.5% growth in expenditure and median variant population

Although about 88% of the population, on average, has been covered with organized drinking water supply in class I cities and class II towns of the country, there is a huge disparity in quantity of water supplied. Of the 299 class I cities, only 77 cities have cent percent water supply coverage. The per capita water supply also ranges from as low as 9 litres per capita per day (lpcd) in Tuticorin to as high as 584 lpcd in Triuvannamalai (CPCB 2000). Similarly, 203 of the 345 class II towns have low per capita supplies of less than 100 lpcd (CPCB 2000). The country's total water requirements by the year 2050 will become 1,422 BCM, which will be much in excess of the total utilizable average water resources of 1,086 BCM. At the national level, it would be a very difficult task to increase the availability of water for use from the 1990 level of approximately 520 BCM to the desired level of 1,422 BCM by the year 2050 as most of the undeveloped utilizable water resources are concentrated in a few river basins such as the Brahmaputra, Ganga, Godavari, and Mahanadi. The Accelerated Rural Water Supply Programme (ARWSP) and Rajiv Gandhi National Drinking Water Mission (RGNDWM). The status of coverage of habitations as on 1 April 1999, shows that about 267347 habitations (18.6% of total) are still either not covered or partially covered. Urban centres contribute more than 25% of the sewage generated in the country. The smaller towns and rural areas do not contribute significant amounts of sewage due to the low per capita water supply. Wastewater generated normally percolates into the soil or evaporates.The CPCB conducted a survey in 1994 - 95 (CPCB 2000, CPCB 2000) on water supply and wastewater generation, collection, treatment and disposal in 299 class I cities and 345 class II towns of the country. The survey findings indicated that, most cities did not have organised wastewater collection and treatment facilities. It also emerged that the class I cities and class II towns of Maharashtra, Delhi, Uttar Pradesh, West Bengal, and Gujarat contributed about 59% of the total wastewater generated in the country.

The annual precipitation including snowfall, which is the main source of the water in the country is estimated to be of the order of 4000 cu.km. For the purpose or rainfall country has been divided into 35 meteorological sub-divisions. The resources potential of the country, which occurs as natural run-off in the rivers is about 1869 cu.km. as per the basin wise latest estimates of Central Water Commission, considering both surface and ground water as one system. Ganga-Brahmaputra-Meghna system is the major contributor to total water resources potential of the country. Its share is about 60 per cent in total water resources potential of the various rivers. Based on 1991 census, the per capita availability of water works out to 220 cubic metre (cu.m.). Due to various constraints of topography, uneven distribution of resource over space and time, it has been estimated that only about 1122 cu.km. of total potential of 1869 cu.km. can be put to beneficial use, 690 cu. km. being due to surface water resources. Again about 40 per cent of utilizable surface water resources are presently in Ganga-Brhamputra-Meghna system. In majority of river basins, present utilization is significantly high and is in the range of 50 per cent to 95 per cent of utilizable surface resources. But in the rivers such as Narmada and Mahanadi percentage utilisation is quite low. The corresponding values for these basins are 23 per cent and 34 per cent respectively.

Table 4.4: Basin wise Surface Water Potential of India

S. No.	Name of the River Basin	Average annual potential in river Cubic Km/Year
1.	Indus (up to Border)	73.31
2.	a) Ganga	525.02
	b) Brahmaputra Barak & Others	585.60
3.	Godavari	110.54
4.	Krishna	78.12
5.	Cauvery	21.36
6.	Pennar	6.32
7.	East Flowing Rivers Between Mahanadi & Pennar	22.52
8.	East Flowing Rivers Between Pennar and Kanyakumari	16.46
9.	Mahanadi	66.88
10.	Brahmani & Baitarni	28.48
11.	Subernarekha	12.37
12.	Sabarmati	3.81
13.	Mahi	11.02
14.	West Flowing Rivers of Kutch, Sabarmati including Luni	15.10
15.	Narmada	45.64
16.	Tapi	14.88
17.	West Flowing Rivers from Tapi to Tadri	87.41
18.	West Flowing Rivers from Tadri to Kanyakumari	113.53
19.	Area of Inland drainage in Rajasthan desert	NEG.
20.	Minor River Basins Drainage into Bangladesh & Burma	31.00
	Total	**1869.35**

The distribution of water resources potential in the country shows that as against the national per capita annual availability of water as 2208 cu. m. the average availability in Brahmaputra and Barak is as high as 16589 cu. m. while it is as low as 360 cu.m. in Sabarmati basin. Brahmaputra and Barak basin with 7.3 per cent of geographical area and 4.2 per cent of population of the country has 31 per cent of the annual water resources. Per capita annual availability for rest of the country excluding Brahmaputra and Barak basin works out to about 1583 cu.m. Any situation of availability of less than 1000 cu. m. per capita is considered by international agencies as scarcity conditions. Cauvery, Pennar, Sabarmati, East flowing rivers and West flowing rivers are some of the basins which fall into this category.

4.3 Groundwater Resources

The importance of groundwater in Indian economy can be hardly overemphasized. One estimate maintains that groundwater sources account for as much as 70% to 80% of the value of farm produce attributable to irrigation. With agriculture contributing roughly 29%of India's GDP and production from irrigated lands claiming the more share in it, a large percentage of India's GDP could actively be seen to be closely tied to the availability of groundwater. Besides, ground water is now the source of four-fifth of the domesticwater supply in rural areas and around half that of urban and industrial uses. Further, in drought seasons ground water happens to be the predominant source of domestic and irrigation. What is more, on account of the share of ground water in raising agricultural yields, its roles as a catalyst of rural development as well as poverty alleviation. While groundwater development has had important implications for the economy of the country the overuse of groundwater has also been exploiting the groundwater table. At an aggregate level, only about 30% of annual utilizable groundwater potential is actually been exploited. While the problem of overexploitation of groundwater is not a major problem at the national level, it is serious problem in a few states like Tamil Nadu and Punjab. Against a critical level of 80%, the level of exploitation is over 98% in Punjab. In Haryana too, the level of exploitation is about 80%. The problem is also becoming increasingly serious in Tamil Nadu where the level of exploitation exceeds 60% and in Rajasthan, where it is 53% (CPCB, 1994). The problem becomes more acute at the district level six districts of Punjab, three districts of Haryana already show a utilization rate well above 100%. The problem is particularly acute in Mehsana district of Gujarat and Coimbatore district of Tamil Nadu, where groundwater aquifers have become permanently dried up because of inadequate recharge by rain harvesting and recycling of domestic and industrial effluents.

Dark,grey and white are the categories used to indicate the level of over exploitation and development of groundwater resources. In dark blocks, the level of exploitation of groundwater exceeds 85%; in grey blocks, it is 65% to 85% and in white it is below 65% of the annual utilizable groundwater potential. At the national level, only 8% of the blocks are characterized as 'Dark' blocks. However, once again, the problem has a spatial dimension. In Punjab for instance, 62% of the blocks as classified as 'dark'; in Haryana, 33% ; in Rajasthan,29%; in Gujarat, 25% and in Tamil Nadu, 26%. Between 1984/85 and 1994/95, the number of dark blocks in these states increased on an average more than threefold (Table 4.5) (CPCB, 1994).

Table 4.5: Blocks With Intensive Exploitation of Groundwater

		Percentage of Blocks using Groundwater Intensively	
S.No.	**States**	**1984/1985**	**1994/2000**
1	Gujarat	3	25
2	Punjab	54	62
3	Rajasthan	9	29
4	Tamil Nadu	14	26

Source : Saleth 1996

Table 4.6 shows the basinwise distribution of groundwater potential of India with cubic kilometers per year. It is shows that the total availability of ground water is about 431.42 cubic meter. It is found to be more in Ganga basin and minimum in Subarnrekha basin.

Table 4.6: Basin wise Groundwater Potential of India

S. No.	Name of Basin	Total Replenishable Groundwater Resources Cubic Km/Year
1.	Brahmai with Baitarni	4.05
2.	Brahmaputra	26.55
3.	Cambai Composite	7.19
4.	Cauvery	12.30
5.	Ganga	170.99
6.	Godavari	40.65
7.	Indus	26.49
8.	Krishna	26.41
9.	Madras and South Tamil Nadu	18.22
10.	Mahanadi	16.46
11.	Meghna	8.52
12.	Narmada	10.83
13.	Northeast Composite	18.84
14.	Pennar	4.93
15.	Subarnrekha	1.82
16.	Tapi	8.27
17.	Western Ghat	17.69

4.4 Water Resources Development

4.4.1 Institutional Arrangements

At the central level the Union Ministry of Water Resources is responsible for development, conservation and management of water as a national resource, *i.e.,* for the general policy on water resources development and for technical assistance to the states on irrigation, multipurpose projects, groundwater exploration and exploitation, command area development, drainage, flood control, water logging, sea erosion problems, dam safety and hydraulic structures for navigation and hydropower. It also oversees the regulation and developments of inter State rivers. These functions are carried out through various Central Organisations.Urban water supply and sewage disposal is handled by the Ministry of Urban Development while Rural Water Supply comes in the purview of Department of Drinking Water under Ministry of Rural Development. The subject of hydroelectric power and thermal power is the responsibility of the Ministry of Power. Pollution environment control, forest resources conservation, water Quality problems in rivers, lakes, ponds, and treatment plants for industrial effluents comes under the purview of the Ministry of Environment and Forests.

Water being a state subject, the state governments have primary responsibility for designated use and control of this resource. The administrative control and responsibility for development of water rests with the various State Departments and Corporations. Major and medium irrigation is handled by the irrigation/water resources departments. Minor irrigation is looked after, partly by water resources departments, minor irrigation corporations, Zilla Parishads, Panchayats and by the other departments such as agriculture. Urban water supply is generally the responsibility of public health departments and panchayats take care of rural water supply. Government tube wells are constructed and managed by the irrigation or water resources department or by tube well corporations set up for the purpose. Hydropower is the responsibility of the State Electricity Boards.

4.4.2 Irrigation

The irrigation projects are classified into three categories viz major, medium and minor. Projects which have a Cultivable Command Area (CCA) of more than 10,000 ha. are termed as major projects, those which have a CCA of less than 10,000 ha. but more than 2,000 ha. are termed as medium projects and those which have a CCA of 2,000 ha. or less are known as minor projects. A broad assessment of the area that can be ultimately brought under irrigation both by surface and groundwater made by the various states in sixties has indicated that ultimate irrigation potential of the country would be of the order of 113 m.ha.. The ultimate potential is 139 m.ha, the increase being primarily due to upward revision in assessed potential of minor groundwater schemes and minor surface water schemes to 64 m.ha and 17 m.ha respectively. Minor irrigation projects have both surface and groundwater as their source, while major and medium projects mostly exploit surface water resources.

The history of irrigation development in India can be traced back to pre-historic times. Vedas and ancient Indian scriptures made reference to wells, canals, tanks and dams which were beneficial to the community and their efficient operation and maintenance was the responsibility of the state. Civilization flourished on the banks of the rivers and harnessed the water for sustenance of life. According to the ancient Indian writers, the digging of a tank or well was amongst the greatest of the meritorious act of a man. Brihaspathi, an ancient writer on law and politics, states that the construction and the repair of dams is a pious work and its burden should fall on the shoulders of rich men of the land. Vishnu Purana enjoins merit to a person who effects repairs to well, gardens and dams.

In monsoon climate and in an agrarian economy like India's where irrigation has played a major role in the production process. There is evidence of the practice of irrigation since the establishment of settled agriculture during the Indus Valley Civilization (2500 BC). These irrigation technologies were in the form of small and minor works, which could be operated by small households to irrigate small patches of land and did not require co-operative effort. Nearly all these irrigation technologies still exist in India with very little technological change, and continue to be used by independent households for small holdings. The lack of evidence of large irrigation works at this time signifies the absence of large surplus that could be invested in bigger schemes or, in other words, the absence of rigid and unequal property rights. While village communities and co-operation in agriculture did exist as seen in well developed townships and economy, such co-operation in the large irrigation works was not needed, as these settlements were on the fertile and well irrigated Indus basin. The spread of agricultural settlements to less fertile and irrigated area led to co-operation in irrigation development and the emergence of larger irrigation works in the form of reservoirs and small canals. While the construction of small schemes was well within the capability of village communities, large irrigation works were to emerge only with the growth of states, empires and the intervention of the rulers. There used to emerge a close link between irrigation and the state. The king had at his disposal the power to mobilize labour which could be used for irrigation works.

In the south, perennial irrigation may have begun with construction of the Grand Anicut by the Cholas as early as in the second century to provide irrigation from the Cauvery river. Wherever the topography and terrain permitted, it was an old practice in the region to impound the surface drainage water in tanks or reservoirs by throwing across an earthen dam with a surplus weir, where necessary, to take off excess water, and a sluice at a suitable level to irrigate the land below. Some of the tanks got supplemental supply from stream and river channels. The entire landscape in the central and southern India is studded with numerous irrigation tanks which have been traced back to many centuries before the beginning of the Christian era. In northern India also there are a number of small canals in the upper valleys of rivers, which are very old (Ministry of Agriculture, 1995).

In the medieval India, rapid advances also took place in the construction of inundation canals. Water was blocked by constructing bunds across streams. This raised the water level and canals were constructed to take water to the fields.These bunds were built by both the state and private sources. Ghiyasuddin Tughluq(1220-250)is credited to be the first ruler who encouraged digging canals. However, it is Fruz Tughlug (1351-86) who inspired from central Asian experience, is considered to be the greatest canal builder before the nineteenth century. Irrigation is said to be one of the major reasons for the growth and expansion of the Vijayanagar empire in southern

India in the fifteenth century. It may be noted that, but for exceptional cases, most of the canal irrigation prior to the arrival of the British was of the diversionary nature. The state, through the promotion of irrigation, had sought to enhance revenue and provide patronage through rewards of fertile land and other rights to different classes. Irrigation also increased employment opportunities and helped in the generation of surplus for the maintenance of the army and the bureaucracy. As agricultural development was the pillar of the economy, irrigation systems were paid special attention to, as irrigation was seen to be a catalyst for enhanced agricultural production. This is demonstrated by the fact that all the large, powerful and stable empires paid attention to irrigation projects. It may be said that the state in irrigation was commensurate with its own interest.

Irrigation development under British rule began with the renovation, improvement and extension of existing works, such as ground anicut. When enough experience and confidence had been gained, the government ventured on new major works, like the Upper Ganga Canal, the Upper Bari Doab Canal and Krishna and Godavari Delta Systems, which were all river-diversion works of considerable size. The period from 1836 to 1866 marked the investigation, development and completion of these four major projects. In 1867, the Government adopted the practice of accepting projects, which promised a minimum net return. Thereafter, a number of projects were taken up. These included major canal works like the Sirhind, the Lower Ganga, the Agra and the Mutha Canals, and the Periyar Dam and canals. Some other major canal projects were also completed on the Indus system during this period. These included the Lower Swat, the Lower Sohag and Para, the Lower Chenab and the Sidhnai Canals, many of which went to Pakistan in 1947.

The recurrence of drought and famines during the second half of the nineteenth century necessitated the development of irrigation to give protection against the failure of crops and to reduce large scale expenditure on famine relief. As irrigation works in low rainfall tracts were not considered likely to meet the productivity test, they had to be financed from the current revenues. Significant protective works were constructed during the period were the Betwa Canal, the Nira Left Bank Canal, the Gokak Canal, the Khaswad Tank and the Rushikulya Canal. Between the two types of works namely productive and protective, the former received greater attention from the government. The gross area irrigated in British India by public works at the close of the nineteenth century was about 7.5 m.ha. Of this, 4.5 m.ha. came from minor works like tanks, inundation canals *etc.* for which no separate capital accounts were maintained. The area irrigated by protective works was only a little more than 0.12 m.ha.

The net irrigated area in the Indian sub-continent, comprising the British Provinces and Princely States, at the time of independence was about 28.2 m.ha. The partition of the country, however, brought about sudden and drastic changes, resulting in the apportionment of the irrigated area between the two countries; net irrigated area in India and Pakistan being 19.4 and 8.8 m.ha respectively. Major canal systems, including the Sutlej and Indus systems fell to Pakistan's share. East Bengal, now Bangladesh, which comprises the fertile Ganga Brahmaputra delta region also went to Pakistan. The irrigation works which remained with India barring some of the old works in Uttar Pradesh and in the deltas of the South, were mostly of a protective nature, meant more to ward off famine than to produce significant yields (CWC, 1993).

In the initial phase of water resources development during the plan period after independence, rapid harnessing of water resources was the prime objective. Accordingly, the state governments were encouraged to expeditiously formulate and develp water resources projects for specific purposes like irrigation, flood control, hydropower generation, drinking water supply, industrial and various miscellaneous uses. As a result, a large number of projects comprising dams, barrages, hydro power structures, canal network CAD *etc.* have come up all over the country in successive Five Year Plans. A milestone in water resources development in India is creation of a huge storage capability. Because of these created storage works it has now become possible to provide assured irrigation in the command area, to ensure supply for hydropower and thermal power plants located at different places and to meet requirement for various other uses. Flood moderation could be effected in flood prone basins, where storage have been provided. Besides, supply of drinking water in remote places throughout the year has become possible in different parts of the country.

At the time of commencement of the First Five year plan in 1951, population of India was about 361 million and annual food grain production was 51 million tonnes which was not adequte. Import of food grains was then inevitable to cover up the shortage. Attaining self sufficiency in food was therefore given paramount importance in the plan period and in order to achieve the objective, various major, medium and minor irrigation and multi-purpose projects were formulated and implemented through successive Five year plans to create additional irrigation potential throughout the country. This drive compounded with green revolution in the agricultural sector, thus transforming India into a food surplus country.

The net irrigated area is 37 % of net sown are and 29% of total cultivable area. As stated earlier, the ultimate potential due to major and medium projects has been assessed as 58 m.ha. of which 60% is estimated to be developed.

India has a vast potential for hydropower generation, particularly in the northern and north-eastern region. As per an estimate of Central Electricity Authority, the potential in the country is assessed as 84,000 MW at 60 load factor, which is equivalent to about 450 billion units of annual energy generation. The basin wise distribution is as given in (Table 4.7). At the time of independence, out of total installed capacity of 1362 MW, hydropower generation capacity stood at 508 MW. The capacity has since been raised to about 13,000 MW. In addition 6,000 MW is available from projects under construction. A potential of about 3,000 MW is contemplated from projects already cleared. The total potential harnessed/under harnessing would thus be about 22,000 MW which is nearly one-fourth of the estimated potential.

Table 4.7: Basin wise Distribution of Potential of Groundwater

S. No	Basins	Potential at 60 load factor (MW)
1.	Indus Basin	20,000
2.	Brahmaputra Basin	35,000
3.	Ganga Basin	11,000
4.	Central India Basin	3,000
5.	West Flowing River System	6,000
6.	East Flowing River System	9,000
	Total	**84,000**

The National Water Policy has assigned the highest priority for drinking water supply needs followed by irrigation, hydro power, navigation industrial and other uses. In the successive five year plans and the intervening annual plans, efforts have been made to rapidly develop water supply and sanitation systems. In the context of the International Drinking Water Supply and Sanitation Decade, the Government of India launched the decade programmes in April, 1981 with a view to achieving population coverage of 100 per cent water supply facilities in urban and rural areas, 80% sanitation facilities in urban areas and 25% sanitation facilities in rural areas respectively by the end of the decade *i.e.* March, 1991. However, due to financial and other constraints the targets originally set for the decade were scaled down to 90 % in the case of urban water supply and 85% in the case of rural water supply, 50% in the case of urban sanitation and 5% 'in the case of rural sanitation respectively. As per policy adopted provisions for drinking water are to be made in all water resources projects. The drinking water requirements of most of the mega cities in India are met from reservoirs of irrigation/multi-purpose schemes existing in near by areas and eve by long distance transfer. Delhi getting drinking water from Tehri Dam and Chennai city from Krishna Water through Telugu Ganga Project are typical example.

Total navigable length of inland waterways in the country is 15,783 km of which maximum stretch lies in the state of Uttar Pradesh followed by West Bengal, Andhra Pradesh, Assam,

Kerala and Bihar successively. Amongst the river system, the Ganga has the largest navigable length followed by The Godavari, The Brahmaputra and the rivers of West Bengal. Waterways are having the unique advantage of accessibility to interior places. Besides this, they also provide cheaper means of transport with far less pollution and communicational obstacles. The waterways traffic movement has gone up progressively from 0.11 m.t. in 1980-81 to 0.33 m.t. in 1994-95.

The development of inland water transport is of crucial importance from the point of energy conservation as well. The ten waterways identified for consideration for being declared as national waterways are namely:

(i) The Ganga-Bhagirath-Hoogli
(ii) The Brahmaputra;
(iii) The Mandavi, Zuari river and the Cumbarjua Canal in Goa
(iv) The Mahanadi
(v) The Godavari
(vi) The Narmada
(vii) The Sunderbans Area
(viii) The Krishna
(ix) The Tapi; and
(x) The West Coast Canal

The Ganga–Bhagirath-Hoogli and Brahmaputra have already been declared as National Waterways. Farakka Navigation Lock has been opened for transport, thus allowing transport for upstream reaches of Ganga with Kolkata. With network of national waterways the carriage and cargo in this sector in the 10 river systems is expected to increase by 35m.t. per year. The consumptive use of water for navigation is not substantial as the wastage is only at the point of terminal storage projects.

A basic necessity of industrial development is adequate availability of water. The Second Irrigation Commission in their report of 1972 recommended a provision of 50 b.cu.m. for industrial purpose for the country as a whole. In 1990, the industrial demand for water was estimated at 15 cubic kilometers just about 2.7% of the total water demand. It is important to note that although the present share of industry in the total demand for water is rather small, that water is used more inefficiently than that in many other countries. For instance, industrial output per unit of water withdrawal in India is only $5 per cubic metre ; this compares unfavourably with not only such developed countires as Japan and Sweden, where the corresponding figures are $25 and $32, but also with a developing country such as Argentina where the figure is about $29. However, a recent assessment indicates that requirement for industrial use during 2000 AD will be about 30 b.cu.m. while it will rise to 120 b.cu.m by 2025 AD.

In a number of cases in both developed and developing countires, it has been demonstrated that regulation combined with tariff and pricing policies has resulted in saving ranging from 20% to 30% or more. In industrialized countries, demand for water does not increase with industrial output; improved technology,the mix of industrial output and increased recycling of liquid effluents serve to keep it in check. In some OECD (Organisation for Economic Cooperation and Development) countries, industrial water use in 2020 will be half of what it was 25 years before. In manufacturing industries in India Similarly, the number of times each cubic metre of water is used went up from 1.8 in 1954 to 3.4 in 1978 and industrial water withdrawal per dollar of value added declined from 0.76 cubic metre in 1955 to 0.54 cubic metre in 1985. Thus, as the industry demands more water, the challenge would be to improve water use efficiency in the industrial sector by alternative techonology such as recycling, bioremediation ,rain water harvesting etc.

As a consequence of water resources development works, apart from the major objectives there has been development in various other sectors as well. Among them, development in inland fish production occupies a prominent place. During 1950-51, total inland fish production stood at 0.22 m.t. which by

1994-95 has gone upto 2.08 m.t. India now has the distinction of being the seventh largest producer of fish in the world and second largest producer of inland fish after China. Amongst the states, West Bengal is the highest producer followed by Andhra Pradesh and Bihar. These three states put together produce about 50% of total inland fish production in the country, while West Bengal along accounts for about one third of the production.

While water is essential for sustenance of human life, it can as well create problems concerning human health being a carrier of vectors for diseases such as typhoid, cholera, diarrhoea, malaria, filariasis, shistosomiasis *etc.* if mismanaged. Water development projects have, however, contributed positively to the human health in the country (Ministry of Health, 1992).

Among the human health benefits, the important one is improved diets resulting from an increased production of staple foods, new opportunity of growing fruits and vegetables and increased purchasing power for foods not produced by those on farm. Other nutrition improvement is due to development of pisciculture and better facilities for feeding and watering the domestic livestock which can also improve diet and income considerably. The development of water development projects not only enabled the country to overcome floods and drought but also have provided enough food and fibre for the ever increasing population.

Water development projects have facilities in providing hygienic water for human consumption, considering scarcity of water now faced in most parts of the country.

Almost all the projects implemented in the country provide water for domestic purpose although primarily some of the projects were not meant for this purpose. With 80-90% precipitation accruing during monsoon only, it has become imperative to store water for designated use. Water supply also has helped to keep populated areas clean and hygienic through better drainage and improved sanitation. Water supply has thus contributed in improvement of health in the country.

As per minor irrigation census carried out in 1987, there are about 1.5 million tanks in various states. The states like Andhra Pradesh, Karnataka, Madhya Pradesh, Maharashtra, Tamil Nadu and West Bengal have greater density. In spite of addition of new tanks during the period 1962-63 to 1985-86, the area under irrigation came down from 4.8 to 3.1 m.ha. It clearly indicates that maintenance of the tanks has been neglected and their capacity has been reduced due to siltation and sedimentation. It has been estimated that about 1.7 m.ha. of net area has been lost under tank irrigation due to drying up of tanks and encroachment of the foreshore area

While the development of irrigation is most essential for increasing food and other agricultural production to meet the needs of the growing population, development of minor irrigation should receive greater attention because of the several advantages they posses like small investments, simpler components as being labour intensive, quick maturing and above all being a farmer friendly system.

Minor Irrigation development programmes in the state is being implemented by many departments organizations like agriculture, rural development, irrigation, social welfare *etc.* At the central level also, different departments launch schemes having minor irrigation component.

The Ministry of Rural Areas and Employment launched a Million Wells Schemes in 1988-89. Till 1997-98, a total of 12,63,090 wells were constructed under MWS with an expenditure of Rs. 4,728.17 crore. It is also implementing Drought Prone Area Programme on watershed development by the same ministry.

The Ministry of Agriculture has been instrumental in providing credit to farmers for the development of minor irrigation through commercial banks, regional rural banks, co-operatives and national bank for agriculture and rural development.

The minor irrigation division of the Ministry of Water Resources monitors the progress of development of irrigation created through minor irrigation project. It implements the centrally sponsored scheme *i.e.* Rationalisation of minor irrigation statistics and conducts census of minor irrigation structures on every year basis with a view to create a reliable database for the development of minor irrigation schemes. It also assists the State Governments in preparation of schemes for posing to external funding agencies for attracting external assistance for minor irrigation schemes.

Groundwater Development is primarily done through individual and co-operation of the farmers with the help of institutional finance and their own savings. Surface water minor irrigation scheme *i.e.* surface lift irrigation schemes and surface flow irrigation schemes are generally funded from the public sector. NABARD provides finance to the banks for installation of minor irrigation projects in the States. In addition, the land development banks provide bank credit to the farmers under their normal programmes also. During the year 1997-98, the total credit disbursement for minor irrigation works out of Rs. 488.65 crores. Further, many old schemes go out of use due to poor maintenance. The irrigation potential created and utilised through groundwater as well as surface water. Minor irrigation schemes are not being recorded systematically in most cases as their schemes are implemented and monitored by individual farmers. Further, the norms being adopted for assessing the irrigation potential of minor irrigation schemes are also not uniform. All the groundwater and surface water schemes having cultivable command area up to 2,000 hectares are included in the minor irrigation sector.

The emerging issues in the management of water resources are chiefly identifying and examining alternative institutional and policy arrangements. In the context of groundwater to address a wide array of environmental, equity and sustainability concerns. On one hand, there is need to identify local institutional arrangements for the management of water resources by users themselves that ensure equitable and sustainable use of water. On the other hand are the issues of institutional reform in the already existing arrangement, such as those for the supply of drinking water. At the same time we need to look at the role of improved technology in augmenting the carrying capacity of water resources. While much is known in terms of the savings that are possible in the use of water by alternative technologies there is a need to examine the applicability of these technologies to Indian conditions, as also to identify policy instruments for influencing technology choice. These are some of the thrust areas that water resources and management policy will have to address in the years to come.

— — —

5

Water Pollution

5.1 Introduction

The source of pollution are many and varied. The most critical are domestic sewage and industrial effluent discharging into rivers, lakes, ponds *etc.* Treatment facilities for domestic sewage in class 1 cities having population of more than 1,00,0000 and class 2 cities having population between 50,000 and 99,999 can process hardly 10% of the wastewater generated. Wastewater treatment facilities are difficult to quantify due to lack of continuous data. On an average, the treatment capacity in class 1 cities can handle only 60% of the wastewater collected and less than 15% of the total volume of wastewater generated.

The Indian industry has grown annually at an average rate of 5.5% during the last 50 years. Among different industrial sectors, water pollution is concentrated with in a few industrial sub-sectors mainly in the form of toxic wastes and organic pollutants. Out of the total pollution contributed by the industrial sub-sectors, 40% to 45% of the total pollutants can be traced to the processing of industrial chemicals and nearly 40% of the total organic pollution to the food products industry alone. Food products and agro-based industries together contribute 65% to 70% of the total industrial wastewater in terms of organic load. Blair T Bower, consultant, the Urban Institute, USA, remarks: "... If substantial further growth of Asia's cities cannot be avoided and if the environmental disasters that could be associated with that growth are to be prevented, there is only one alternative: urban environmental quality management must be substantially improved throughout the region".

The total quantity of water used by the domestic and industrial sectors is much less than that consumed for irrigation. However, the wastewater released from the above sectors has a great concentration of pollutants, and is discharged at specific disposal points. Thus, the wastewater generated from domestic and industrial projects causes much more water pollution as compared to any other source. The share of different industries in respect of biological oxygen demand is presented in fig 5.1.

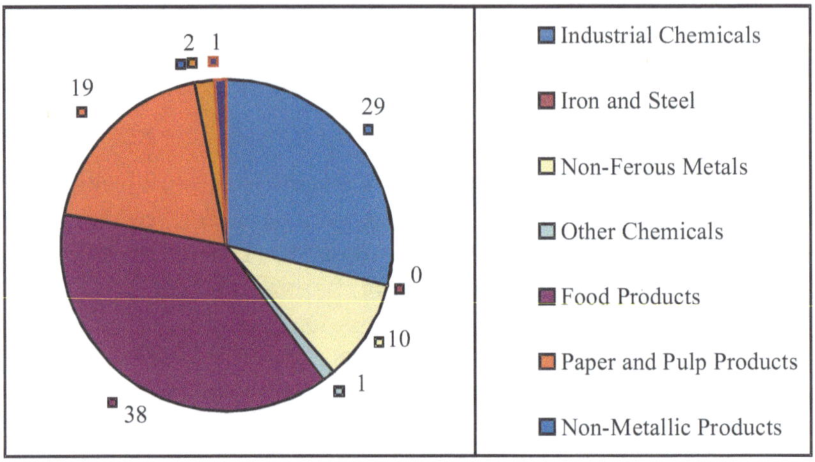

Figure 5.1: Contribution of different industries in water pollution (in terms of biochemical oxygen demand)
Source: World Bank 1996

5.2 Surface Water Pollution

The stress on water resources is from multiple sources and the impact can take diverse forms. The growth of urban megalopolises, increased industrial activity and dependence of the agricultural sector on chemicals and fertilizers has led to the overcharging of the carrying capacity of our water bodies to assimilate and decompose wastes. Deterioration in water quality and contamination of lakes, rivers, ponds, reservoirs and groundwater aquifers has therefore been the result. The need is to bring about a perceivable shift in our philosophy to address water pollution problems. Water resource managers and professionals are beginning to focus on the use of existing infrastructure to meet the demands of a growing population by improving efficiency, reallocating of water for different designated uses, prioritizing the water demand sector-wise and adopting policies and practices that check resource degradation.

Discharge of untreated domestic and industrial wastewater is a predominant source of pollution of aquatic ecosystems in India. Further more, the facilities constructed to treat wastewater do not function properly and remain closed most of the time due to improper design and poor maintenance, together with a non-technical and unskilled approach of the operators. For example, metro cities are drain in carrying wastewater . Rural sanitation is a state subject, and is looked after by the State Governments under the MNP (Minimum Needs Programme) and supplemented by the CRSP (Centrally Sponsored Rural Sanitation Programme) aiming at increased coverage and eradicating manual scavenging. It has been targeted to achieve at least 60% coverage by the end of Tenth plan period.

With government policies that provide hardly any incentive to encourage efficient usage, water has conventionally been considered as a free commodity. Distribution losses of treated water range between 25% and 40%; losses in irrigation are even to the extent of 45% due to seepage and excess application and storage losses are estimated to be about 15%. It shows such a case of resource loss due to water overflow in the irrigation. Industrial output per unit of water withdrawal in India is only $5 per cubic metre as against output at $25 and $32 for such developed countries as Japan and Sweden. Even in the domestic sector, areas with high per capita water availability are known for poor water utilization. The subsidy regime in the domestic sector further leaves the service providers with insufficient funds for proper upkeep of the system and finally affects the quality of service and its efficiency.

Comparing water availability in the country's basins with the standard definition by Engleman and Roy, only four of the twenty basins had more than 1,700 cubic meter per capita per year renewable fresh water resources, nine basins had between 1,000 to 1,700 cubic meter, five basins had between 500 to 1,000 cubic meter, and two basins had less than 500 cubic meter in 1991. In 1997, at an Agro-Ecological Zone 2 (AEZ) level, availability exceeded requirements throughout the country with the exception of AEZ 2 (western plains and Kachchh) and AEZ 9 where it is less than the demand. By 2047 it is anticipated that demand will exceed availability in five of the twenty AEZs and of these, the situation will be particularly critical in AEZs 2, 9, and 15 (Bengal and Assam plains) where availability is less than 75% of the total demand (TERI 2001). Despite the fact that the National Water Policy accords top priority to drinking water, the coverage of population for safe water supplies is still less than 100 % in most urban and rural areas. Though maximizing water availability, water pricing and water zoning for proper management of resources have all been addressed in this national document, poor execution presents a diametrically opposite picture on ground. Further, with water being a state subject and with the absence of water policies at the state level, resource management and conflict resolution ultimately affect resource availability. Inadequate legal framework for withdrawals also affects resource accessibility due to over-exploitation.

The major rivers of the country have generally retained pristine water quality in the less densely populated upper stretches where the likelihood of getting affected by man's interference is minimal. As the rivers enter the plains, these start getting exploited for irrigation and receiving pollution discharges due to human activities such as intensive agriculture, According to a standard definition, for water availability from 1000 cubic meter /capita/year to 1700 cubic meter /capita/year, shortage will be local and rare. Below 1000 cubic meter per capita per year, water supply begins to hamper health, economic development and human well-being. At less than 500 cubic meter per capita per year, water supply is primary constraint to life. Twenty zones into which the country has been divided on the basis of physiological features, soil type, climate *etc.* to facilitate easy accounting of natural resources. Use of fertilisers and insecticides, domestic sewage, industrial effluents *etc.* Thus in the middle stretches, the rivers are most affected both, due to increased water requirement for various consumptive and non-consumptive uses, and degraded water quality. Increased quantity of wastes of a more complex nature finds way into the river and tends to deteriorate the water quality. This makes the situation grave especially during the lean flow season when the amount of dilution water available is less. The Central Pollution Control Board has been monitoring water quality of national aquatic resources in collaboration with concerned State Pollution Control Boards at 507 locations (CPCB 1999), of which 430 stations are under MINARS (Monitoring of Indian National Aquatic Resources), 50 stations are under GEMS (Global Environmental Monitoring Systems) and 27 stations under the YAP (Yamuna Action Plan). The polluted stretches identified in some of the major rivers are based on regular monitoring. The water quality and desired water quality have been classified as A, B, C, D, and E, which reflect the best use of the water. The water quality monitoring results obtained during 1998 indicate that organic and bacterial contamination still continues to be critical sources of pollution in Indian aquatic resources. The number of observations in different broad ranges of observed values for BOD, total coliform and faecal coliform at different locations. The results show that BOD concentrations below 3 mg/l were observed in 61% of the samples as against 65% in 1997. BOD between 3 to 6 mg/ l was observed in 24% of the samples as against 28% in 1997 and BOD exceeding 6 mg/l was observed in 14% of the samples, which is the same as in 1997. The number of observations having high coliform density increased in 1998 against 1997. The Yamuna river is the most polluted in the country having high BOD and coliform in the stretch between Delhi and Etawah. Other severely polluted rivers are the Sabarmati at Ahmedabad, Gomti at Lucknow, Kali, Adyar, Cooum (entire stretches), Veghai at Madurai, and Musi d/s of Hyderabad (CPCB 1999).

In an effort to assess the health of a water bodies, CPCB is developing a bio-monitoring methodology under the Indo-Dutch Collaboration Programme on the Environment. Intensive exercises have been carried out for the Yamuna River and the methodology has been developed and tested for other rivers. In the first phase, 215 locations have been selected for the introduction of bio-monitoring on the basis of the interpretation of physico-chemical data at different locations (CPCB 1999). CPCB has also carried out limited water quality monitoring of the wells in different states and calculated per cent violations over the desired levels of water quality in terms of pH, dissolved oxygen, BOD and total coliform. Certain locations in these states reported 100% violation over the desired levels for dissolved oxygen and total coliform (CPCB 1999). CWC's studies on chemical composition of groundwater in phreatic zones have revealed that in many cases anomalously high concentrations of nitrates, potassium and even phosphates are present in contrast to their virtual absence or low concentration (nitrate and potassium < 10 mg/l) in semiconfined and confined aquifers. The unsystematic use of synthetic fertilisers coupled with improper water management has affected the groundwater quality in many parts of the country. The statewise brief account of the incidence of groundwater pollution also reflects the occurrence of high concentrations of heavy/toxic metals, fluoride and nitrates at different locations around the country moreover the presence of zinc in shallow aquifers of Delhi has also been reported.

Water has been included in India's Constitution as Entry 17 of the state list. The current institutional arrangement for managing water resources in India involves various government agencies. At the central level, the Ministry of Water Resources is responsible for developing, conserving and managing water as a national resource covering areas as diverse as irrigation, ground water exploitation, drainage and flood control. The MWR functions through the Central Water Commission, National Water Development Agency and Central Groundwater Board. The Ministry of Environment and Forests is the nodal agency for water quality and environmental matters. Water supply in urban and rural areas is coordinated by the Ministries of Urban Affairs and Rural Development, respectively. Besides this water is also a subject of several other ministries and departments such as the Ministry of Agriculture, Power, Health and Family Welfare, Surface Transport and the Inland Waterways Authority. Major policies and legislations guiding the management of water resources and its quality and initiatives taken have been discussed. The government explicitly enacted the Water (Prevention and Control of Pollution) Act, 1974, with the primary objective of Preventing and controlling of water pollution. The Water Act established the Central Pollution Control Board and the state pollution control boards for its implementation. The Water Act empowers the state pollution control boards to lay down and maintain location and source specific standards for discharge of wastewater. The actual provisions for enforcement such as penalties, imprisonment *etc.* are confined to source-specific standards for individual polluters. The Environment Protection Act, 1986, is an umbrella act providing for the protection and improvement of environment and for matters connected therewith. It authorizes the central government to intervene directly in order to protect the environment and also allows public interest litigation for the same purpose. The nature of penalties under this act is similar to those authorised under the Water Act. The government has also introduced, as a supplementary measure, major economic incentives for pollution abatement, besides the 'command and control' regulatory mechanism. The Water Cess Act was introduced in 1977, empowering the state pollution control boards to levy a cess on local authorities supplying water to consumers and on consumption of water for certain specified activities. The Act also provides for a rebate on the cess payable if the local authority or industry concerned installs a plant to treat sewage or trade effluent. The cess rates were increased three fold in February 1992. A rebate of 25% on the cess payable has been provided to those industries whose wastewater discharge does not exceed the quantity declared by them and which also comply with the effluent standards prescribed under the Water Act and the Environment Protection Act. Under the 1994 EIA notification, an Environmental Impact Assessment has been made mandatory for 30 categories of development activities involving investments of more than Rs 500 million and above and environmental clearance for activities is given by the Ministry of Environment and Forest. Under the National River Action Plan, certain stretches of major rivers with high or intermediate levels of pollution were identified by the CPCB. Sewage collection and treatment works being created to reduce the pollution load to these rivers include schemes for better sewage interception and diversion, construction of sewage treatment plants, provisions for low cost sanitation and other schemes. In the first phase, in the GAP (Ganga Action Plan), 29 towns were selected along the river and 261 schemes of pollution abatement were sanctioned. At present, 156 towns are being considered under the NRAP, out of which about 74 towns are located on the river Ganga, 21 on the river Yamuna, 12 on the Damodar, 6 on the Godavari, 9 on the Cauvery, 4 each on Tungbhadra and Satlej, 3 each on the Subarnarekha, Betwa, Wainganga, Brahmini, Chambal, Gomti, 2 on the Krishna and one each on the Sabarmati, Khan, Kshipra, Narmada, and Mahanadi.

To focus on urban lakes subjected to anthropogenic pressures, the National Lakes Conservation Plan (NLCP), 1993 was prepared. Bhoj Lake of Madhya Pradesh is already getting assistance under funds provided by OECF, Japan. Under the World Bank aided Industrial Pollution Control project there is a provision of loan and grant assistance to proposals of construction of Common Effluent Treatment Plants (CETP) for the treatment of sewage and trade effluents from a cluster of Industries particularly of small scale (CPCB 1999). Besides, there are other acts that have a bearing on the water policy. The Easement Act, 1882 allows rights to use the groundwater by viewing it as an attachment to land. It also provides that all surface water is to be treated as state property. The Transfer of Property Act, 1994 provides that ownership in groundwater can be given to one only if ownership in land overlying is also transferred. Thus groundwater is viewed essentially as an attachment to land.

The major bottleneck in an effective policy formulation and implementation is the current institutional setup involving various government agencies. Further, there is a separation of responsibilities on the basis of water quality and quantity. As many as eight agencies are involved in collecting data on the following waterrelated parameters: quality of surface water, groundwater quality, monitoring of drinking water quality, sanitation and drinking water supply. Such a fragmentary approach, both at the central and state levels, results in duplication and ambiguity of functions and discourages unitary analysis of this scarce resource. For instance, the CPCB monitors the water quality at 507 locations and the CWC separately measures water quality at another 300 locations. However, the much needed co-ordination between the two agencies in fixing the monitoring locations and defining monitoring protocols is missing. Water being a state subject, the states are empowered to enact laws or frame policies related to water. Even then, only some of the states have set up organizations for planning and allocating water for various purposes. Though water policy for the country has been prepared by the Ministry of Water Resources, only four of the states have their own respective state water policies. A proper legal framework for regulating withdrawals of groundwater is not in place. Though efforts have been made to check the over-exploitation of groundwater through licensing, credit or electricity restrictions, these restrictions are directed only at the creation of wells. Even the licenses do not monitor or regulate the quantum of water extracted. The water cess in industries is potentially an effective instrument for inducing abatement, but the rates of raw water are so low that the rebate has been as much of an incentive so far. Market based instruments to encourage resource conservation mainly in the agriculture and domestic sector have not been really tried. This when accompanied with the subsidy regime in these sectors has resulted in poor resource usage efficiency. It was realised during the later stages of implementation of the Ganga Action Plan, that the local authorities were not able to operate and maintain these assets due to inadequate resources and skills. The level of commitment required from the state agencies was also missing. The pollution arose from a number of diffused sources either urban or rural.

Water quality monitoring by CPCB is at present being carried out at 507 locations, as against 77 stations in 1977. The 476 stations at which monitoring was carried out in 1996 and 1997 comprised 407 stations on rivers, 20 on wells, 33 on lakes, 9 on canals, 2 on ponds, 3 on creeks, and 2 on tanks. Water quality monitoring at 383 locations is conducted on a monthly basis, on a quarterly basis at 121 stations and annually for 3 locations through the involvement of several agencies. The maximum, minimum, and mean values of the parameters and the percentage violations for select parameters are reported. However, specific information is not available for water quality in these water bodies for seasons with lean flow. The frequency of monitoring and number of monitoring stations also is not representative of the quality of the water body specifically in the non-monsoon period. The CWC also monitors the water quality for 47 parameters at about 300 locations. Though there is a dedicated staff for monitoring the water quality at these three times in a month, published data are not available. Information is available only at the regional office level and that too, on request. Information on the availability of groundwater and its quality is limited. Though groundwater availability maps have been prepared for certain locations, extraction rates have not been defined. Much of the information is quantitative as well as qualitative, on water supplied, coverage of population, quality of service and sanitation both in the urban and rural areas is not available. Besides, information gaps on water consumption and effluent discharge patterns for industries also exist.

With water being a subject under the state list, the present approach to water related matters restricts the issue only to political boundaries, involving a number of agencies and ministries with overlapping responsibilities. Instead a river basin or sub-basin based approach to water management is called for. This would ensure that aspects such as water allocation, pollution control, protection of water resources, and mobilisation of financial resources are not dealt in isolation and decisions on the overall development process and landuse planning flow from this. The administrative mechanisms of these authorities need to be defined and operationalised in coordination with relevant state government departments, the central government, and representatives from the community, ensuring that the delegation of authority from the existing departments is consistent and avoids any overlapping. Further, for effective co-ordination, apex level bodies need to be created, as in other countries, to co-ordinate the functioning of different agencies. For instance, the National Water Commission (NWC) in Mexico was established in 1989 as the sole authority with offices in all 31 states and co-ordinates with the river basin organizations for each of the six basins. Plug weaknesses in the current policy and legal framework State specific water policies need to be prepared for all issues concerning a state. Various individual development projects and proposals, water allocation priorities and guidelines for resource management need to be area specific and formulated by the states within the framework of such an overall plan. Revision in the National Water Policy, 1987 also needs to be finalized at the earliest. Similarly, weaknesses in the current legal framework, specifically with regard to groundwater regulations, arise from the absence of certain laws and inadequate provisions. Groundwater legislation aiming at equity and sustainability in access to groundwater and its development needs to be enacted in all states. It is important to assess the effectiveness of the various legislative acts and work out measures that improve their applicability and outcomes. Incentives under the Water Cess Act, for instance, have to be made more attractive to make the industries undertake pollution control measures.

The need is to develop surface irrigation sources and undertake measures for rainwater harvesting and preventing water run-offs. With the rivers of the country carrying about 80% of the flow during the monsoon months of June-September and generally in excess of 90% during the period of June-November, the run-off can be tapped by building appropriate water harvesting structures in the lower reaches to trap the water. However, constraints associated with rainwater harvesting in terms of the capacity of soil to absorb large quantities of water in a short time frame, quality of the harvested water for drinking water purpose, and the cost involved with building such harvesting structures, need to be looked into, as well. The concept of watershed development has also to be adopted more rigorously, which will effectively contribute to the revival of local level traditional water control works. Micro-watershed development provides a medium for revival and integration of traditional water control measures. This type of integrated planning helps to make investments the function to more effectively and economically but it is also more demanding on both the government and the affected people. Obviously a major effort in public education and training of local people to impart the basic understanding and skills necessary for eliciting such participation is imperative. The government should also consider providing technical and financial support for rainwater harvesting, especially in the rural areas. Water being a state subject, pricing is done by the state governments and water prices vary from state to state. With water demand in the agricultural sector as high as 95% of total demand and no proportions between the water rates and consumption patterns, water usage efficiency is only 30%–35%. Such poorly targeted subsidies send the wrong signals to users causing a wasteful use of resources and sub-optimal choices by consumers. An appropriate tariff structure for water services will encourage wise usage of the resource and generate additional support for the funds starved service providers as well.

Together with the measures towards pollution abatement it is imperative to further intensify efforts for conservation of water to prevent over-exploitation of existing resources and reduce the quantity of wastewater generated. As water tariffs are very low, the consumer has little incentive to conserve water. There is a need to take a fresh look at the existing water pricing structure. Additionally, there is a need to develop and implement cost-effective water appliances such as low flow cisterns and faucets and formulate citizen forum groups to encourage and raise awareness on water conservation. Besides the Water Cess Act, efforts have to be made to introduce and implement the Zero discharge concepts, which would enhance recycle and reuse of effluent discharge.

In order to enhance effective treatment of wastewater, there is a need for better collection and interception of sewage. The existing large number of scattered sources of pollution from high-density low-high-income communities need to be converted into concentrated point sources that are easier to monitor and intercept for any further treatment. Many low cost and effective technologies for waste water treatment, *e.g.* UASB, duckweed ponds, and horizontal filters have been developed in other parts of the world but are applied to a limited extent in India. There is a need to explore the associated advantages in terms of the negligible amount of energy required, beneficial uses of by products (sludge as manure and biogas), lower operation and maintenance costs, *etc.* Adoption of cleaner technologies by the industry would go a long way in safeguarding the quality scarce resources. Policy initiatives can aid the diffusion and implementation of clean technologies by encouraging their procurement by the public sector and other government owned organizations leading to development of a domestic market demand for the product.

Baseline information quantitative as well as qualitative needs to be collected for water supply and sanitation both in the urban and rural areas and then used for formulating strategies to address these and prioritizing the action plan. Exercises such as performance measurement of the service provider, specifically in the urban areas need to be undertaken to benchmark operational efficiencies related to water treatment and distribution. This will also help in critically reviewing the various water and wastewater treatment processes and then coming out with some best practice guidelines for operation and maintenance of different types of systems. Similarly, information on water consumption and effluent discharge patterns for industries could be used to benchmark resource consumption and increase the productivity levels per unit of water consumed. A basin wise analysis of the availability of utilizable resources, demand levels and consumption patterns needs to be made. This will help in identifying pockets or states over using water, basins that have poor water utilization rates and priorities an action plan for implementing projects like watershed management to increase the resource availability. Such an analysis would also assist in developing a Water Zoning Atlas to guide decisions related to the sitting of industries and other economic activities.

Community management is the key to an overall successful performance of the water sector. It has been amply demonstrated that projects with community inputs are more successful in reaching the greatest number of affected people with long lasting services. Other benefits include lower costs, greater acceptance of the technology, and better maintenance of the facilities by the users. In order to regulate pollution, changes in government policies are required and community participation is also necessary to ensure the success. However, one needs to maintain some degree of caution while adopting either 'community participation' or 'community management' approaches. Community-based management goes one step beyond just simple involvement of the people in the process .It empowers the community to control its systems. This would require a number of committed volunteers and trained staff to carry out the tasks. At the micro-level, the delegation of integrated water resources development and management procedures to the lowest appropriate levels would lead to redressal of the problems of the affected people within their own social and regional domains. The NGOs can provide a very important link between the community and government institutions. The NGOs can offer their services in capacity building of the relevant stakeholders, R&D for low-cost and effective water supply and sanitation facilities, and timely enforcement of policies.

5.3 Coastal Water Pollution

The various sources that cause pollution of coastal water arise from the discharges of domestic sewage and industrial effluents and rubbish from ships, transportation of oil and exploration and exploitation of the coastal bed and ocean floor. Since the tendency of self-purification of the sea is high due to different factors such as dilution, dispersion in temperature *etc.*, and pollution of the coastal water is not considered as serious as river pollution.

India is one of the growing industrial countries in the world. (Ministry of Industries 1994) of industries revealed that there are 8432 large and medium industries existing in the country but the number was about half a decade ago. With regard to industrial settlement in the country the leading states are Goa, Maharashtra, Karnataka, Tamil Nadu, Andhra Pradesh, Uttar Pradesh, Madhya Pradesh, Punjab, Rajasthan and West Bengal. Where Tamil Nadu the leader in the east coast (20%) and Maharashtra in the west (16%). With regard to distribution of large and medium industries in the littoral states, there are, in total, 491 industries located in both the coast of which 52% in the west coast and the remaining 48% in the east. A study was made in 1994/95 to assess the pollution potential of coastal industries in the country. Under this study, a coastal landmass of 25km in shore (in the land ward side) was considered. It has been observed that there is a good concentration of large and medium industries in the narrow coastal belt. Statewise coastal length, area and number of large and medium industries as also aquacultural farms (may be regarded as industries) located in the coastal area with in 25 km land ward along with the number of industries under 17 categories (in parenthesis) are given in (Table 5.1). It may be observed that 308 large and medium industries are located within the coastal belt of the country which are likely to discharge their liquid and solid wastes directly or indirectly into the coastal waters. Out of these, 233 industries are located in the west coast and 75 on the east coast. In addition, from the available information, there are 138 aquaculture farms predominantly for shrimp farming located along the east coast, alone which is more than 75% of the total number of such farms in the country.

Table 5.1: Details of Industries in Coastal India

Sr. No.	Coastal State	Coastal length (km)	Area up to 25 km from shoreline	Industries	Aquaculture farms
1.	Gujarat	1663	41,575	35(29)	-
2.	Maharashtra	720	18,000	167(38)	-
3.	Goa	140	3,500	2(1)	
4.	Karnataka	290	7,250	3(2)	-
5.	Kerala	560	14,000	26(12)	-
6.	Tamil Nadu	860	21,500	30(15)	20
7.	Pondicherry	24	600	4 (4)	-
8.	Andhra Pradesh	930	23,250	30(24)	88
9.	Orissa	450	11,250	4(2)	20
10.	West Bengal	200	5,000	7(4)	10

5.3.1 Western Coast

Gujarat

Of all the maritime states, the state of Gujarat has the largest coastline. Important rivers outfall are Sabarmati, Mahi, Narmada, Tapi, Purna, Saraswati, Indola, Ambika, Par, Kolak and Daman Ganga.

Not less than 35 important industries including seven industrial estates are located far or near the coast of which chemicals; petrochemicals, refinery, fertilizers, pharmaceuticals, pesticides textiles and power plants are predominated. Major industrial locations are Atul, Utran, Hazira, Vapi and Vadodara. Besides release of effluents from coastal industries and untreated domestic wastes into the coastal water, the port activities at Kandla, Porbandar,Okha and Surat including dredging, navigation and transport of crude oil are the sources of potential threats to the coastal waters.

Maharashtra

The coastal zone of the state is traditionally known as Konkan. The coastal zone is mainly rocky and broacken by small creeks and fringed with islands. Mentionable small rivers outfall are Ulhas, Patalganga, Vogeswar, Amba, Kundalika, Savitri, Vasishtha. Major industial locations are Mumbai- Thane complex and Ratnagiri. Out of a total 167 industries major types of industries are chemical, petrochemicals, pharmaceuticals, textiles, engineering and metallurgy are located in these regions. Besides industrial activities, the port related activities at Mumbai,JNPT and Nhavasheva and transport of crude oil also contribute substantially to the total contaminant load in the coastal waters.

Goa

In general, the coast of Goa is sandy. The prominent river outfalls are Mandovi and Zuari. The prime importance of the coast is that it has an extensive beach resource of international tourist interest. Only a pharmaceutical unit and a sewage treatment plant is located at Panaji and Corlim. One of the major concern in the system generating from the mine rejects dumped along the shore which are ultimately transported into coastal seas.

Karnataka

The coastline is well defined and almost straight but broken at numerous points by rivers, creeks, and bays. River outfalls in the coast are formed by small rivers namely, Kalinadi, Bedti, Sharavati, Swarnanadi. The coast is almost free from industries. Only three industries of chemicals, fertilizers and Iron ore are located at Mangalore and Karwar region. Besides waste generated from 12 coastal towns. The port related activities of New Mangalore and Bharkal including a number of fishing harbours also form the potential sources of coastal pollution.

Kerala

The coastal planes of Kerala is endowed with brackish water lagoons interconnected with natural and manmade canals as also 41 rivers outfalls. The conspicuous feature is that it is a small state but has utilizable coastline of about 14km per 100 sq.km land area. Major industries in the coastal zone are in the category of chemical, petrochemical and fish processing mainly located in the three regions like Calicut, Cochin, Udhyogmandal-Ambala mugal area. Besides industrial waste and municipal waste generated from 14 coastal towns, heavy traffic of marine vessels for fishing, port activities at Cochin, Alleppy, Calicut and Defense related activities at Cochin also form the variable sources of pollution in the coastal water.

5.3.2 Eastern Coast

Tamil Nadu

The coastline of Tamil Nadu is mostly facing the Bay of Bengal to the east with only a smaller part facing the Arabian Sea. The plain is mostly alluvial formed by the important tributaries namely Vellor and Coleroon has formed an extensive deltaic mass at the coast fringed with mangroves. Other important river outfalls are Palar, Cheyyar, Amarabati, Pennar and Tamraparni. The coastal belt is predominantly occupied by the aquaculture farms and sea food processing industries. Other industries like fertilizers, petro and agro-chemicals and chemicals are mainly located at Chennai, Ennore, Cuddalor, Avadayaikoil, Ottapidaram and Tuticorin. Besides industries and municipal waste, port related operation with busy traffic of marine vessels at Chennai, Tuticorin, Karaikal including oil transport as allows the waste of aquaculture farms are increasingly posing threats to the coastal water quality.

Pondicherry

The Union Territory of Pondicherry is surrounded by Tamil Nadu state on the landward side and Bay of Bengal in the east. The coastline is very small. Only four large and medium industries are located along the coast of which a distillery and paper mill contribute substantially to the total contaminant load in the coastal water.

Andhra Pradesh

The coastal geomorphology of Andhra Pradesh coast is characterized by sandrifts in the north, rocky cliff in the south with way headlands, the prominents of which is known as 'Dolphin noise' behind this occure coastal march with mud flats and salt pans. Two broad delta have been formed by the Godavari and Krishna rivers. Other important rivers are Pennar, Nagavalli and Vamsadhara. Major types of coastal industries namely sugar, distilleries, chemicals, refinery, fertilizers, paper and large number of aquacultureal forms and marine food processing industries are located in the regions-Bhogapuram, Bhimunupatram, Visakhapatnam, Rambillimondal, Nakkapalli-mondal, Kothapatnam and Allura. In addition, the port activites at Visakhapatnam and Kakinada also form the potential sources of coastal pollution.

Orissa

The coast planes of Orissa has two districts topographical features. The zone from the State of West Bengal to the north of

Poladeep is concave and very shallow with sandy beaches. The area is characterized by major river outfalls namely Subarnarekha, Brahmanii, Baitarani and the Mahanadi. The remaining part of Paradeep which is near Paradeep to the State of Andhra Pradesh is protrudingly exposed to the sea with rocky beds at places. The coastal area is relatively free from industries except a phosphate and distillery industries at Paradeep and a chemical and rare earth industry near Gopalpur. Besides industrial and municipal wastes from coastal towns, the other important potential sources of coastal pollution are port activities at Gopalpur and Paradeep. Intensive mechnised fishing and waste of good number of aquaculture farms.

West Bengal

The coast of West Bengal, unlike the remaining coastal fronts of India, exhibits a distinctive physiographical feature. The Ganga, Brahmaputra river system, transporting huge suspension load, has created a vast inter-tidal deltaic mass 'Sundarbans' the largest delta in the world with extensive mangrove forests. The Hugli-Malta river system and six others esturies with tidal creeks and channels forms and extensive network in the lower Bengal. Although the state is very rich in industrial settlement, the coastal belt in almost devoid of industries. However an industrial complex at Haldia Hoogly about 40 km from the coastline has grown up. Like remaining coast in the east, the coastal aquacultural fariming has also been a prominent activity along the West Bengal coast. The major sources of pollution in the West Bengal coast are the sewage of Kolkata metropolis and port operations at Haldia and Kolkata including growing traffic of oil tankers.

As regards liquid and solid waste generation, the total quantity of about 1.35 million cubic meters of effluent and about 34,500 tonnes of solid waste are generated by the coastal industries every day. State wise coastal industries and their respective waste generation are given in Table 5.2. It may be observed that the largest concentration of effluent in industries is in Maharashtra followed by Gujarat, Tamil Nadu, Andhra Pradesh and Kerala. On the other hand, the largest concentration of aquaculture farms is in Andhra Pradesh, Tamil Nadu and Orissa in the east coast. Out of the total solid waste of 34,476 tonnes generated per day about 44% in the west coast though the number of industries there is about three tonnes that in the east coast where 56%. This disproportionate generation of waste may be attributed to the power plants and steel mills located in the states of Tamil Nadu and Andhra Pradesh. In the west coast, generation of large quantities of solid waste in Gujarat is also due to the similar reason.

In the generation of liquid waste, out of the total quantity of 1.35 million cubic meters per day, about 0.85 million cubic meters per day is from west coast industries, in which by far the largest quantity is generated in Gujarat. The east coast industries generated the total quantity of about 0.5 million cubic meters per day, in which Andhra Pradesh alone contribute 0.35 million cubic meters per day, followed by Tamil Nadu that ie 0.125 million cubic meters per day. The liquid waste generation from aquacultural farms from east coast only, in absent of data on west coast , is the tune of 2.37 million cubic meters per day, out of which Andhra Pradesh has the lion share of about 2.12 million cubic meters per day.

From the pollution point of view, the 17 categories of industries (of highly polluting in nature) comprise a total of 131 in the coastal area. Out of which 38 are located in Maharashtra, 29 in Kerala and remaining 13 being distributed in other 4 states

Table 5.2: State wise coastal industries (Large and Medium) waste generation

State	Industries (Nos.)	Industrial Effluent (million /day)	Industrial Solid waste (T/day)	Aquaculture farms(Nos.)	Aquaculture farms waste (million/day)
Gujarat	35	0.566	95066	-	-
Maharashtra	167	0.080	2628	-	-
Goa	2	0.012	1.4	-	-
Karnataka	3	0.043	76	-	-
Kerala	26	0.515	2431	-	-
Tamil Nadu	30	0.125	9112	20	0.253
Pondicherry	4	0.006	1.25	-	-
Andhra Pradesh	30	0.350	7191	88	2.12
Orissa	4	0.001	3505	20	-
West Bengal	7	0.022	25	10	-
East coast	75	0.50	19834	138	2.37
West coast	233	0.85	14642	-	-

and one Union Territory. The state wise distribution of 12 categories are given in (Table 5.2).

5.4 Ocean Pollution

India has a coastline of 7515 km out of its 820 million population; nearly 25% live in the coastal areas. Many highly populated and industrial cities like Mumbai, Chennai, Kolkata, Cochin, Visakhapatnam are located along near the coastal areas. The demographic pressure, rapid industrialization, urbanization in the coastal cities and towns has added variety environmental problems.

Demographic pressure in the urban cities and towns has resulted in the production of enormous amounts of domestic waste anaferials. These material reach the marine environment rather directly or indirectly through rivers, ereeks,bays *etc.*, The domestic sewage contributes to the largest amount of waste and it has been estimated that approximately 18,240 ml as of 1994 reach the coastal environment, of the country.

Water pollution plays a vital role in recent past due to scarcity of available healthy water in our country. To conserve water from pollution by recycling industrial effluent through biological means such as secondary treatment like bio-reactors. The organic pollutant is converted by oxygenated through bacterial population and plants.

— — —

6

Forest Resources

6.1 Introduction

The state of India's forests is important in many ways, whether it be as a source of fuel and fodder for rural citizens, of industrial inputs for a growing economy, as a habitat for thousands of plant and animal species, a sink for carbon dioxide emissions, or as a protective cover for its soils.

The forest resources forms an ecological system consisting of tree dominated vegetative associations. Forests not only provide timber, fuel wood, pulpwood fodder and fiber grasses, and non wood forest produce and support industrial and commercial activities but also maintain the ecological balance and life support systems essential for food production, health, and all round human development. The innate complexity and inherent diversity of forest ecosystems make it difficult to establish clear cause-and effect relationship or to predict the outcomes of a given intervention accurately. Figure 6.1 shows that the percentage of land mass with forest covered and non forest area in India

The wide range of economic and environmental services and products that forests provide can be classified as follows.

- Services of consumptive direct-use-value *e.g.*timber, fuelwood, fodder and fibre grasses, and a wide range of non-timber products derived from plants and animals.
- Services of option value, *e.g.* a natural habitat for biodiversity and a repository of genetic wealth.

— Services of non-consumptive direct use value, *e.g.* recreation and eco-tourism services of local indirect-use value, *e.g.* watershed protection, regulation of water regimes, flood protection services and soil retention.

— Services of global indirect -use value, *e.g.* carbon saturation.

— As demands for forest products increase with population and with increasingly consumptive lifestyles, it no longer possible to meet them out for the annual incremental growth. Supplies are also affected because of the diversion of forest lands to other uses.

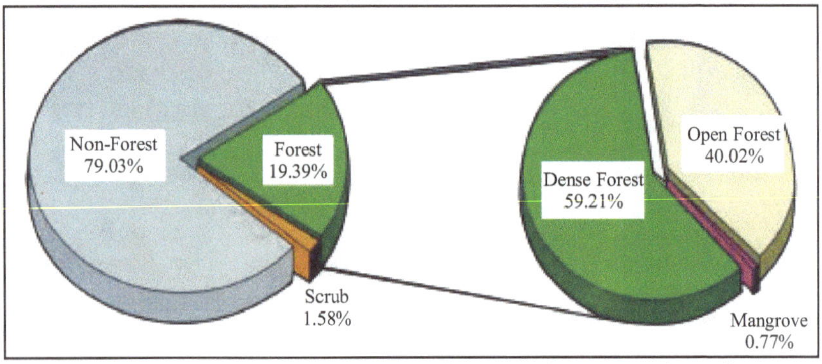

Figure 6.1: Percentage of forest and non-forest area in India

At the Earth Summit at Rio De Genero in 1992, issues related to deforestation were a major concern. The agenda 21 declaration of the UNCED (United Nations Conference on Environment and Development) stated: 'Deforestation is a result of many causes; some natural, but mainly due to human development, such as inappropriate land tenure systems and incentives, expansion of agricultural areas, increasing forest product demand and lack of information about and understanding of the value of forest In the case of India, particularly a review of available literature suggests the following pressure on India's forest.

The sustainable extractable quantity of fuel wood from India's forest is far below the requirement of the population.

Livestock population of India is greater than can be sustainable supported by the available land and forest resources.

The demand for industrial wood and other wood, part of which is currently being met by imports, will continue to rise with industrial development and economic growth.

Unregulated and increased harvesting of non-wood forest produce will result in loss of biodiversity and gene wealth in the forest ecosystem.

Expansion of protected area networks will result in increasing pressure on the existing productive forests by human intervention.

6.2 Forest Area In India

This chapter attempt to study the nature, extent and intensity of changes in Indian forests over the lost fifty years, the competing demands on forest resources and future trends in demands and resources, the best utilization of forest trees for the purification of industrial effluents and selective method for the various trees from the forest. It also addresses most critical resource related problems that have serious ecological, economic and social implication which, if ignored now, could lead to a crisis in the future.

The rapid and impressive progress made by India in agriculture, industry and development of infrastructure has had a significant impact on the forest resources by *Jhum* cultivation *etc*.

With growing population, the relentless pressure to convert forest lands for agriculture, industries, power and irrigation projects, housing and urban development has gone up substantially, trapping the country in a vicious spiral of deforestation, land degradation, and poverty. To produce more food, fuel wood, fodder, timber and non-wood forest produce from a dwindling biomass resources base and, at the same time, to maintain the minimum area required to be under forests to ensure environmental and ecological stability, is a discourage challenge in the Indian forests.

6.2.1 Forest Policy

Scientific management of forests was initiated in India in 1864. India's first forest policy originated in 1894 under a colonial administration, which accorded priority to commercial exploitation and state custodianship and placed greater emphasis on permanent cultivation than forestry, allowing forest land to be diverted to agriculture. The National Forest Policy formulated in 1952 (Ministry of Food and Agriculture, 1952) had envisaged increasing of forest area to one third of the total land area. It has not been possible, however, to implement this policy. On the contrary, forest land had to be used for Hydropower projects, minor irrigation projects, industries, residential settlements, rehabilitation of landless people, construction of roads and other systems for communication. In the late 1950s and early 1960s, forest land was also allotted to people for farming under the 'Grow More Food' Programme, which was latter stopped. Rehabilitation of refugees who came to India after the partition also made large-scale deforestation for human settlement.

The National Forest Policy provided a functional classification of forests and brought under its purview the conservation of wildlife. Forest legislation was brought on the concurrent list in 1977. The enactment of the Forest (Conservation) Act of 1980 put a hurdle on the uncontrolled diversion of forest land for other designated uses.

Only those forest owned by forest departments have a well defined legal status. Such forests are of three categories, namely reserve forests, protected forests and unclassed forests.

6.2.2 Reserve Forests

Reserve forests are the most important category to conservation or scientific management of forest, and have been properly demarcated and notifies under provisions of the Indian Forest Act (1927) or other laws in force. These forest benefits from the highest degree of state control and the exercise of its proprietary rights. Generally, local villagers do not have any rights in the reserve forests.

6.2.3 Protected Forests

Protected forest are similar to reserve forests but the state exercise a lower degree of control and proprietary rights. Local villagers can exercise some rights, unless specifically prohibited by notification.

6.2.4 Unclassed Forests

All publicly-owned forests other than reserve and protected forests are categorized as unclassed forest. The state government exercise the least degree of control over such forests, and they are usually in a state of severe degradation. There is gradual process to bring unclassed forests into the category of reserve and protected forests. The administrative classification of recorded forest in 1995 is shown in Table 6.1.

Table 6.1: Administrative classification of recorded forests in 1995

S. No.	Category of forest	Area	
		(Million Hectare)	As % of total forest area
1.	Reserved Forests	41.65	54.4
2.	Protected Forests	22.33	29.2
3.	Unclassed Forests	12.54	16.4
	Total Forest Area In India	**76.52**	**100**

Source : Forest Survey of India, 1987

The figure 6.1 shows the area covered by forest in India. It shows dense forests, open forests, mangrove forests and scrub jungle forests. The following Table 6.2 shows distribution of forests area in state wise and union territory wise. It is found to be maximum in Andaman & Nicobar Islands forests and minimum area is to be in Delhi forests areas.

6.2.5 Evolution of Forest Policies and Acts

The history of formulation of forest policy in India in recent past may be traced back to the creation of the Imperial Forest Department in 1864 under the colonial rule. The main objectives for setting up this department was to ensure sustained availability of large number of sleepers required for railways. The establishment of this department marked a beginning of the shift in the management of forests in India from communities to the State.

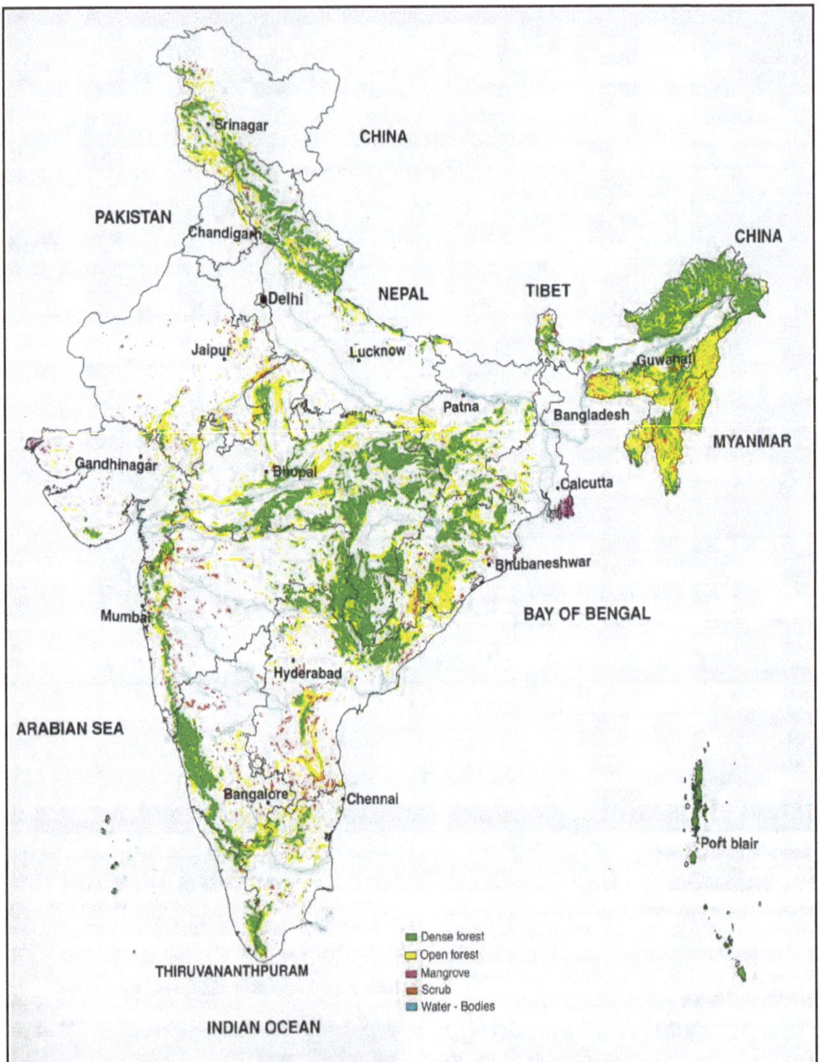

Figure 6.2: Forest Cover in India

Table 6.2: Distribution of recorded forest area in States/UTs (sq.km)

State/UT	Geographic Area	Reserved	Protected	Unclassed	Total	Per cent
Andhra Pradesh	275,068	50,479	12,365	970	63,814	23.20
Arunachal Pradesh	83,743	15,321	8	36,211	51,540	61.54
Assam	78,438	18,242	3,934	8,532	30,708	39.15
Bihar	173,877	5,051	24,168	7	29,226	16.81
Delhi	1,483	78	7	0	85	2.83
Goa	3,702	165	0	1,259	1,424	38.46
Gujarat	196,024	13,819	997	4,577	19,393	9.89
Haryana	44,212	247	1,104	322	1,673	3.78
Himachal Pradesh	55,673	1,896	31,473	2,038	35,407	63.60
Jammu & Kashmir	222,235	20,182	–	–	20,182	9.08
Karnataka	191,791	28,611	3,932	6,181	38,724	20.19
Kerala	38,863	11,038	183	–	11,221	28.87
Madhya Pradesh	443,446	82,700	66,678	5,119	154,497	34.84
Maharashtra	307,690	48,373	9,350	6,119	63,842	20.75
Manipur	22,327	1,463	4,171	9,520	15,154	67.87
Meghalaya	22,429	981	12	8,503	9,496	42.34
Mizoram	21,081	7,127	3,568	5,240	15,935	75.59
Nagaland	16,579	86	507	8,036	8,629	52.04
Orissa	155,707	27,087	30,080	17	57,184	36.73
Punjab	50,362	44	1,107	1,750	2,901	5.76
Rajasthan	342,239	11,585	16,837	3,278	31,700	9.26
Sikkim	7,096	2,261	285	104	2,650	37.34
Tamil Nadu	130,058	19,486	2,528	614	22,628	17.40
Tripura	10,486	3,588	509	2,196	6,293	60.01
Uttar Pradesh	294,411	36,425	1,499	13,739	51,663	17.54
West Bengal	88,752	7,054	3,772	1,053	11,879	13.38
A&N Islands	8,249	2,929	4,242	0	7,171	86.93
Chandigarh	114	31	0	0	31	27.19
Dadra & Nagar Haveli	491	198	5	0	203	41.34
Daman & Diu	112	0	0.7	0	0.7	0.62
Lakshdweep	32	0	0	0	0	0
Pondicherry	493	0	0	0	0	0
Total		**416,547**	**223,321**	**125,385**	**765,253**	**23.28**

Source: State/UT Forest Department, 1987.

6.2.6 *Forest Act, 1865*

The first Forest Act was enacted in 1865 mainly to facilitate the acquisition of forest areas that could supply timber to the railways without abridging the existing rights of the people. The forest in this Act was defined as "land covered with trees, brushwood and jungle".

6.2.7 *Forest Act, 1878*

The next Forest Act was enacted in 1878 after realising that many of the provisions made in the previous Act were not adequate for an effective control by the State. The definition of the forest itself inhibited raising of plantations by the State on barren lands. The Forest Act of 1878, therefore, reversed almost all provisions of the Forest Act of 1865 except the provision of "arrest without warrant". Some of the important provisions of the new Act were as follows: (1) any land whatsoever could be designated as forest, (2) treatment of customary rights of Indian villager as based on privilege and not on right, (3) a bar to accrual of any further rights of people on Reserved Forests, (4) conversion of Protected Forests into Reserved Forests as and when required, and (5) constitution of a third category of forests as Village Forests. This Act provided a great deal of flexibility to the forest settlement officers that resulted in large variations between different regions in terms of rights of forest dwellers.

6.2.8 *Forest Policy, 1894*

A resolution on forest policy was made for the first time in 1894. The salient features of the policy were as follows:

1. The sole object with which State forests are administered is public benefit. In general, the constitution and preservation of a forest involve the regulation of rights and the restriction of privileges of the user in the forest by the neighbouring population
2. Forests situated on hill slopes should be maintained as protection forests to preserve the climatic and physical conditions of the country and to protect the cultivated

plains that lie below them from the devastating action of hill torrents

3. Forests which are the reservoirs of valuable timbers should be managed on commercial lines as a source of revenue to the Central and States

4. Wherever an effective demand for culturable land exists and can only be supplied from forest area, the land should ordinarily be relinquished without hesitation, subject to the following conditions

   Honey combing of a valuable forest by patches of cultivation should not be allowed

   Cultivation must be permanent and must not be allowed to an extent as to encroach upon minimum area of forest that is needed to meet the reasonable forest requirements, present and prospective and

5. Forest that yield only inferior timber, fuel wood or fodder, or are used for grazing, should be managed mainly in the interest of local population. Care being taken to see that the user is not exercised so as to annihilate its subject and the people are protected against their own improvidence.

6.2.9 Forest Act, 1927

The Indian Forest Act 1927 largely involved redrafting of some clauses of the Forest Act 1878. One major change is stated to be its reference to individuals and not individuals or communities while referring to rights on forests.

6.2.10 National Forest Policy, 1952

A resolution on the first post-independence era Forest Policy was issued in 1952. While this policy retained the basic thrust of the earlier policy, it emphasized a balance across economic, ecological and social benefits from the forests. It thus proposed to classify the forests on a functional basis into (i) protection forests, (ii) national forests,(iii) village forests, and (iv) tree lands.

While the functions of protection forests and village forests were the same as laid down in the earlier policy, the national forests were meant for meeting the requirements of defence, communications and industry with a progressively increasing sustainable yield, and the tree lands were proposed for improving physical and climatic conditions and for promoting general well being of people. The provision of centralised management was continued.

6.2.11 National Forest Policy, 1988

It was only about 25 years later that the Forest Policy 1988 underscored community participation in protection and development of forests. The objectives of the Forest Policy 1988 have been stated as (i) maintenance of environmental stability through preservation and restoration of ecological balance, (ii) conservation of natural heritage, (iii) check on soil erosion and denudation in catchment areas of rivers, lakes and reservoirs, (iv) check on extension of sand dunes in desert areas of Rajasthan and along coastal tracts, (v) sustainable increase in forest tree cover through massive afforestation and social forestry programmes, (vi) steps to meet requirement of fuelwood, fodder, minor forest produce and timber of rural and tribal populations, (vii) increase in productivity of forest to meet the national needs, (viii)encouragement to efficient utilisation of forest produce and optimum substitution of wood, and (ix) steps to create massive people's movement with involvement of women to achieve the objectives and minimise pressure on existing forests.

India has a recorded forest area of 76.52 million hectares that is 23.28 % of its total geographical area. The ownership of this forest area rests largely with the Government. It is estimated that 92.47 % of the recorded forest area is owned by the Forest Departments, 3.18 percent by other Government Departments, 2.45 % by corporate bodies, and 1.91 % by others (Sagreiya 1994, p 45). The total forest area has been classified into three categories, namely, Reserved Forests (54.44%), Protected Forests (29.18%), and Unclassed Forests (16.38%). There are 87 National Parks and 485 Wildlife Sanctuaries created for in situ conservation of bio-diversity. These National Parks and Wildlife Sanctuaries covering 4.75 % (15.60 m.ha.) of the total geographical area are referred together as Protected Areas. The network of Protected Areas also include 23 Tiger Reserves spread over 3.30 million hectares overlapping with National Parks and Wildlife Sanctuaries. There are 11 Biosphere Reserves with an area of 4.76 million hectares part of which goes even beyond Protected Areas. Table 6.3 shows the comparative account of forests cover of states and union territories during 1997 and 1999 assessments. Few states show the decreasing area of forests and some show increasing forests area.

Table 6.4: Comparative account of forest cover of States/UTs in 1997 & 1999 assessments.

State/UT	1997 Assessment		1999 Assessment		
	Data period	Forest (sq.km.) cover	Data period	Forest cover (sq.km.)	Change (sq.km.)
Andhra Pradesh	Oct.93	43,290	Nov.98-Jan.99	44,229	+939
Arunachal Pradesh	Nov.94-Nov.95	68,602	Dec.98-Feb.99	68,847	+245
Assam	Dec.93, Apr.-Nov.94	23,824	Dec. 98	23,688	-136
Bihar	Nov.-Dec.94	26,524	Dec.95, Jan.96	26,474	-50
Delhi	Oct.-Nov. 92 & 94	26	Oct.-Nov. 98	88	+62
Goa	Dec.93-.94	1,252	Dec.95-Jan.96	1,251	-1
Gujarat	Oct.- Dec.94	12,578	Oct.-Dec. 96 & 97	12,965	+387
Haryana	Oct.-Nov. 92 & 94	604	Nov.-Dec. 96	964	+360
Himachal Pradesh	Oct.94-Nov.95	12,521	Oct. -Dec.98	13,082	+561
Jammu & Kashmir	Nov.94-95	20,440	Oct.-Dec. 96 & 97	20,441	+1
Karnataka	Dec.93 , Jan.94	32,403	Dec. 95-Jan. 96	32,467	+64
Kerala	Mar.-Apr., 95	10,334	Jan. Mar. 96	10,323	-11
Maharashtra	Oct.-Nov.93	46,143	Oct. –Nov.96	46,672	+529
Manipur	Dec.93-Feb.94	17,418	Dec. 98	17,384	-34
Meghalaya	Dec.93	15,657	Dec. 98	15,633	-24

State/UT	1997 Assessment		1999 Assessment		
	Data period	Forest (sq.km.) cover	Data period	Forest cover (sq.km.)	Change (sq.km.)
Mizoram	Dec.93-Feb.94	18,775	Dec. 98	18,338	-437
Nagaland	Dec.93-Oct.94	14,221	Dec. 98	14,164	-57
Orissa	Oct.-Nov.93	46,941	Nov.-Dec. 95	47,033	+92
Punjab	Oct.94- Jan 95	1,387	Nov.-Dec. 96	1,412	+25
Rajasthan	Nov.-Dec.94	13,353	Oct.-Dec. 96	13,871	+518
Sikkim	Sep.94	3,129	Nov. 98	3,118	-11
Tamil Nadu	Mar.94	17,064	Jan., Mar., Sep. 96	17,078	+14
Tripura	Dec.93	5,546	Dec. 98	5,745	+199
Uttar Pradesh	Oct.-Dec.94	33,994	Oct.-Dec. 96	34,016	+22
West Bengal	Oct.-Dec.93	8,349	Dec. 95-Feb.96	8,362	+13
A&N Islands	Dec.94	7,613	Dec. 96 Mar.97 & Jan.-Mar. 98	7,606	-7
Chandigarh	Oct.-Nov.94	7	Jan. 99	7	0
D & N Haveli	Oct.-Dec.94	204	Nov.-Dec. 98	202	-2
Daman & Diu	Oct.-Dec.94	3	Oct. 96	3	0
				Total	+3,896

* No discernible forest cover.

Fig 6.3 shows sources of supply of fuel and wood during 1995 from Indian forests. It shows that the maximum fuel wood is coming from forestlands; figure 6.4 shows percentage of fuel wood in India by state wise distribution. It is distributive evenly.

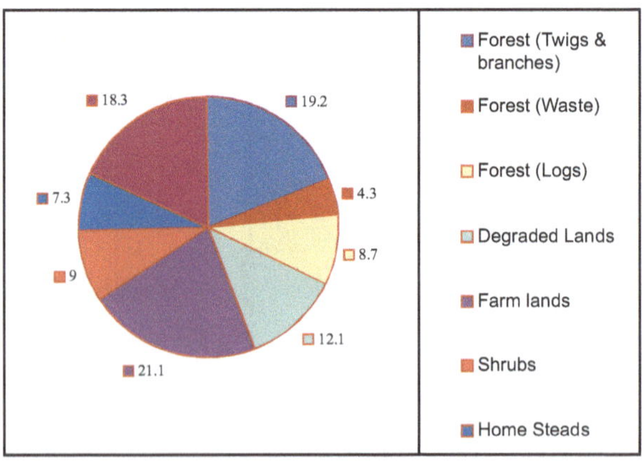

Figure 6.3: Sources of Supply of Fuel Wood During 1995

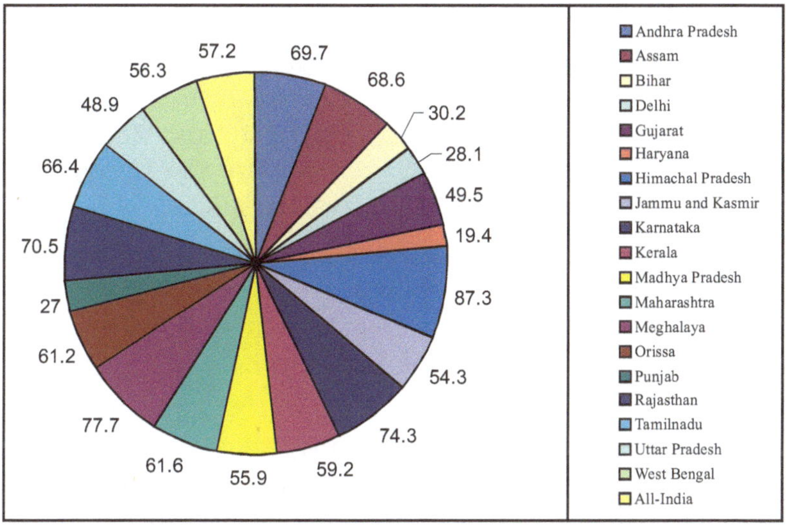

Figure 6.4: Percentage of Fuel Wood In India During 1985

Figure 6.5 shows share of fuel wood in total domestic energy consumption in rural area. It elaborated about contribution to energy consumption in rural areas.

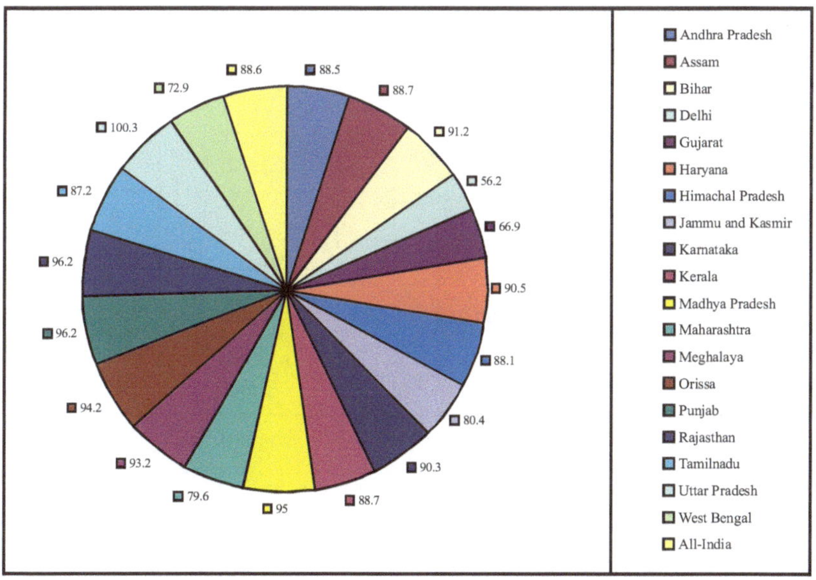

Figure 6.5: Share of Fuel Wood In Domestic Energy Consumption In Rural Areas (1978/79).

6.3 Tamil Nadu Forest Resources

Tamil Nadu has a geographic area of 13 million ha which constitutes 3.96% of the land area of the country. It lies between latitude 8° 04' and 13° 34' N and long. 76° 14' and 80° 21' E. The main rivers flowing through the state are the Cauveri, the Pennaiyar and the Vaigai, Tamirabarani, Pallar *etc.*

The south-west monsoon feeds the plateau and the retreating north-east monsoon brings rain to the east coast. The temperature in the state ranges from 1.9° C to 45.6° C. The average rainfall ranges from 925 mm to 1,170 mm.

The total population of the state is 55.86 million (1991 census), which constitutes 6.60% of the country's population. The urban population constitutes 34.15% and rural 65.85%. Population density is 429 persons per sq.km. Fig 6.5 showed land use pattern in Tamil Nadu in percentage it shows maximum (42.21%) from forests.

Table 6.4: Land use pattern in Tamil Nadu.

Land use	Area in '000 ha	Percentage
Total Geographical area	13006	
Forests	2,141	16.47
Not available for cultivation	2,418	18.60
Permanent Pasture & Grazing land	125	0.96
Land under misc. tree crops & groves	226	1.74
Culturable waste land	345	2.65
Fallow land other than current fallows	1,229	9.46
Current fallows	1,028	7.91
Net area Sown	5,486	42.21

Source : Land use statistics at a Glance 1996-97, Ministry of Agriculture, GOI, 2000

The recorded forest area is 2.26 million ha which constitutes 17.40% of the land area of the state. Reserved Forest comprises 86.12%, Protected Forest 11.17% and Unclassed Forest 2.71%. The forest types occurring in the Tamil state are Tropical Wet

Evergreen, Tropical Semi-Evergreen and Tropical Moist Deciduous, Littoral and Swamp, Tropical Dry Deciduous, Tropical Thorn, Sub-Tropical Broadleaved and Montane Wet Temperate Forests.

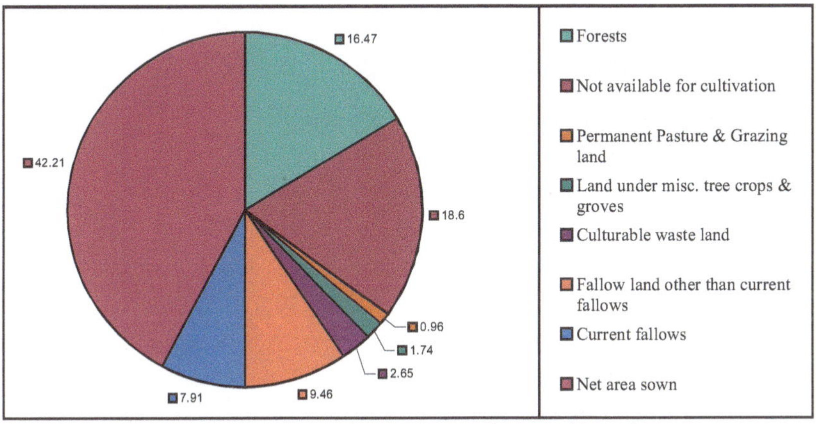

Figure 6.6: Land use Pattern in Tamil Nadu

6.3.1 Protected Area

The state is having 5 National Parks and 20 Wildlife Sanctuaries spread over 0.29 million ha, which constitutes 2.24% of the geographic area. Kalakad Mundanthurai tiger reserve is in the state. Tamil Nadu shares the Nilgiri Biosphere Reserve with the states of Karnataka and Kerala.

6.3.2 Forests in villages

There are 15,822 villages in the state of which 1,405 have forest as a land use. The area of forests in these villages is 1.92 million ha. The total population of these villages is 3.11 million. The villages having less than 100 ha, between 100-500 ha and more than 500 ha forest in each village constitute 48%, 33 % and 19% of the total villages, respectively. It provides details of villages by forest area and population.

— — —

7

Forest Degradation

7.1 Introduction

The rapid population and industrial growth experienced beginning in the middle part of this century has led to spiraling increases in the demand for forest wood. Historical data reveal that there was a 159.6% increase in overall wood production between 1970 and 1993. Wood is defined simply as wood in the rough, and includes trees felled for any purpose. The majority of total wood production has been for use as fuel wood and charcoal, much of which is harvested by villagers, and to some degree urban squatters.

Since 1970, there has been a 160% increase in fuel wood and charcoal production. The largest portion (104%) occurred between 1970 and 1980, which may be attributed to the introduction of fuel wood species earlier, during the Second Five Year Plan period. Looking at the decades to come, the demand for fuel wood is likely to continue growing in pace with future increases in population, which is growing at the rate of 24 % per decade. It is estimated that by the year 2010, demand for fuel wood and charcoal will exceed 33 million cubic meters (FAO, 1993). Since there is expected to be little further change in the area under potential productive forests, there will be an increasing probability of a shortage of wood production in India (Planning Commission, 1992).

7.2 Physical Degradation

The damage to the forest by physical means such as cutting of trees and shrubs, tree felling, collection of minor forest produce by encroaching to the forests. This type of degradation is simple and control easily. It should be given awareness to the tribal peoples about importance of forests and conservation.

7.3 Chemical Degradation

The forest damage by chemical means such as forest fires, quarrying in the forest by applying mechanical instruments *etc.* to induce fires. This type of degradation is very dangerous and uncontrollable due to the vast area get damaged easily.

7.4 Biological Degradation

The biological degradation means that the cattle and animals, and other biosystem can be destroyed the forest area. The people are encroaching the forest land for cultivation and grazing by cattle, is some of the cause of forest degradation.

While data for standing forest cover were not collected until relatively recently, it is well known that India has historically experienced a significant problem of deforestation and the conversion of land to environmentally degrading and unsustainable uses. Out of India's total geographical area of 329 Million hectares (Mha), only 305 Mha is the reporting area. Forests and wood lands occupy about 67 Mha. Surprisingly, the data reveal that since 1947, about 27 Mha has been added to forest area, mostly through acquisition of private forest lands from zamindars (Bali, 1994). However, these figures, which reflect geopolitical accounting modifications more than improvements in the plight of Indian forests, fail to reveal the true seriousness of the picture.

The afore mentioned pressures have led to a wide gap between the demand and supply of fuelwood and charcoal. Already this demand is being met by the unsustainable clearing of forest lands, which is partially responsible for increasing soil degradation in the areas (% area under forest: 1987-1989) shows the %age of remaining forest cover by states in India. The western and northwestern states of Gujarat, Rajasthan, Haryana, Punjab, and Jammu & Kashmir have particularly sprase forest cover, while only the northeastern states could be said to have abundant forests.

In addition to the steady decrease in scrub lands since 1981, there has been an increase in dense forest cover, accompanied by a decrease in open forest cover. This can be attributed to revisions in accounting methods, as well as gains in forest cover in previously accounted-for areas, and in particular, community protected areas.

A further concern related to the sate of forest resources is that of biodiversity and extinction of species. At present, India is home to several thousand animal species that are considered threatened, including over 500 mammals, 700 fishes, and one thousand birds species (Wildlife Institute of India, 1993). It is understood that destruction of habitat is the primary reason for this problem, and future damages to ecosystems will have accelerating negative impacts.

Although much of the discussion regarding forest resources in India has centered on deforestation, there has been a persistent focus by the Government of India on increasing the country's forest cover through afforestation. The planned economic development of the country started in the year 1951 with the First Five Year Plan, which envisaged afforestation for the purpose of soil conservation (Planning Commission, 1951). Subsequent plans included the introduction of a National Forest Policy, which emphasized the need to expand the forest cover to a minimum of 33% of the total geographical area; the afforestation of industrial economic species and plantations of fuel wood and fodder trees; and plantations of fast-growing species. In the past, forests were leased out to contractors and wood-based industries, but in recent years, public undertakings, in the form of forest corporations, have been established by each State Forest Department to take over extraction. The Forest Conservation Act (1980) was a landmark in Indian Forestry. It put a check on the conversion of forest land to non-forest uses from an average of 1440 km^2/year from 1951-1980, almost 5000 km^2/year between 1986 and 1986, finally arriving at a negative net deforestation rate at the end of that decade (Forest Survey,

1987). Nevertheless, while a negative net deforestation rate is desirable, one must keep in mind that forest plantations typically consist of monospecific, even growth stands, and thus are poor contributors to biodiversity.

7.5 Himalayan Forest Degradation

The total forested area of the Himalayan region is reported to be 30%. In reality the Himalayas have been deforested to a larger extent. The floods in the plains of the sub-continent are its direct result. Every year, vast areas in Bangladesh and many parts of our country are submerged resulting in devastation of standing crops, loss of human life and damage to immovable property worth millions of rupees. The colossal amount spent by the Government by way of relief to the adversely affected people virtually goes down the drain as nothing can halt the floods and improve the situation except re-afforestation of watershed areas in the Himalayas that have been denuded of forest cover by indiscriminate felling over the years.

The Indus Water Treaty with Pakistan has no provision regarding re-afforestation of Indus watershed areas by either India or Pakistan or both. Regrettably, the Government of India has also not so far entered into any international agreement with Nepal about re-afforestation of the Himalayas falling in the latter's territory. Until some effective steps to remedy the situation are taken, the floods in Uttar Pradesh, Bihar, West Bengal will continue to create havoc in these states.

Prior to the 16th century AD the forests in Jammu & Kashmir formed a part of fiefdoms ruled by chieftains. After the late Maharaja Gulab Singh established the rule of law and consolidated the state that the squatters gave up their holdings in the forests and settled down in the plains. Earlier, forests were administered by the civil authority, the Wazir-i-Wazarat (head of district administration). The Tehsildar under him used to manage the affairs of a tehsil. The Girdawar used to collect "Rasum" (forest dues) initially from individuals and later on from village communities as a whole for various forest produces consumed and utilised by them. The "Rasum" used to be collected at the will of the administration and the protection of forest was not thought of. There was no control over the quantity of forest produce consumed by the locals so long as "Rasum" was paid

Thus the forests were only worked with the object of securing increasing revenue from them. The departmental felling for timber export began sometime in 1885, originally through traders from Punjab and later by local contractors. The "Pattas" were issued to traders on payment of a fixed sum per tree in advance to fell certain number of trees without specifying the area. As a result, trees were felled at places that were convenient and economical for extraction. It resulted in heavy illicit felling. The State Forest Department was set up in 1881. The forests were divided into compartment blocks which were grouped into various ranges and effective steps were taken to check illicit felling. The State Council passed the Forest Regulation No. 1 of 1884. Survey and demarcation of forest boundaries were initiated. Gradually the Forest Department expanded to cope with the increasing workload. In 1904, the departmental working of forests was abandoned and the practice, obtaining in the other Forest Departments in the country, of auctioning standing trees was adopted.

With the practice of auctioning standing trees to private parties on royalty basis, the process of devastation of forests in the Jammu & Kashmir started. Indiscriminate felling of trees by lessees, in collusion with forest officials, over and above the yield prescribed by the Working Plan became common. It continued unabated till forests were nationalised by the Act of the State Legislature in 1986. After 1947, the number of forest lessees increased manifold because of increased demand for timber both inside and outside the state. It resulted in unprecedented exploitation of virgin forests. However, the maximum gain from uncontrolled felling has been to forest lessees with the state exchequer getting very little. This malpractice continued unabated till 1985-1986.

The Government has been consistent pressing the Forest Department to earn as much annual revenue as could be raised from the auction of forests. It cared least for the regeneration of forests. The denudation of high ranges is the result of this unplanned working. 95% of fires that destroy forests are because of careless or deliberate acts by human beings. Unfortunately, no effective steps have been taken all these years to prevent intentional or accidental forest fires. The greedy forest lessees set fire to forest blocks after exploiting it and then claiming right to fell trees in other ones. The forest officials collude with the lessees in this game.

The worst victim of the explosive population growth and the hunger for land is forest land, which continues to be treated as "nobody's land". The forest in close proximity of villages and urban centres has been extensively encroached upon with impunity.

7.6 Western Ghats Forest Degradation

Western Ghat forest area constitutes from Maharashtra to Kerala facing Arabian Sea. There are many evergreen forest and semi evergreen forest in this ghat. The Western Ghat forest is a continuous forest with height more than 3000 m from mean sea level. Tribal of this area ignoring about the importance of forest, destroy the forest by cattle grazing, forest fires, felling of trees and extension of urban centers are some of the cause of forest degradation.

7.7 Eastern Ghats Forest Degrdation

Eastern Ghat forest area constitute from West Bengal in the north to Tamil Nadu in the south. This ghat is not a continuous forest batch of hill and lesser elevation compared to Western Ghat. There are semi evergreen forest types, deciduous forest types, and mangroves forest, scrub jungle forest types. Tribal of this region and people of this region are cutting the valuable trees, inducing forest fires, clearing for domestic cultivation, Jhum cultivation, are few cause of forest degradation in this ghat.

The Himalayan forest, Western and Eastern Ghats are degraded vigorously due to many reasons. It should be protected by some conservation measures like declared as protected forests from non-protected forests and unclassed forests.

— — —

8

Industries : Their Effluents & Treatments

8.1 Introduction

Contamination of drinking water supplies from industrial waste is a result of various types of industrial processes and disposal practices. Industries that use large amounts of fresh water for processing have the potential to pollute waterways through the discharge of their waste into streams and rivers, or by run-off and seepage of stored wastes into nearby water sources. Other disposal practices, which cause water contamination, include deep well injection and improper disposal of wastes in surface impoundments.

Industrial wastes consists of both organic and inorganic substances. Organic wastes include pesticide residues, solvents and cleaning fluids, dissolved residues from fruits and vegetables, and lignin from pulp and paper to name a few. Effluents can also contain inorganic wastes such as brine salts and metals. This is an incentive for industry to pre-treat their water by neutralizing the chemically active components, recycling, dilution or extraction and collection for proper disposal.

The waste disposal practices, which presently pose a threat to drinking water supplies, include deep well injection of wastes and wastes that are dumped and retained in surface impoundments or evaporation ponds. (Ministry of Industries, 1994).

In keeping with the functions delegated to the Central Pollution Control Board under the Water (Prevention & Control of Pollution) Act, 1974, they covered a number of industries, their production and location with details of receiving water besides details on the raw material they used, the process they adopted to process them, inplant control systems, pollution control system provided and the future requirement with cost implications, monitoring system *etc.*

These documents are also aimed at developing standards for effluents and emissions as Minimal National Standards that can be adopted uniformly throughout the country. The State Pollution Control Boards (SPCBs) can tighten the standards, wherever the local situation demands.

While implementing these standards, the status of technologies adopted by the industries and further requirements to meet the overall objective of pollution control have been assessed. The technology requirement for pollution control industry wise has been presented in the following groups of industry categories.

8.2 Textile Industries: Their Regions and Effluents

The textile industry encompasses a range of industrial units, which use a wide variety of natural and synthetic fibers to produce fabrics. The textile industry can be broadly classified in two groups, namely cotton industry and woolen industry.

The effluent generated from textile industries contains various dyes, chemicals, auxiliary chemicals, sizing materials *etc.* The effluent is usually treated by physico-chemical treatment followed by biological treatment process. However, such treatment systems are not effective for removal of colour, dissolved solids, trace metals *etc.* Inplant control measures such as process change, recovery/re-use of chemicals, chemical substitutes can significantly reduce pollution from this sector. There are described below:

8.2.1 Process change and its sources of effluent

Sizing

Starch is the most commonly used as sizing material for cotton textiles. During sizing, the starch eliminates the possibility of its recovery. It also contributes high BOD. *Recovery of Sizing Material*; The other types of sizing material, such as Carboxymethyl Cellulose (CMC), Polyvinyl Acetate (PVA) are comparatively more expensive but are recoverable.

Mercerizing

Waste contains about 4% caustic. Few textile industries have provision for its recovery. *Recovery of Caustic*: Spent caustic from mercerizing as well as other units can be recovered and reused either by membrane separation technology or by most commonly used evaporation method.

Dyeing

The textile industry uses various types of dyes to impart the desired quality in the fabrics, which generates coloured effluent. No specific treatment is given before it is discharged. *Reuse of dye bath*: Instead of discharging the exhausted dye bath, it can be reconstituted by adding appropriate amount of make-up dyes and auxiliary chemicals. The reconstituted dye bath can be reused for dyeing successive batches.

Printing

The conventional printing involves colour paste application to fabric and subsequent dye fixation. After this, all chemicals other than the dye need to be removed from fabric. This increases effluent generation. *Transfer Printing*: The transfer printing transfers dyestuff, previously printed on paper, on the fabric. Only the dyestuff and other chemicals are transferred on the fabric thus eliminating the after-washing. Figure 8.1 shows major textile centers in India. It shows that the major centre is situated around, Tamil Nadu, Gujarat and West Bengal.

8.2.2 Wastewater Treatment

The wastewater is treated by physico-chemical and/or biological treatment process. Some industry uses filtration alongwith physico-chemical treatment to reuse the specific effluent streams. *Recycling of Treated Wastewater*: The effluent can

Figure 8.1: Major Textile Centers in India

be further treated by activated carbon adsorption process or other advanced treatment process so that the treated effluent can be recycled/reused.

8.3 Dyeing Industries: Their Regions and Effluents

Dyes and Dye Intermediates industry is an important sector of the Indian Chemical Industry. This sector has grown at a very fast pace after independence and nearly half of its production is being exported today. A remarkable feature of the Indian dyestuff industry is the co-existence of units in the small, medium and large sectors, actively involved in the manufacture of dyestuffs and their intermediates. The pollution that accompanies this industry in its nature and extents, particularly, because of the non-biodegradable nature of the dyes as well as due to the presence of acid/ alkali/ toxic trace metals/ carcinogenic aromatic amines in the effluents. In addition to effluent, gaseous emissions such as SO_2, NOx, NH_3 and HCl and solid wastes in the form of iron sludge, gypsum and sludge from treatment facilities are generated. The available pollution control systems and the requirements are tabulated below (Table 8.1).

Table 8.1: Pollution control system and requirements for dyeing industries

Technologies/Current Practices	Requirements
Effluent treatment comprising primary (physico-chemical) and secondary (biological) systems are in practice. Some of the units have also provided tertiary treatment and incinerators for non-biodegradable waste.	Possibilities for adaptation of cleaner process options for reducing the water consumption and effluent generation; better management practices for segregation and reuse/ recycle of the treated effluent; effective utilisation of raw materials; improvement in efficiency of process; and recovery of by-products. The effluent generated from manufacturing of some of the dyes and intermediates such as H-acid is not biodegradable, which requires process change.
Gaseous emissions such as SOx, NOx, HCl and NH_3 are generally scrubbed.	Properly designed scrubber with recovery reuse of scrubbed liquid is required.
Gypsum, iron sludge and sludge from ETP are generated as solid waste. The gypsum and iron sludge can be used in the cement and pigment industries. The sludge is either disposed off on land/secured landfill or sent to other user industries.	Cleaner process technologies e.g. catalytic hydrogenation, use of spent acid after nitration for acidification of fusion mass, which can eliminate generation of iron and gypsum sludge.

8.4 Paper Industries: Their Regions and Effluents

The pulp and paper industries can be classified into three-categories *i.e.* large-scale pulp and paper mills, agro based pulp and paper mills and waste paper based mills having installed capacity of 4.25 million tonnes. Environmental problems associated with pulp and paper industries vary with the size and category of the mill. Although all the large-scale pulp and paper mills have adequate treatment systems but still some of the problems like colour in the effluent and solid waste disposal problem still persists. The colour problem is basically due to spillage of black liquor during its handling which ultimately joins the effluent stream. The effluent that emanates from the bleaching section of the mill also contributes the colour. The toxicity is another problem, which is mainly due to use of elemental chlorine during the bleaching. In small scale agro-based pulp and paper mills, major cause of pollution is discharge of black liquor which is otherwise taken to chemical recovery plant by large scale pulp and paper mills. The absence of chemical recovery plant in small-scale pulp and paper mills is due to their smaller size and high cost involved in its installation.

In waste paper based mills, zero discharge is possible through recycling of wastewater after suitable treatment. But due to poor waste treatment and old fibre recovery technologies, the industries are unable to recycle the effluent. Table. 8.2 presents practices adopted by the pulp and paper mills along with the technology requirements are outlined.

8.5 Leather Industries: Their Regions and Effluents

Tanning is an integral part of leather making process, which converts the raw hides and skins to finished leather, which is used for manufacturing various leather goods.

Tanning industries can be classified into two categories with respect to the kind of tanning practised: vegetable or EI tanning and chrome tanning. Further these processes can be classified into different processes each depending upon the level of tanning a particular industry adopts.

Table 8.2: Pollution control system and requirements for paper industries

Technologies/Current Practices	Requirements
Use of elemental chlorine in bleaching of pulp which is resulting in generation of toxic effluent containing chloro compounds of lignin. It results in generation of AOX, which is highly toxic and carcinogenic.	Bleaching techniques, which avoid the use of elemental chlorine, should be adopted. Use of chlorine dioxide and use of oxygen at alkali extraction stage should be preferred. It reduces generation of AOX by about 70%. The use of oxygen/ ozone as bleaching agents makes the effluent recyclable from this section with no colour
Use of kraft pulping process for delignification of wood/bamboo raw material in large-scale mills.	Use of modern pulping process like RDH pulping, Oxygen delignification should be practised. These processes produce pulp of low kappa number and high brightness, which require low bleach chemicals. Low steam requirement with high pulping yield are the attempted benefits.
Land disposal of lime sludge by the mills having chemical recovery plant	Most of the large-scale mills dispose lime sludge on land. Lime kiln should be used for recalcination of lime sludge so that it can be reused in the process.
Discharge of black liquor by the small scale agro-based pulp and paper mills	Chemical Recovery Plant (CRP) is required to be installed by such mills. The black liquor can be taken to CRP for recovery of pulping chemicals. Some agro-based pulp and paper mills have installed CRP and running it successfully. The installation of CRP by all units is necessary to control pollution and colour.
Removal of colour through lignin precipitation by adding poly-electrolyte	For the industry where chemical recovery is not feasible economically and problem of colour persists, the removal of lignin through precipitation and its conversion into useful and marketable product e.g. binders should be practised.
Use of obsolete technologies like conical save-all *etc.* as fibre recovery system	Dissolved air floatation based fibre recovery systems and micro-filters. Use of micro-filters improves the recycling of wastewater significantly.

8.5.1 Vegetable tanning

(a) Raw hide to vegetable tanned semi-finished leather

(b) Vegetable tanned semi-finished leather into finished leather.

For Chrome tanning

(a) Raw hide to chrome tanned semifinished leather

(b) Raw hide to finished leather by chrome tanning

(c) Chrome tanned leather into finished leather.

In India, mostly chrome tanning is practised.

The effluent generated from tanning process contains very high TDS, chromium (where chrome tanning is practised), high BOD & COD. So far, the practice to reduce TDS in effluent has been to segregate soak liquor and to minimise the total volume by solar evaporation. The chromium can be reduced by two ways i.e. chemical precipitation or chrome recovery. The biological treatment (anaerobic followed by aerobic) is practised to reduce BOD & COD. The technologies available and the requirements are described below:

(i) Chrome Recovery

Adoption of chrome recovery in case of raw hide to finished processes especially is practiced by some of the medium and large-scale tanneries. It comprises collection of spent chrome liquor after basification and recovery of chrome from the same. This results in substantial saving besides reducing the concentration of chrome in the trade effluent. The supernatant liquor after recovery of chrome can be used for soaking. The recovered chrome can be used alongwith regular basic chrome sulphate for chrome tanning.

Large and medium units should provide individual chrome recovery system barring those which are practising semi-chrome finished to finished leather. The small-scale units need to adopt the chrome recovery system in a group of 4 to 5 units.

(ii) Soaking

Soaking consists of dirt soak and main soak. The main soak is retained and used for dirt soak for the next batch.

(a) *Addition of soaking enzymes :* Soaking enzymes @ 0.4% of w/s wt. can be added to achieve uniform and thorough soaking.

(b) *Drum soaking instead of pit soaking :* Drum soaking instead of pits soaking which reduces the water consumption besides bringing down the soaking time from 12 hrs. to 3 hrs.

(c) *Reuse of dirt soak :* Possibilities of collection of dirt soak liquor and adding polyelectrolyte to flocculate and settle the suspended solids need to be explored. Soak liquor after treatment and filtration can be reused partially in liming/ deliming washes and picking. Modern plants are providing these facilities.

(iii) Liming

(a) *Substitution of paste lime by 85% pure calcium oxide (CaO):* This can bring down the quantity of consumption of powered lime to one third of its original quantity. It can also reduce the frequency of cleaning the primary settling containing the lime sludge.

(b) *Provision of slight slope in the pasting area :* By providing a slight slope in the pasting area, the excess liming paste can be effectively collected and used, which is otherwise washed away in the drain by lime yard workers.

(c) *Reuse of relime liquor :* 50% of relime liquor can be retained and reused for liming of subsequent batches. This also reduces water consumption.

Other than optimization of chemical consumption in this section, fleshing can be used for production of high-grade protein. This, if achieved, will solve the problem of solid waste disposal from the liming section.

Use of Liming Enzymes : Use of liming enzymes @ 0.4% can reduce Sodium Sulphide (Na_2S) consumption by 40%. Use of soaking and liming enzymes can improve liming quality resulting in cleaner and flatter pelts. The marginal increase in cost is more than offset by increase in yield achieved in Wet Blue as well as reduction in Na_2S consumption. At higher enzyme levels, hair can be shaved off without burning which can be screened and used as a fertiliser. However some tanneries are practising it while others should be encouraged to do so.

(iv) Deliming

Efforts can be made to reduce water consumption in this section by implementing the following measures:

a. Use of deliming agents.
b. Use of first delimes wash for liming.,
c. Proper deliming agents need to be identified.

(v) Pickling

Use of drained float for next batch

Normally after desired pH is obtained in pickling, 1/3rd float is drained to ensure better chrome exhaustion at lower floats. This liquor can be collected and used for next batch to reduce consumption of salt and acids. Such facilities need to be installed in selected units for demonstration purposes. Technologies for waste minimization in tanneries.

Manual/mechanical techniques for desalting prior to soaking

— Reducing hydraulic load in soaking
— Counter current recycling of soak liquors
— Lime-free Beam house operations
— Enzyme assisted less-sulfide unhairing
— Recycling of lime liquor/washings
— Ammonia-free deliming process
— Salt-less picking
— Pickle-free chrome tanning

— Closed loop pickle-chrome recycling methods involving high exhaust chrome tanning
— Less chrome and chrome-free tanning methods
— Full chrome tanning methods
— Use of Eco-benign post tanning auxiliaries
— Optimization of float volumes in processing
— Formaldehyde-free finishing techniques
— Use of newer finish application systems
— Use of Roller Coater for improved transfer efficiency
— Split finishing

8.6 Distillery Industries: Their Regions and Effluents

The main source of pollution from distilleries is the spentwash, which is produced as a result of fermentation and distillation of the molasses. Spentwash is acidic in nature having very high BOD (40,000 - 50,000 mg/l) and COD (10,000-125,000 mg/l). The different treatment technologies for treatment of distillery effluent have been adopted depending upon the availability of land; filler material for compost and mode of disposal of treated effluent. The existing technologies and technologies required are given below.

Table 8.3: Pollution control systems and requirements for distillery industries

Technologies/Current Practices	Requirements
Bio-methanation followed by Secondary Biological treatment system. Large number of industries has provided the system wherein methane gas produced can be used into boilers which saves the fuel to the tune of 60%, besides removing BOD in the order of 80-90%. The secondary biological treatment such as activated sludge process or extended aeration system after bio-methanation brings down	Two stage secondary biological treatment system is needed preferably using diffused aeration system for better efficiency and saving in power. The treated effluent when utilised on land for irrigation should meet the requirement of TDS by mixing with the irrigation water from other sources.

Contd...

Table 8.3: Contd...

Technologies/Current Practices	Requirements
the BOD in the range of 300-500 mg/l. The final effluent after mixing with the other wastewater can be used on land for irrigation.	
Composting In this process, press mud generated from sugar mill is utilised to produce compost by mixing distillery effluent. Both anaerobic and aerobic composting systems are practised. In some plants composting with treated effluent treated through bio-methanation plant is also practised. This system can achieve zero effluent if the press mud quantity matches with the effluent generated.	Adequate capacity of composting facility is needed and the compost quality is required to be checked periodically. There should be adequate holding capacity of effluent so that at no time effluent finds way into the drain or in the ground water. Ground water monitoring is also necessary to ensure that there is no seepage from the composting site.
Incineration Following drying of spentwash and using dried material in the boiler for steam generation.	Use of the spent wash alongwith baggasse/biomass for generation of power.

8.7 Refining Industries: Their Regions and Effluents

In a refinery, crude oil is processed in Crude Distillation Unit, consisting of atmospheric distillation and vacuum distillation columns. In addition, various chemical conversion processes *viz.* catalytic cracking, hydro-cracking, thermal cracking, *viz.*, breaking, *etc.*; purification processes *viz.* hydrodesulphurisation, desalting, sulphur recovery, *etc.*; and utilities & auxiliary facilities *viz.* water, power, steam, hydrocarbon slop treatment, *etc.* are also in use in refineries.

Various unit processes in the refining of petroleum oil cause significant amount of air and water pollution and also generate solid wastes. The type and quantum of the pollutants, generated from an oil refinery, will depend on type of crude and processes in use. The major pollutants emanated are emissions of Oxides of Sulphur (SO_x) and Hydrocarbons (HC); liquid effluent containing oil, phenol, sulphide with significant concentration of BOD and COD; and solid waste including oily sludge. The available pollution control technologies and the requirements are tabulated below.

Table 8.4: Pollution control systems and requirements for refining industries

Technologies/Current Practices	Requirements
Effluent treatment comprising primary (physico-chemical), secondary (biological) & tertiary (*e.g.* activated carbon) systems.	Possibilities (implant measures) for reducing water consumption and effluent generation; and better management practices for reuse/recycle of the treated effluent.
Part of the oil is recovered from oily sludge and the sludge is disposed off through a secured landfill.	Technology is required for minimising the generation of oily sludge and proper handling of oily sludge and more efficient recovery of oil from sludge using improved adsorbent.

8.8 Aluminum Industries: Their Regions and Effluents

The manufacturing of aluminium involves two important stages (i) refining bauxite to aluminium oxide (alumina) by the Bayer process and (ii) reducing alumina in Hall-Heroult electrolytic cells to the aluminium metal. In Bayer process the bauxite material is crushed and digested in a heated caustic solution. The solution is then filtered to remove insoluble residue (red mud) and the pregnant liquor is cooled so that precipitation of aluminium oxide occurs. The precipitated material is removed from the process stream by filtration and calcined to produce aluminium oxide. In the Hall-Heroult process, aluminium oxide is dissolved in an electrolytic bath composed mainly of cryolite, sodium aluminium fluoride and aluminium fluoride. The electrolytic cells consist of open steel vessels, that are lined with carbon. The carbon lining serves as the cathode for electrical conductance. Consumable carbon anodes (Soderberg or prebaked type) are used to provide a carbon source to react with the oxygen liberated in the electrolysis.

The major pollutants/wastes generated are (i) red mud (solid waste) from refining of bauxite; (ii) fluoride emission (air pollutant) and spent pot lining (solid waste) from electrolytic stage. The red mud is highly alkaline and hence needs special precaution while disposing to avoid pollution of surface as well ground water resources. The specific generation of red mud in our country is 1.16 – 1.4 T/T of alumina production. The total generation of red mud in India is about 2 million TPA. The specific generation rate for spent pot lining in our country varies from 43 to 62 Kg per tonne of aluminium produced. The spent pot lining carbon portion contains 4-8% leachable fluoride as well 0.01-0.025% leachable cyanide, requiring handling and management as per Hazardous Wastes (Management & Handling) Rules, 1989. The existing pollution control/waste management systems and the requirements are tabulated below.

Table 8.5: Pollution control systems and requirements for aluminium industries

Existing Environmental Management System	Requirements
Red Mud: a) *Wet disposal* : In this method, washed red mud slurry containing 10- 30% solids is pumped to the pond. b) *Dry disposal* : In this method, the red mud disposed contains 30 – 50% moisture and also known as thickened tailing disposal	Dry disposal in secured land fill, as dry disposal requires much less space (1/3 to 1/5 of Wet disposal) and less seepage is expected.
Spent Pot Lining: a) *Flouride recovery* followed by use as fuel. b) *Disposal in secured* landfill to avoid leakage of fluoride and cyanide.	a) Fluoride recovery followed by reuse for carbon portion (Impact of such reuses need to be investigated). b) Disposal in secured landfill for refractory portion.

8.9 Steel Industries: Their Regions and Effluents

Iron and steel is one of the largest sectors of industries in India. Though the production of steel is vital for the economic growth but its production is a major source of pollution. The production of steel causes water, air and noise pollution and generation of solid wastes including hazardous waste. The main units of steel industry causing pollution are coke oven and by-product plant, steel melting shop, sintering plant, blast furnace, refractory material plant and captive thermal power plant (Fig. 8.2).

Figure 8.2: Metal industries in India

8.10 Coke Oven By-product Plants

In coke ovens plants, the volatile materials released during cooking flows from the oven to the by-product plants where ammonia, benzol, xylene, toluene, tar, pitch and tar acids are recovered. Table 8.6 shows the pollution control systems and requirements of coke oven by product plants in India.

Table 8.6: Pollution control systems and requirements for coke oven industries

Technologies/Current Practices	Requirements
Coke Oven In coke ovens the volatile materials released during cooking flows from the oven to the by-product plants where ammonia, benzol, xylene, toluene, tar, pitch and tar acids are recovered. The operations are associated with fugitive and stack emissions. The PAH compounds released during cooking operation as fugitive emissions are carcinogenic in nature. The technologies available to control the pollution are - HPLA system - Hydraulic door and door frame cleaner - Doors with double knife edge and rope sealing - Water sealed AP caps - Screw feeder	- Land based pushing and charging emission control with dust extraction system - Automation for process operations - Self sealing air cooled doors - Possibility of coke dry quenching needs to be tried out Effluent treatment plant to treat cyanide, phenol, ammonia, COD etc. - Hazardous waste (tar sludge and ETP sludge) handling and disposal following Hazardous Waste Handling, Rules; or, tar sludge / ETP sludge charging alongwith the coal fines in the coke ovens
Sintering Plant - ESP / bag filter / wet scrubber for process emissions - ESP / bag filter / wet scrubber for work zone environment	- ESP / bag filters with higher efficiency of removal for process emissions.
Thermal Power Plant - ESP for the emissions	- Proper management and utilisation of fly ash
Steel Melting Shop - ESP/ bag filter wet scrubber for the process emissions - Effluent treatment comprising settling unit and re-circulation system for the treated effluent	- Proper operation and maintenance of air emission control and effluent treatment systems.

Contd...

Table 8.3: Contd...

Technologies/Current Practices	Requirements
Blast Furnace - ESP / bag filter / wet scrubber for air emissions	- Proper operation and maintenance of ESP / bag filter / wet scrubber for air emissions - BF slag utilisation
Lime / dolomite plant - ESP bag filter / multiclones for process and work zone dust emissions	- Effective operation and maintenance of ESP / bag filter / multiclones for process and work zone dust emissions
Mills - Oil & Grease traps and settling tanks for waste water treatment	- API separators and settling tanks for wastewater treatment
Raw material handling units - Enclosures and water sprinkling system	- Improvements in the systems for controlling fugitive emissions.

8.11 Bulk Drug Manufacturing Industry

Environmental pollution control in bulk-drug manufacturing industry requires high skilled manpower due to its nature of pollutants. In general, it has been observed that the final product's purity is of major concern to the industry. Thus, the rejects (unreacted/converted portion of raw materials) contribute to the major pollution load from the industry. The industry involves several batch reactors to get required product and each reaction yields different kinds of pollutants depending upon particular reactants and process. There are number of streams with different characteristics which emanate from the various sections of the industry, requiring segregation and corresponding treatment instead of the conventional end-of-pipe treatment system for combined effluent. The air pollution potential is also significant, though quantity of air pollutants may not be much. However, the toxic emissions (fugitive and channelised) are required to be properly collected and treated. The solid waste generated from the industry falls under hazardous categories, thus the compliance as per hazardous waste management rules is required. The following table shows the existing pollution control systems and requirements for the bulk drug manufacturing plants.

Table 8.7: Pollution control systems and requirements for bulk drug industries

Technologies/Current Practices	Requirements
Wastewater treatment Collection of all the streams and providing collective treatment (end-of-the-pipe treatment) as follows: • Collection tanks - For separation of carbon black (usually used for the colour removal of the final product). • Oil & Grease trap - conventional separator • Equalisation tank • Neutralisation • Primary clarification • Biological treatment (mostly activated sludge process and lagoons) • Secondary clarifier	***Wastewater treatment*** • In-plant pollution control measures • Process optimisation/ modifications to avoid untreatable pollutants generation • Segregation of effluent streams and characterisation for separate treatment as necessary is shown on next page. • Salt recovery from high TDS (inorganic) containing streams through forced evaporation system. • Efficient solvent recovery systems.

Combi-nation	Quality of Effluent	Treatment Options
1	Waste is not easily bio-degradable but toxic	1. Thermal decomposition (based on calorific value) 2. Chemical oxidation by hydrogen peroxide, ozone etc. 3. Evaporation + Secure land-fill
2	May be toxic; not suitable for biological treatment; mostly inorganic salts	1. Chemical treatment (recovery, precipitation etc.) 2. Evaporation + Secure land-fill of evaporated residue
3	Highly organic effluent fully biodegradable	1. Anaerobic + Aerobic treatment 2. If quantity is less, incineration

Table 8.7: Contd...

Combination	Quality of Effluent	Treatment Options
		(based on calorific value) + Secure land-fill of incineration ash
4	Only inorganic salts, no need for biological treatment	1. Solar evaporation 2. Forced evaporation (after separation of volatile organic matter) 3. Reverse osmosis
5	Highly organic effluent, may not be easily biodegradable	1. Thermal decomposition 2. Chemical oxidation by hydrogen peroxide or ozone or sodium, hypochlorite etc. 3. Chemical + biological treatment
6	Highly inorganic effluent, not suitable for biological treatment	1. Chemical recovery 2. Chemical oxidation + biological treatment
7	Organic effluent, fully biodegradable	Anaerobic + aerobic treatment
8	Low organic and low inorganic effluent	Recycle and reuse (after preliminary treatment)

8.12 Pesticides Industries

Pesticides manufacturing involves various toxic chemicals as raw materials and a number of unit operations to get required technical grade product. In a unit process, due to impurities in raw materials, variations in operational parameters of the reactor vessels and thermodynamic limitations, 100% conversion of raw materials into products is impracticable. Hence, excess chemicals are fed into the reactor to get the required efficiency and quantity of final product. The unconverted reactants from each unit process generate wastes in the form of effluents, emissions and solids. The table 8.8 shows the pollution control systems in current practices and their future requirements.

Table 8.8: Pollution control systems and requirements for pesticides industries

Technologies/Current Practices	Requirements
Wastewater Treatment • pH correction • Solar evaporation ponds for high TDS/inorganic effluent • Incinerator for high organic waste	*Wastewater Treatment* • In-plant pollution control measures • Process optimisation/ automation to avoid discarded products, and to reduce pollutants generation • Segregation of streams and providing treatment as follows: • Inorganic streams - recovery of salts through forced evaporation or membrane separation • Highly organic streams (toxic effluents) which cannot be treated biologically are to be chemically treated or incinerated, depending on calorific value. • medium organic streams are to be biologically treated (preferably extended aeration). • Efficient solvent recovery systems • Identification of compatible streams for neutralisation to avoid chemical closing and formation of additional total dissolved solids concentrations. • Homogenisation of effluent, before feeding into biological systems • Usage of pure oxygen, ozonation, chemical wherever necessary.

8.13 Caustic Soda Industries

There are 40 units manufacturing caustic soda in India with an installed capacity of 2.27 million tonnes per annum, and the actual production in the year 1998 has been about 1.49 million tonnes. 34% of the capacity is based on the mercury cell process, and 66% on the membrane process. The major environmental problems posed by this industrial sector is from the mercury cell process and although this metal is not supposed to get consumed as per the chemistry of the production, it gets entrapped into the circulating brine solution and all the product and bye-product streams. This leads to contamination of the water, wastewater, air and solid wastes generated from the production activities. Also, since the quantity of mercury involved in the production is very large, its leakage, spillage and even evaporation of the spilled mercury are observed to be very common and require proper and timely attention. A limit of 0.01 mg/l has been prescribed for the levels of mercury in the effluent alongwith a limitation of a maximum of 10 cum effluent per tonne of product. The CPCB experience gathered through visits and in-depth studies of the mercury cell based chlor-alkali plants confirm that a major part of mercury escaping into the environment is due to the lack of good housekeeping practices specially in the cell house and related activities. It has also to be noted here that the efficiency of any of the control measures which mostly involve the end-of-pipe treatment technology, can be affected by the lack of attention in attending the mercury leakage/ spillage or even floor washings in the cell room. Special attention needs to be given to all the mercury cell-based chlor-alkali plants looking at the manner in which the return brine from the electrolysis cells is treated soon after the power failures. This is because the mercury concentration in the return brine after power failures may go upto even 200 mg/l as against a concentration of about 7 mg/l in the brine in the normal running of the plant. There has been a practice of adding Sodium Sulphide to the brine after power failures for avoiding the chlorine nuisance but this addition of Sodium Sulphide results into a bigger nuisance as the high level of mercury present in the brine gets precipitated as Mercury Sulphide and the subsequent brine sludge from the clarifier may contain upto over 1000 mg/kg of mercury. The escape of mercury in the brine sludge in a single power failure can be as much as 10 times the loss in the sludge produced in a day under the normal running of the plant.

The commissioning/expansion of caustic soda units based on mercury cell process has already been banned by the Government and the existing mercury cell based plants are also in the process of switching over to the membrane process. However, there is no mandatory target existing for this conversion and the mercury cell based units need to take proper attention for their mercury bearing wastes including the disposal of the brine sludge. The pollution control measures, existing as well as waiting to be incorporated, are given below as table (8.9).

Table 8.9: Pollution control measure and requirements for caustic soda industries

Technologies/Current Practices	Requirements
Caustic Soda production through Mercury Cell as well as Membrane Cell Process	Conversion of Mercury Cells into Membrane Cells in a phased manner
Addition of sodium sulphide to the brine to avoid chlorine nuisance after power failures	Stand-by Power supply for dechlorination of the return brine in the existing mercury cell pants after power failures, instead of adding sodium sulphide to eliminate chlorine. This dechlorinated brine should be stored and recycled directly to the cells in a controlled manner to ensure conversion of the high amount of the dissolved mercury back into the elemental mercury.
Rejection of the cell cleaning water as effluent for treatment with final effluent	Collection of the washings immediately after the start of the cell cleaning operation and recycle of the washings into the brine system.
Floor Washings with fresh water	Collection of the wastewater from cell house in a amply dimensioned sedimentation tank, providing a

Technologies/Current Practices	Requirements
	pump with nipple and hose pipe arrangements in the discharge line and use of this collected water for floor washings as well as its recycle into the brine system as and when possible with the help of same pumping arrangements (Chemical Age of India 37 (11) : 1986). Also, the floor should be preferably swept and the wet washings should be avoided as far as possible.
The collection and washing of the solid wastes generated from the cell house for mercury recovery	The solid wastes resulting from the cell room should be heated in a closed system and the mercury should be recovered through condensation (indirect cooling).
Scrubbing of the uncondensed gases from the HCl production system.	The hydrogen gas should be treated at source with the help of activated carbon adsorption technique (Chemical Age of India 37 (12):1986). This will eliminate the involvement of the mercury in the HCl production system. The hydrogen produced can also be used for hydrogenation of the oils and the mercury free HCl produced from this hydrogen will be useful even for the food and pharmaceuticals sector.
Utilisation of excess chlorine with caustic soda or lime slurry	The production of caustic soda should be optimised on the basis of the demand, and the chlorine neutralisation should be minimised as far as possible. If at all required, the use of caustic soda or lime slurry should be

Technologies/Current Practices	Requirements
	made on the basis of the use of resulting Calcium hypochlorite or Sodium hypochlorite.
Disposal of sludge cake from the brine recovery drum filter into authorised landfills	Each of the mercury cell chlor-alkali plant need to study the level of excess chlorine which can be maintained in the circulating brine of the production system as the presence of chlorine in brine avoids precipitation of mercury into the brine sludge. Also, the disposal of brine sludge should be made in a secured landfill with proper arrangements for the collection and recycle of the leachate.
Sodium sulphide precipitation, filtration followed by ion exchange or activated carbon adsorption method of the mercury from the final effluent	The mercury bearing streams should be segregated at the source itself in the plant and recycled into the brine system. This will result into minimisation of mercury input load to the final treatment system, and the steps like precipitation, ion exchange etc. can be decided by individual plants depending upon the level of mercury control that can be achieved at source.

8.14 Industrial Pollution Control Along the Rivers and Lakes

8.14.1 Programme and Developments

A programme was also initiated in 1993-94 to identify polluting industries along the rivers in India for priority actions for control of industrial discharges into rivers. While this process of inventorisation continued, the National River Conservation Authority (NRCA) in its meeting held on July 12, 1997 under the Chairmanship of the Hon'ble Prime Minister, decided that the polluting industries which are discharging their effluents into rivers and lakes should be directed to install the requisite effluent treatment systems within three months, failing which closure notices should be issued. Accordingly, the Chairman, Central Board at the instance of MoEF issued directions under Section 18(1) (b) of the Water (Prevention & Control of Pollution) Act, 1974, to all the SPCBs/PCCs on July 14, 1997, requiring them to :

1. submit (within 10 days) a list alongwith the names and addresses of Grossly Polluting Industries (GPI)* discharging their effluents into rivers and lake which have taken requisite measures for meeting the respective effluent standards prescribed;
2. submit (within 10 days) a list alongwith the names and address of GPIs discharging their effluent into rivers and lakes which have not taken requisite measures for meeting the respective effluent standards prescribed; and direct the defaulting industries to take necessary action for effluent treatment within 3 months failing which closure notices shall be issued against the defaulting industries.

The figure 8.3 shows the statewise distribution of industries. Maximum industries situated in Tamil Nadu and minimum in Pondicherry. The programme was further intensified and four Regional Committees of experts were constituted to monitor the compliance of the directions issued by the CPCB to the SPCBs/PCCs in this regard. A series of discussions have been held since then by the expert committees with the concerned SPCBs/PCCs to monitor the progress of implementation of the programme and to ensure issuance of appropriate directions to the defaulting industries by the concerned SPCBs/PCCs. The important decisions taken in these meetings and also communicated to the various Boards/Committees for implementation include (i) the

*industries discharging 100 kg per day or more of BOD

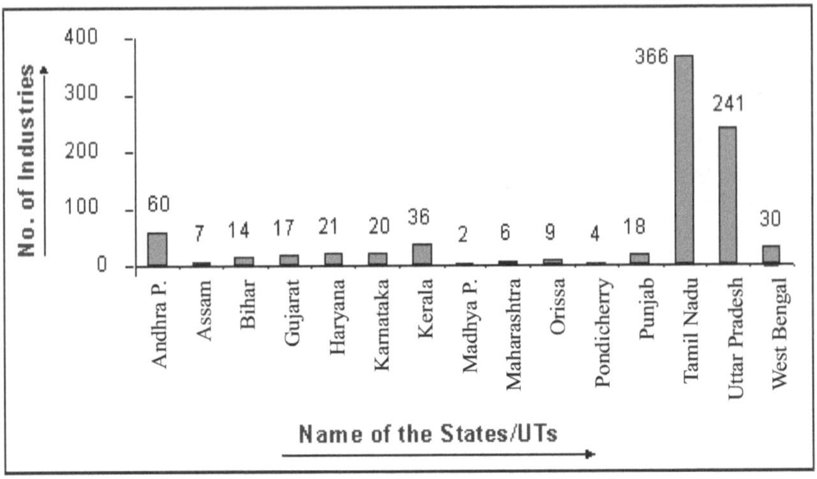

Figure 8.3: State wise Distribution of Industries
Present Status - Statewise (as on August 31, 2003)

industries where the commissioning of ETPs are going on satisfactorily are to be given a reasonable time extension, (ii) the industries which have neither shown sufficient progress nor complying with the standards are to be issued closure notices, (iii) the industries which are closed are to be directed not to restart till they provide requisite ETPs, and (iv) the industries where there is no ETP are to be issued confirmed orders for their closure with immediate effect (Fig.8.4).

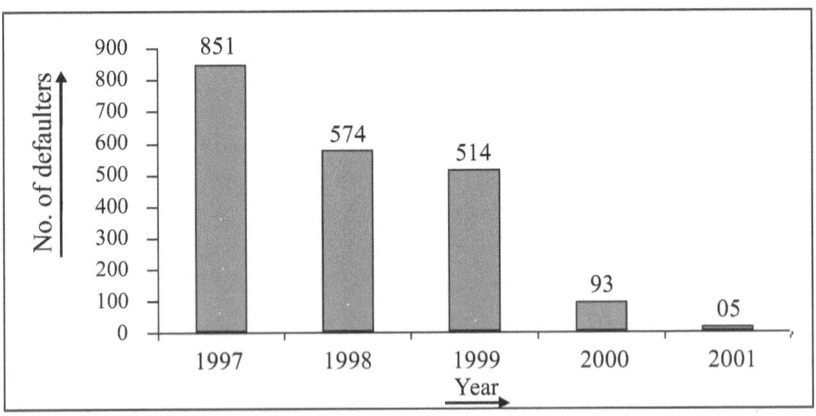

Figure 8.4: Year wise defaulting industries in India

The programme is being continued since then, and the monitoring of the progress include feed back from the SPCBs/ PCCs and direct action against the industries by CPCB in cases needing special attention.Industries Identified A total of 851 industries which are discharging 100 kg/day or more of BOD without adequate treatment got identified under this programme in 1997.

— — —

9

Effects of Industrial Effluents

9.1 Introduction

The sources and types of chemical pollution to which freshwater systems can be exposed are many and varied. The origins of pollutants entering these systems range from those that are predominantly point sources (*i.e.,* industrial effluents) to those that are mainly diffuse, such as agricultural run-off and acid deposition. Some of these are effectively continuous, whereas others are intermittent or episodic.

Pollutants can also be characterized by their quality: general organic loading, specific organic toxicants, inorganic toxicants, and acids. While most of the sources listed above produce mixtures of these characteristics, particular components are enhanced. Industrial effluents generally are the source of specific toxicants, but might also lead to general organic loading.

Some consideration should also be given to the types of system exposed to these pollutants. Most freshwater systems flow, but some more rapidly than others; that is, lakes and ponds have a slow throughput, the so called lentic systems whereas that for rivers and streams is rapid. Because they flow rapidly, the so-called lotic systems have been used for the transport of materials, such as removing industrial pollutants from factories and organic effluents from sewage works.

A view exists that lotic systems that depend substantially on organic inputs from terrestrial ecosystems as a basis for their economy should have the capacity for self-cleansing of at least organic pollutants. However, this perception has been challenged recently (Royal Commission on Environmental Pollution, 1992). Of course, "still" or so-called lentic waters may also be important repositories of pollutants, and are certainly exposed to diffuse inputs from agricultural land leading to eutrophication.

Thus, the challenge for aquatic ecotoxicology is to develop methods that can not only assess but also estimate the ecological impact of chemicals on a variety of complex ecosystems under diverse and complicated circumstances (*e.g.*, periodic perturbations or steady trickles, and mixtures of varying complexity). The predictive approach is important in risk assessment used in the regulation of chemical pollutants. Assessment, at times referred to as a "retrospective approach," is used to determine whether particular contaminants have an impact on specified natural ecosystems. This chapter reviews current methods, first predictive and then retrospective approaches, to address such problems. Initially, one must define what is to be measured, for it has relevance to both approaches.

9.2 What to Measure

Effects of contaminants can be identified across the entire biological hierarchy from subcellular systems to ecosystems. Moving down in scale, effects are usually measured more quickly and with more experimental rigour and control. Moreover, in this direction, systems are more general; most organisms contain DNA, but most ecosystems differ considerably in species composition. Since ecotoxicology is concerned with protecting ecological systems, this generally means consideration of populations and communities that compose ecosystems.

Considerable debate continues about the ecological relevance of observations in individual organisms and of the processes functioning within them. One view is that ecological processes are driven "bottom up," so that specific functional links can be made between effects observed at the organismic and suborganismic levels and those at the population-community levels. Thus, any impact on the physiological materials and energy flows in organisms can be linked with consequences for developmental rates, survival chances, and reproductive output;

these then can be linked to consequences in population dynamics and, alternatively, to the role of a species or population within the community. By contrast, the impact of a pollutant on keystone predators is likely to alter the interaction between prey species in a way that could not have been predicted from ecotoxicological observations on the species individually.

The relative values of "bottom-up" and "top-down" regulation may vary from one ecosystem to another, and may depend upon the extent to which particular ecosystems are structured. Thus flowing-water systems that may be relatively unstructured, because of their temporal dynamism (Peckarsky, 1984; Hildrew & Townsend, 1987), might be subject predominantly to "bottom-up" control. This outcome could be a justification for use of organismic-suborganismic test systems in defining the hazards associated with chemicals to which the organisms are likely to be exposed. More research is needed to clarify these relationships.

Even for ecosystems difficult questions have to be considered to decide which attributes should be measured. Unlike for organisms, ecosystem "goal states" are unlikely, although states related to ecosystem stability and resilience are known to exist. Traditionally in ecotoxicology, measurements of effects have been made of physicochemical variability, species composition and diversity *i.e.* and, less commonly, functional features (Odum, 1983). Yet food-web structure might be as important, as might be the analysis of functional components and their ability to maintain balance of energy flow and of material cycles within systems. Protecting species deemed important for humans might also be important.

9.3 Predictive Tests

These theoretical considerations notwithstanding, single-species tests have dominated studies in aquatic ecotoxicology for the past 20 years. Moreover, certain taxa, particularly the daphnids, have dominated these single-species studies, because single species tests can be accomplished more quickly and easily and, in principle, daphnids are easily maintained in laboratory culture for such tests.

9.3.1 Single-species Tests

These tests can be classified according to either (1) the form of the response measured: discontinuous or quantal (*i.e.*, death or cessation of a specified behaviour) or continuous (*e.g.*, a reduction in growth or reproduction) or (2) the relationship between the time-course of the response and the generation time (GT) of the test organism, may be short or long relative to GT. Tests are usually referred to as acute (quantal and short term) or chronic (continuous or long term).

Most tests in aquatic ecotoxicology have been performed with a single species and of acute duration. Both acute and chronic test systems have been incorporated into legislation concerned with the assessment of ecological hazards of both new and existing chemicals. Their use has arisen largely from the convenience of some post hoc justification of relevance. Thus, the use of daphnids as test organisms can be justified by (1) the key roles that they and their taxonomic associates play in freshwater ecosystems such as zooplankton (interestingly, not often the case for lotic systems) and (2) their proven sensitivity relative to other freshwater species.

Convenience has been a criterion in the choice of test systems, because it enables tests to be executed on a routine basis and to be standardized. The latter is paramount, since without the ability to get the same result from the same test system in different laboratories, something not always possible even for daphnids, the whole legal and scientific basis of the test is undermined.

For the following reasons, attention must also be paid to the ecological relevance of the test. First, demonstrating that the test species is pivotal to estimating broad environmental consequences, its ecological legitimacy would be strengthened. However, often too little understanding exists of the structure of freshwater ecosystems to know if keystone species exist at all. Second, ecological relevance might be claimed if the test species were known to be more sensitive than most other species. The daphnids appear to be quite sensitive, but much variation in sensitivity to numerous toxicants is apparent even between genotypes of Daphnia magna. The concept of the more sensitive indicator species seems to have been undermined. Much more needs to be known about the distribution of sensitivities to toxicants both within and between species in communities.

Moreover, the emphasis on pelagic organisms also needs careful consideration. Epibenthic and sediment systems may be as important, if not more so, in freshwaters as are pelagic ones; yet, because of difficulties in manipulation, sediments have been relatively neglected.

Given the predominance of acute tests and the interest in using them to set priorities and environmental standards through the application of safety factors, the relationships between acute and chronic responses must be well understood. To increase scientific confidence, the mechanistic basis of the relationship between acute short-term and chronic longer-term responses needs to be supported by additional data.

9.3.2 *Multi-species Tests*

Two reasons that multi-species systems might bring more ecological relevance to ecotoxicity tests include:

1. The test results may expose crucial emergent effects that arise out of species interactions.
2. The test findings from testing in complex milieu may provide insight into the distribution (fate) of toxicants between various compartments of the systems (*i.e.*, sediment and water column) and hence on bioavailability.

If a divergence occurs between single and multi-species responses, knowing whether it arises from basis 1 or 2 above would prove useful.

Multi-species tests can certainly be conducted for a variety of scales and using a number of alternative microcosms and macrocosms. However, no generally accepted distinction exists among systems based solely on size. They can be based indoors or outdoors, and they can be closed or open. Closed systems are observed more frequently than are open ones, largely because of the complexity of the "plumbing" needed for open systems; however, both indoor and outdoor artificial streams have been constructed and used.

Mesocosms have been used in a legislative context for pesticide registration in the US where the USEPA can require a mesocosm analysis if information from other tests is insufficient to "negate a presumption of risk" or indicates that significant biological populations will be at risk. The best practice in this context has been evaluated in Workshops organized by the Society of Environmental Toxicology and Chemistry for the use of both microcosms and mesocosms. Standard multi-species ecotoxicological test systems have been described.

For the effort and expense involved in establishing and managing these systems, careful consideration needs to be given to their usefulness and relevance. Three major problems are apparent: (1) because of the size and complexity of these systems, data obtained from them are difficult to replicate, so rigorous statistical analysis is not always possible; (2) methods of construction differ sufficiently to increase the difficulty in reproducing results; and (3) uncertainty exists over exactly which properties should be measured, as it does for natural ecosystems.

Multi-species systems can either be set up by (1) sampling from natural systems (*e.g.* enclosing a sample of plankton in a closed flask) or (2) colonization (*e.g.*, leaving the pond or stream open for colonisation) or (3) by deliberate construction. Techniques (1) and (2) cannot guarantee reproducibility, and the enclosing effects in (1) and (3) could lead to peculiar dynamics that interact with or potentially mask other perturbations. These effects need to be thoroughly investigated in control systems. These features mean that standardization is probably difficult to achieve, and ecological relevance may be illusory.

9.4 Application of Toxicants

Most of the single- and multi-species test systems apply the toxicant continuously; however, episodic events are also common in freshwater systems. A few studies have been conducted in which the toxicant was applied as a pulse. The effects of fluctuating ammonium on trout, and concluded that, over a 96-hour period, they could withstand a fixed concentration of ammonia better than fluctuating concentrations with the same mean. By contrast, found that, with either zinc or mixtures of zinc and ammonia, no significant difference in survival was observed for trout exposed either continuously or alternately to low and high concentrations.

To distinguish between standard toxicity tests and those including post-exposure mortality. The use of median lethal exposure time (*i.e.,* time required to kill half the population within a predetermined post-exposure period). A similar index, median-post-exposure-lethal time (*i.e.,* time from end of exposure period by which 50 per cent of the animals are dead).

Within the context of episodic events, more careful consideration needs to be given to the effects of amplitude, duration, and frequency of pulse of the dose on populations and communities, not only in terms of survivorship but also of developmental rates and reproductive output.

A further complication to be addressed is that test substances are most often applied singly to test systems, because complex mixtures' are more difficult to handle and because regulations focus predominantly on single substances. All the most appropriate mixtures and conditions in the field for carrying out tests would be impossible to imagine, let alone construct experimentally. Yet interest in the effects of complex effluents on natural systems has directed attention to this problem. Many mixtures of organic chemicals appear to act primarily by simple, sometimes joint, actions so that the contribution of the components to the total mixture are additive however, not all toxicants produce this effect. Understanding of basic mechanisms of ecotoxicological action needs to be extended to ascertain how toxicants exert their primary effects and how toxicants might interfere with or enhance each other's actions.

9.5 Retrospective Assessment

Assessments can be carried out on different scales: (1) surveying the general state of fresh waters regionally, nationally and, locally; (2) assessing impacts of contamination at a particular site; and (3) monitoring effluent on a site on a continuous basis to assess quality. In principle, all these activities can be carried out using effects at all biological levels described previously; often, however, organismic and suborganismic responses are convenient to use in limited studies, whereas community and ecosystem properties are more convenient in the more extensive ones. In all, ecological relevance remains a critical determinant.

Chemical analyses on their own are rarely adequate in assessments, because the dynamic complexity of inputs means that samples taken at specific times (the norm for chemical analysis) may be misleading. Also, the qualitative complexity of inputs implies extreme difficulty in assessing ecological impact from a database comprised of only those substances present. Biological systems, however, integrate effects over time of complex mixtures of contaminants.

Two key issues in designing and interpreting retrospective biological assessments are: (1) what to measure and (2) how to identify cause from correlation (related to problems of design of sampling programmes).

9.6 The Measurement Problem Revisited

Are there characteristics of healthy ecosystems that can be defined and against which divergences can be gauged? As noted previously, while "goal states" are not appropriately applied to ecosystems, steady or stable states might be. One approach based on an attempt to define a characteristic assemblage of benthic invertebrates for a particular river habitat is the River Invertebrate Predictive And Classification System (RIVPACS). This system defines relationships between physicochemical variables and species assemblages on the basis of an initial survey of clean sites, and then uses the model based on the results to estimate expected assemblages at particular sites from observation of the physico-chemical variables. The deviation of observed from predicted findings is considered an index of disturbance that can be used for both surveys and impact assessments. However, this and similar approaches developed for other taxa (*i.e.,* fish) are based on correlations between what is presumed to be dependent and independent variables thus, deviations from expectation that correlate with an extra variable (*i.e.,* presence of a contaminant) need not be causally related.

Another approach focuses not so much on the details of species occurrence as on the general properties of ecological diversity. Disputes on how this property should be measured remain, and certainly no a priori theory that predicts what levels of diversity might be expected in particular habitats exists. How diversity should respond¾ either positively or negatively¾to stress is simply unclear; that is, diversity of plankton appears to diminish continuously with organic enrichment, and to increase and then diminish for benthic invertebrates.

The expectations for the functional organization of ecosystems and how it might change under stress are defined relatively easily: for any stable ecosystem, the input of energy (either autochthonous or allochthonous) should balance output. Organic loading can destabilize the balance by causing input to exceed output; alternatively, toxic stress can destabilize this process by causing output to exceed input, resulting from the increased metabolic work needed to counteract this kind of pollution. This situation leads to changes in ecosystem functional ratios involving production, biomass, and respiration (Odum, 1983). Such changes will also be closely linked to the cycling and spiralling of specific nutrients, a topic beginning increasingly to attract attention.

The extent to which structure and function are coupled in ecosystems is problematic, so that the one probably cannot be used as a surrogate for the other. This situation means that a choice has to be made either to measure either structural or functional responses, but not both, or to combine structural and functional indices as a basis for inferences about divergences from the norm. For the latter approach, care has to be taken to ensure that the different indices are not autocorrelated.

A close coupling exists between functioning and trophic structure embodied in food webs. The properties of these are coming under increased scrutiny. Structural-functional attributes are likely to be identified for use in defining relative stability as well as resilience to disturbance in ecosystems. Benthic invertebrates have been classified into trophic functional groups, and predictable shifts in the relative abundance of these along rivers (from shredders to collectors) have been claimed as part of the River Continuum Concept. Thus, deviations from these could signal disturbances. Two caveats persist: (1) predictions are not yet precisely defined, and the RCC theory is not universally accepted; and (2) causation should not be mistaken for correlation.

If ecosystem properties and processes are difficult to measure, an alternative is to use alterations in individual species populations as indicators of change. Searching for key species may be tempting; however, "key" species may have several definitions: sensitivity, functional role, or impact on the dynamics of other species. Approaches relying on indicator species (involving presence or absence of a single species; ratios of sensitive to tolerant species; and biotic scores) are based largely on the construct of "sensitive" species, a philosophy whose difficulties have already been noted. Moreover, separated populations within species can display considerable variation in response to pollutants based possibly on differential local conditions and selection pressures. Shifts from sensitive to tolerant forms of organisms (both inter- and intra-species) have been used independently as indicators of stress as is the case for the Pollution Induced Community Tolerance (PICT) system.

9.7 Cause or Only Correlation?

In complex field situations, defining confidently causal links from direct observations is always difficult. Usually a change is observed to be correlated with a variable of interest (*e.g.*, a reduction in diversity or density downstream of an effluent), but to say that one caused the other is unjustified without further research, because important contributing variables may be present but hidden from view.

However, without some a priori yardstick against which to compare observed systems, divergences from normal have to be judged comparatively by reference to the state of the system before the presumed disturbances or with similar systems in habitats not exposed to the pollutants of interest (*e.g.*, upstream and downstream comparisons). Some profound problems are associated, however, with being able to distinguish between natural variation through space and time and that caused by the putative disturbance¾the so-called sampling problem of pseudodesign.

The only way to identify causal links with more certainty is to associate the field observations with an experimental programme. Testing ecological hypotheses derived from field observations in more rigorously controlled experimental circumstances can be used widely in ecology, and ought to be used more in ecotoxicology. For example, conclusions about putative interactions between contaminants and organisms in field situations could be tested using classical dose- response experiments. The reverse is sometimes undertaken; that is, quantitative dose-response comparisons can result from simple laboratory tests using the more complex microcosms, mesocosms, and with true ecosystems.

9.8 Planted Systems

Planted systems are often used to monitor effluents or even whole rivers in which physiological or behavioral features are used to signal change in systems that range from caged fish to microbes.

Planted systems can also be used in upstream-downstream, before-after studies as in situ bioassays. They avoid problems of pseudodesign, because in principle all replicates start in the same condition. Of course, these systems raise questions of relevance. Careful choice of a system and of effects may help to overcome this difficulty. The Gammarus Scope for Growth Bioassay serves to illustrate this point: the organism, G. pulex was chosen as the test animal because of its relative sensitivity to a wide range of toxicants and because of its important role in the decomposer food chain is of considerable importance in the economy of flowing-water systems. Furthermore, a physiological response involving the net energy available for somatic and reproductive products was chosen, because it is sensitive to contaminants, can be linked causally to population dynamics, and is obviously related to important ecosystem processes in the decomposer food chain.

— — —

10

Analysis of Industrial Effluents

10.1 Introduction

Industrial effluents, which are deteriorate their quality, and push them to the brink of extinction in the process of unplanned discharge, giving rise to the need for suitable conservation strategies for the receiving water body. Unfortunately, over the years, less attention has been given to industrial effluents world over. The degradation of the industrial effluents has altered their functions, affecting the ecological balance. The objectives of carrying out the physico-chemical and biological analyses of water bodies are as follows:

1. Generally, industrial effluent functions directly relate to their physical, chemical and biological integrity. Water quality evaluation for industrial effluent leads to information about their misuse by indicating the pollution status. 1st define water quality objectives as the overall direction and purpose of the industrial effluent and furthermore define goals as milestones to be met during the course of a book. Since the quality of aquatic life depends on the water quality, a thorough assessment of the water quality is an integral part of industrial effluent toxicity evaluation. The assessment of the chemical criteria of the industrial effluent helps in:

(a) Evaluating the chemicals that cause toxicity to aquatic life.

(b) Studying the long-term effects on the ecosystem.

(c) Conducting the status and monitoring of industrial discharges by studying their physico-chemical and biological parameters.

2. Designate uses that protect the structure and function of fresh water for protection of fish, birds, wildlife, and recreation. The baseline values attached to fresh water in terms of designating the viable usage of these water bodies based on established standards protecting their functions is also attempted.

3. Analyse the qualitative and quantitative aspects of plankton population of the industrial effluent. The biological integrity of the fresh water is the driving force for their sound ecological functioning. Fresh water bodies that support a vast diversity of fish, birds, mammals, etc., depend directly on it by supporting vast and diverse forms of plankton providing a nutrient base and a complex food-web. In many cases, planktons also act as the biological indicators of pollution being very sensitive to changes in water quality.

Water is a dynamic medium and its quality varies spatially and temporally. In order to characterise any water body, studies on the major components, hydrology, physico-chemical and biological characteristics, should be carried out based on Standard methods for waste water analysis (APHA,1995), 19th Edition.

10.2 Hydrological Features

A thorough knowledge of the hydrological properties of the industrial effluents must be acquired before an effective water quality monitoring system is established. Each of the receiving is characterised by unique hydrological features such as:

— ***Rivers:*** characterised by unidirectional current with relatively high average velocity (0.1 – 1.0 m/S). In general, thorough and continuous vertical mixing is achieved in rivers due to the prevailing currents and turbulence.

— ***Lakes:*** characterised by low, average current (0.001 to 0.01 m/S) giving higher residential time for water. Currents within a lake are multi-directional with mixing regulated by the climatic conditions and lake depth.

— ***Ground water:*** characterised by a steady flow pattern both in direction and speed that is largely governed by the porosity of the geological material as a result of which the mixing is poor.

— ***Reservoirs:*** intermediate between rivers and lakes.

Large variations in the water residence time occur in different types of inland water bodies. The hydrodynamic characteristics of each type of water body are highly dependent on the size of the waterbody, climatic conditions, currents, waves, sediment, dynamics and the drainage pattern associated with it. Groundwater greatly depends on the recharge regime *i.e.* infiltration through unsaturated aquifer zone, that allows renewal of the groundwater.

10.3 Physical, Chemical and Biological Properties

The physical and chemical properties of industrial effluent are characteristic of the climatic, geochemical, geomorphological and pollution conditions (largely) prevailing in the drainage basin and the underlying aquifer and industrial processes. The biota in the surface water is governed entirely by various environmental conditions that determine the selection of species as the physiological performance of the individual organisms. The primary production of organic matter, in the form of phytoplankton and macrophytes is more intense in lakes and reservoirs than in rivers. In contrast to the chemical quality of water bodies, which can be measured by suitable analytical methods, biological quality is a combination of both qualitative and quantitative characterisation. This can be carried out in two levels:

— Response of individual species to changes in its environment.

— Response of biological communities to changes in their environment.

10.4 Sampling

The sample collected should be small in volume, enough to accurately represent the whole water body. The water sample tends to modify itself to the new environment. It is necessary to ensure that no significant changes occur in the sample and preserve its integrity till analysed (by retaining the same concentration of all the components as in the water body). The essential objectives of water quality assessment are to:

1. Define the status and trends in water quality of a given water body.
2. Analyse the causes for the observed conditions and trends.
3. Identify the area specific problems of water quality and provide assessments in the form of management to evaluate alternatives that help in decision-making.

Sampling sites for the industrial effluents are selected to represent the water quality at different points and depths. Generally three sampling sites are selected for monitoring.

Inlet: the point where the principal feeder opens into the industries.

Center: the point that gives the general water quality of the industrial water pipelines.

Outlet: the place where the outlet occurs to discharge into any water body.

10.4.1 Types of Sampling

Generally three types of sampling are adopted for collecting water samples.

Grab or Catch sampling: the sample is collected at a particular time and place that represents the composition of the source at that particular point and time.

Composite sampling: a mixture of grab samples is collected at the same sampling point at different time intervals.

Integrated sampling: a mixture of grab samples collected at different points simultaneously.

10.4.2 Sampling Frequency

The quality of water varies with time in a water body due to various natural and human induced factors. The monitoring has to be done in a way that records all the changes in the quality. The sampling frequencies generally adopted in monitoring are:

1. Weekly sampling for one year.
2. Consecutive day sampling during study period.
3. Hourly sampling for 24 hours.
4. Monthly sampling at predefined time.
5. Seasonal sampling at predefined time
6. Yearly integrated sampling at predefined time
7. Continuous sampling up to more than a year

Variations in water quality are mainly due to changes in the concentrations of the components of the water flowing into the water body. These variations can be man-made or natural and can either be cyclic or random.

Random variations: due to spasmodic, often unpredictable events such as accidental oil spills, sewage leaks, overflows, etc.

Cyclic variations: may be a result of regular seasonal changes triggering certain natural processes such as rainfall, snowmelts and seasonal temperature changes, altering the ecosystem. Seasonal growth and decay of vegetation will also rise due to cyclic changes in the composition of water.

In lakes, the mass of water and good lateral mixing provide inertia against any rapid modifications due to inputs and outputs.

10.4.3 Sampling Container

The sampling container should not react with the sample, be of adequate capacity to store the sample and be free from contamination. The following table 10.1 shows the different containers used for various parameters.

Table 10.1: Sampling containers

Parameters	Containers
BOD, DO,	BOD bottles
Inorganic	Plastic bottles
Heavy metals	Plastic bottles with out reacted by Heavy metals
Other parameters	Preferably plastic cans

10.4.4 Sampling Method

Grab sampling was done at the inlet, center and outlet in most of the water bodies studied to assess their physical and chemical qualities at monthly intervals, expect during some seasons when the center of the lake was not accessible due to excessive growth of water hyacinth. The samples were collected in thoroughly cleaned 2.5-litre inert plastic containers, which were rinsed with distilled and lake/tank water before collection.

Water samples were collected in a sampling bottle avoiding floating materials. The stoppers of the sample containers were closed properly to prevent outside contamination by immersed in the water body. The container was labelled describing the name of the water body, date, time, sampling-point, and conditions under which it was sampled.

10.4.5 Preservation of the Sample

Between the time a sample is collected and analysed in the laboratory, physical, chemical and biochemical reactions may take place in the sample container leading to changes in the intrinsic quality of the sample, making it necessary to prevent or minimize these changes with suitable preservatives such as alcohol and mercuric chloride. Highly unstable parameters such as pH, temperature, transparency, free carbon di oxide, dissolved oxygen, etc. are measured at the sampling site. The preservation procedure includes keeping the samples in the dark, adding chemical preservative, lowering the temperature to retard reactions, or combinations of these. The preservation methodologies showed in table 10.2.

Table 10.2: Preservation methods for various parameters

Experiment	Preservative	Max. Holding Time
BOD	Cool, 4° C	4 hours
Calcium	Cool, 4° C	7 days
Chloride	Cool, 4° C	7 days
COD	Cool, 4° C	24 hours
Dissolved Oxygen	Fix on site	6 hours
Fluoride	Cool, 4° C	7 days
Magnesium	Cool, 4° C	7 days
Nitrate + Nitrite	Cool, 4° C	24 hours
PH	None	6 hours
Phosphorus		
Dissolved	Filter on site using 0.45μm filter	24 hours
Inorganic	Cool, 4° C	24 hours
Ortho	Cool, 4° C	24 hours
Total	Cool, 4° C	1 month
Potassium	Cool, 4° C	7 days
Specific conductance	Cool, 4° C	24 hours
Sodium	Cool, 4° C	7 days
Heavy metals		
Cadmium	2 ml conc. Nitric acid/L sample	6 months
Chromium	2 ml conc. Nitric acid/L sample	6 months
Copper	2 ml conc. Nitric acid/L sample	6 months
Iron	2 ml conc. Nitric acid/L sample	6 months
Lead	2 ml conc. Nitric acid/L sample	6 months
Nickel	2 ml conc. Nitric acid/L sample	6 months
Zinc	2 ml conc. Nitric acid/L sample	6 months

(*Source:* USEPA, 1983, Sample preservation. pp.xv-xx.

10.5 Analyses of Physical, Chemical and Biological Parameters

The parameters analysed to assess the water quality are broadly divided into:

Physical parameters: Colour, Temperature, Transparency, Turbidity and Odour.

Chemical parameters: pH, Electrical Conductivity (E.C), Total Solids (TS), Total Dissolved Solids (TDS), Total Suspended Solids (TSS), Total Hardness, Calcium Hardness, Magnesium Hardness, Nitrates, Phosphates, Sulphates, Chlorides, Dissolved Oxygen (D.O), Biological Oxygen Demand (BOD), Chemical Oxygen Demand (COD), Fluorides, Free Carbondioxide, Potassium and Sodium.

Heavy metals: Lead, Copper, Nickel, Iron, Chromium, Cadmium and Zinc.

Biological parameters: The biological parameters involved the qualitative analyses of planktons (zooplankton and phytoplankton).

Field measurement

The field parameters measured include pH, conductivity, dissolved oxygen, temperature and transparency.

10.6 Physical Parameters

In natural water, colour is due to the presence of humic acids, fulvic acids, metallic ions, suspended matter, plankton, weeds and industrial effluents. Colour is removed to make water suitable for general and industrial applications and is determined by visual comparison of the sample with distilled water.

Visual comparison: About 20 ml of the sample and 20 ml of distilled water were taken in two separate wide mouthed test tubes. The results were tabulated (as clear, greenish, greyish, brownish, blackish, *etc*) by comparing the colour of the sample with distilled water.

Temperature

Impinging solar radiation and atmospheric temperature brings about spatial and temporal changes in temperature, setting up convection currents and thermal stratification. Temperature plays a very important role in wetland dynamism affecting the various parameters such as alkalinity, salinity, dissolved oxygen, electrical conductivity etc. In an aquatic system, these parameters affect the chemical and biological reactions such as solubility of oxygen, carbon-di-oxide-carbonate-bicarbonate equilibrium, increase in metabolic rate and physiological reactions of organisms, etc. Water temperature is important in relation to fish life. The temperature of drinking water has an influence on its taste.

Apparatus required: Thermometer- 0.1° C division.

Procedure: Temperature measurement is made by taking a portion of the water sample (about 1litre) and immersing the thermometer probe into it for a sufficient period of time (till the reading stabilizes) and the reading is taken, expressed as °C.

Transparency (Light Penetration)

Solar radiation is the major source of light energy in an aquatic system, governing the primary productivity. Transparency is a characteristic of water that varies with the combined effect of colour and turbidity. It measures the light penetrating through the water body and is determined using Secchi disc.

Apparatus required: Secchi disc, a metallic disc of 20cm diameter with four quadrats of alternate black and white on the upper surface. The disc with centrally placed weight at the lower surface, is suspended with a graduated cord at the center.

Procedure: Transparency is measured by gradually lowering the Secchi disc at respective sampling points. The depth at which it disappears in the water (X_1) and reappears (X_2) is noted. The transparency of the water body is computed as follows:

Transparency (Secchi Disc Transparency) = $(X_1 + X_2)/2$

Where, X_1 = Depth at which Secchi disc disappears

X_2 = Depth at which Secchi disc reappears

Turbidity

Turbidity is an expression of optical property; wherein light is scattered by suspended particles present in water (Tyndall effect) and is measured using a nephelometer. Suspended and colloidal matter such as clay, silt, finely divided organic and inorganic matter; plankton and other microscopic organisms cause turbidity in water. Turbidity affects light scattering, absorption properties and aesthetic appearance in a water body. Increase in the intensity of scattered light results in higher values of turbidity.

Apparatus required: Nephelometer (It detects scattered light at 90° to the incident beam of light. It consists of a light source for illuminating the sample. One or more photoelectric detectors with a display unit indicate the intensity of light scattered at 90° to the path of incident light.), sample cells, lab-glass wares and Monopan balance.

Principle: Nephelometric measurement is based on comparison of the intensity of scattered light of the sample with the intensity of light scattered by a standard reference suspension (Formazin polymer) under similar conditions.

Reagents

Distilled water and Stock primary Formazin suspension

Solution 1: 1.0 g Hydrazine sulphate is dissolved in 100ml of distilled water.

Solution 2: 10.0g of Hexa methylnetetramine is dissolved in distilled water and made up to 100 ml in a volumetric flask.

Stock Turbidity Suspension: 5 ml of solutions 1 and 2 are mixed in a volumetric flask and allowed to stand for 24 hrs at about 25° C (±3° C) and diluted to 1000 ml with distilled water to give a 400 NTU suspension.

Standard Turbidity Suspension: 10 ml of the stock solution is diluted to 100 ml with distilled water to give a standard solution of 40 NTU.

Procedure: The nephelometer is calibrated using distilled water (Zero NTU) and a standard turbidity suspension of 40NTU. The thoroughly shaken sample is taken in the nephelometric tube and the value is recorded.

Turbidity (NTU) = (Nephelometer readings) (Dilution factor*)

* If the turbidity of the sample is more than 40 NTU, then the sample is diluted and the dilution factor is accounted in final calculations.

10.7 Chemical Parameters

pH:

The effect of pH on the chemical and biological properties of liquids makes its determination very important. It is one of the most important parameter in water chemistry and is defined as -log $[H^+]$, and measured as intensity of acidity or alkalinity on a scale ranging from 0-14. If free H^+ are more it is expressed acidic (*i.e.* pH<7), while more OH^- ions is expressed as alkaline (*i.e.* pH> 7).

In natural waters pH is governed by the equilibrium between carbon dioxide/bicarbonate/carbonate ions and ranges between 4.5 and 8.5 although mostly basic. It tends to increase during day largely due to the photosynthetic activity (consumption of carbon-di-oxide) and decreases during night due to respiratory activity. Waste water and polluted natural waters have pH values lower or higher than 7 based on the nature of the pollutant.

* The colorimetric indicator method can be used only for approximate pH values.

Apparatus required

pH indicator (BDH) method: BDH Indicator (Universal Indicator) and test tubes.

Electrometric method: Glass electrode, reference electrode (mercury/calomel or silver/silver chloride) and pH meter.

Procedure

Colorimetric method: About 10ml of the sample is taken in a wide mouth test tube, 0.2ml of BDH indicator is added, and shaken gently. The color developed is matched with the chart and the pH noted.

Electrometric method: The pH is determined by measuring the Electro Motive Force (E.M.F) of a cell comprising an indicator electrode (an electrode responsive to hydrogen ions such as a glass electrode) immersed in the test solution and the reference electrode (usually a mercury/calomel electrode). Contact between the test solution and the reference electrode is usually got by means of a liquid junction, which forms a part of reference electrode. E.M.F of this cell is measured with pH meter, that is a high impedance voltmeter calibrated in terms of pH. The electrode is allowed to stand for 2 minutes to stabilize before taking reading for reproducible results (at least ±0.1 pH units).

Electrical Conductivity

Conductivity (specific conductance) is the numerical expression of the water's ability to conduct an electric current. It is measured in micro Siemens per cm and depends on the total concentration, mobility, valence and the temperature of the solution of ions. Electrolytes in a solution disassociate into positive (cations) and negative (anions) ions and impart conductivity. Most dissolved inorganic substances are in the ionised form in water and contribute to conductance. The conductance of the samples gives rapid and practical estimate of the variation in dissolved mineral content of the water supply. Conductance is defined as the reciprocal of the resistance involved and expressed as mho or Siemen (s).

$$G = \frac{1}{R}$$

where

G - Conductance (mho or Siemens) and R - Resistance

Apparatus required: Conductivity meter

Procedure: The electrode of the conductivity meter is dipped into the sample, and the readings are noted for stable value shown as mS/cm.

Total Solids

Total solids is the term applied to the material residue left in the vessel after evaporation of the sample and its subsequent drying in an oven at a temperature of 103-105°C. Total solids include Total Suspended Solids (TSS) and Total Dissolved Solids (TDS).

Principle: A known volume (50 ml) of well-mixed sample is evaporated in a pre-weighed dish and dried to constant weight in an oven at 103-105° C. The increase in weight over that of the empty dish gives the total solids.

Apparatus: Evaporating dishes-100 ml porcelain dish, steam bath, drying oven, desiccator, Monopan balance and measuring jars.

Procedure: A known volume of the well-mixed sample (50 ml) is measured into a pre-weighed dish and evaporated to dryness at 103° C on a steam bath. The evaporated sample is dried in an oven for about an hour at 103-105° C and cooled in a desiccator and recorded for constant weight.

Calculation

$$\text{Total solids (mg/L)} = \frac{(W_1 - W_2)(1000)}{\text{Sample volume (ml)}}$$

W_1 = Weight of dried residue + dish

W_2 = Weight of empty dish

Total Dissolved Solids

Dissolved solids are solids that are in dissolved state in solution. Waters with high dissolved solids generally are of inferior palatability and may induce an unfavourable physiological reaction in the transient consumer.

Principle: The difference in the weight of total solids and the total suspended solids expressed in the same units gives the total dissolved solids.

Apparatus: Glass-fiber filter disks, membrane filter funnel, filtration apparatus, suction flask and pump, drying oven and Grooch crucible.

Procedure: The difference in the weights of Total Solids (W_1) and Total Suspended Solids (W_2) expressed in the same units gives Total Dissolved Solids (TDS).

Calculation

$$\text{Total Dissolved Solids (mg/L)} = \frac{(W_1 - W_2) \times 1000}{\text{Sample volume (ml)}}$$

W_1 = Weight of total solids + dish
W_2 = Weight of total suspended solids

Total Suspended Solids

Suspended solids are the portions of solids that are retained on a filter of standard specified size (generally 2.0 μ) under specific conditions. Water with high-suspended solids is unsatisfactory for bathing, industrial and other purposes.

Principle: A well - mixed sample is filtered through a weighed standard glass fibre filter and the residue that is retained on the filter is dried to a constant weight at 103-105 °C. The increase in the weight of the filter determines the total suspended solids.

Apparatus: Porcelain dish (100 ml capacity), glass fiber filter disk, suction pump and flask, measuring jar, membrane filter funnel, oven and filtration apparatus.

Procedure: The known volume of vigorously shaken sample (50 ml) is filtered into a pre-weighed glass fibre filter disk fitted to suction pump, and washed successively with distilled water. The filter is carefully removed from the filtration apparatus and dried for an hour at 103-105 °C in an oven, cooled in dessicator and weighed for constant weight.

Calculation

$$\text{Total Suspended Solids (mg/L)} = \frac{(W_1\text{-}W_2)\ (1000)}{\text{Sample volume (ml)}}$$

W_1 = Weight of dried glass fibre filter + residue

W_2 = Weight of glass fibre filter disk before filtering

Total Hardness

Hardness is predominantly caused by divalent cations such as calcium, magnesium, alkaline earth metal such as iron, manganese, strontium, *etc*. The total hardness is defined as the sum of calcium and magnesium concentrations, both expressed as $CaCO_3$ in mg/L. Carbonates and bicarbonates of calcium and magnesium cause temporary hardness. Sulphates and chlorides cause permanent hardness. Table 10.3 shows the classification of hardness ranging from 0 to 180 mg/L.

Table 10.3: Classification of hardness

Soft	0 - 60 mg/L
Medium	60 -120 mg/L
Hard	120 - 180 mg/L
Very Hard	> 180 mg/L

Principle: In alkaline conditions EDTA (Ethylene-diamine tetra acetic acid) and its sodium salts react with cations forming a soluble chelated complex when added to a solution. If a small amount of dye such as Eriochrome black-T is added to an aqueous solution containing calcium and magnesium ions at alkaline pH of 10.0 ± 0.1, it forms wine red colour. When EDTA is added as a titrant, all the calcium and magnesium ions in the solution get complexed resulting in a sharp colour change from wine red to blue, marking the end point of the titration. Hardness of water prevents lather formation with soap rendering the water unsuitable for bathing and washing. It forms scales in boilers, making it unsuitable for industrial usage. At higher pH>12.0, Mg^{++} ion precipitates with only Ca^{++} in solution. At this pH, murexide indicator forms a pink color with Ca^{++} ion. When EDTA is added Ca^{++} gets complexed resulting in a change from pink to purple indicating end point of the reaction.

Apparatus required: Lab glassware-burette, pipette, conical flask, beakers etc.

Reagents

Buffer solution: 16.9 g of ammonium chloride and 1.25 g of magnesium salt of EDTA is dissolved in 143 ml of concentrated ammonium hydroxide and diluted to 250 ml with distilled water.

Eriochrome black-T indicator: 0.5 g of Eriochrome black-T indicator is dissolved in 100 g of triethanolamine.

Standard EDTA titrant: 0.01M or Ng AR grade EDTA is dissolved in distilled water and diluted to 1000 ml and is standardised against standard calcium solution, 1 ml = 1 mg $CaCO_3$.

Standard Calcium Solution: 1.0 g of AR grade $CaCO_3$ is weighed into a 250ml conical flask, to which 1+1 HCl is added till all $CaCO_3$ is dissolved completely. 200 ml of distilled water is added and boiled to expel carbon-di-oxide, and diluted to 1000 ml. 1 ml = 1 mg $CaCO_3$.

Procedure: Exactly 50 ml of the well-mixed sample is pipetted into a conical flask, to which 1ml of ammonium buffer and 2-3 drops of Eriochrome black -T indicator is added. The mixture is titrated against standard 0.01M EDTA until the wine red colour of the solution turns pale blue at the end point.

Calculation

$$\text{Total hardness (mg/L)} = \frac{(T)(1000)}{V}$$

Where, T = Volume of titrant

V = Volume of sample

Calcium Hardness

The presence of calcium (fifth most abundant) in water results from passage through or over deposits of limestone, dolomite, gypsum and such other calcium bearing rocks. Calcium contributes to the total hardness of water and is an important micro-nutrient in aquatic environment and is especially needed in large quantities by molluscs and vertebrates. It is measured by EDTA titrimetric method. Small concentration of calcium carbonate prevents corrosion of metal pipes by laying down a protective coating. But increased amount of calcium precipitates on heating to form harmful scales in boilers, pipes and utensils.

Principle: When EDTA (Ethylene-diamine tetra acetic acid) is added to the water containing calcium and magnesium, it combines first with calcium. Calcium can be determined directly with EDTA when pH is made sufficiently high such that the magnesium is largely precipitated as hydroxyl compound (by adding NaOH and iso-propyl alcohol). When murexide indicator is added to the solution containing calcium, all the calcium gets complexed by the EDTA at pH 12-13. The end point is indicated from a colour change from pink to purple.

Apparatus required: Burettes, pipette, conical flask, beakers and droppers.

Reagents

Sodium hydroxide (8%): 8g of sodium hydroxide is dissolved in 100ml of distilled water.

Murexide indicator (ammonium purpurate): 0.2 g of murexide is ground well with 100 g of sodium chloride thoroughly.

Standard EDTA titrant, 0.01 M: 3.723 g of EDTA (disodium salt) is dissolved in distilled water and made up to 100 ml with the same.

Procedure: A known volume (50 ml) of the sample is pipetted into a clean conical flask, to which 1ml of sodium hydroxide and 1ml of iso-propyl alcohol is added. A pinch of murexide indicator is added to this mixture and titrated against EDTA until the pink color turns purple.

Calculation

$$\text{Calcium as Ca (mg/L)} = \frac{T \times 400.5 \times 1.05}{\text{Sample taken, ml}}$$

Where, T= volume of titrant, ml

$$\text{Calcium hardness (mg/L as } CaCO_3) = \frac{T \times 1000 \times 1.05}{\text{Sample taken, ml}}$$

Magnesium Hardness

Magnesium is a relatively abundant element in the earth's crust, ranking eighth in abundance among the elements. It is found in all natural waters and its source lies in rocks, generally present in lower concentration than calcium. It is also an important element contributing to hardness and a necessary constituent of chlorophyll. Its concentration greater than 125 mg/L can influence cathartic and diuretic actions.

Principle: Magnesium hardness can be calculated from the determined total hardness and calcium hardness.

Calculation

Magnesium = (T - C) x 0.243 (as mg/L)

where, T = Total hardness mg\L (as $CaCO_3$)

C = Calcium hardness mg\L (as $CaCO_3$)

High concentration of magnesium proves to be diuretic and laxative, and reduces the utility of water for domestic use while a concentration above 500 mg/L imparts an unpleasant taste to water and renders it unfit for drinking. Chemical softening, reverse osmosis and electro dialysis or ion exchange reduces the magnesium hardness to acceptable levels.

Nitrates

Nitrates are the most oxidized forms of nitrogen and the end product of the aerobic decomposition of organic nitrogenous matter. The significant sources of nitrates are chemical fertilizers from cultivated lands, drainage from livestock feeds, as well as domestic and industrial sources. Natural waters in their unpolluted state contain only minute quantities of nitrates. The stimulation of plant growth by nitrates may result in eutrophication, especially due to algae. The subsequent death and decay of plants produces secondary pollution. Nitrates are most important for biological oxidation of nitrogenous organic matter. Certain nitrogen fixing bacteria and algae have the capacity to fix molecular nitrogen in nitrates. The main source of polluting nitrates is domestic sewage. Nitrates may find their way into ground water through leaching from soil and at times by contamination. They can be measured by the phenoldisulphonic method.

Principle: Nitrates react with phenoldisulphonic acid and produce a nitrate derivative, which in alkaline solution develops yellow colour due to rearrangement of its structure. The colour produced is directly proportional to the concentration of nitrates present in the sample.

Apparatus required: Nessler's tube, pipettes, beakers, spectrophotometer, cuvettes, measuring jar and hot water bath.

Reagents

Phenol disulphonic acid: 25 g of phenol is dissolved in 150 ml of concentrated sulphuric acid, to which 85ml of sulphuric acid is further added and heated for about 90 min on a water bath and stored in dark bottles upon cooling.

Sodium hydroxide: About 50g of sodium hydroxide is dissolved in 150-200 ml of water and cooled.

Conc. Ammonium hydroxide

Nitrate solution

Stock nitrate solution: 721.8 mg (0.722g) of AR potassium nitrate is dissolved in distilled water and made up to 100ml for stock solution.

Standard nitrate solution: Standard nitrate solution is prepared by evaporating 50ml of the stock solution to dryness in the water bath. The obtained residue is dissolved in 2 ml of phenol disulfonic acid and diluted to 500 ml, to give 1 ml = 10 mg. The solution of various strengths ranging from 0.0 (blank) to 1.0 mg/L at the intervals of 0.2 mg/L is prepared by diluting stock solution with distilled water.

Procedure: A known volume (50 ml) of the sample is pipetted into a porcelain dish and evaporated to dryness on a hot water bath. 2 ml of phenol disulphonic acid is added to dissolve the residue by constant stirring with a glass rod. Concentrated solution of sodium hydroxide or conc. ammonium hydroxide and distilled water is added with stirring to make it alkaline. This is filtered into a Nessler's tube and made up to 50 ml with distilled water. The absorbance is read at 410 nm using a spectrophotometer after the development of colour. The standard graph is plotted by taking concentration along X-axis and the spectrophotometric readings (absorbance) along Y-axis. The value of nitrate is found by comparing absorbance of sample with the standard curve and expressed in mg/L.

Calculation

$$\text{Nitrates (as mg/L)} = \frac{\text{Absorbance of sample} \times \text{Conc. of Std} \times 1000}{\text{Absorbance of Std.} \times \text{Sample taken}}$$

Phosphates

Phosphates occur in natural or wastewaters as orthophosphates, condensed phosphates and naturally found phosphates. Their presence in water is due to detergents, used boiler waters, fertilizers and biological processes. They occur in solution in particles or as detritus. They are essential for the growth of organisms and a nutrient that limits the primary productivity of the water body. Inorganic phosphorus plays a dynamic role in aquatic ecosystems; when present in low concentration is one of the most important nutrients, but in excess along with nitrates and potassium, causes algal blooms. It is calculated by the stannous chloride method.

Principle: In acidic conditions orthophosphate reacts with ammonium molybdate forming Molybdophosphoric acid, reduced further to molybdenum blue by stannous chloride. The intensity of the blue colour is directly proportional to the concentration of phosphate. The absorbance is noted at 690 nm using spectrophotometer.

Apparatus required: Spectrophotometer, lab glassware, hot plate and Nessler's tube.

Reagents

Ammonium molybdate reagent: 25 g ammonium molybdate is dissolved in 175 ml distilled water. 280 ml concentrated sulphuric acid is added to 400 ml distilled water and cooled. Molybdate solution is added and the mixture diluted to 1000 ml.

Stannous chloride reagent: 2.5 g fresh stannous chloride is dissolved in 100 ml glycerol, heated on water bath and stirred with the glass rod to hasten dissolution.

Standard phosphate solution: 219.5 mg of dried AR potassium hydrogen phosphate is dissolved in distilled water and made up to 1000 ml, where 1 ml = 50.0 mg. of phosphate. 10 ml of the stock solution is made up to 1000 ml to give 1 ml = 0.05 mg. Standards of strength ranging from 0 (blank) to 0.05 mg/L at intervals of 0.01 mg is prepared by diluting the stock with distilled water.

Procedure: To 50 ml of the filtered sample, 4ml of ammonium molybdate reagent and about 4-5 drops of stannous chloride reagent is added. After about 10 min but before 12 min, the colour developed is measured photometrically at 690 nm and calibration curve is prepared. A reagent blank is always run with same treatment with distilled water as sample. The value of phosphate is obtained by comparing absorbance of sample with the standard curve and expressed as mg/L.

Calculation

$$\text{Phosphates (as mg/L)} = \frac{\text{Absorbance of sample} \times \text{Conc. of Std} \times 1000}{\text{Absorbance of Std.} \times \text{Sample taken}}$$

High phosphorus content causes increased algal growth till nitrogen becomes limiting, although blue green algae continues to dominate because of its ability to utilize molecular nitrogen. Besides sedimentation, high uptake by phytoplankton is one of the reasons for fast depletion of phosphorus in water.

Sulphates

Sulphates are found appreciably in all natural waters, particularly those with high salt content. Besides industrial pollution and domestic sewage, biological oxidation of reduced sulphur species also add to sulphate content. Soluble in water, it imparts hardness with other cations. Sulphate causes scaling in industrial water supplies, and odour and corrosion problems due to its reduction to hydrogen sulphide. It can be calculated by turbidometric method.

Principle: Sulphate ions are precipitated in acetic acid medium with barium chloride to form barium sulphate crystals of uniform size. The scattering of light by the precipitated suspension (barium sulphate) is measured by a Nephelometer and the concentration is recorded.

Apparatus required: Nephelometer, magnetic stirrer, Nessler's tubes and lab glassware.

Reagents

Conditioning reagent: 50 ml of glycerol was mixed in a solution containing 30 ml of conc. hydro chloric acid, 300ml distilled water (10% HCl), 100 ml of 95% ethyl alcohol or isopropyl alcohol and 75g NaCl.

Barium Chloride

Standard sulphate solution: 147.9 mg of AR grade sodium sulphate was dissolved in distilled water and made up to 1000 ml, to give 1 ml = 100 mg sulphate.

Procedure: 100 ml of the sample is filtered into a Nessler's tube containing 5 ml of conditioning reagent. About 0.2 g of barium chloride crystals is added with continued stirring. A working standard is prepared by taking 1 ml of the standard, 5 ml of conditioning reagent and made up to 100 ml, to give 100 NTU. The turbidity developed by the sample and the standards are measured using a Nephelometer and the results are tabulated.

Calculation

Sulphate (as mg/L) = (Nephlometric reading) (0.4) (Dilution Factor)

Chlorides

The presence of chlorides in natural waters can mainly be attributed to dissolution of salt deposits in the form of ions (Cl). Otherwise, high concentrations may indicate pollution by sewage, industrial wastes, intrusion of seawater or other saline water. It is the major form of inorganic anions in water for aquatic life. High chloride content has a deleterious effect on metallic pipes and structures, as well as agricultural plants. They are calculated by Argentometric method.

Principle: In alkaline or neutral solution, potassium chromate indicates the endpoint of the silver nitrate titration of chlorides. Silver chloride is quantitatively precipitated before the red silver chromate is formed.

Apparatus required: Lab glassware.

Reagents

Potassium chromate indicator solution: 50 g of potassium chromate is dissolved in minimum amount of distilled water and silver nitrate is added drop wise till a red precipitate is formed. The mixture is allowed to stand for about 12 hours and diluted to 1000 ml with distilled water.

Silver nitrate solution (0.014N): 2.395 g of silver nitrate is dissolved in distilled water and made up to 1000 ml.

Procedure: A known volume of filtered sample (50 ml) is taken in a conical flask, to which about 0.5 ml of potassium chromate indicator is added and titrated against standard silver nitrate till silver dichromate ($AgCrO_4$) starts precipitating.

Calculation

$$\text{Chlorides } (Cl^-) = \frac{(A-B)\,(N)\,(35.45)}{\text{Sample taken in ml}}$$

Where,

A - Volume of silver nitrate consumed by the sample

B - Volume of silver nitrate consumed by the blank

N - Normality of silver nitrate (Standard methods, APHA, 16th edn, pp 286-88)

Dissolved Oxygen

Oxygen dissolved in water is a very important parameter in water analysis as it serves as an indicator of the physical, chemical and biological activities of the water body. The two main sources of dissolved oxygen are diffusion of oxygen from the air and photosynthetic activity. Diffusion of oxygen from the air into water depends on the solubility of oxygen, and is influenced by many other factors like water movement, temperature, salinity, *etc.* Photosynthesis, a biological phenomenon carried out by the autotrophs, depends on the plankton population, light condition, gases, *etc.* Oxygen is considered to be the major limiting factor in water bodies with organic materials. Dissolved oxygen is calculated by many methods.

Method 1: Membrane electrode method

Principle: The membrane electrode has a sensing element protected by an oxygen-permeable plastic membrane that serves as a diffusion barrier against impurities. Under steady conditions the electric current read is directly proportional to the D.O concentrations (electric current is directly proportional to the activity of molecular oxygen).

Apparatus required: Oxygen-sensitive membrane electrode and lab glassware.

Procedure: The calibrations are carried out following the manufacturer's calibration procedure. The electrode is dipped into the sample, and the reading noted.

Method 2: Winkler's method (modified).

Principle: Oxygen present in the sample oxidizes the dispersed divalent manganous hydroxide to the higher valency to precipitate as a brown hydrated oxide after addition of potassium iodide and sodium hydroxide. Upon acidification, manganese reverts to its divalent state and liberates iodine from potassium iodide, equivalent to the original dissolved oxygen content of the sample. The liberated iodine is titrated against N/80 sodium thiosulphate using fresh iodine as an indicator.

Apparatus required: BOD bottles-300 ml capacity, sampling devices, lab glassware - measuring cylinder, conical flasks, *etc.*, and Bunsen burner.

Reagents

Manganese sulphate: 480 g of manganous sulphate tetrahydrate is dissolved and made up to 1000 ml with distilled water (Discarded if it changes colour with starch).

Alkaline iodide-azide reagent: 500 g of sodium hydroxide and 150 g of potassium iodide along with 10 g of sodium azide (NaN_3) is dissolved and made up to 1000 ml with distilled water.

Conc. sulphuric acid

Starch indicator: 0.5 g of starch is dissolved in distilled water and boiled for few minutes.

Stock sodium thiosulphate: 24.82 g of sodium thiosulphate pentahydrate ($Na_2S_2O_2 . 5H_2O$) is dissolved in distilled water and made up to 1000 ml.

Standard sodium thiosulphate (0.025N): 250 ml of the stock sodium thiosulphate pentahydrate is made up to 1000 ml with distilled water to give 0.025N.

Procedure: The samples are collected in BOD bottles, to which 2 ml of manganous sulphate and 2 ml of potassium iodide are added and sealed. This is mixed well and the precipitate allowed to settle down. At this stage 2 ml of conc. sulphuric acid is added, and mixed well until all the precipitate dissolves. 203 ml of the sample is measured into the conical flask and titrated against 0.025 N sodium thiosulphate using starch as an indicator. The end point is the change of colour from blue to colourless.

Calculations

203 ml because (200) (300)/ (200-4) = 203 ml.

1ml of 0.025N Sodium thiosulphate = 0.2mg of Oxygen

$$\text{Dissolved Oxygen (as mg/L)} = \frac{(0.2)\ (1000\ \text{ml of Sodium thiosulphate})}{200}$$

Biological Oxygen Demand

Biological Oxygen Demand (BOD) is the amount of oxygen required by micro organisms for stabilizing biologically decomposable organic matter (carbonaceous) in water under aerobic conditions. The test is used to determine the pollution load of wastewater, the degree of pollution and the efficiency of wastewater treatment methods. 5-Day BOD test being a bioassay procedure requires the addition of nutrients and maintaining the standard conditions of pH and temperature and absence of microbial growth inhibiting substances.

Principle: The method consists of filling the samples in airtight bottles of specified size and incubating them at specified temperature (20 °C) for 5 days. The difference in the dissolved oxygen measured initially and after incubation gives the BOD of the sample.

Apparatus required: BOD bottles - 300 ml capacity, air incubator - to be controlled at 20 °C -\+ 1 °C, oximeter and magnetic stirrer.

Reagents

Preparation of dilution water: To 1000 ml of water, 1 ml each of phosphate buffer, magnesium sulphate, calcium chloride and ferric chloride solution is added, before bringing it to 20 °C and aerating it thoroughly.

Procedure: The sample having a pH of 7 is determined for first day DO. Various dilutions (at least 3) are prepared to obtain about 50% depletion of D.O. using sample and dilution water. The samples are incubated at 20 °C for 5 days and the 5th day D.O is noted using the oximeter. A reagent blank is also prepared in a similar manner.

Calculation

$$\text{BOD (in mg/L)} = \frac{(DO_1 - DO_5) - (B_1 - B_2) \times f}{p}$$

DO_1 - 1st day D.O of diluted sample

DO_5 - 5th day D.O of diluted sample

P - decimal volumetric fraction of sample used.

B_1 - 1st day D.O of control

B_2 - 5th day D.O of control , f - Constant

Chemical Oxygen Demand

Chemical oxygen demand (COD) is the measure of oxygen equivalent to the organic content of the sample that is susceptible to oxidation by a strong chemical oxidant. The intrinsic limitation of the test lies in its ability to differentiate between the biologically oxidisable and inert material. It is measured by the open reflux method.

Principle: The organic matter in the sample gets oxidized completely by strong oxidizing agents such as potassium dichromate in the presence of conc. sulphuric acid to produce carbon-di-oxide and water. The excess potassium dichromate remaining after the reaction is titrated with Ferrous Ammonium Sulphate (FAS) using ferroin indicator to determine the COD. The dichromate consumed gives the oxygen required for the oxidation of the organic matter.

Apparatus required: Reflux apparatus, Nessler's tube, Erlenmeyer flasks, hot plate and lab glassware.

Reagents

Standard potassium dichromate solution (0.250M): 12.25 g of potassium dichromate dried at 103 °C for about 2 hours is dissolved in distilled water and made up to 1000 ml.

Standard ferrous ammonium sulphate (FAS) 0.25N: 98 g of FAS is dissolved in minimum distilled water to which 20 ml of conc. sulphuric acid is added and made up to 1000 ml using distilled water to give 0.25 N of ferrous ammonium sulphate.

Ferroin indicator: 1.485 g of 1,10-Phenanthroline monohydrate and 695 mg of ferrous sulphate is dissolved in 100 ml of distilled water.

Conc. sulphuric acid

Silver sulphate crystals

Mercuric sulphate crystals

Procedure: 15ml of conc. sulphuric acid with 0.3 g of mercuric sulphate and a pinch of silver sulphate along with 5 ml of 0.025 M potassium dichromate is taken into a Nessler's tube. 10 ml of sample (thoroughly shaken) is pipetted out into this mixture and kept for about 90 minutes on the hot plate for digestion. 40 ml of distilled water is added to the cooled mixture (to make up to 50 ml) and titrated against 0.25 M FAS using ferroin indicator, till the colour turns from blue green to wine red indicating the end point. A reagent blank is also carried out using 10 ml of distilled water.

Calculation

$$\text{COD (mg/L)} = \frac{(\text{Blank reading - Sample reading}) \times N \times F \times 1000}{\text{Sample taken, ml}}$$

To calculate F,

$$F = \frac{10000}{\text{Titrant value of blank.}}$$

Fluoride

Fluorides have dual significance in water supplies. High concentration causes dental fluorosis and lower concentration (<0.8 mg/L) causes dental caries. A fluoride concentration of approximately 1mg/L in drinking water is recommended. They are frequently found in certain industrial processes resulting in fluoride rich wastewaters. Significant sources of fluoride are found in coke, glass and ceramic, electronics, pesticide and fertiliser manufacturing, steel and aluminium processing and electroplating industries. It is calculated by SPADNS method.

Principle: The colorimetric method of estimating fluoride is based on the reaction of fluorides (HF) with zirconium SPADNS solution and the 'lake' (colour of SPADNS reagent), which is greatly influenced by the acidity of the reaction mixture. Fluoride reacts with the dye 'lake', dissociating (bleaching) the dye into a colourless complex anion (ZrF_6^{2-}). As the amount of fluoride increases, the colour produced becomes progressively higher or of different hue.

Apparatus required: Spectrophotometer and lab glassware.

Reagents

Standard fluoride solution.

Stock: 221.0 mg of AR grade sodium fluoride was dissolved in distilled water and made up to 1000 ml to give 1 ml = 100 mg of F^-

Working Standard: 100 ml of the stock fluoride was diluted to 1000 ml to give 1 ml = 10 mg of flouride.

SPADNS Solution: 958 mg of SPADNS is dissolved in 500 ml of distilled water.

Zirconyl-acid reagent: 133 mg Zirconyl chloride octahydrate ($ZrOCl_2 .8H_2O$) was dissolved in about 25 ml of distilled water. 350 ml of conc. HCl was added and diluted to 500 ml with distilled water.

Zirconyl acid-SPADNS reagent: Equal volume of SPADNS and zirconyl acid reagent was mixed.

Procedure: A standard graph is prepared by using fluoride concentrations ranging from 0.005 mg/L to 0.150 mg/L at 570 nm. A reference solution is prepared by adding 4 ml of acid zirconyl-SPADNS reagent to 21 ml of distilled water. A known volume of filtered sample (21 ml) is taken in a test tube, 4 ml of acid zirconyl-SPADNS reagent is added to the sample along with a reference solution. The mixture is left for about 30 min for complete colour development and the optical density is read at 570 nm.

Calculation

$$F\ mg/L = \frac{(\text{O.D sample})\ (\text{Conc. of the Standard})\ (1000)}{(\text{O.D Standard})\ \ (\text{sample taken})}$$

Free Carbon dioxide

The important source of free carbon dioxide in surface water bodies is mainly from respiration and decomposition by aquatic organisms. It reacts with water partly to form calcium bicarbonate and in the absence of bicarbonates gets converted to carbonates releasing carbon dioxide.

Principle: Free carbon dioxide reacts with sodium carbonate or sodium hydroxide to form sodium bicarbonate. The completion of the reaction is indicated by the development of pink colour, characteristic of phenolpthalein indicator at an equivalent pH of 8.3

Apparatus required: Lab glassware - measuring jar, pipette, conical flask etc.

Reagents

Sodium hydroxide solution (0.22N): 1 g of sodium hydroxide was dissolved in 100 ml of distilled water and made up to 1000 ml to give 0.22 N.

Phenolpthalein indicator

Procedure: A known volume (50ml) of the sample is measured into a conical flask. 2-3 drops of phenolpthalein indicator is added and titrated against 0.22 N sodium hydroxide till the pink colour persists indicating the end point.

Calculation

$$\text{Free } CO_2 \text{ (mg/L)} = \frac{(Vt)\,(1000)}{Vs}$$

Where, Vt - volume of titrant (ml)

Vs - volume of the sample taken (ml)

Potassium

Potassium ranks seventh among the elements in order of abundance, behaves similar to sodium and remains low. Though found in small quantities (<20 mg/L) it plays a vital role in the metabolism.

Principle: Trace amount of potassium can be determined by direct reading of flame photometer at a specific wavelength of 766.5nm by spraying the sample into the flame. The desired spectral lines are then isolated by the use of interference filters or suitable slit arrangements. The intensity of light is measured by the phototube.

Working principle of Flame photometer: The emission of characteristic radiations by alkali and alkaline earth metals and the correlation of the emission intensity with the concentration of the element form the basis of flame photometry. The principle of the flame photometer depends on the "Emission Spectroscopy" in which the electrons of the metals after absorbing energy get excited from ground state to higher energy level and return back to the ground state with emission of light. The sample under test is introduced into flame in solution by means of atomizer. The radiation from the flame enters a dispersing device and isolates it (radiation) from the flame to the desired region of the spectrum. The phototube measures the intensity of isolated radiation, which is proportional to the concentration of the element present in the sample.

Apparatus required: Flame photometer, lab glassware and Whattman filter paper.

Reagents

Deionised distilled water.

Stock potassium solution: 1.907 g of dried Potassium chloride, is dissolved in 1000ml of distilled water, to give 1 ml = 1 mg of potassium

Working Potassium solution: Working standards of suitable strengths are prepared from the stock solution.

Procedure: The filter of the flame photometer is set at 766.5 nm (marked for Potassium, K) the flame is adjusted for blue colour. The scale is set to zero and maximum using the highest standard value. A standard curve of different concentration is prepared by feeding the standard solutions. The sample is filtered through the filter paper and fed into the flame photometer. The concentration is found from the standard curve or as direct reading.

Sodium

Sodium is one of the most abundant elements and is a common constituent of natural waters. The sodium concentration of water is of concern primarily when considering their solubility for agricultural uses or boiler feed water. The concentration ranges from very low in the surface waters and relatively high in deep ground waters and highest in the marine waters. It is calculated by flame photometric method.

Reagents

Deionised water

Stock sodium solution: 2.542 g of Sodium chloride of dried (at 140° C) was dissolved in 1000 ml distilled water to give 1 ml = 1mg of sodium.

Working Potassium solution: Working standards of suitable strengths were prepared from the stock solution.

Procedure: The filter of the flame photometer is set to 589nm (marked for Sodium, Na). By feeding distilled water the scale is set to zero and maximum using the standard of highest value. A standard curve between concentration and emission is prepared by feeding the standard solutions. The sample is filtered through filter paper and fed into the flame photometer and the concentration is found from graph or by direct readings.

10.8 Heavy Metals

Heavy metals are elements (properties of metals satisfied) of high atomic numbers. They have high utilities in industrial applications from papers to automobiles, by their very characteristic properties. They are found in the deep bowels of the earth as ores (complexes of mixtures). The metals are segregated from these ores, leaving behind the tailings that find their way into the environment as toxic pollutants. They get into the water bodies directly from point sources as sewage, and non-point sources as runoff and more insidiously as atmospheric deposition that are transported from long distances. Heavy metals affect every level of the food web, from producers in the trophic levels to the highest order carnivore by residing in the system and magnifying at every trophic status.

Atomic Absorption Spectrophotometer (AAS)

Working principle: Atomic absorption spectrometer's working principle is based on the sample being aspirated into the flame and atomized when the AAS's light beam is directed through the flame into the monochromator, and onto the detector that measures the amount of light absorbed by the atomized element in the flame. Since metals have their own characteristic absorption wavelength, a source lamp composed of that element is used, making the method relatively free from spectral or radiational interferences. The amount of energy of the characteristic wavelength absorbed in the flame is proportional to the concentration of the element in the sample.

Procedure: The sample is thoroughly mixed by shaking, and 100 ml of it is transferred into a glass beaker of 250 ml volume, to which 5 ml of conc. nitric acid is added and heated to boil till the volume is reduced to about 15-20 ml, by adding conc. nitric acid in increments of 5 ml till all the residue is completely dissolved. The mixture is cooled, transferred and made up to 100ml using metal free distilled water.

Operations for analysing heavy metals

Lamp selection

Lamp for the element to be detected is selected.

Operating current is suitably adjusted.

The lamp is aligned for the visible beam to fall on the slit of the monochromator

Wave length selection and slit adjustment:

Appropriate wavelength for the element to be detected is selected. The wavelength controller is moved clockwise or anti-clockwise slowly to get maximum percentage of transmittance.

The slits are adjusted to get closest to the required wavelength and avoid excess stray light.

Flame adjustment

On selecting suitable wavelength, the acetylene-air mixture is lit at the recommended pressure.

The burner level is so adjusted that the beam from the cathode crosses 1cm from the top of the burner and the beam is stabilized.

Analysis

A calibration graph is obtained by feeding the standard solutions of suitable concentration.

The samples are aspirated by feeding them through the capillary and the readings are noted. (Distilled water is aspirated between samples).

Apparatus required: AAS and lab glassware.

Reagents

Air-Acetylene flame

Metal free water

Standard metal solutions

Lead

Lead is relatively a minor element in the earth's crust but is widely distributed in low concentrations in uncontaminated soils and rocks. Lead concentration in freshwater is generally much higher. High concentration of lead results from atmospheric input of lead originating from its use in the leaded gasoline or from smelting processes. Industrial processes such as printing and dyeing, paint manufacturing, explosives, photography and mine or smelter operations may contain relatively high values in lead. Lead is toxic to aquatic organisms.

Principle: Lead can be determined at a wavelength of 283.3 nm by AAS with aspiration of the sample into the oxidising air-acetylene flame. When the aqueous sample is aspirated, the sensitivity for 1% absorption is 0.5 mg/L and the detection limit is 0.05 mg/L.

Standard lead solution: 1.598 g of lead nitrate is dissolved in about 200 ml of water containing 1.5 ml of conc. nitric acid and diluted to 1000 ml of metal free water to give 1 ml = 1 mg lead. A series of standards ranging from 1 mg to 5 mg were prepared from the stock and a standard graph was made.

Copper

Copper is a widely distributed trace element because most copper minerals are relatively insoluble and is sorbed to solid phases, hence only low concentrations are normally present in natural waters. Because of the presence of sulphide, copper would be expected to be even less soluble in anoxic systems. The presence of higher concentrations of copper can usually be attributed to corrosion of copper pipes, industrial wastes or particularly in reservoirs, which uses copper as algaecides. Copper is an essential trace element in the nutrition of plants and animals including man. It is required for the function of several enzymes and is necessary in the biosynthesis of chlorophyll. High levels are toxic to organisms but the response varies greatly with species.

Principle

Copper can be determined at a wavelength at 324.7 nm by AAS with aspiration of the sample into an oxidising air-acetylene flame. When the aqueous sample is aspirated, the sensitivity for 1% absorption is 0.1 mg/L and the detection limit is 0.01 mg/L.

Standard copper solution: 1g of copper salt is dissolved in 15ml of 1+1 nitric acid and diluted to 1000ml to give 1ml = 1mg copper. A series of standards ranging from 1mg to 5mg are prepared from the stock and a standard graph prepared.

Nickel

The nickel element is abundant in the chrome plating industrial effluent and the chrome plating industrial effluent discharged into the water body gets the nickel content. Nickel can be determined at a wavelength at 232 mm by APS with aspiration of the sample in to cum oxidising air-acetylene flame.

Standard nickel solution: 1.273 g of nickel oxide is dissolved in a minimum quantity of 10% HCl and diluted to 1000 ml with distilled water to give 1 ml = 1 mg of nickel. A series of standards ranging from 1 mg to 5 mg are prepared from the stock and analyzed.

Iron

Iron is an abundant element in the earth's crust, but exists generally in minor concentrations in natural water systems. Iron is found in the +2 (ferrous) and +3 (ferric) states depending on the oxidation-reduction potentials of the water. The ferric state of iron imparts orange strain to any settling surfaces, including laundry articles, cooking and eating utensils, and plumbing fixtures.

Principle: Iron can be determined at a wavelength of 248.3 nm by AAS with aspiration of the sample into an oxidising air-acetylene flame. Under standard conditions, iron produces 1% absorption at 0.12 mg/L and a linear response up to about 5 mg/L.

Standard iron solution: 1g of iron is dissolved in 50 ml of 1+1 nitric acid and diluted to 1000 ml with distilled water to give 1 ml = 1 mg of iron. A series of standards ranging from 1 mg to 5 mg are prepared from the stock and analysed.

Chromium

The concentration of chromium in natural waters is usually very low. Elevated concentrations of chromium can result from mining and industrial processes. Chromate compounds are routinely used in cooling waters to control erosion. Chromium in water supplies is generally found in the hexavalent form.

Principle: Total chromium can be determined at a wavelength of 357.9 nm by atomic absorption with aspiration of sample into a reducing air-acetylene flame. Under standard concentrations, chromium produces 1 % absorption at 0.25 mg/L and is detectable down to 0.003 mg/L.

Standard chromium solution: 2.828 g of AR grade potassium dichromate is dissolved in about 200 ml of distilled water, with 1.5 ml of conc. nitric acid and made up to 1000 ml with the same to give 1 ml = 1 mg of chromium. A series of standards ranging from 1 mg to 5 mg are prepared from the stock and analysed.

Cadmium

Cadmium is largely found in nature in the form of sulphide, and as an impurity of zinc - lead ores. The abundance of cadmium is much less than that of zinc. Cadmium may enter the surface waters as a consequence of mining, electroplating plants, pigment works, textile and chemical industries, and is toxic to man. There is evidence that cadmium affects reproductive organs in humans and is also a potential carcinogen. A specific disease called "itai-itai" has been absorbed in Japan due to excess cadmium. In addition, due to bioaccumulation, certain edible organisms may become hazardous to the ultimate consumer.

Principle: Cadmium can be determined at a wavelength of 228.8 nm by atomic absorption with aspiration of sample into an oxidising air-acetylene flame. When the aqueous sample is aspirated, the sensitivity for 1 % absorption is 25 mg/L and the detection limit is 2 mg/L.

Standard cadmium solution: 1.000 g of cadmium metal is dissolved in minimum volume of 1+1 HCl and made up to 1000ml with distilled water to give 1 ml = 1 mg of cadmium. A series of standards ranging from 1 mg to 5 mg are prepared from the stock and analysed.

Zinc

Zinc is an abundant element in rocks and ores and is present in natural waters only as a minor constituent. The main industrial use of zinc is in galvanizing and may enter the drinking waters from galvanized pipes. Another important use is in the preparation of alloys, including brass and bronze. It is an essential element in human nutrition. Food provides the main source of zinc to the body. Zinc may be toxic to aquatic organisms but the degree of toxicity varies greatly depending on water quality characteristics as well as the species being considered.

Principle: Zinc can be determined at a wavelength of 213.9 nm by AAS aspiration of the sample into an oxidizing air-acetylene flame. When the aqueous sample is aspirated, the sensitivity for 1% absorption is 20 mg/L and the detection limit is 5 mg/L.

Standard zinc solution: 1.000 g of zinc metal is dissolved in 20 ml of 1+1 HCl and diluted to 1000ml in distilled water, to give 1 ml = 1 mg of zinc. A series of standards ranging from 1 mg to 5 mg are prepared from the stock and analysed. Table 10.4 shows wave lengths for different heavy metals.

Table 10.4: Heavy metals with their wave length

S. No	Element	Wavelength (in nm)
1	Lead	283.3
2	Copper	324.7
3	Iron	248.3
4	Chromium	357.9
5	Cadmium	228.8
6	Zinc	213.9
7	Nickel	232

10.9 Biological Parameters

Plankton Analysis

The physical and chemical characteristics of water affect the abundance, species composition, stability and productivity of the indigenous populations of aquatic organisms. The biological methods used for assessing water quality includes collection, counting and identification of aquatic organisms; biomass measurements; measurements of metabolic activity rates; toxicity tests; bioaccumulation; biomagnification of pollutants; and processing and interpretation of biological data. The work involving plankton analysis would help in:

1. Explaining the cause of colour and turbidity and the presence of objectionable odour, tastes and visible particles in waters.
2. The interpretation of chemical analyses.
3. Identifying the nature, extent and biological effects of pollution.
4. Providing data on the status of an aquatic system on a regular basis.

Plankton: A microscopic community of plants (phytoplankton) and animals (zooplankton), found usually free floating, swimming with little or no resistance to water currents, suspended in water, nonmotile or insufficiently motile to overcome transport by currents, are called "Plankton".

Phytoplankton (microscopic algae) usually occurs as unicellular, colonial or filamentous forms and is mostly photosynthetic and is grazed upon by the zooplankton and other organisms occurring in the same environment. Zooplankton principally comprise of microscopic protozoans, rotifers, cladocerans and copepods. The species assemblage of zooplankton also may be useful in assessing water quality.

The structure of photosynthetic populations in the aquatic ecosystems is dynamic and constantly changing in species composition and biomass distribution. An understanding of the community structure is dependent on the ability to understand the temporal distribution of the different species. Changes in species composition and biomass may affect photosynthetic rates, assimilation efficiencies, rates of nutrient utilization, grazing, etc.

Plankton, particularly phytoplankton, has long been used as indicators of water quality. Because of their short life spans, planktons respond quickly to environmental changes. They flourish both in highly eutrophic waters while a few others are very sensitive to organic and/or chemical wastes. Some species have also been associated with noxious blooms causing toxic conditions apart from the tastes and odour problems.

Plankton net: The plankton net is a field-equipment used to trap plankton. It has a polyethylene filter of a defined mesh size and a graduated measuring jar attached to the other end. A handle holds the net. The mesh size of the net determines the size range of the plankton trapped. The mesh number 30 of size 60 mm was used for collecting samples.

Sampling Procedure: The manner in which sampling is done should conform to the objectives of the study. The "surface samples" (samples collected from the surface) are collected as close to the water surface as possible, mostly towards the center of the lake at regular monthly intervals. A known volume of the sample, 5 L to 50 L is filtered and planktons are filtered and preserved for further analysis.

Labels: The sample label has the date, time of sampling, study area-lake name and the volume measured and pasted on the containers of 50 ml capacity.

Preservation: The samples collected into the 100 ml polyethylene vials were preserved by adding suitable amounts of 1ml chloroform to act as the narcotizing agent and 2 ml of 2% formalin for preservation and analyses.

Concentration technique: The plankton nets are used to collect samples for the qualitative and quantitative estimation of the plankton, by filtering a known volume of water (5-50 liters) through the net depending on the plankton density of the tanks.

Qualitative and quantitative evaluation of plankton: Detailed analyses of phytoplanktonic populations are done by estimating the numbers in each species. The phytoplankton consisting of individual cells, filaments and colonies are counted as individual cells. When colonies of species are counted, the average number of cells per colony is counted, and in filamentous algae, the average length of the filament has to be determined.

Sedimentation and enumeration by microscope: Preserved samples in bottles are mixed uniformly by gentle inversion and then exactly 1ml of the sample is pipetted out into the S-C cell for analysis.

Microscope

Compound microscope

A monocular compound microscope is used in the counting of plankton with different eyepieces such as 10X, 15X and 20X. The microscope is calibrated using plankton-counting squares.

Counting

Counting cell- Sedgwick-Rafter (S-R) cell:

The Sedgwick-Rafter cell is a devise used for plankton counting and is about 50 mm long by 20 mm wide and 1mm deep. The cell is covered by a relatively thick cover slip and is calibrated to contain exactly 1.0 ml.

Phytoplankton Counting Units: Some plankton are unicellular while others are multicellular (colonial), posing a problem for enumeration. For analysis, a colony of plankton is accounted as a single count. The large forms that cross two or more boundaries of the grid are counted separately at lower magnification and their number included in the total count.

Method

Filling the cell

The cover slip is placed diagonally across the S-R cell and filled with the sample carefully without air bubbles with a large bore pipette. The sample is allowed to settle for about 5 minutes before the actual counting begins.

Note: Since the configuration of the S-R cell does not allow the use of high power microscope objectives, the identification of organisms smaller than 10 - 15 mm is difficult or impossible, limiting the usage to only larger forms of relatively dense populations.

Strip counting

A "strip" is the length of the cell that constitutes a volume approximately 50 mm long, 1-mm deep accounting to the volume of 25 mm^3 or 1/40 (2.5%) of the total cell volume. By moving the mechanical stage from left to right, the organisms can be examined in a systematic manner. By knowing the surface area of the portion counted in relation to that of the total, a factor is determined to expand the average counts of the plankton to the total area of the counting surface. This total area represents the number of organisms present per given volume of the sample. This volume expanded to an appropriate factor yields the organisms per litre of water for the lake.

The total number of planktons in the S-R cell is obtained by multiplying actual count in the strip by the number (enumeration factor) representing the portion of the S-R cell counted. The number of the strips counted is a function of the precision desired and the number of units (cells, colonies) for the strips measured. In this study, 500 cells were counted for estimation.

The plankton count in the S-R cell is got from the following,

$$\text{Number/ml} = \frac{C \times 1000 \text{ mm}}{L \times D \times W \times S}$$

Where,

C = Number of organisms counted

L = Length of each strip (S-R cell length) mm

D = Depth of a strip (S-R cell depth) mm

W = Width of a strip in mm

S = Number of strips counted

V_1 = (50)(1)(W = mm^3).

The plankton counts per strip are then determined by multiplying the actual count by the factor representing the counted portion of the whole S-R cell volume.

Number/ml = (C) (1000 mm^3) / (L) (D) (W) (S)

Where

C = Number of organisms counted.

L = Length of each strip in mm (of S-R cell)

D = Depth of the strip in mm (S-R cell)

W = Width of the strip in mm (Whipple grid image width), S = Number of strips counted.

The above physico-chemical and biological parameters of water including industrial effluents are essential to analysis for the assessment of water quality studies.

— — —

11

Treatments of Industrial Effluents

11.1 Introduction

Generally, except particular cases, the typical civil wastewater do not present substantial differences according to the town where they are produced, therefore the type and the sequence of water treatment are nearly the same.

Conversely, the industrial wastewater characteristics are extremely varying according to the type of activity. For example, the oil industry wastewater will contain high concentrations of oily substances and hydrocarbons, the galvanic industry will produce heavy metal polluted wastewater, a food industry will produce wastewater containing biodegradable substances and so on. Consequently also the whole cycle of treatment, being aimed at the removal of particular pollutants, will be different according to kind of industry. The individual treatments of a wastewater treatment plant can be classified in different ways. According to the functioning principle it is possible to distinguish biological, physical and chemical treatments.

Biological plants are more commonly used to treat domestic or combined domestic and industrial wastewater from a municipality. They use basically the same processes that would occur naturally in the receiving water, but give them a place to happen under controlled conditions, so that the cleansing reactions are completed before the water is discharged into the environment.

Physico-chemical plants are more often used to treat industrial wastewaters directly, because they often contain pollutants which cannot be removed efficiently by micro-organisms— although industries that deal with biodegradable materials, such as food processing, dairies, breweries, and even paper, plastics and petrochemicals, may use biological treatment. And biological plants generally use some physical and chemical processes, too.

According to sequence, wastewater treatment processes can be classified as preliminary, primary, secondary or tertiary.

- Preliminary treatment aiming at separating substances which can cause problems to purification plant equipment (non-organic solid waste, oils, sands).
- Primary treatments, where only the solid and heavier part of wastewater, called settleable solids is separated
- Secondary treatments, where a separation of dissolved organic substance and suspended non settling substance is operated.

Tertiary treatments, aiming at finishing the organic material purification and reducing the load of eutrophying elements present in the wastewater. There can also be a final disinfecting treatment to remove the residual pathogen organisms. A typical plant scheme presenting primary and secondary treatments is shown in the figure below(Fig. 11.1):

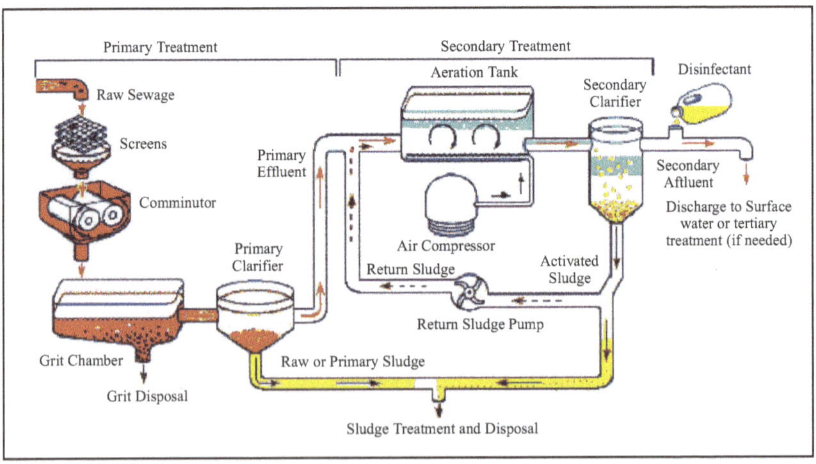

Figure 11.1: A Typical Treatment Plant

11.2 Criteria for the Choice of the Purification Process

After the removal of the suspended solids from the wastewater it is deduced from the BOD_5/COD ratio whether to proceed with a biological or chemical treatment.

- $BOD_5/COD < 0,2$ non biodegradable
- $0,2 < BOD_5/COD$ biodegradable wastewater with selected micro-organisms
- BOD_5/COD 0,6 biodegradable wastewater

  The BOD value is also used to guide the choice between the aerobe and the anaerobe method.

- $BOD_5 < 4000$ ppm aerobic process
- $BOD_5 < 4000$ ppm anaerobe process

During the aerobic purification the oxidised organic substances in the catabolism supply a lot of energy, allowing a strong biosynthesis with a rapid growth of cells mass, that will form the settling flake.

During the anaerobic purification instead the catabolic processes supply little energy, which makes the biosynthesis, and consequently the cellular mass growth less quick. There is also the formation of intermediate metabolites produced by the fermentation processes.

The most basic answer is to make dirty water clean. Treatment facilities simply compress the organic decomposition processes which take place in nature. This is performed by a combination of physical, biological, and chemical treatment stages. Nature (receiving waters) can only accept small amounts of effluent before becoming polluted, that is, natural bacteria feed on the Effluent organics and create an abnormal amount of dissolved oxygen uptake. Dissolved oxygen which exists in minute amounts (10 parts per million @ 20°C), is required by all marine life for survival. One of the principle objectives of wastewater treatment is to prevent as much of this "oxygen-demanding" organic material as possible from entering the receiving water.

Other objectives of wastewater treatment include, removal of objectionable items, nutrients and heavy metals.

The degree or level of treatment required often depends upon:

- The nature and quality of the receiving water, *i.e.*, salt water, inland fresh water bodies, estuaries. Federal/ Provincial regulations. Quantity of flow from the treatment plant. Uses and existing quality of receiving waters. The amount of mixing between a plant effluent and receiving waters.
- Assimilation capacity of the receiving water.

11.3 Common Terms Used in Wastewater Treatment

Preliminary or pretreatment is the very first stage, it is the removal of larger materials and grit that if not removed could hinder subsequent treatment processes. It is accomplished through the use of equipment such as bar screens, macerators, comminutors, racks and grit removal systems.

Primary treatment is usually comprised of preliminary treatment followed by primary clarifiers which remove approximately 50% suspended solids and 35-40% $B.O.D_5$ This is accomplished by channeling flows through large tanks with residence times of 2-4 hours, thus allowing suspended solids to settle.Post disinfection and a biosolids treatment process are normally included. Enhanced primary treatment can be performed by the addition of a coagulant such as ferric chloride along with a polymer, improving the degree of Suspended Solids and Biological Oxygen Demand removal to 80% and 60% respectively.

Primary wastewater treatment is carried out with primary settling basins, where the water flows slowly for up to a few hours, to allow organic suspended matter to settle out or float to the surface. Most of this material has a density not much different from that of water, so it needs to be given enough time to separate. For this treatment rectangular or cylindrical tank are used. They are endowed with a cone at the base where the settled sludge is collected. A bridge crane equipped with a scraping device rotates at the bottom and conveys the sludge towards an outlet pipe, while a surface skimmer removes the floating materials.

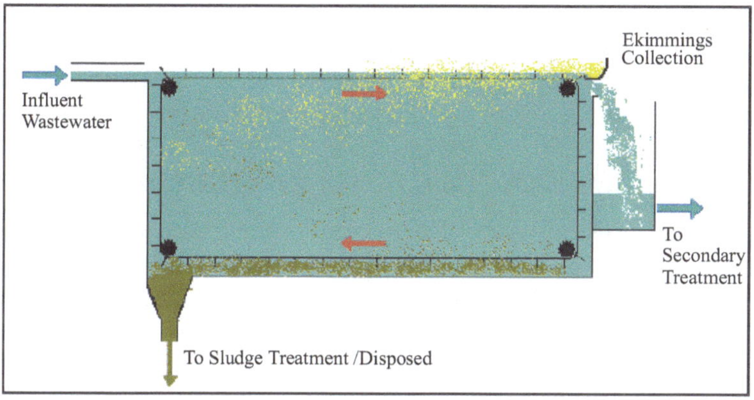

Figure 11.2: A Primary Settling Basin

Secondary treatment involves a primary process and a biological treatment stage. There are many biological processes in the treatment operation with the majority being variations of fixed film and mixed culture applications. The activated sludge process (mixed) is achieved by establishing large diversified cultures of bacteria. The bacteria metabolizes and provides the enzymatic breakdown of organic components, ie., liquids, carbohydrates, proteins and cellulose, in the wastewater. 90% removal rates of B.O.D. and suspended solids are typical of secondary treatment. As for these treatments a first distinction is to be done between:

- Attached biomass systems, represented by percolator filters, biodisks, and fluidised beds
- Suspended biomass systems, represented by biological ponds, actived sludge system, and anaerobic digesters.

11.4 Attached Biomass Systems

11.4.1 Percolator Filters

The percolator systems are usually preceded by a primary settler separating the settling solids existing in the rough sewage.

The filter consists of a tank, usually cylinder-shaped, filled with porous inert material on which a *bacteria* film develops. The effluent is put into it by overhead sprinkling and slowly percolates through the porous bed; the film, those ones in solution pass through it and are degraded by the bacteria, absorbs the organic materials suspended in the effluent . At the bottom of the *percolating filters* the sludge and water are collected, and conveyed to a secondary settler separating the two fractions.

11.4.2 Rotating Biological Contacters (RBC's)

The classic scheme of this plant provides the delivery of wastewater after a preliminary *sedimentation* to a biological oxidation basin where a roller is installed consisting of a certain number of disks, opportunely spaced from each other and mounted on a shaft set into rotation by a motor. The disks have generally 1 to 3 m. *diameter*, spaced about 2-3 cm from each other. Afterwards the effluent is directed to the final sedimentation phase, where it occurs the sedimentation of sludge, in general consisting mainly of the "*biodisk*" stripping film. The biological *oxidisation* occurs through the direct contact with the sludge film forming *spontaneously* on the disks, partially submersed in the Effluent themselves, and set into slow rotation. Thanks to this latter there alternately occur the phases of organic matter oxidisation (submersion), and of bacterial flora oxygenation (phase of air exposition). The biological film of these *sludge* keeps on developing until attained a certain thickness. After than, it automatically comes off the disk surface. This type of plant is particularly suitable for small and average use, where there are considerable load jumps, and where a management as simple as possible is required (Hammer & Bastian, 1989).

11.4.3 Fluidised Beds

In the *fluidised beds* (or submerged bacterial beds) the support material (generally sand) on which a *biomass* film is formed, is crossed from the bottom upwards by the Effluent to be purified. This creates a physical state in which the particles are free to move in the whole volume of the reactor. This allows to obtain biomass concentrations higher than those attainable in the dispersed biomass reactors. But it has a disadvantage given by the difficulty in supplying the high quantities of oxygen necessary to the process.

11.5 Suspended Biomass Systems

11.5.1 Biological Ponds

The biological ponds (or lagoons) are very simple treatment systems, being they formed by big artificial basins where the Effluent to be treated is put in; the solids settle, while the non settling and dissolved fractions are partly degraded by the bacteria. The Effluent put in the basins are usually with a very low organic load (BOD_5) while the standing time is long, producing a well stabilised sludge. The basins are usually excavated in the soil, and have to be waterproofed in order to avoid infiltration in the underground. The biological pond requires the availability of wide surfaces in comparison to the quantity of treated sewage, but the there are no technological devices and no energetic consumption. 4 main types of biological ponds can be distinguished according to the depth and the presence or not of an anaerobic environment :

- Anaerobic ponds, characterised by higher depth, by a relatively high organic load, and by the absence of oxygen. The purification processes to be established are anaerobic, and the microbial fauna is like that of the anaerobic digesters.
- Ventilated ponds, about 3 m deep, kept in aerobic conditions at any depth by an artificial aeration system. The organic loads are relatively high, and the microbial population is traceable to that of active sludge plants.
- Optional ponds, having a lower depth than the previous ones, with a higher aerobic zone, where the oxygen is supplied by the algae, and a lower anaerobic one. The bacterial populations are different at the two depths.
- Aerobe ponds have a completely aerobe environment thanks to the low depth, allowing a complete spreading of the oxygen. Abundant algae are formed on the surface layer. (House *et.al.*, 1991).

11.5.2 *Activated Sludge Process*

The active sludge process in its different versions, can be used both as a secondary treatment after the primary sedimentation, and as direct treatment on the effluent such as it is.

11.5.2.1 Microorganisms of the activated sludge

A lot of bacteria species, varying both with the chemical characteristics of the medium and with the physical characteristics, such as the temperature, participate in the sludge formation. A high concentration of proteins favours bacilli like *Zoogloea ramigera* and the geni *Alcaligenes* and *Flavobacterium*. An high concentration of carbohydrates favours *bacilli* of the genus *Pseudomonas*, a vigorous oxygenation and a low concentration of organic substances favours bacteria of the genera *Nitrobacter, Nitrosomonas*, and *Bacillus*; the presence of sulphur fosters the growth of bacteria of the genus *Thiotrix*.

The most important one among all these seems to be the *Zoogloea ramigera*, as the sludge flakes are mostly formed by colonies of this bacillus.

The protozoon are bacteria predators: if there are protozoon there must be also the bacteria. They therefore become indirect indicators of the condition of the waters and of the sludge on the way to purification.

The Amoeba indicate bad oxygenation, while those of bigger dimensions are characteristic of poorly active sludge. The zooflagellate resist in little oxygenated media, and are sometimes the only ones to populate the industrial wastewater sludge, containing the phenols or other organic compounds; they are the first to develop, and are characteristic of young sludge.

The ciliates are very important and can freely swim (floating) like Paramecium accompanying the little oxygenated flakes, or stick to a support like Opercularia, and Vorticella very useful in the water clarification phase. Vorticella is particularly characteristic of mature sludge, and indicates by its presence a good oxygenation. There exist also ciliates moving on the flake

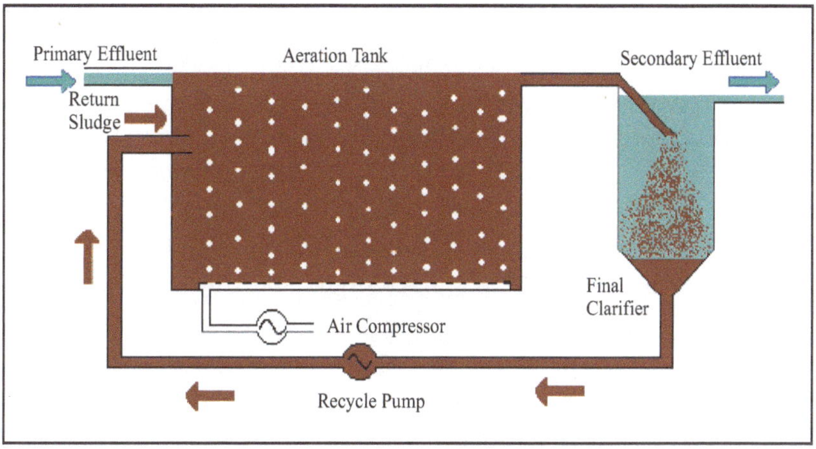

Figure 11.3: Activated Sludge Process

through filiform apparatus (basically movable) like Euplotes and Aspidisca. Among the algal protists Euglena and chlorella are almost always present especially in the stabilisation tanks, where they provide by photosynthesis part of the oxygen necessary to the bacterial oxygenation.

Among the higher multicellular organisms there are Rotiferi and Nematodes. The former are very susceptible to the toxic substances and to the excessive variations of the wastewater composition, develop in old sludge if only well oxygenated. They are therefore indicators of oxygenation prolonged in time. The nematodes are characteristic of old sludge now in course of mineralization, that is to say near the anaerobic digestion.

11.5.2.2 Functioning of an Activated Sludge Process

As before said, the active sludge is nothing else than bacterial biomass, dispersed in form of little flakes. The flocculation process consists of the aggregation of solid particles finely dispersed in the liquid, in flakes of such dimension and weight as to be separated by settling. The bacteria present in the flake metabolise both the particulate organic substance and the dissolved one using it for growth - producing more microorganisms - and for respiration, which results mostly in the formation of carbon dioxide and water. The process can also be set up to provide biological removal of the nutrients nitrogen and phosphorus

Moreover In the activated sludge are also present sessile ciliate protozoon tied to the flake by a peduncle, movable ciliate protozoon, rotifers and nematodes. As their main nourishment is made up by bacteria dispersed in the liquid (also pathogen ones), they contribute to the attainment of an high purity in the final Effluent by removing the dangerous bacteria.

The first stage of this purification system consists of the passage to an aeration tank (see figure), in order to pass then to a secondary tank (clarifier) where the sludge are separated, and the outgoing liquid results purified.

The separated sludge in the clarifier are partly put in again in the aeration tank, in order to keep in it an adequate bacterial biomass. However since the amount of microorganisms increases as a result of this process, some must be removed on a regular basis for further treatment and disposal, adding to the solids produced in primary treatment.

An aerobe environment is constantly kept in the aeration tank, consenting to obtain a better efficiency of the bacteria action. The aeration is ensured by mechanical equipment placed on the surface (turbines, rotating brushes) or by direct air insufflations. These systems produce turbulence in the liquid mass, ensuring the aeration and the complete remixing.

11.5.2.3 Biotic index and protozoon indicator role in sludge

The ciliate protozoon are very numerous in all kinds of wastewater aerobic treatment processes, and most of them present in the purification plants feed on dispersed bacteria. According to their behaviour they can be distinguished into three functional groups:

1. Floating, that float in the liquid fraction and stay in suspension in the sedimentation tank;
2. Basically movable, living on the sludge flake surface on which they move.

3. Sessile, that are firmly fixed through a peduncle to the sludge flake, and therefore precipitate with it during the sedimentation.

It has been proved that the ciliate protozoon improve the effluent quality through the predation of most dispersed bacteria, and that continuously get into the system with the wastewater.

In the purification plants belonging to the typology of active sludge process, the analysis of microfauna as a plant efficiency indicator is to be included among the routine analysis. It is able to give useful and ready indications about the active sludge biological activity, according to the micro-organisms community developing in it. It has therefore been set up an index appraising the active sludge quality, inspired by EBI applicable to all type of active sludge plants.

The sludge biotic index (SBI) is based both on the different sensitivity shown by some microfauna groups to the main physical, chemical, and managerial parameters, and on the abundance and variety of the existing species. This allows defining the sludge biological quality through conventional numeric values.

The index is obtained through the use of a two-entry table. The dominant groups are taken into consideration in the rows, while in the columns they are associated to a sludge biological quality, decreasing downwards. The species that are considered in the higher part of the columns, represent the sludge microfauna (except the flagellates), and the thickness of flagellates counted in the Fuchs-Rosenthal room. For the determination of SBI values it is necessary to select the line containing the dominant species considering the total microfauna thickness, and intersecting it with the column containing the species total number measured and the thickness of flagellates being taken, so assigning the value 1 to 10 taken with the intersection. This is to be included in the appropriate conversion table that will give the whole estimation.

11.5.2.4 Flake formation in the activated sludge process

An important condition for the success of this process is the formation of a type of culture which will flocculate naturally, producing a settling sludge and a reasonably clear upper, or supernatant layer. If the sludge does not behave this way, a lot of solids will be remain in the water leaving the clarifier, and the quality of the effluent wastewater will be poor.

The following factor can hinder the flakes formation, thus impairing water purification:

- *Flakes bulking:* the filamentary organisms extend towards the flake exterior, becoming gelatinous and retaining water; the sedimentation is hindered.
- *Formation of biological foams:* they themselves are due to filamentary organisms, growing on the tank surface forming rigid masses troubling the sedimentation.
- *Dispersed growth:* because of the existing surface-active or toxic substances the bacteria do not adhere to each other, and do not cause the flake formation any more.
- *Formation of too small flakes:* the Effluent is muddy, the solids remain in suspension and there occurs no separation of sediment.

11.5.2.5 Anaerobic digester

Secondary wastewater treatment can be carried out also by anaerobic digestion, with the same equipment for the sludge anaerobic digestion.

Tertiary treatment is comprised of a three stage process which further improves effluent quality past the primary and secondary treatment phases (see above examples). Usually 95-98% removal rates are achieved. Often, nutrient removal is included with both secondary and tertiary systems.

The main objective of the tertiary treatments is the removal of dissolved nitrogen and phosphorous compounds of the purification plant effluent, with the aim to limit their eutrophying effect in the receiver water body. Also the phytodepuration treatments can be considered tertiary treatments. There can also be a final disinfecting treatment, when the receiver water body is intended for an use requiring a particular hygienic-sanitary safeguard (*e.g.* bathing).

11.5.2.6 Nitrogen removal

Nitrogen is found in industrial wastewater mostly in the form of ammonia and organic nitrogen. Its removal is a process of biological nature and occurs in two phases. 1) In the first phase called nitrification the ammonia is oxidised to nitrate, thanks to a series of bacteria mediated reactions: NH_3, NO_2^-, NO_3^-. In this phase the Nitrosomonas oxidise the ammonia to nitrite and the nitrifying bacteria oxidize the nitrite to nitrate. In the second phase the nitrates are denitrified to molecular nitrogen by means of different genus of bacteria (*Pseudomonas, Bacillus*) using the nitrates as oxidising compound in place of oxygen. The first phase has to occur in aerobic environment, and a tank similar to that for the active sludge is used , while the second phase has to occur in anoxic environment in such a way that the bacteria use the nitrate instead of oxygen, as electron acceptor.

There are also physical/chemical processes which can remove nitrogen, especially ammonia; they are not as economical for domestic wastewater, but might be suited for an industrial location where no other biological processes are in use. (These methods include alkaline air stripping, ion exchange, and "breakpoint" chlorination).

11.5.2.7 Phosphorus removal

Phosphorous removal is most commonly done by chemical precipitation with iron or aluminum compounds, such as ferric chloride or alum (*aluminum sulfate*). The solids which are produced can be settled along with other sludges, depending on where in the treatment train the process takes place. ("Lime", or calcium hydroxide, also works, but makes the water very alkaline, which has to be corrected, and produces more sludge.). There is also a biological process for phosphorus removal, which depends on designing an activated sludge system in such a way as to promote the development of certain types of bacteria which have the ability to accumulate excess phosphorus within their cells. The basic principle of the phosphorous biological removal systems contemplates a depurative unit where it is alternated an anaerobic condition and an aerobic one, inducing an high phosphorous intake by the bacteria.

These methods mainly convert dissolved phosphorus into particulate form. For treatment plants which are required to discharge only very low concentrations of total phosphorus, it is common to have a sand filter as a final stage, to remove most of the suspended solids which may contain phosphorus.

11.5.2.8 Disinfection

Disinfection, usually the final process before discharge, is the destruction of harmful (pathogenic) microorganisms, *i.e.* disease-causing germs. The object is not to kill every living microorganism in the water but to reduce the number of harmful ones to levels appropriate for the intended use of the receiving water.

The most commonly used disinfectant is chlorine, which can be supplied in the form of a liquefied gas which has to be dissolved in water, or in the form of an alkaline solution called sodium hypochlorite, which is the same compond as common household chlorine bleach. Chlorine is quite effective against most bacteria, but a rather high dose is needed to kill viruses, protozoa, and other forms of pathogen. Chlorine has several problems associated with its use, among them: that it reacts with organic matter to form toxic and carcinogenic chlorinated organics, such as chloroform, chlorine is very toxic to aquatic organisms in the receiving water and it is hazardous to store and handle. Hypochlorite is safer, but still produces problems 1 and 2. Problem 2 can be dealt with by adding sulfur dioxide (*liquefied gas*) or sodium sulfite or hydrogen-sulfite (solutions) to neutralize the chlorine. The products are nearly harmless chloride and sulfate ions.

A more powerful disinfectant is ozone. Ozone is too unstable to store, and has to be made as it is used. It is produced by passing an electrical discharge through air, which is then bubbled through the water. While chlorine can be dosed at a high enough concentration so that some of it remains in the water for a considerable time, ozone is consumed very rapidly and leaves no residual. It may also produce some chemical byproducts, but probably not as harmful as those produced by *chlorine*.

The other commonly used method of disinfection is ultraviolet light. The water is passed through banks of cylindrical, quartz-jacketed fluorescent bulbs. Anything which can absorb the light, such as fouling or scale formation on the bulbs' surfaces, or suspended matter in the water, can interfere with the effectiveness of the disinfection. Some dissolved materials, such as iron and some organic compounds, can also absorb some of the light. Ultraviolet disinfection is becoming more popular because of the increasing complications associated with the use of *chlorine*.

11.5.2.9 Sludge treatments

Sludge from primary settling basins, called primary or "raw" sludge, is a noxious, smelly, gray-black, viscous liquid or semi-solid. It contains very high concentrations of bacteria and other microorganisms, many of them pathogenic, as well as large amounts of biodegradable organic material. Because of the high concentrations, any dissolved oxygen will be consumed rapidly, and the odorous and toxic products of anaerobic biodegradation (*putrefaction*) will be produced. The greasy floatable skimmings from primary treatment are another portion of this putrescible solid waste stream.

In addition to the primary sludge, wastewater plants with secondary treatment will produce a "secondary sludge", consisting largely of microorganisms which have grown as a result of consuming the organic wastes. While not quite so objectionable, due to the biodegradation which has already taken place, it is still very high in pathogens and contains much material which will decay and produce odors if not treated further.

Therefore sludge must be stabilized in order to reduce pathogen load, putrefactive processes and water content. Afterward they can be used as compost production of for land filling. However sludges from physical-chemical treatment of industrial waste streams containing heavy metals and non-biodegradable toxic organic compounds often must be handled as hazardous wastes. Some of these will end up in hazardous waste landfills, or may be chemically treated for detoxification - or even for recovery of some components for recycling. Recalcitrant organic compounds can be destroyed by carefully controlled high-temperature incineration, or by other innovative processes, such as high-temperature hydrogen reduction. Biological digestion is a common method for treating wastewater sludge. In this process organic material of the sludge is metabolized (digested) from internal microbial population.

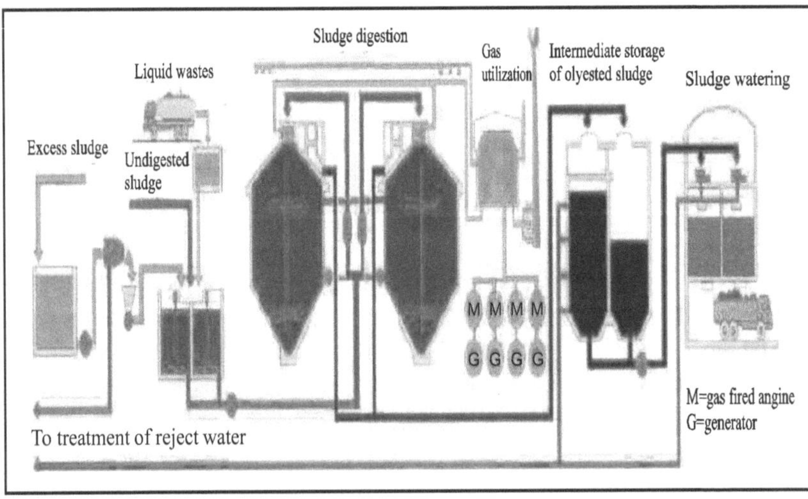

Figure 11.4: A Typical sludge processing

11.6 Aerobic Digestion

Aerobic digestion requires supplying oxygen to the sludge; it is similar to the activated sludge process, except no external "food" is provided.

11.6.1 Anaerobic Process and Biogas Production

The anaerobic digestion produces a gas which is mostly a mixture of methane and carbon dioxide. The gas has a fuel value, and can be burned to provide heat to the digester tank and even to run electric generators. Some localities have compressed the gas and used it to power vehicles. Digestion can reduce the amount of organic matter by about 30 to 70 percent, greatly decrease the number of pathogens, and produce a liquid with an inoffensive, "earthy" odor. The anaerobic digestion is a process commonly used as sludge biological stabilisation treatment as well as for the treatment of effluent having a high BOD value (>4000 ppm). The digesters are made up by big cylindrical tanks having a dome top, sometimes floating in a way that the higher part of the digester can be used for the biogas collection. Anaerobic digesters. The process can be a one or two phase process. The monophase plant is characterised by the fact that the digestion occurs in only one unit, at room temperature, and without stirring. In a digester of this type various zones can be distinguished: a higher one where the supernatant liquor is collected, an intermediate one where the digestion process occurs, a lower one where the digested sludge is accumulated. The gas developing in the intermediate zone, by rising drags oils and fats forming the layer of floating foams. Being without stirring the process is slow, and is usually supplied in a discontinuous way, sending the supernatant liquor to active sludge process. (Patrick, 1976).

In the two-phase digester instead the first phase is intended for the sludge digestion, while the second one is used for the separation of the digested sludge, besides completing the biological process. The first reactor is mixed, and for such operation it can be used the biogas produced during the digestion. The *reactors* can be heated at a temperature between 30 and 60°C by always recycling the produced biogas. Biochemistry of the anaerobic process.

The biochemical phases involved in the biogas production are :

1. *Hydrolysis and fermentation:* the process occurs still in the presence of oxygen, that remains imprisoned in the digester during the load. The aerobe and microaerophilic bacteria attack the complex molecules making the mass more fluid. This phase products are sugars, fatty acids, amino acids, being catabolised at CO_2 and H_2O. Also micro-organisms able to degrade the cellulose are present. The oxygen being used up, the anaerobes operate to further degrade the cellulose, to ferment sugars, fatty acids, amino acids. The products deriving from these fermentations are lactic acid, ethanol, succinate, acetate, formate, and propionate.

2. *Acetogenic dehydrogenation:* the compounds previously produced are catabolised through processes called dehydrogenation with CO_2 and H_2 formation

3. *Acetogenic hydrogenation:* in this phase the anaerobe bacteria synthesise acetic acid from CO_2 and H_2 by a process called hydrogenation.

4. *Methanogenesis:* in this phase there occurs an abundant production of methane, as well as of CO_2. The methanogene bacteria are strictly anaerobe, and their ideal substratum is the acetic acid produced in the previous phase. For the methane production also substrata like formic acid or methanol can be used.

11.6.2 Sludge dewatering

A liquid sludge, which might contain 3 to 6% dry weight of solids, can be dewatered to form a drier sludge cake of maybe 15 to 25 percent solids, which can be hauled as a solid rather than having to be handled as a liquid. Equipment used to dewater sludge includes centrifuges, vacuum filters, and belt presses or plate-and-frame presses. Chemical coagulants are commonly added to help form larger aggregates of solids and release the water. Further processes such as composting and heat drying can produce a drier product with lower pathogen levels. Another approach involves treatment with lime (calcium oxide), which kills pathogens due to its highly alkaline nature as well as the heat that is generated as it reacts with the water in the sludge; this also results in a drier product. A final disposal method which eliminates all of the pathogens and greatly reduces the volume of the sludge is incineration. This is not considered a beneficial use, however, and is becoming less popular due to public concerns over air emissions.

11.6.3 Phytodepuration (Constructed Wetlands)

The phytodepuration is used for the finishing and removal of nutrients (nitrogen and phoshorus) in the biological purified effluents, or for the clarified Effluent coming from septic tanks. Algae or aquatic macrophytes are used in simple systems from the building viewpoint and with low energy consumption. Three phytodepuration systems can be distinguished:

11.6.4 Macrophyte Systems

They consists of artificial "wetlands" where the macrophytes "contribute" with the micro-organisms to the water purification. The wastewater to be treated generally come from an active sludge purificator or from septic tanks. There exist two different treatment systems:

a) Surface flow (FWS - free water surface). The water runs in low depth basins (1-1,2 m) housing floating *macrophytes* like water hyacinth or duckweeds (Lemna), or rooted macrophytes like bulrush, marsh reed, Typha. The floating macrophytes are mostly used for the removal of *eutrophying nutrients;* the rooted ones are used like a support to the biofilm, adhering to stems and leaves, real protagonist of the purification. The macrophytes biomasses are periodically harvested in order to avoid the basin filling.

b) Sub-surface flow (SF - sub-surface). It consists of a trench excavated in the soil, filled with inert material (medium) with different texture (crushed stone, gravel, sand), where emerging rooted macrophytes like *Typha, Phragmites,* Scirpus grow. The plants grow forming a thick tangle. The Effluent coming out of a septic tank crosses the medium remaining submersed, that is to say under the topsoil. The effluent is purified through mechanical filtration and through bacterial degradation by the film forming around the macrophytes.

11.6.5 Planktonic Micro-algae Systems

Biologically purified wastewater are placed in basins where the load of eutrophying elements is reduced by the activities of micro-algae. These organisms show a very good removal capacity and a certain alimentary interest due to their protein content. The main question is that of the final separation of the algae, for which technological solution like centrifugation, micro-sieving, *etc.* are to be used.

11.6.6 Artificial Lagoons with Controlled Food Chains

The algal biomass and the macrophytic one operating the purification help the maintenance of a food chain having at its top species of economic interest.

11.6.7 The Extensive Purification Techniques (Rural Purification of Waters or Lagooning)

The extensive techniques of purification fit particularly for the treatment of Effluents of small communities where the building of conventional municipal plants should be to expensive.

These techniques

— are adapted to the treatment of waters with weak polluting loads;

— support the seasonal fluctuations generated by tourism;

— have weak maintenance expenses;

The main disadvantage is that they require large surfaces. These techniques of purification are based on the purification properties of the aquatic *biocenoses* (bacteria, fauna and flora).

The organic pollutant decomposition relies on the metabolism of the bacteria (identical to biological purification achieved in the conventional purification stations). The mineral elements, produced by the bacterial metabolism, are absorbed by the plants (the most of the time by algae) which produce O_2(photosynthesis) necessary to the bacteria. There is natural control of the development of algae and bacteria by the aquatic fauna that consumes them.

11.6.8 The Lagooning Technique

Practically, waters to be treated pass, after simple netting, in successive lagoons represented by shallow basins (of 50 cm to 1 m). This reduced depth permits to get, for a certain volume of water, a big surface in contact with air. It will speed up the oxygenation and the the light exposure which photosynthesis depends on. The dividing of the total surface in several reduced size basins permits to get a better purification as if with only one lagoon. Every lagoons is thus colonized by microorganisms adapted to the different stages of the purification). The flora developing in lagunes can be:

— microphytes (algae, seaweeds....)

— macrophytes or superior plants rooted to at the bottom of the lagoon (*Scirpus, Thypha, Phragmites,...*)

The excess vegetation can be easily reapped and extracted. It will be treated respecting the foreseen norms. The purification by lagooning is slow (about 60 days) as water to be purified has therefore to stay quite a long time in these ponds. The artificial ventilation of the lagoon by air insufflation permits an acceleration of the purification. The purification being faster, the size of the lagoons could be reduced (1 to 3 m^3 by E.I.). An average of 10 m^3 by equivalent - inhabitant (E.I.). or 1 ha of reservoir by 100 inhabitants.

An interesting example of purification by lagooning with the Lemna system is shown in Figure 11.5.

Figure 11.5: A Typical Lagooning System.

Figure 11.6: A Typical Lagooning With Lemna System

The traditional lagooning system has been improved by the setting up of two floors: a first part equipped with air blowers at the bottom where most of the organic matter is decomposed and a stabilization where the purification is refined.

The originality of the system lies in the conception of the last basin covered with duckweeds (Lemna). The duckweeds

(Lemna) are floating macrophytes. They form a layer that covers the surface of the lagoon. A steady ecological system settles because of the absence of light. It prevents the growth of parasite algae and prevents the diffusion of the smells while creating a layer rich in oxygen between the water and the atmosphere.

A Lemna tank therefore consist of:

— An anaerobic zone, deep situated, where the bacteria decompose the organic materials.

— A thin aerobe zone of some centimeters, situated under the layer of plants. The by-products of the decomposition are oxidized there.

— A layer of floating duckweeds, that assimilate the nutriments (nitrates, ammoniums, phosphates) serving for their growth. A periodic harvest of the duckweeds, made by means of a floating reaper, regularly removes these nutriments. Lemnas are then composted.

The Lemna lagoons are some meters deep and are excavated in the ground. They are protected from the infiltrations by a tightness membrane. A metal lattice stops the rodents from damaging the membrane. A hydraulic partition separates the lagoon into the two parts. The maintenance must be regular and should consider " outfencing ", checks of the water inflow equipments and the harvest of the Lemnas. The Lemna system suits small and middle communities, if the necessary land (3 m^2 by inhabitant) is available at a reasonable price.

11.6.9 Leachates Treatment In An Aerated Lagoon

Leachate treatment in an aerated lagoon is been studied a technique to reduce the organic an the nitrogen load of leachates. Leachates should be first characterized: flow rates, concentrations and loads, The concentrations of some compounds (COD, BOD) vary inversely with influent flow rate. Other compounds as NH_4^+ and humic acid have a concentration nearly independent of the flow rate. Moreover we can observe rather important seasonal variations, probably due to the degradation activity in the landfill. Performances analysis of the aerated lagoon is given as concentration evolution with time and outlet frequencies distributions of the level of COD, BOD, $N\text{-}NH_4^+$ and humic acid. Standards at the outlet are respected but efficiency decreases as the biodegradable part of the leachates is becoming less important. In that case efficiency for COD is rather poor. As far as nitrogen compounds are concerned, there is an important decrease of total nitrogen between inlet and outlet. But biological nitrification is limited and occurs only during summer. Most of the nitrogen is eliminated by striping. More detailed analysis should be done about possible complexation and precipitations processes that can occur in the aerated lagoon and how they can be managed.

Anyway an appropriate system for aerobic treatment of leachates should :

— Be dimensioned to the treatment of compounds with a load that will be decreased with time;

— Be dimensioned to drastically decrease the $N\text{-}NH_4^+$ concentration in the Effluent, especially to avoid fish toxicities in the receiving waters;

— Be dimensioned to work in a high Cl^- concentration environment and where precipitations and incrustations will occur.

The treatment of industrial effluent is well described by physical, chemical and biological treatment using various methods such as screening, grating, chemical treatment such as addition of alum, bioreactors, trickling filters using plants such as lemna, trees.

— — —

12

Volatile Organic Compounds

12.1 Introduction

Volatile Organic Compounds (VOCs) are chemicals that evaporate easily at room temperature. The term "*organic*" indicates that the compounds contain carbon. VOC exposures are often associated with an odor while other times there is no odor. Both can be harmful. There are thousands of different VOCs produced and used in our daily lives.

Many products emit or "off -gas" VOCs. Some examples of VOC emission sources are:

— Benzene
— Toluene
— Methylene
— Chloride
— Formaldehyde
— Xylene
— Ethylene glycol
— Texanol
— 1,3-butadiene

12.2 Emission Sources

— Paints
— Varnishes
— Moth balls
— Solvents
— Gasoline

— Newspaper
— Cooking
— Cleaning Chemicals
— Vinyl floors
— Carpets
— Photocopying , Upholstery Fabrics
— Adhesives
— Sealing Caulks
— Cosmetics
— Air Fresheners
— Fuel Oil
— Vehicle Exhaust
— Pressed Wood Furniture
— Environmental Tobacco Smoke (Secondhand smoke)

Organic compounds are chemicals that contain carbon and are found in all living things. Volatile organic compounds, sometimes referred to as VOCs, are organic compounds that easily become vapors or gases. Along with carbon, they contain elements such as hydrogen, oxygen, fluorine, chlorine, bromine, sulfur or nitrogen.

Volatile organic compounds are released from burning fuel, such as gasoline, wood, coal, or natural gas. They are also released from solvents, paints, glues, and other products that are used and stored at home and at work.

Many volatile organic compounds are also hazardous air pollutants. Volatile organic compounds, when combined with nitrogen oxides, react to form ground-level ozone, or smog. Examples of volatile organic compounds are gasoline, benzene, formaldehyde, solvents such as toluene and xylene, and perchloroethylene (or *tetrachloroethylene*), the main solvent used in dry cleaning. Many volatile organic compounds are commonly used in paint thinners, lacquer thinners, moth repellents, air fresheners, hobby supplies, wood preservatives, aerosol sprays, degreasers, automotive products, and dry cleaning fluids.

Volatile organic compounds are common air pollutants found in most of the air in the United States. It can be exposed to volatile organic compounds outdoors by breathing polluted air that contains them. You are most likely to be exposed to volatile organic compounds outdoors in the summer, when the sun and hot temperatures react with pollution to form smog,.

Indoors, products that contain volatile organic compounds release emissions when you use them, and to a smaller degree, when they are stored. It can be exposed to volatile organic compounds at home if the people use cleaning, painting, or hobby supplies that contain them. It can also be exposed if you dry-clean your clothes with home dry-cleaning products; if you dry-clean your clothes at a professional dry-cleaners; or if the people use graphics and crafts materials such as glues, permanent markers, and photographic solutions.

At work, it can be exposed at a dry-cleaner, a photography studio, or an office that uses copiers, printers, or correction fluids. It can also be exposed if you work in chemical manufacturing or with petroleum-based products.

The health effects of volatile organic compounds can vary greatly according to the compound, which can range from being highly toxic to having no known health effects. The health effects of volatile organic compounds will depend on nature of the volatile organic compound, the level of exposure, and length of exposure.

According to the 10th Report on Carcinogens, benzene is known to be a human carcinogen; formaldehyde and perchloroethylene are "reasonably anticipated to be carcinogens." People at the highest risk of long-term exposure to these three volatile organic compounds are industrial workers who have prolonged exposure to the compounds in the workplace; cigarette smokers; and people who have prolonged exposure to emissions from heavy motor vehicle traffic.

Long-term exposure to volatile organic compounds can cause damage to the liver, kidneys and central nervous system. Short-term exposure to volatile organic compounds can cause eye and respiratory tract irritation, headaches, dizziness, visual disorders, fatigue, loss of coordination, allergic skin reactions, nausea, and memory impairment.

12.3 Nitrogen Oxides

Nitrogen oxides are a group of gases that are composed of nitrogen and oxygen. Two of the most common nitrogen oxides are nitric oxide and nitrogen dioxide. The chemical formula for nitric oxide is NO; for nitrogen dioxide, it is NO_2.

Nitric oxide is a gas with a sharp, sweet smell; it is colorless to brown at room temperature. Nitrogen dioxide is a colorless to brown liquid at room temperature, with a strong, harsh odor. It becomes a reddish-brown gas at temperatures above 70° F.

Nitrogen oxides are released into the air from motor vehicle exhaust, or the burning of coal, oil, and natural gas, especially from electric power plants. They are also released during industrial processes such as welding, electroplating, engraving, and dynamite blasting.

Nitrogen oxides, when combined with volatile organic compounds, form ground-level ozone, or smog. Nitric oxide is used to bleach rayon and produce nitric acid. Nitrogen dioxide is used to produce rocket fuels, explosives, and other chemicals. Nitrogen dioxide is sometimes used to bleach flour.

Nitrogen oxides are common pollutants found in most of the air in the United States. It can be exposed to nitrogen oxides outdoors by breathing air that contains it, especially if you live near a coal-burning electric power plant or areas with heavy motor vehicle traffic. It can be exposed to higher levels if air pollution and smog levels are high. It can be exposed at home or at work, indoors or outdoors, through smoking cigarettes or breathing second-hand cigarette smoke. It can be exposed at work if you work in a facility that produces nitric acid, explosives such as dynamite and TNT, or welded metals.

Exposure to high industrial levels of nitric oxide and nitrogen dioxide can cause death. It can cause collapse, rapid burning and swelling of tissues in the throat and upper respiratory tract, difficult breathing, throat spasms, and fluid build-up in the lungs. It can interfere with the blood's ability to carry oxygen through the body, causing headache, fatigue, dizziness, and a blue color to the skin and lips.

Industrial exposure to nitrogen dioxide may cause genetic mutations, damage a developing fetus, and decrease fertility in women. Repeated exposure to high levels of nitrogen dioxide may lead to permanent lung damage. Industrial exposure to nitric oxide can cause unconsciousness, vomiting, mental confusion, and damage to the teeth. Industrial skin or eye contact with high concentrations of nitrogen oxide gases or nitrogen dioxide liquid can cause serious burns.

Long-term exposure to nitrogen oxides in smog can trigger serious respiratory problems, including damage to lung tissue and reduction in lung function. Exposure to low levels of nitrogen oxides in smog can irritate the eyes, nose, throat, and lungs. It can cause coughing, shortness of breath, fatigue, and nausea.

12.4 Ozone

Ozone is a gas that occurs both at the earth's ground level, and in the earth's upper atmosphere. Its chemical formula is O_3. The ozone in the atmosphere occurs naturally and protects life on earth from the sun's harmful ultraviolet rays.

The ozone that occurs on the ground level is formed when sunlight reacts with pollution from motor vehicles, power plants, industrial boilers, refineries, chemical plants, and other industrial sources. Ground-level ozone is the main ingredient of smog, a kind of air pollution found in many U.S. cities.

Ozone can also be industrially manufactured. Manufactured ozone is a colorless to blue gas with a pungent odor. It is used for purifying air and drinking water; treating industrial waste; drying varnishes and printing inks; deodorizing feathers; bleaching waxes; and making oils and other chemicals. It is used to control mold and bacteria in cold storage, and to age liquor and wood.

It is most likely to be exposed to ozone in the summer, when the sun and hot temperatures react with pollution to form ozone. You can be exposed to ozone if you exercise or work outdoors during the summer.

As levels of ozone increase, more people are exposed, especially if "ozone alerts" are issued by local governments to warn of dangerous ozone levels. You will be exposed to more ozone in the middle of the day, when ozone levels are highest. Active children are likely to be exposed to ozone if they spend a lot of time playing outdoors in the summer. You will be more sensitive to ozone if you exercise or work vigorously outdoors, if you are elderly, or if you have asthma or other respiratory diseases. You can be exposed to ozone at work if you work in a facility that exposes you to gasoline vapors, chemical solvents, or processes that produce ozone. Repeated exposure to ozone may cause permanent damage to the lungs, especially in children whose lungs are still developing. It can cause reproductive and genetic damage. Exposure to ozone may increase the risk of damage to a developing fetus.

Exposure to ozone can aggravate chronic lung diseases such as emphysema and bronchitis, and reduce the immune system's ability to fight off infections in the respiratory system. Exposure to ozone can aggravate asthma and heart disease, reduce lung capacity, and cause a build-up of fluid in the lungs, causing difficulty breathing. Exposure to ozone can irritate your respiratory system, causing you to cough, feel irritation in your throat, or feel uncomfortable in your chest. Breathing ozone can cause headache, upset stomach, congestion, fatigue, and vomiting. Having skin or eye contact with liquefied ozone in the workplace can produce severe burns. Moderate exposure to ozone can cause eye irritation, burning of the throat and eyes, and a bitter taste and smell.

12.5 Toluene

Toluene is a clear, colorless liquid with a strong, sweet, and pungent odor. It occurs naturally in crude oil. Toluene has a chemical formula of C_7H_8. Toluene is used as a solvent, and to make aviation gasoline, spray and wall paints, paint thinner, medicine, dyes, explosives, detergents, fingernail polish, spot removers, lacquers, adhesives, rubber, and antifreeze. It is also used in some printing and leather tanning processes. The largest industrial use of toluene is in the production of benzene, a chemical used to make plastics and synthetic fibers. Toluene is also used to boost the octane of gasoline. You can be exposed to toluene by breathing automobile exhaust, pumping gasoline, consuming contaminated food or water, or using other products that contain toluene, such as kerosene, heating oil, paints, and lacquers. You can be exposed to toluene at work by breathing contaminated air, or having skin contact with it. You can be exposed to toluene in your community if toluene is released in a fire or spill, or has been contaminating water or air for a long time.

Inhaling high levels of toluene can cause death or unconsciousness. Repeatedly breathing toluene over long periods of time at work, or through deliberately "sniffing" or "huffing" glue or paint, can cause death, permanent brain damage, or depression. If you are pregnant, repeated exposure to toluene may increase the risk of damage to the fetus. Exposure to high levels of toluene may affect your kidneys, nervous system, liver, brain, and heart. Direct, prolonged contact with liquid toluene or vapor can irritate the eyes, and cause dry skin and skin rashes. Ingesting toluene can cause vomiting, diarrhea, and difficult breathing. Exposure to low to moderate levels of toluene can cause confusion, light-headedness, dizziness, headache, fatigue, weakness, memory loss, nausea, appetite loss, coughing, wheezing, and hearing and color vision loss.

12.6 Benzene

Benzene, also known as benzol, is a colorless liquid with a sweet odor, and can be described as a volatile organic compound. The chemical symbol for benzene is C_6H_6. Benzene is formed from both natural processes and human activities. It is produced from volcanoes and forest fires, and is a natural part of crude oil, gasoline, and cigarette smoke. Benzene is one of the 20 most widely used chemicals in the United States. It is used to make other chemicals that are then used to make plastics, resins, nylon, and other synthetic fibers. It is used to make explosives, photographic chemicals, rubber, lubricants, dyes, adhesives, coatings, paint, detergents, drugs, and pesticides. It is used in printing, lithography, and food processing. It has been used as a gasoline additive in the past, but that use has been greatly reduced in the United States since the 1990s.

Benzene is found in the air, water, and soil. You can be exposed to small amounts of benzene outdoors, where the air can contain low levels from tobacco smoke, automotive service stations, vehicle exhaust, and industrial emissions. You can be exposed to higher levels of benzene near gas stations, hazardous waste sites, or industrial facilities. You can be exposed to benzene indoors at home, where the air can contain higher levels of benzene than outdoor air, from products such as glue, paint, furniture wax, and detergent. Approximately half the national exposure to benzene comes from smoking cigarettes or being exposed to cigarette smoke, indoors or outdoors. You can be exposed to benzene by drinking or using well water that has been contaminated by leaking underground gasoline storage tanks or hazardous waste sites, though those levels are usually less than those from industrial facilities and smoking cigarettes.

You can be exposed to higher than normal levels of benzene at work if you work at a facility that makes or uses benzene, including petroleum refining sites, pharmaceutical plants, petrochemical manufacturing facilities, rubber tire manufacturing facilities, or gas stations. You may be exposed if you are a steel worker, printer, shoemaker, laboratory technician, or firefighter.

Benzene is classified as a carcinogen by the National Toxicology Program because it has been known to cause cancer. Long-term exposure to high levels of benzene can cause leukemia.

Breathing very high levels of benzene, or eating or drinking foods contaminated with high levels of benzene, can cause death. Eating or drinking foods contaminated with high levels of benzene can also cause vomiting and stomach irritation. Small amounts of benzene, which are not harmful, can be found in fruit, fish, vegetables, nuts, dairy products, beverages, and eggs. Short-term exposure to high levels of benzene by breathing or eating affects the central nervous system, and can cause paralysis, coma, convulsions, dizziness, sleepiness, rapid heart rate, tightness of the chest, tremors, and rapid breathing.

If you work at a facility that uses benzene, breathing high levels of benzene can cause irreversible brain damage, unconsciousness, cardiac arrest, blurred vision, headaches, tremors, confusion, and fatigue. In women, it can shrink ovaries and cause menstrual irregularity. Spilling benzene on your skin can cause redness, sores, scaling, and drying of the skin. If benzene contacts the eyes, it can cause irritation and damage to the cornea. Long-term exposure to benzene can decrease red blood cells, leading to anemia. It can also cause excessive bleeding and affect the immune system, increasing the chance of infection.

The U.S. Environmental Protection Agency (EPA) estimates that VOCs are present in one-fifth of the nation's water supplies. They can enter ground water from a variety of sources. Benzene, for example, may enter ground water from gasoline or oil spills on the ground surface or from leaking underground fuel tanks. Other examples of commonly detected VOCs are dichloromethane (*methylene chloride*), an industrial solvent; trichloroethylene, used in septic system cleaners; and tetrachloroethylene (*perchloroethylene*), used in the dry-cleaning industry.

Volatile organic compounds may have a variety of harmful health effects. At high levels of exposure, many VOCs can cause central nervous system depression (drowsiness, stupor). All can be irritating upon contact with the skin, or to the mucous membranes if inhaled. For each chemical, EPA has established a maximum contaminant level (MCL). Water containing a chemical in an amount lower than the MCL is considered safe to drink. Drinking water containing one or more VOCs at levels above standards should not be consumed. In addition, because little is known about the additive effects of these chemicals, special attention should be paid to detecting and eliminating VOC sources if two or more chemicals are found in water. In any case, sources of VOC contamination should be eliminated if possible.

The most effective method for preventing VOC contamination is to ensure that these compounds are not used or disposed of near wells or surface water supplies. Protecting your water source is the most effective method to eliminate exposure to these chemicals. Be sure that your well is constructed properly and is protected to prevent surface water from moving down the well casing into your drinking water supply.

Public water systems are required to be monitored on a routine basis for contamination. For private water supplies, however, it is the homeowner's responsibility to regularly have water quality evaluated. If VOCs or other contaminants are found at levels approaching or above drinking water standards, the source of contamination should be eliminated. Prior to transfer of property, the prospective owner may wish to request in writing that well water be analyzed to determine water quality. This testing is especially important in cases where the property is a current or former agricultural or industrial site, or where buried fuel tanks are located nearby.

Options for homeowners with contaminated water include preventing further contamination, locating an alternative water supply, or treating water to remove contaminants. Identifying and removing the contamination source is the safest and most permanent solution. However, it is not always possible to identify and eliminate the source.

In some cases, ground water is contaminated to the extent that cleanup may take many years and be extremely expensive. Alternative water supplies include new wells, public water systems, and bottled water. If a new well is constructed, be sure that it is not susceptible to contamination from the same source as the polluted well.

Bottled water can be used as a short-term source of drinking water. Keep in mind, however, that VOCs may also enter the body through skin absorption or through inhalation of water vapor.

Home filter systems may provide a high-quality water supply if properly installed and maintained. Filters may be purchased for point-of-use (POU) treatment at the faucet or point-of-entry (POE) treatment where water enters the home. POE treatment systems are recommended for VOC removal to ensure that all water used for drinking, cooking, cleaning, and bathing is free of contamination. There are a variety of filter systems available. Before purchasing a filter system, it is wise to consult with several reputable water treatment companies to ensure that the equipment purchased will treat the specific water quality problem.

Granular activated carbon (GAC) filters are typically used to reduce VOC levels in home drinking water. The effectiveness of carbon filters is related to (1) the type and amount of contaminant, (2) the rate of water usage, and (3) the type of carbon being used. Large contaminant concentrations and high water use rates reduce the carbon life. The manufacturer's guidelines for replacing carbon filters should be followed. Water entering and leaving the filter should be tested periodically to ensure that the treatment system is working properly.

Bacteria may grow on the surface of a carbon filter. Water should be disinfected after it passes through the filter to ensure its safety. Many types of disinfection systems are available. Ultraviolet (UV) radiation is one type of system shown to work effectively and efficiently to eliminate bacteria problems in water.

Methyl tert-butyl ether (MTBE) was detected in source water used by 8.7 % of randomly selected community water systems (CWSs) in the United States at concentrations that ranged from 0.2 to 20 micrograms per liter (μg/L). The Random Survey conducted by the U.S. Geological Survey, in cooperation with the Metropolitan Water District of Southern California and the Oregon Health & Science University, was designed to provide an assessment of the frequency of detection, concentration, and distribution of MTBE, three other ether gasoline oxygenates, and 62 other volatile organic compounds (VOCs) in ground- and surface-water sources used for drinking-water supplies. The Random Survey was the first of two components of a national assessment of the quality of source water supplying CWSs sponsored by the American Water Works Association Research Foundation. A total of 954 CWSs were selected for VOC sampling from the population of nearly 47,000 active, self-supplied CWSs in all 50 States, Native American Lands, and Puerto Rico based on a statistical design that stratified on CWS size (population served), type of source water (ground and surface water), and geographic distribution (State).

At a reporting level of 0.2 μg/L, VOCs were detected in 27 % of source-water samples collected from May 3, 1999 through October 23, 2000. Chloroform (in 13 % of samples) was the most frequently detected of 42 VOCs present in the source-water samples, followed by MTBE. VOC concentrations were generally less than 10 μg/L—95 % of the 530 detections—and 63 % were less than 1.0 μg/L. Concentrations of 1,1-dichloroethene, tetrachloroethene, trichloroethene, vinyl chloride, and total trihalomethanes (TTHMs), however, exceeded drinking-water regulations in eight samples.

Detections of most VOCs were more frequent in surface-water sources than in ground-water sources, with gasoline compounds collectively and MTBE individually detected significantly more often in surface water. Use of personal and commercial motorized watercraft on surface-water bodies that are drinking-water sources is probably the reason for the elevated detections of gasoline contaminants relative to ground water. MTBE detections demonstrated a seasonal pattern with more frequent detections in surface water in summer months, which is consistent with seasonal watercraft use.

The detection frequency of most VOCs was significantly related to urban land use and population density. Detections of any VOC, non-trihalomethane compounds, gasoline compounds collectively, the specific gasoline compounds benzene, toluene, ethylbenzene, and xylenes (BTEX), MTBE, solvents, and refrigerants were significantly greater in areas with more than 60 % urban land use and (or) population density greater than 1,000 people per square mile than in source waters from less urbanized or lower population-density areas. MTBE detections were five times more frequent in source waters from areas with high MTBE use than in source waters from low or no MTBE use, but, unlike other gasoline compounds, MTBE detections were not significantly related to the density of gasoline storage tanks near drinking-water sources.

As of July, 2003 neither Minnesota nor the Federal Government have set standards for VOC levels in non-occupational settings. However, some guidelines are available. MDH has established Health Risk Values (HRVs) for some contaminants in air for several different exposure situations. Many studies have shown VOC levels are higher in indoor air than outdoor air. The U.S. Environmental Protection Agency (EPA) Total Exposure Assessment Methodology (TEAM) studies have found indoor VOC levels that were 2 to 5 times higher than outdoors.

Levels of VOC Exposure in indoor air vary widely depending on:

— the volume of air in the room/building
— the rate at which the VOC is off-gassed
— the building ventilation rate
— outdoor concentrations
— time spent in the effected *environment*

12.7 Acute Impacts

— Eye irritation / watering
— Nose irritation
— Throat irritation

— Headaches
— Nausea / Vomitting
— Dizziness
— Asthma exacerbation

12.8 Chronic Impacts

— Cancer
— Liver damage
— Kidney damage
— Central nervous system damage

Most studies till date have been conducted on single chemicals. Less is know about the health effects of combined chemical exposure. The best health protection measure is to limit your exposure to products and materials that contain VOCs when possible. If you think you may be having health problems caused by VOC exposure consult an occupational/ environmental health physician who specializes in this area. Persons with respiratory problems such as asthma, young children, elderly, and persons with heightened sensitivity to chemicals may be more susceptible to illness from VOC exposure.

Some home screening kits are available to measure total volatile organic compound (TVOC) levels, and some individual VOCs. These home sampling kits should be viewed as providing "ballpark" amount of VOCs in the indoor air. Conditions such as ventilation, temperature and humidity can cause VOC concentrations to fluctuate daily.

Prior to testing conduct an inspection of your home for some common sources of VOCs such as:

— New carpeting
— New furniture
— Idling automobile in attached garage
— Recent painting
— Chemicals stored in the home
— Recently applied adhesives
— New plastic or electronic devices

Once you determine the probable source of VOCs, steps can be taken to reduce your exposure. If you are unable to determine the source, a professional indoor air quality investigator / industrial hygienist can be consulted. MDH has a residential service provider list along with recommendations on selection. MDH also has a guidance document that can be used for investigating possible VOC contamination entitled Indoor Air Sampling at VOC contaminated sites.

Most products containing VOCs will off gas within a short period of time although some will continue to give off trace amounts of VOCs for a long period of time. The best means of reducing VOC exposure is to eliminate products containing VOCs or use low emitting VOC products. Some steps you can take to reduce your exposure to VOC in the home are:

— Source control
  - eliminate products from home that have high levels of VOCs.
  - purchase new products that contain low or no VOCs (Environmentally Preferable Purchasing).

— Ventilation - open doors and windows, use fans.

— Control climate - as temperature and humidity increase some chemicals will off gas more.

— Treat the source - airtight sealers can be used to coat over some products. However, caution is advised in choosing the coating product as this could introduce new VOCs into the air while controlling for others.

— Air cleaners - look for ones with activated charcoal filtration designed to remove chemicals from the air.

— Purchasing environmentally responsible cleaning chemicals.

— Remove unused chemicals from the home. Check with city or county for household hazardous waste collection sites.

— — —

13

World Bank Standards

13.1 Introduction

The World Bank Standards for water quality parameters show important because the acute and chronic impact on aquatic ecosystem causes very dangerous to the animals and human beings. It describes about the level of toxic concentration would be allowed to the aquatic ecosystem to survive living beings. The Indian standards also describes about the limit of toxic constituent, which are harmful to the aquatic living beings.

13.2 Federal Water Pollution Control Act (Clean Water Act)

33 U.S.C. 1251-1387, October 18, 1972, as amended 1973-1983, 1987, 1988, 1990-1992, 1994, 1995 and 1996.

The Federal Water Pollution Control Act, popularly known as the Clean Water Act, is a comprehensive statute aimed at restoring and maintaining the chemical, physical and biological integrity of the nation's waters. Enacted originally in 1948, the Act was amended numerous times until it was reorganized and expanded in 1972. It continues to be amended almost every year.

Even prior to the enactment of the 1972 version of the Act, the Act authorized the Public Health Service to prepare comprehensive programs for eliminating or reducing the pollution of interstate waters and tributaries and improving the sanitary condition of surface and underground waters. Due regard was to be given to improvements necessary to conserve waters for public water supplies, propagation of fish and aquatic life, recreational purposes, and agricultural and industrial uses. A number of other provisions found in the current Act were adopted prior to 1972.

Primary authority for the implementation and enforcement of the Clean Water Act now rests with the U.S. Environmental Protection Agency (EPA). In addition to the measures authorized before 1972, the Act authorizes water quality programs, requires federal effluent limitations and state water quality standards, requires permits for the discharge of pollutants into navigable waters, provides enforcement mechanisms, and authorizes funding for wastewater treatment works construction grants and state revolving loan programs, as well as funding to states and tribes for their water quality programs. Provisions have also been added to address water quality problems in specific regions and specific waterways.

Important for wildlife protection purposes are the provisions requiring permits to dispose of dredged and fill materials into navigable waters. Permits are issued by the Army Corps of Engineers under guidelines developed by EPA. What is known as Section 404 permitting applies to many wetlands, which has proven controversial.

13.2.1 Findings/Policy

The objective of the Clean Water Act is to restore and maintain the chemical, physical and biological integrity of the nation's waters. Among the national goals stated in the Act are the elimination of the discharge of pollutants into navigable waters by 1985 and, where attainable, the achievement by mid-1983 of an interim goal of water quality sufficient to provide for the protection and propagation of fish, shellfish, and wildlife and for recreation in and on the water.

It is the policy of Congress to recognize the primary responsibilities and rights of states to prevent, reduce and eliminate pollution. Congress also intends that the states manage the wastewater treatment works construction grants program and implement the discharge permit programs under the Act.

The federal government will support research and provide technical services and financial aid to state and interstate agencies and municipalities. Congress emphasized that the authority of each state to allocate quantities of water within its jurisdiction are not superseded, abrogated or otherwise impaired by the Act.

It is also the policy of Congress that the President will take such action as may be necessary to insure that, to the fullest extent possible, foreign countries take meaningful action to prevent, reduce and eliminate pollution in their waters and in international waters 1251.

Except as otherwise provided, the Administrator of the EPA administers the Act. EPA, in cooperation with other federal agencies, states, interstate agencies, municipalities and industries, is to develop comprehensive programs for preventing, reducing or eliminating pollution and improving the sanitary condition of surface and underground waters. Due regard must be given to the improvements necessary to conserve these waters for the protection and propagation of fish and aquatic life and wildlife, recreational purposes, and the withdrawal of water for public water supply, agricultural, industrial and other purposes 1251 and 1252.

Biological monitoring: the determination of the effects of the discharge of pollutants on aquatic life using certain techniques and procedures at appropriate frequencies and locations. Discharge of a pollutant: the addition of any pollutant to navigable waters from a point source and the addition of a pollutant to the waters of the contiguous zone or the ocean from a point source other than a vessel or other floating craft. The word discharge, when used without qualification, refers to the discharge of a pollutant or pollutants. Effluent limitation: any restriction imposed by a state or EPA on quantities, rates and concentrations of chemical, physical, biological, and other constituents which are discharged from point sources into navigable waters, the waters of the contiguous zone, or the ocean, including schedules of compliance. Municipality: Includes a city, town, county, district, or other public body created by or under state law and having jurisdiction over disposal of sewage or other wastes. Also includes an Indian tribe or authorized Indian tribal organization. Navigable waters: the waters of the U.S., including the territorial seas. Point source: any discernible, confined and discrete conveyance, but does not include agricultural storm water discharges and return flows from irrigated agriculture. Pollutant: dredged soil, solid waste, incinerator residue, sewage, garbage, sewage sludge, munitions, chemical wastes, biological materials, radioactive materials, heat, wrecked or discarded equipment, rock, sand, cellar dirt and industrial, municipal and agricultural waste discharged into water, but the term does not include sewage from vessels or a discharge incidental to the normal operation of a vessel of the Armed Forces with the meaning of 1322, or, in some cases, water or oil injected into wells for oil or gas production purposes. Pollution: the man-made or man-induced alteration of the chemical, physical, biological and radiological integrity of water. Toxic pollutant: those pollutants which, after discharge and upon exposure, ingestion, inhalation or assimilation into an organism will, on the basis of information available to EPA, cause death, disease, behavioral abnormalities, cancer, genetic mutations, physiological malfunctions or deformations in the organism or its offspring. Treatment works: any devices and systems used in the storage, treatment, recycling and reclamation of municipal sewage or industrial wastes of a liquid nature or necessary to recycle or reuse water at the most economical cost over the estimated life of the works. It also means any other method or system for preventing, abating, reducing, storing, treating, separating or disposing of municipal waste, which includes stormwater runoff, or industrial waste, which includes waste in combined stormwater and sanitary systems 1292 and 1362.

13.2.2 Research and Related Programs

The Act authorizes a number of research programs and studies on the prevention, reduction and elimination of pollution, as well as the issuance of grants for these purposes. For example, EPA must conduct research on the harmful effects of pollutants in water on health and welfare in conjunction with the U.S. Fish and Wildlife Service (USFWS) and other federal agencies. This research is to emphasize the effect that the bioaccumulation of pollutants in aquatic species has on the value of aquatic commercial and sport fisheries, and must explore methods to reduce and remove these pollutants from the affected species so as to restore and enhance valuable resources. The Act also authorizes research on the effect of pollution on estuaries and estuarine zones, as well as on the nature of river systems 1254 and 1254a.

The Act authorizes grants to states and interstate agencies for the prevention, reduction and elimination of pollution, including enforcement activities. Beginning in 1974, EPA was not permitted to make grants under this section to any state which, among other things, had not provided for the establishment and operation of devices, methods, systems and procedures to monitor and to compile and analyze data on the quality of navigable waters and, to the extent practicable, ground waters, including biological monitoring 1256.

Various provisions of the Act address specific regions or waterways. Examples include: Alaska village demonstration projects; a Hudson River reclamation demonstration project; continuation of the Chesapeake Bay program; continuation of the Management Conference of the Long Island Sound Study; establishment of a Lake Champlain Management Conference to develop a comprehensive pollution prevention, control and restoration plan for Lake Champlain. The Great Lakes are discussed in the next paragraph 1263, 1266, 1267, 1269 and 1270.

13.2.3 Great Lakes Programs

The Great Lakes are addressed with a number of programs. The Act authorizes EPA to enter into agreements with states and other public bodies to carry out projects to demonstrate new methods and techniques and develop preliminary plans for the elimination or control of pollution within all or any part of the watersheds of the Great Lakes. A demonstration wastewater management program for the rehabilitation and environmental repair of Lake Erie was specifically authorized. The Act also established a Great Lakes National Program Office within EPA and a Great Lakes Research Office within the National Oceanic and Atmospheric Administration (NOAA). Related federal agencies, including the USFWS, are required to report to EPA annually regarding agency activities affecting compliance with the 1978 Great Lakes Water Quality Agreement. As part of the Great Lakes program, EPA, in conjunction with USFWS and NOAA, is to conduct research on the harmful effects of pollutants on the general health and welfare 1258 and 1268.

13.2.4 *Aquatic Sediment*

In 1992, Congress adopted a requirement that EPA, in consultation with NOAA, conduct a comprehensive survey of data on aquatic sediment quality in the U.S. and report to Congress in two years on the results of the survey, with recommendations for actions necessary to prevent contamination of aquatic sediments and to control sources of contamination. EPA was also instructed to conduct a monitoring program to assess aquatic sediment quality, which would, among other things, identify locations where pollutants in sediment may pose a threat to the quality of drinking water supplies, fisheries resources and marine habitats. The report on the findings of the monitoring program is due two years after the survey results are due and biennially thereafter. Related provisions on aquatic sediment can be found in the ocean dumping provisions of the Marine Protection, Research, and Sanctuaries Act of 1972.

13.2.5 *Waste Treatment Management Plans and Grants*

The Act is intended to require and assist in the development and implementation of waste treatment management plans and practices to achieve the goals of the Act. Plans and practices must provide for treatment of waste using the best practicable technology before there is any discharge of pollutants into receiving waters, as well as the confined disposal of pollution so that it will not migrate to cause water or other environmental pollution. To the extent practicable, waste treatment management is to be on an areawide basis and is to provide for the control or treatment of all point and non-point sources of pollution. Among other things, the Administrator shall encourage waste treatment management which combines open space and recreational considerations with such management 1281.

To encourage and facilitate the states development of areawide waste treatment management plans, Congress directed EPA to publish guidelines for the identification of areas with substantial water quality control problems. These areas require an areawide waste treatment management plan and a continuing planning process. No national pollution discharge elimination system (NPDES) permit may be issued which is in conflict with an approved plan.

The provisions of the Act on the planning process are wide-ranging. Among other things, USFWS is to provide technical assistance to states requesting help in developing and implementing their plans. Congress also authorized the appropriation of $6 million to the Secretary of Interior to complete the National Wetlands Inventory by 1982, and to provide information to states as it becomes available to assist the states with their programs. Other provisions direct the Secretary of Agriculture, acting through the Soil Conservation Service and other agencies, to establish a program for entering into contracts with owners and operators of rural land, in states or areas for which a plan has been approved, for the purpose of encouraging the use of best management practices to control nonpoint source pollution 1288.

13.2.6 Construction Grants and Loans

The Act outlines a program of grants to state, municipalities or intermunicipal or interstate agencies for the construction of publicly owned treatment works (POTWs). There are extensive provisions on the requirements, prerequisites and conditions for the grants, which can also be awarded to privately owned treatment works under certain limited conditions. Funds are allotted among the states by formula, with reservations of funds for small communities, innovative and alternative projects, water quality management planning, nonpoint source pollution programs and marine estuaries 1281-1287 and 1289-1299.

In 1987, Congress began to change its focus from the use of direct grants for the construction of wastewater treatment facilities to the concept of capitalization grants. The Act as amended provides for EPA to make grants to states for the purpose of establishing water pollution control revolving loan funds, which would provide assistance for the construction of POTWs, for implementing nonpoint source management programs under 1329, and for developing and implementing conservation and management plans for estuaries under 1330. The Act reduces the level of funding authorized for capitalization grants each year, with $1.2 billion authorized for 1989 and only $.6 billion authorized for 1994 1381-1387.

13.2.7 Effluent Limitations and Water Quality Standards

The Act prohibits the discharge of pollutants except in compliance with the effluent limitations and other provisions of the Act. Effluent limitations from point sources other than POTWs must be treated using best practicable control technology. Toxic pollutants, defined and otherwise described in the Act, require treatment using the best available technology which is economically achievable. If the source discharges into a POTW, it must comply with applicable pretreatment requirements. Notwithstanding any other provisions, the Act makes it unlawful to discharge any radiological, chemical, or biological warfare agent, any high-level radioactive waste, or any medical waste into navigable waters.

Effluent limitations must be determined for point sources which are consistent with state water quality standards, including toxic and pretreatment standards. Procedures for state assurance of water quality standards must be established, guidelines to identify and evaluate the extent of nonpoint source pollution must be developed, and water quality inventory requirements must be set. The Act also requires EPA to develop national standards of performance for the control of discharge of pollutants from new sources.

When discharges of pollutants from a point source or group of point sources under established effluent limitations would interfere with the attainment or maintenance of water quality necessary to assure protection of public health, public water supplies, agricultural and industrial uses, and the protection and propagation of a balanced population of shellfish, fish and wildlife, and allow recreational activities in and on the water, EPA must establish effluent limitations for the point source or sources which can reasonably be expected to contribute to the attainment or maintenance of water quality 1311, 1312, 1314, 1316 and 1317.

The Act provides for states to adopt water quality standards and for EPA to adopt standards for the states which do not. States also are required to develop strategies for cleanup of toxic pollutants in waters where the application of best available technology discharge standards is not sufficient to meet state water quality standards. The state must establish a total maximum daily load for those pollutants suitable for maximum daily load measurements. Further, states must identify waters for which controls on thermal discharges under 1311 are not stringent enough to assure protection and propagation of a balanced indigenous population of shellfish, fish and wildlife. The state is to estimate the total maximum daily thermal load required to assure appropriate protection and propagation. The states must report on their water quality biennially 1313 and 1315.

EPA is expected to provide information and guidelines to assist states in adopting water quality standards, including information on: the identifiable effects on health and welfare, including plankton, fish, shellfish, wildlife, plant life, shorelines, beaches, esthetics and recreation, which may be expected from the presence of pollutants in a body of water, including ground water; the concentration and dispersal of pollutants, or their byproducts, through biological, physical and chemical processes; the effects of pollutants on biological community diversity, productivity and stability. In addition, the Administrator must publish information, for example, on factors necessary to restore and maintain the chemical, physical and biological integrity of all navigable waters, ground waters, waters of the contiguous zone and the oceans, on the factors necessary to the protection and propagation of shellfish, fish and wildlife, and factors to allow recreation activities in and on the water 1314.

The Act imposes requirements regarding recordkeeping and reporting, and allows for inspections. It also contains extensive provisions on enforcement, with administrative, civil and criminal penalties available for violations 1318 and 1319.

Applicants for federal permits or licenses for activities involving discharges into navigable waters are to provide certification from the state that the proposed activity will not violate applicable effluent limitations and water quality standards. Licenses and permits may not be granted if the state or interstate certification has been denied 1341.

13.2.8 Discharge Permits

One of the most significant features of the 1972 Act is the creation of a national pollutant discharge elimination system (NPDES). Except as otherwise provided in the Act, industrial sources and publicly owned treatment works may not discharge pollutants into navigable waters without a permit. The Administrator may issue a permit for discharge upon condition that the discharge meets applicable requirements, which are outlined extensively in the Act and which reflect, among other things, the need to meet federal effluent limitations and state water quality standards. The Act also provides that, with EPA approval, a state may administer its own permit program in lieu of the federal program. There are special provisions on municipal and industrial stormwater discharges 1342.

EPA was required, by mid-1973, to promulgate guidelines for determining the degradation of the waters of the territorial seas, the contiguous zone and the oceans. These guidelines were to include, for example: the effect of disposal of pollutants on human health or welfare, including but not limited to plankton, fish, shellfish, wildlife, shorelines and beaches; the effect on marine life, changes in marine ecosystem diversity, productivity and stability, or species and community population changes; the effect of disposal of pollutants on aesthetic, recreation and economic values. Discharge permits may not be issued except in compliance with the guidelines 1343.

13.2.9 Section 404 Permits

Section 1344 of the Act as codified originated as Section 404 of the Act as adopted by Congress. The requirement that persons wanting to dispose of dredged or fill material in navigable waters obtain a permit from the Army Corps of Engineers is important to the current debate over the protection of wetlands.

The Act directs the EPA Administrator to adopt guidelines for disposal sites. Applying these guidelines, the Corps may issue permits on an individual basis or may issue general permits on a state, regional or national basis. A general permit may be issued for any category of activities that are similar in nature, will cause only minimal environmental effects when performed separately, and will have only minimal cumulative adverse impact on the environment. The Secretary of the Army is required to notify USFWS when an application for an individual permit is received and when the Secretary proposes to issue a general permit. USFWS must submit any comments on the application or the proposed general permit within 90 days.

EPA is authorized to prohibit the use of a site for disposal if discharges would have an unacceptable adverse effect on municipal water supplies, shellfish beds, fishery areas, and wildlife or recreational uses. On the other hand, permits are not required for certain types of activity, such as the discharge of dredged or fill material resulting from ordinary farming, silviculture and ranching activities.

The Act establishes procedures for state assumption of the program. It includes a requirement that the Director of USFWS, as well as the Corps of Engineers, provide advice to the Administrator regarding transfer of the program to a state.

13.2.10 Sewage Sludge

The Act regulates the disposal and use of sewage sludge. The disposal of sewage sludge resulting from the operation of a treatment works is prohibited whenever it would result in a pollutant entering navigable waters, except in accordance with a permit issued by EPA or an approved state program. The Administrator is directed to issue regulations governing the issuance of permits and requiring for these permits the use of the standards and procedures applicable to NPDES permits. By regulation, EPA is required to identify uses for sludge, including disposal, specify the factors to consider in determining measures and practices applicable to each use or disposal, and identify concentrations of pollutants which interfere with each use or disposal 1345.

13.2.11 Oil and Hazardous Substance Liability

U.S. policy, as stated in the Act, is that there should be no discharges of oil or hazardous substances into or upon the navigable waters of the U.S., on adjoining shorelines or into or upon the waters of the contiguous zone, or which may affect natural resources belonging to, appertaining to, or under the exclusive management or authority of the U.S. The President, by regulation, shall determine the quantities of oil and hazardous substances the discharge of which may be harmful to the public health or welfare or the environment, including but not limited to fish, shellfish, wildlife, public and private property, shorelines and beaches.

The Act imposes liability for the costs of the removal of oil and hazardous substances that have been discharged, as well as for natural resource damages. It also imposes administrative and civil penalties for unlawful discharges and for failure to carry out orders issued under the Act. The word removal refers to the containment and removal of oil or hazardous substances from the water and shorelines or the taking of other actions necessary to minimize or mitigate damage to the public health or welfare, including, but not limited to, fish, shellfish, wildlife, and public and private property, shorelines, and beaches.

The Act also establishes a national response system and requires the preparation of a National Contingency Plan by the President to provide for efficient and coordinated action to minimize damage from oil discharges, including containment, dispersal and removal. The Oil Spill Liability Trust Fund established under 26 U.S.C. 9509 is made available for purposes of the Act. Further provisions on oil discharges can be found in the Oil Pollution Act, 1321.

13.2.12 Marine Sanitation Devices

The Act requires that EPA develop performance standards for marine sanitation devices, that is, equipment installed on board vessels to receive, retain, treat or discharge sewage, and any process to treat sewage. In consultation with the Secretary of the department in which the Coast Guard is operating and after giving consideration to the economic costs involved and the limits of available technology, the Administrator of EPA is to adopt standards designed to prevent the discharge of untreated or inadequately treated sewage into navigable waters; the Secretary of the department in which the Coast Guard is operating must promulgate regulations consistent with EPA's standards. Manufacturers may not sell marine sanitation devices unless they are certified by the Secretary as meeting the standards and regulations.

In the Clean Vessel Act of 1992, codified as a note to this section, Congress observes that there is an inadequate number of pumpout stations for the type of marine sanitation devices used by recreational vessels and that sewage discharged by recreational vessels because of an inadequate number of pumpout stations is a substantial contributor to localized water degradation. The 1992 Act is intended to provide funds to states for the construction, renovation, operation, and maintenance of pumpout stations and waste reception facilities. The program is described in the editor's note to the summary of the Federal Aid in Sport Fish Restoration Act, and its funding referred to in 777c and 777 g of that Act.

1996 amendments to the Clean Water Act require that the Administrator of EPA and the Secretary of Defense jointly determine the extent to which marine pollution control devices should be used by military vessels to mitigate adverse impacts on the environment of discharges (other than sewage) which are incidental to normal operations. The Secretary of Defense must require the use of a device on board vessels whenever it is determined that the use of a device is reasonable and practical. The Act also provides for some state involvement in the control of discharges from vessels of the Armed Forces 1322 and 1322 note.

13.2.13 Federal Facilities

Federal facilities are subject to all federal, state, interstate and local requirements, administrative authority and sanctions respecting the control and abatement of water pollution to the same extent as any nongovernmental entity 1323.

13.2.14 Clean Lakes Program

The Act establishes a clean lakes program. States must, on a biennial basis, prepare and submit to EPA for approval an identification and classification, according to eutrophic condition, all publicly owned lakes in the state and a description of the procedures, processes and methods being used to control sources of pollution and restore quality. The states' reports on the water quality of lakes must include methods to mitigate the harmful effects of high acidity. A demonstration program will be funded, with funds to be distributed to the states based on relative acidity problems. 1324.

13.2.15 Thermal Discharges

While 1313 allows for more stringent requirements for thermal discharge when necessary, the Act also permits owners and operators of point sources to propose less stringent limits when appropriate. They need to demonstrate that the effluent limitations established by EPA or the state are more stringent than necessary to assure the protection and propagation of a balanced, indigenous population of shellfish, fish and wildlife. Water quality standards must require that the location, design, construction and capacity of cooling water intake structures reflect the best technology available for minimizing adverse environmental impact 1326.

13.2.16 Non-point Source Pollution

As amended in 1987, the Act is paying increased attention to nonpoint source pollution. It provides for states to prepare reports and propose management plans for the control of non-point source pollution for approval by EPA, and encourages the development of plans on a watershed-by-watershed basis. States with approved management programs are eligible, on a cost-sharing basis, for federal grants to assist in the implementation of the program. Grants are also available to states with approved plans to assist the states in carrying out ground water quality protection activities which will advance the state toward the implementation of a comprehensive nonpoint source pollution control program. Appropriations were authorized for the first several years of the grant program, from $70 million for fiscal year 1988 to $130 million for fiscal year 1991, 1329.

13.2.17 Estuaries

The Act authorizes a state/federal cooperative program to nominate estuaries of national significance and to develop and implement management plans to restore and maintain the biological and chemical integrity of estuarine waters. NOAA is directed to conduct water quality research and a trends assessment in estuaries of national significance 1330.

13.2.18 Administration of the Act

Several sections of the Act are devoted to its administration, to the creation of a Water Pollution Control Advisory Board, to employee protection, to federal procurement, to administrative review and procedure, and to reports to Congress. Citizen suits are permitted under the guidelines and procedures set forth in 1365. The Act provides further that states, their political subdivisions and interstate agencies are not preempted from adopting or enforcing standards, limitations or requirements as long as they are no less stringent than their federal counterparts. Under 1377, EPA is authorized to treat Indian tribes as states for purposes of water quality standards and numerous other provisions of the Act. 1361-1377.

13.2.19 Appropriations Authorized

Numerous sections of the Act provide for the authorization of funds to be appropriated for programs and requirements established by the Act, 1254-1258, 1262-1270, 1287-1289, 1324, 1325, 1329, 1330, 1345, 1376 and 1387.

13.3 Indian Standards

In a coastal segment marine water is subjected to several types of designated uses. Depending of the types of uses and activities, water quality criteria have been specified to determine its suitability for a particular purpose. Among the various types of uses there is one use that demands highest level of water quality/purity and that is termed a "designed best use" in that stretch of the coastal segment. Based on this, primary water quality criteria have been specified for following designated best uses(Table 13.1) (CPCB, 1995).

Table 13.1: Water Quality Criteria(BIS)

Designated-Best-Use	Class of water	Criteria
Drinking Water Source without conventional treatment but after disinfection	A	1. Total Coliforms Organism MPN/100ml shall be 50 or less 2. pH between 6.5 and 8.5 3. Dissolved Oxygen 6mg/l or more 4. Biochemical Oxygen Demand 5 days 20°C 2mg/l or less
Outdoor bathing (Organised)	B	1. Total Coliforms Organism MPN/100ml shall be 500 or less 2. pH between 6.5 and 8.5 3. Dissolved Oxygen 5mg/l or more 4. Biochemical Oxygen Demand 5 days 20°C 3mg/l or less

Designated-Best-Use	Class of water	Criteria
Drinking water source after conventional treatment and disinfection	C	1. Total Coliforms Organism MPN/100ml shall be 5000 or less 2. pH between 6 to 9 3. Dissolved Oxygen 4mg/l or more 4. Biochemical Oxygen Demand 5 days 20°C 3mg/l or less
Propagation of Wild life and Fisheries	D	1. pH between 6.5 to 8.5 2. Dissolved Oxygen 4mg/l or more 3. Free Ammonia (as N) 1.2 mg/l or less
Irrigation, Industrial Cooling, Controlled Waste disposal	E	1. pH betwwn 6.0 to 8.5 2. Electrical Conductivity at 25°C micro mhos/cm Max.2250 3. Sodium absorption Ratio Max. 26 4. Boron Max. 2mg/l
	Below-E	Not Meeting A, B, C, D & E Criteria

— — —

14

Phytosociology

14.1 Introduction

The observation of phytosociology deals with the germination of growth on tree species in the industrial effluents. It shall be calculated germination potential based on germination capablility of the seeds. The growth parameters are measured then calculated leaf weight ratio, stem weight ratio, root weight ratio, top dry weight, sturdiness quatient, volume index and quality index. The following sub chapters dealing with formulae used to calculate the above parameters. The data so collected is then analyzed. The usual methods, which are employed in analysing the data, are averages, dispersion, skew ness, correlation, *etc*. The leaf weight ratio, stem weight ratio and root weight ratio are calculated by using the following formulae made by Kumaran (1991).

14.2 Calculation of Germination Potential

To assess the germination potential of the seeds, germination percentage, germination value, germination energy period and maximum germination speed are calculated using the following formulae (Czabator, 1962).

$$\text{Germination Percentage} = \frac{\text{Total Number of seeds germinated}}{\text{Total number of seeds sown}} \times 100$$

Germination Value = Final mean daily germination x Peak value

Germination Energy Period = up to the day of peak Germination

$$\text{Germination Speed} = \frac{\text{Cumulative germination Percentage Period}}{\text{Days since sowing}}$$

14.3 Leaf Weight Ratio

The leaf weight ratio is the ratio between the weights of the leaves with other parts of a plant *i.e.* Stems and roots. It is a statistical parameter for estimating the mass of the leaves for the desired period.

$$\text{Leaf Weight Ratio} = \frac{\text{Laef Mass Weight}}{\text{Weight of Remaing}} \times 100$$

14.4 Stem Weight Ratio

The stem weight ratio is the ratio between the weights of the stem with other parts of a plant *i.e.* leaves and roots. It is a statistical parameter for estimating the mass of the stem for the desired period.

$$\text{Stem Weight Ratio} = \frac{\text{Stem Mass Weight}}{\text{Weight of Remaing}} \times 100$$

14.5 Root Weight Ratio

The root weight ratio is the ratio between the weights of the root with other parts of a plant i.e. Stems and leaves. It is a statistical parameter for estimating the mass of the leaves for the desired period.

$$\text{Root Weight Ratio} = \frac{\text{Root Mass Weight}}{\text{Weight of Remaing}} \times 100$$

14.6 Top Dry Weight

The top dry weight is the weight of the stem and leaves It is a statistical parameter for estimating the mass of the above ground for the desired period.

Top Dry Weight = Leaf Weight (Gm) + Stem Weight(gm)

The three indices are calculated from the observed data such as above ground height, basal diameter, fresh weight, dry weight and moisture content.

14.7 Sturdiness Quotient

$$\text{Sturdiness Quotient} = \frac{\text{Above ground height(cm)}}{\text{Basal Diameter (cm)}}$$

14.8 Volume Index

Volume index = Above ground height (cm) X Basal diameter (cm)

14.9 Quality Index

$$\text{Quality index} = \frac{\text{Seedlings dry weight(g)}}{\text{(Height(cm)/Diameter(cm) + Top dry weight(g)/ Root dry weight(g)}}$$

The observation of phytosociology were carried out for the selected tree species to assess the recycling capabilities of industrial effluents particularly textile industrial effluents. The results show the incremental growth in the treated effluent irrigation and medium growth in raw effluent irrigation when compared to tap water irrigation. It shows the recycling of industrial effluent by forest tree species are determined for a period of three seasons such as pre monsoon, monsoon and post monsoon seasons.

— — —

15

Biostatistics

15.1 Introduction

Statistics is mostly used as a tool for assessing the capability of the system. Statistics refers to facts shown in numbers. Modern statistical methods and data are being found increasingly useful in research in different fields such as hydrology, biology, water quality and forestry *etc.* Statistics when used effectively becomes so intertwined in the whole fabric of the subjects to which it is applied. Statistics assists in planning the initial observations, organizing them and formulating hypothesis from them and in judging whether the new observations agree sufficiently well with the predictions from the hypothesis. In statistical methods, there is an operation of multiple causes and the investigator has only limited control over there. But statistical methods are found extremely useful in predicting the consequences of a situation. It requires skill for acquiring and handling data. There is a methodology to deal with the data and analysis of data is based on scientific and engineering strategies (Ramakrishnan, 1995).

In a huge rainfall data over a period of 300 years, it is not possible to observe all the items. Statistical methods are developed to estimate the error or deflection from the true or real value when we are taking inference from a sample for a hydrological data.

In the modern world where life sciences is getting more and more importance. To meet our environmental problems and energy requirements due to rapid industrialization and population growth, scop of life science has taken its new shape. Based on statistical analysis, new field like environmental sciences, hydrology, genetic engineering, biotechnology and bio-sociology have been evolved. Experiments about crop yields with different types of fertilizers and different types of soils or the growth of animal life and plant life under different environmental conditions and diets are very often designed and analyzed according to statistical method. Even in the field of medicine and public health, statistical methods are used for testing the efficacy of new medicine and method of treatments. As a matter of fact, for a research worker in any field, which is concern with numerical results, a study of statistical method is not only useful but also necessary. Hence it can be rightly by remarked *"Science without statistics bears no fruit, statistics without science have no root"*.

Modern biological investigations have become quantitative in which a vast array of biological observations consists of numerical facts called data. As the biological observations are measured or counted, it becomes clear that some objective verifying the research data. The statistical method applied to biology of the environmental problems is called as Biostatistics. The term biometry is also used, which means "biological measurement".

The purpose of this chapter is to explain and discuss the fundamental principles and methods of statistics in simple and comprehensive manner for the environmentalists, foresters, students of environmental sciences to understand the complex environmental phenomenon like evapotranspiration, biofilter, mineral cycles, nutrient cycle, pollutant transport in the natural cycles.

For any statistical enquiry, the basic problem is to collect facts and figures relating to a particular phenomenon under study, whether the enquiry is in business, economic or sciences. The phenomenon under study is known as 'statistical enquiry' or ' statistical investigation'. Care must be exercised in collecting data because the data constitute of the foundation on which the statistical analysis is built. The success of an enquiry is based upon the proper collection of data.

Statistical investigations consists of systematic collection of data and analyzing it with the help of different statistical methods. Thus, one may collect the output data of few industrial units over a number of years and make forecast about their future growth on the basis of their past performance. Similarly the research works in sciences can be assessed on the basis of past finding in the research activity (CMIE, 1994).

Statistical investigation is a long and comprehensive process. It extends over various stages from planning to the final preparation of the report. The various stages can be listed as follows:

1. Planning of statistical investigation
2. Collection of data
3. Editing of data
4. Presentation of data
5. Analysis of data
6. Interpretation of data and preparation of report

The various stages and their component parts can be summarized as in Fig 15.1

15.2. Planning of Statistical Investigation

Before starting actual collection of data, various components of statistical investigation should be clearly defined; e.g. the object and scope of enquiry, the unit of study, the time and type of investigation and the degree of accuracy desired.

a) Object and scope of statistical investigation

Before starting a statistical investigation the first and foremost task is to know the nature, object and scope of the investigation. It is to be decided whether the enquiry in view is to serve a general purpose or a specific one. The correct determination of the purpose helps in removing a number of complexities and difficulties. So it should be done with minimum wastage of time, money and energy. In deciding the object and scope of investigation we should not over estimate out aims, be unmindful of the money and time available to us.

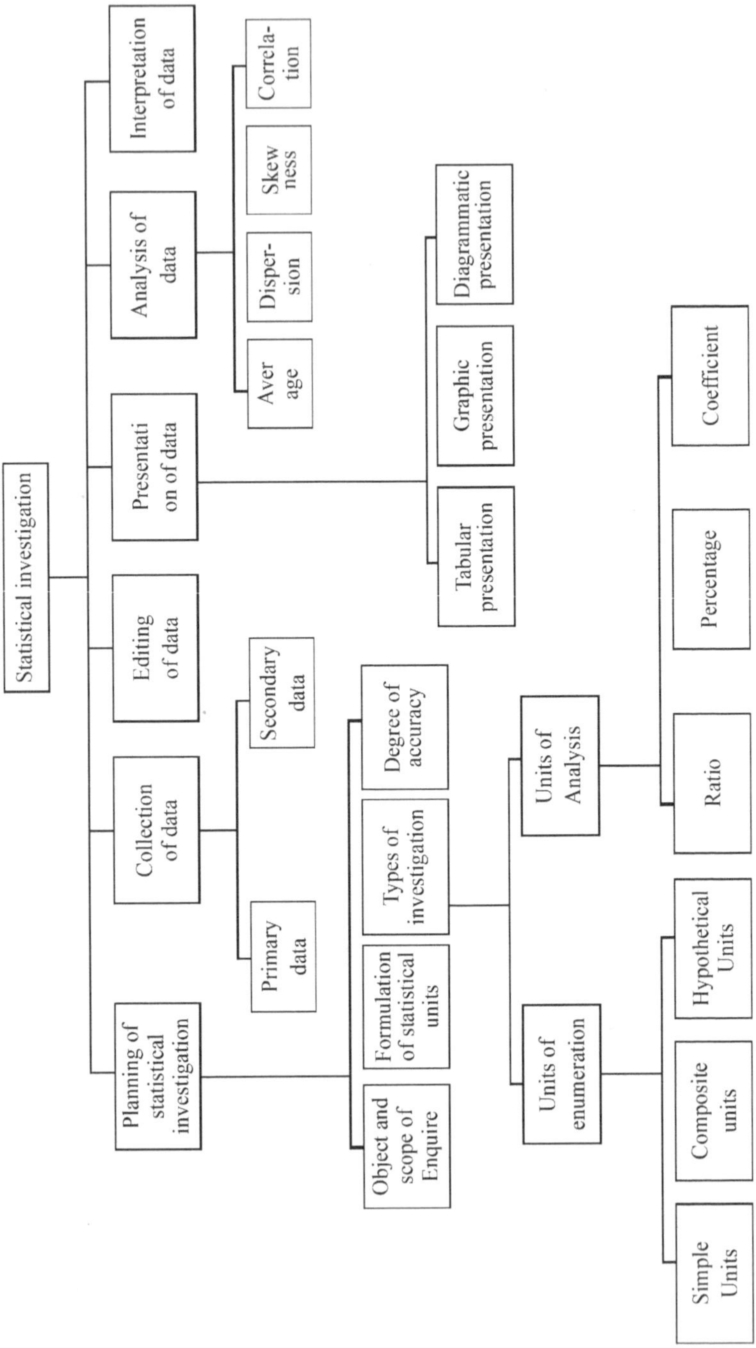

Figure 15.1: Stages of statistical investigation

The scope of statistical investigation depends upon the object on investigation, which, in turn, will determine the area of coverage of enquiry.

b) Formation of statistical Units

A statistical unit is the unit of measurement in terms of which the magnitude of a variable is expressed. Quantitative data can be collected accurately only when the unit in which it is to be counted, measured, or estimated, has been correctly defined. According to Prof. King" it is not only desirable but strictly essential that the units be accurately and unambiguously defined. Definition of unit is necessary to avoid any misunderstanding and to bring homogeneity in data. The need for defining unit is all the more felt because of the quantitative nature of the unit and lack of standard connotations" the ideal statistical unit should possess the following main characteristics.

1. It should be suitable to the specific purpose of investigation.
2. It should be unambiguous and specifics
3. It should be complete in itself
4. It should be homogeneous and not heterogeneous
5. It should be easily understandable as well as easy to use

There are various types of investigations which are used in different situations. Each type of investigation has got its own merits and demerits. Hence, the right type of investigation must be chosen with reference to its objectives.

15.3 Collection of Data

The process of accounting and the systematic recording of the results obtained after concluding the investigation is called the collection of statistical data. The statistical data on the basis of collection can be grouped into two types:

1) Primary data
2) Secondary data

The primary data is collected by the investigator himself for a specific purpose of investigation. On the other hand, if the data is already collected, tabulated and presented by some one is utilized by a second person for some other purpose is known as secondary data. Thus, the distinction between primary and secondary data is a relative one.

15.4 Editing of Data

The collected data must be edited before it is used because it contains some irrelevant matter which may not be needed for the study. Editing is done to make the data consistent and uniform, complete and accurate. In editing the data, a higher level of skill and scientific knowledge is needed. On the object and utility of editing the data. Professors like, Crum, Pattan and Tebbutt have remarked, " the process of editing is by no means an unimportant and routine operation; rather it requires marked ability, scrupulous and rigid adherence to scientific objectivity".

15.5 Presentation of Data

After having collected that data, it is classified and presented in tabulated forms to make it intelligible. We may also make use of visual methods like graphics and diagrammatical representations to represent it.

15.6 Primary and Secondary Data Sources

Methods of Collecting Primary Data

1. Direct Personal investigation
2. Indirect oral investigation
3. Information through correspondents
4. The questionnaire method

1. Direct Personal investigation

The investigator has to contact the sources of information directly and personally. This method of collecting data is suitable: (a) When the area of investigation is limited (b) When a higher degree of accuracy is needed (c) When the results of the investigation are to be kept confidential (d) Where the area of investigation is complex and heterogeneous (e) Where a greater degree of intellectual power, experience and labour are required.

Merits

1. Original data is collected.
2. Reliable information is obtained.
3. There is uniformity in the collection of information.
4. This method is elastic because the investigator can use his influence and different techniques as the situation demands.
5. The method yields more accurate results.
6. It can be most useful when the area of investigation is very small.

Demerits

1. This method is unsuitable when the area of investigation is large.
2. It is more expensive and time consuming.
3. The chances of personal bias are more.
4. It is more complex and places a heavy burden upon the sources of the investigator.

Precautions

1. In the use of this method, precautions must be taken in regard to the nature, behaviour and personality of the investigator. The investigator must posses the aptitude necessary for conducting personal interviews.
2. The success of this method mainly depend upon the qualities of the investigator, *viz.* efficiency, consistency, farsightedness and impartiality.
3. The questions should be limited in number. Only relevant question should be asked.

15.7 Indirect Oral Investigation

There are certain situations when the information cannot be approached directly. In such situations we have to collect data from those persons who may possess some knowledge about the investigation. Such persons are known as 'witness'. This method is suitable in the following situations:

(a) When the area of investigation is large, (b) when the information cannot be obtained directly from the informants (c) When expertise in collection of data is required to be used. The Governments and other such institutions generally make use this method.

Merits

1. It can be used when the area of investigation is large.
2. It is a simple and convenient method of investigation.
3. It is economical and saves time, money and labour.
4. More complex data can be analyzed.
5. It is not open to bias.
6. It is possible to obtain complete and adequate information regarding the enquiry.

Demerits

1. The results may not always be true and accurate; these may be open to suspection and doubt.
2. The informants may not be serious in furnishing the proper replies and hence degree of accuracy can be affected.

Precautions

1. It must be ascertained that the informants possess the require knowledge and are interested in providing the correct information.
2. The number of informants is not biased and is obtain reliable results.
3. It must be ascertained that informants are not biased and are providing correct and true information only.

15.8 Information Through Correspondents

In this method the investigator does not collect the information directly from the respondents. The task is handled over to a few persons or a group of persons, who are known as correspondents. The method is suitable in the following situations. (a) When the area of investigation is very large (b) When regular and continues information is required (c) When the degree of accuracy is only of secondary importance. This method is generally employed by newspapers, magazines, broadcasting agencies, and various governmental agencies requiring information on regular basis.

Merits

1. It is the most economical and extensive method of investigation.
2. It is a very convenient method of collecting information from far-off area.
3. It is useful where the information is needed from time to time.

Demerits

1. There is lack of originality in data.
2. The information can be biased.
3. Degree of accuracy is generally very low.
4. Information made available may be out of date.
5. There may not be uniformity in the collected data.

Precautions

1. Only properly trained correspondents should be appointed.
2. Efforts should be made to reduce the personal bias of the correspondents. This bias may arise due to caste, religion, *etc.*
3. The consistency of information should be verified at regular intervals.

15.9 Questionnaire Method

In this method the information is obtained from the information through questionnaires, this method is of two forms:

(a) Questionnaires sent through post

In this method, the questionnaire is mailed to the informants. It also carries a request for the quick response and lays down the aims and objectives of collecting the information. In this method, the return postage expenses are generally borne by the investigator. This method is suitable in the following situations:

(a) When the area under investigation is very large; and (b) When the informants are educated and are likely to co-operated

Merits

1. It can conveniently be used when the area of investigation is very large.
2. It is economical and involves less labour and time.
3. Collected information may be more reliable.
4. Original data can be obtained directly from the informants.

Demerits

1. It is not possible to determine the degree of accuracy of data.
2. Informants may prove unco-operative, and hence may refuse to part with proper information.
3. Informants may be biased.
4. Informants may not like to provide written information.
5. If the questionnaire is complex, it may not be responded.
6. If may involve a long time-lag in answering the questionnaire.

Precautions

1. Goodwell and Co-operation on informants is a prime requisite.

2. Questionnaire should be simple, attractive and unambiguous.
3. Language used in the questionnaire should be polite and effective.
4. The efforts should be made to extract the information as quickly as possible.

15.10 Questionnaire Sent Through Enumerators

The enumerators go to the informants with a prepared questionnaire and get the replies to the questions. This method is generally used by public organisations like FICCI, NCAER *etc*. for the research projects that need a high rate of response.

Merits

1. There is no chance of non-response since the enumerators give to all the informants.
2. Personal contact makes it possible to collect reliable data.
3. Personal bias is minimized.
4. Illiterate informants can also be approached.

Demerits

1. This is a very costly method, as the enumerators have to be paid their services.
2. It is time consuming.
3. Personal bias of enumerators may lead to false results.
4. This method can be used only by big organizations.

Precautions

1. The success of this method lies on the caliber of enumerators.
2. The enumerator should be (a) wise, honest, laborious and active (b) educated and technically trained (c) unbiased (d) interested in research work (e) well-versed in local language, customs traditions *etc*.
3. The number of questions should be small.

Biostatistics and its applications are very useful for any studies related to scientific and engineering strategies. It shall be of optimum usages for recycling of industrial effluents by forest trees. With respect to this studies many ratios and indices are calculated and presented in the chapters 14 and 21.

— — —

16

Recycling Technology

16.1 Conservative Technology

Recycling technology being practiced by ancient times by the people who used for municipal industrial effluent. In India the people in rural area, they collected cow dung in a pit. They applied a layer of soil on the cow dung to composting. After three to four months period, they used as manure for the agricultural fields. In a household waste, they collected as organic waste from a kitchen, store a pit allow it for decompose for conversion of compost. People who are residing in house constructed in a plot, they used to generate industrial effluent in a pit and cultivate a kitchen garden like vegetable crops and banana trees *etc.* in ancient times, the amount organic waste is limited and self purification is taken in small amount of organic waste therefore no organic pollution occurs in rural India.

16.2 Alternate Technology

In recent times, the amount of organic and inorganic waste is unlimited and demand of more self purification processes, but the self purification processes is limited by sun light and atmosphere geases. The load of organic pollution is increasingly day by day and needs to made many alternate technology such as bio reactors, using many phytoplankton, algae rotifers lemna *etc.*

Conventionally mechanized waste water plants involving primary and secondary treatment systems require large capital investment, and demand high operation and maintances costs and hence do not seems to work in our country. Besides mechanical treatment options do not consider the value of renewing organic waste resources and do not promote front end recycling of treated water. Therefore alternate waste water treatment technologies are required to enable communities to own, operate and maintain the processes equipment and the technology for waste water management and at the same time, offer ecological, enviormental and social benefits. Therefore, it is meaning full to give a clear sketch the adequacy and candidature of treatment systems. Several features can characteristics of alternate wastewater treatment technologies.

1. The technology should be low cost and have minimum possible mechanization which rduce the risk of malfunctions.
2. The technology should be simple to operate locally manufactured as well as labour intensive. It should not relay upon expensive chemical inputs and should be able to recover and reuse the resources as far as possible.
3. The technology should be capable of being incrementally upgraded s user defined.

16.3 Recent Trends in Recycling Technology

Freshwater has been used for an economic or beneficial purpose such as domestic, industrial processes, it is generally discarded as waste. In many countries, these wastewaters are discharged, either as untreated waste or as treated effluent, into natural watercourses, from which they are abstracted for further use after undergoing "self-purification" within the natural resources. Through this system of indirect recycling, wastewater may be recyling up to a dozen times or more before being discharged to the water ecosystems. Such indirect recycling is common in the larger river systems of India like Ganges, Yamuna, Narmadha, and Cauvery. However, more direct recycling is also possible: the technology to reclaim wastewaters as potable or process waters is a technically feasible option for agricultural, cultivation of forest trees and some industrial purposes such as for cooling water or sanitary flushing, and a largely experimental option for the supply of domestic water. Wastewater recycling for drinking raises public health, and possibly religious, concerns among consumers. The adoption of wastewater treatment and subsequent recycling as a means of supplying freshwater is also determined by economic factors.

In many countries, water quality standards have been developed governing the discharge of wastewater into the environment. Wastewater, in this context, includes industrial effluent, storm water runoff, and industrial effluent discharges. The necessity to protect the natural environment from wastewater-related pollution has led to much improved treatment techniques. Extending these technologies to the treatment of wastewaters to potable standards is a logical extension of this protection and augmentation process.

One of the most critical steps in any recycling program is to protect the public health, especially that of workers and consumers. To this end, it is most important to neutralize or eliminate any infectious agents or pathogenic organisms that may be present in the wastewater. For some recycling applications, such as irrigation of non-food crop plants, secondary treatment may be acceptable. For other applications, further disinfection, by such methods as chlorination or ozonation, may be necessary. Table 16.1 presents a range of typical survival times for potential pathogens in water and other media.

Table 16.1: Typical Pathogen Survival Times at 20 - 30°C (in days)

Pathogen	Freshwater and industrial effluent	Crops	Soil
Viruses	< 120 but usually <50	<60 but usually < 15	<100 but usually <20
Bacteria	<60 but usually <30	<30 but usually < 15	<70 but usually < 20
Protozoa	<30 but usually <15	<10 but usually < 2	<70 but usually < 20
Helminths	Many months	<60 but usually < 30	Many months

Source: U.S. Environmental Protection Agency, Process Design Manual: Guidelines/ or Water Recycling. Cincinnati, Ohio, 1992 (Report No. EPA-625/R-92-004).

A typical two examples of wastewater recycling are the system at the Sam Lords Castle Hotel in Barbados and at Jamaica. The industrial Effluent consisting of toxic material is collected in a sump, from which it is pumped, through a comminutor, to an aeration chamber. No primary sedimentation is provided in this system, although it is often desirable to do so. The aerated mixed liquor flows out of the aeration chamber to a clarifier for gravity separation. The industrial effluent from the clarifier is then passed through a 16-foot-deep chlorine disinfections chamber before it is pumped to an automatic sprinkler irrigation system. The irrigated areas are divided into sixteen zones; each zone has twelve sprinklers. Some areas are also provided with a drip irrigation system. Sludge from the clarifier is pumped, without thickening, as a slurry to suckwells, where it is disposed of. Previously the sludge was pumped out and sent to the Bridgetown Industrial effluent Treatment Plant for further treatment and additional desludging.

For health and aesthetic reasons, recycling of treated industrial effluent is presently limited to non-potable applications such as irrigation of non-food crops and provision of industrial cooling water. There are no known direct recycling schemes using treated wastewater from sewerage systems for drinking. Indeed, the only known systems of this type are experimental in nature, although in some cases treated wastewater is recycling indirectly, as a source of aquifer recharge. Table 16.2 presents some guidelines for the utilization of wastewater, indicating the type of treatment required, resultant water quality specifications, and appropriate setback distances. In general, wastewater recycling is a technology that has had limited use, primarily in small-scale projects in the region, owing to concerns about potential public health hazards.

Wastewater recycling in the Caribbean is primarily in the form of irrigation water. In Jamaica, some hotels have used wastewater treatment effluent for golf course irrigation, while the major industrial water users, the bauxite/alumina companies, engage in extensive recycling of their process waters In Barbados, effluent from an extended aeration industrial effluent treatment plant is used for lawn irrigation Similar use of wastewater occurs on Curaçao.

In Latin America, treated wastewater is used in small-scale agricultural projects and, particularly by hotels, for lawn irrigation. In Chile, up to 220 l/s of wastewater is used for irrigation purposes in the desert region of Antofagasta. In Brazil, wastewater has been extensively recyling for agriculture. Treated wastewaters have also been used for human consumption after proper disinfection, for industrial processes as a source of cooling water, and for aquaculture. Wastewater recycling for aquacultural and agricultural irrigation purposes is also practiced in Lima, Peru. In Argentina, natural systems are used for wastewater treatment. In such cases, there is an economic incentive for reusing wastewater for reforestation, agricultural, pasturage, and water conservation purposes, where sufficient land is available to do so. Perhaps the most extensive recycling of wastewater occurs in Mexico, where there is large-scale use of raw industrial effluent for the irrigation of parks and the creation of recreational lakes.

Table 16.2: Guidelines for Water Recycling

Type of Recycling	Treatment Required	Reclaimed Water Quality	Recommended Monitoring	Setback Distances
Agricultural	Secondary Disinfection	pH = 6-9	pH weekly	300 ft from potable water supply wells
Food crops commercially processed		BOD 30 mg/l	BOD weekly	
		SS = 30 mg/l	SS daily	
Orchards and Vinerds		FC 200/100 ml	FC daily	100 ft from areas accessible to public
		Cl_2 residual = 1 mg/l min.	Cl_2 residual continuous	
Pasturage	Secondary Disinfection	pH = 6-9	pH weekly	300 ft from potable water supply wells
Pasture for milking animals		BOD 30 mg/l	BOD weekly	
		SS 30 mg/l	SS daily	
Pasture for livestock		FC 200/100 ml	FC daily	100 ft from areas accessible to public
		Cl_2 residual = 1 mg/l min.	Cl_2 residual continuous	

Forestation	Secondary Disinfection	pH = 6-9	pH weekly	300 ft from potable water supply wells
		BOD 30 mg/l	BOD weekly	
		SS 30 mg/l	SS daily	
		FC 200/100 ml	FC daily	100 ft from areas accessible to the public
		Cl_2 residual = 1 mg/l min.	Cl_2 residual continuous	
Agricultural	Secondary Filtration Disinfection	pH = 6-9	pH weekly	50 ft from potable water supply wells
Food crops not commercially processed		BOD 30 mg/l	BOD weekly	
		Turbidity 1 NTU	Turbidity daily	
		FC = 0/100 ml	FC daily	
		Cl_2 residual = 1 mg/l min.	Cl_2 residual continuous	
Groundwater Recharge	Site-specific and use-dependent	Site-specific and use-dependent	Depends on treatment and use	Site-specific

Source: USEPA, Process Design Manual: Guidelines for Water Recycling, Cincinnati, Ohio, 1992, (Report No. EPA-625/R-92-004).

In the United States, the use of reclaimed water for irrigation of food crops is prohibited in some states, while others allow it only if the crop is to be processed and not eaten raw. Some states may hold, for example, that if a food crop is irrigated in such a way that there is no contact between the edible portion and the reclaimed water, a disinfected, secondary-treated effluent is acceptable. For crops that are eaten raw and not commercially processed, wastewater recycling is more restricted and less economically attractive. Less stringent requirements are set for irrigation of non-food crops.

International water quality guidelines for wastewater recycling have been issued by the World Health Organization (WHO). Guidelines should also be established at national level and at the local/project level, taking into account the international guidelines. Some national standards that have been developed are more stringent than the WHO guidelines. In general, however, wastewater recycling regulations should be strict enough to permit irrigation use without undue health risks, but not so strict as to prevent its use. When using treated wastewater for irrigation, for example, regulations should be written so that attention is paid to the interaction between the effluent, the soil, and the topography of the receiving area, particularly if there are aquifers nearby.

The operation and maintenance required in the implementation of this technology is related to the previously discussed operation and maintenance of the wastewater treatment processes, and to the chlorination and disinfection technologies used to ensure that pathogenic organisms will not present a health hazard to humans. Additional maintenance includes the periodic cleaning of the water distribution system conveying the effluent from the treatment plant to the area of recycling; periodic cleaning of pipes, pumps, and filters to avoid the deposition of solids that can reduce the distribution efficiency; and inspection of pipes to avoid clogging throughout the collection, treatment, and distribution system, which can be a potential problem. Further, it must be emphasized that, in order for a water recycling program to be successful, stringent regulations, monitoring, and control of water quality must be exercised in order to protect both workers and the consumers.

The private sector, particularly the hotel industry and the agricultural sector, are becoming involved in wastewater treatment and recycling. However, to ensure the public health and protect the environment, governments need to exercise oversight of projects in order to minimize the deleterious impacts of wastewater discharges. One element of this oversight should include the sharing of information on the effectiveness of wastewater recycling. Government oversight also includes licensing and monitoring the performance of the wastewater treatment plants to ensure that the effluent does not create environmental or health problems.

Cost data for this technology are very limited. Most of the data relate to the cost of treating the wastewater prior to recycling. Additional costs are associated with the construction of a dual or parallel distribution system. In many cases, these costs can be recovered out of the savings derived from the reduced use of potable freshwater (*i.e.,* from not having to treat raw water to potable standards when the intended use does not require such extensive treatment). The feasibility of wastewater recycling ultimately depends on the cost of recycled or reclaimed water relative to alternative supplies of potable water, and on public acceptance of the reclaimed water. Costs of effluent treatment vary widely according to location and level of treatment. The degree of public acceptance also varies widely depending on water availability, religious and cultural beliefs, and previous experience with the recycling of wastewaters.

The effectiveness of the technology, while difficult to quantify, is seen in terms of the diminished demand for potable-quality freshwater and, in the Caribbean islands, in the diminished degree of degradation of water quality in the near-shore coastal marine environment, the area where untreated and unreclaimed wastewaters were previously disposed. The analysis of beach waters in Jamaica indicates that the water quality is better near the hotels with wastewater recycling projects than in beach areas where recycling is not practiced: Beach #1 in Table 16.3 is near a hotel with a wastewater recycling project, while Beach #2 is not. From an aesthetic point of view, also, the presence of lush vegetation in the areas where lawns and plants are irrigated with reclaimed wastewater is further evidence of the effectiveness of this technology.

Table 16.3: Water Quality of Beach Water in Wastewater Recycling Project in Jamaica

Site	BOD	TC	FC	NO_3
Beach # 1	0.30	<2	<2	0.01
Beach # 2	1.10	2.400.00	280.00	0.01

Source: Basil P. Fernandez, Hydrogeologist and Managing Director, Water Resources Authority, Kingston, Jamaica.

This technology has generally been applied to a small-scale projects, primarily in areas where there is a shortage of water for supply purposes. However, this technology can be applied to larger-scale projects. In many developing countries, especially where there is a water deficit for several months of the year, implementation of wastewater recycling or recycling by industries can reduce demands for water of potable quality, and also reduce impacts on the environment.

Large-scale wastewater recycling can only be contemplated in areas where there are reticulated sewerage and/or stormwater systems. Urban areas generally have sewerage systems, and, while not all have stormwater systems, those that do are ideal localities for wastewater recycling schemes. Wastewater for recycling must be adequately treated, biologically and chemically, to ensure the public health and environmental safety. The primary concerns associated with the use of industrial effluent effluents in recycling schemes are the presence of pathogenic bacteria and viruses, parasite eggs, worms, and helminths like all biological concerns and of nitrates, phosphates, salts, and toxic chemicals, including heavy metals (all chemical concerns) in the water destined for recycling (House, 1995).

This technology reduces the demands on potable sources of freshwater. It may reduce the need for large wastewater treatment systems, if significant portions of the waste stream are recyling or recycled. The technology may diminish the volume of wastewater discharged, resulting in a beneficial impact on the aquatic environment. Capital costs are low to medium, for most systems, and are recoverable in a very short time; this excludes systems designed for direct recycling of industrial effluent water. Operation and maintenance are relatively simple except in direct recycling systems, where more extensive technology and quality control are required. Provision of nutrient-rich wastewaters can increase agricultural production in water-poor areas. Pollution of seawater, rivers, and groundwaters may be reduced. Lawn maintenance and golf course irrigation is facilitated in resort areas. In most cases, the quality of the wastewater, as an irrigation water supply, is superior to that of well water.

If implemented on a large scale, revenues to water supply and wastewater utilities may fall as the demand for potable water for non-potable uses and the discharge of wastewaters is reduced. Recycling of wastewater may be seasonal in nature, resulting in the overloading of treatment and disposal facilities during the rainy season; if the wet season is of long duration and high intensity, the seasonal discharge of raw wastewaters may occur. Health problems, such as water-borne diseases and skin irritations, may occur in people coming into direct contact with recyling wastewater. Gases, such as sulfuric acid, produced during the treatment process can result in chronic health problems. In some cases, recycling of wastewater is not economically feasible because of the requirement for an additional distribution system. Application of untreated wastewater as irrigation water or as injected recharge water may result in groundwater contamination.

A large percentage of domestic water users are afraid to use this technology to supply of potable water (direct recycling) because of the potential presence of pathogenic organisms. However, most people are willing to accept recycling wastewater for golf course and lawn irrigation and for cooling purposes in industrial processes. On the household scale, recycling of wastewaters and manures as fertilizer is a traditional technology.

Expansion of this technology to large-scale applications should be encouraged. Cities and towns that now use mechanical treatment plants that are difficult to operate, expensive to maintain, and require a high skill level can replace these plants with the simpler systems; treated wastewater can be recyling to irrigate crops, pastures, and lawns. In new buildings, plumbing fixtures can be designed to recycling wastewater, as in the case of using gray water from washing machines and kitchen sinks to flush toilets and irrigate lawns. Improved public education to ensure awareness of the technology and its benefits, both environmental and economic, is recommended (Pescod, 1992).

Sam Lord's Castle Hotel is located on the southeastern coast of Barbados, in the parish of St. Philip. It lies within the coral-covered portion of the island, with a coral cap thickness of about

80 ft. With an average annual rainfall of 45 inches, this is one of the driest areas of the island (the average annual rainfall for the whole island is 60 inches). In this area, except for 4 months of the year (August to November), the average evapotranspiration rate, 4.5 inches/month, exceeds the monthly rainfall figures. The groundwater resources in this area consist of a thin freshwater lens floating on top of saline water.

The hotel was formerly supplied with freshwater from a groundwater well, but because of the high water demand, especially for the irrigation of large expanses of lawns and garden plants, saline groundwater intruded into it to the point where the freshwater supply was virtually exhausted. A decision was made then to abandon the use of the well and the hotel sent an application to the Ministry of Health and Environment seeking permission to use the treated effluent from its extended aeration industrial effluent treatment plant for irrigating lawns and garden plants. Permission for wastewater recycling was granted and treated wastewater was diverted to irrigation use from its former disposal site in four deep suckwells.

Effluent consisting of kitchen, laundry, and domestic industrial effluent is conveyed to a collection chamber, from which it is pumped through a comminutor to an aeration chamber. No primary sedimentation is provided. The aerated mixed liquor then flows out of the aeration chamber through a rectangular opening at one end into a clarifier for gravity separation of solids. The effluent from the clarifier chamber is then passed through a 16-foot-deep chlorine disinfection chamber and pumped to an automatic sprinkler irrigation system. The irrigated areas are sub-divided into 16 zones with 12 sprinklers each. Some areas also have a drip irrigation system Sludge with a high water content is pumped from the sludge chamber to the suckwells for disposal without thickening. Previously this sludge was pumped to the Bridgetown Industrial effluent Treatment Plant for further treatment and additional desludging. This pumping incurred additional transportation costs. The packaged wastewater treatment plant was designed abroad and constructed using local contractors. The drip and sprinkler irrigation systems were designed and installed in part by a local irrigation system consulting company and in part by the hotel's maintenance personnel. The Environmental Engineering Division (EED) of the Ministry of Health and Environment was responsible for approving, monitoring, and controlling the operation of the packaged plant. Thus, despite the absence of effluent standards enacted into law, some conditions were placed on the system before permission was granted for irrigation recycling. The approval process involved consultations with the Town and Country Planning Offices and the Barbados Water Authority (BWA).

At present, there are twelve wastewater treatment facilities in use in Barbados, ranging in size from 2 860 gpd to 37 400 gpd for hotel facilities and to 594 000 gpd for the Barbados Water Authority plant. The combined total treatment capacity amounts to 786 280 gpd. Eight of these plants are extended aeration plants, three are rotating biological contactor plants, and one, the Barbados Water Authority plant, is a contact stabilization plant. Two more BWA sewerage systems are planned for the south and west coasts, with the intention of reusing their wastewater effluents.

Recycling of treated wastewater for the irrigation of garden plants and lawn grass is limited at present to Sam Lord's Castle Hotel. Another, the Almond Beach Village Hotel, formerly Heywoods Hotel, in St. Peter on the west coast, is almost ready to start irrigating a 9-hole golf course. Other applications for the recycling of wastewater on golf courses Westmoreland, Kingsland, and Bushy Park are pending, and a number of major hotels have indicated their interest in applying for permission to recycling their effluent. In addition, plans are in place to recycling some of the treated effluent from the BWA Bridgetown Industrial effluent Treatment Plant for flushing sewer lines.

According to the report of a survey on the Operational Aspects of Wastewater Treatment Plants in Barbados undertaken by A. Vlugman of PAHO in 1990, the operational status of the Sam Lord's Castle Hotel plant was considered to be moderate. The plant is about twelve years old and the operator reports few problems; those that have occurred are considered minimal (due to grease). There does not seem to be any problem with obtaining spare parts. However, no design or construction drawings are available to help with the operation and maintenance of the plant, and the basic skills required to operate and maintain the plant, such as some knowledge of microbiology, some electrical/ mechanical skills to repair the equipment, and some understanding of the treatment process and the impact of poor performance on the whole scheme, are generally lacking.

Considering the small size of most packaged wastewater treatment plants, it may not be cost-effective for each hotel to employ a qualified operator. However, it might be possible for a number of hotels to employ collectively one qualified operator to look after a number of plants. Alternatively, the Barbados Hotels and Tourism Association (BHTA) could employ an environmental officer or sanitary engineer to oversee or advise the various hotels on wastewater treatment and effluent recycling.

The operation and maintenance required consists of turning the pumps that do not run continuously (such as the sludge pumps) on and off, and checking to ensure that all systems are running smoothly without any blockages. There are no flow meters installed and no laboratory facilities of any kind are provided to document the technical performance of the plant. Any operational monitoring of plant and process by the operator is limited to visual inspections. Plant performance is evaluated by the operator on the basis of the color of the mixed liquor in the aeration chamber; a brownish color is an indicator of good performance. Nevertheless, BOD and TSS analyses are done monthly during inspections by the EED.

The only government involvement in this program is licensing, monitoring and administrative control, exercised through the EDD, which is charged with the responsibility of approving and monitoring the performance of packaged wastewater treatment plants. The Sam Lord's Castle Hotel plant is entirely privately owned and operated, except for the monthly inspections and sampling for BOD and TSS conducted by the EED.

Based on 1989 and 1990 results, BOD and TSS removal efficiencies of 86%, and of 98% and 83%, respectively, are achievable. Data on the microbiological quality of the effluent are not available; two chlorine tablets are put into the chlorination chamber each week, regardless of effluent quality or quantity. Hence there is need to evaluate in detail the effectiveness of the disinfection before the effluent is used for irrigation. However, from an aesthetic point of view, the irrigation of lawns and plants seems to be very successful, as evidenced by the lush greenery surrounding the hotel. This is a great improvement compared to the period before the effluent recycling program was put into place.

The applicability of this technology depends on the nature of the land. In Barbados, owing to the karstic nature and topography of the coral rock aquifer system, groundwater contamination by recyling wastewater can be avoided only if the wastewater is properly treated. At present, there are very few facilities with a suitable effluent quality. However, the hotels in the belt along the south and west coast, downgradient from the line of public water supply wells, would be obvious candidates for application of this recycling technology, posing the least danger of contamination to the groundwater. The hotel belt also has the advantage of being situated next to the BWA wastewater treatment plants.

The use of the treated effluent results in substantial savings in irrigation water costs and reduces the likelihood of water pollution, assuming that the effluents would otherwise have been disposed of through sea outfalls. This technology eliminates the need to use potable water supplied by the BWA public domestic supply system for irrigation and makes it available for other uses.

Inadequate operation and maintenance may pose some health risks. The WHO criteria on wastewater recycling for recreational purposes with possible human contact may not be fully met in this case. These criteria (effluents should not contain more than 100 coliform organisms/100 ml in 80% of samples, and should not contain chemical contaminants that lead to the irritation of mucous membranes and skin) require primary and secondary treatment and sand filtration, or the equivalent. Provision of such treatment would significantly increase the cost of this technology. The potential environmental impacts associated with this technology are contamination of groundwater, human skin irritations caused by bacteria or viruses in inadequately disinfected effluent sprayed on lawns or gardens, and mineral buildup (salination) in the soil, none of which are currently monitored on an adequate and continuous basis. (Because of the proximity of the application area to the coast, there is little risk to the domestic groundwater supply from the Sam Lord's Castle Hotel recycling scheme; however, the flow to the sea could still adversely affect the coastal marine ecosystem. In this case, the irrigation is timed to minimize the health risk to the hotel guests.)

The technology is well developed; however, local engineers and scientists need to familiarize themselves with it and evaluate its suitability for use elsewhere in Barbados, with any necessary modifications. There is also a need to evaluate the effectiveness of the disinfection process (chlorination by gas or chlorine tablets) in eliminating bacteria and viruses. It is very probable that, in future, more hotels will want to recycling effluent from the packaged treatment plants, especially in the light of proposals to change the domestic water tariff structure. Special training programs, in association with the BWA wastewater treatment facilities, should be developed to improve plant performance and monitoring.

Recycling of industrial effluent is now being practiced by several industries to reduce the demands on freshwater resources and to reduce pollution of the environment. The recycling of industrial effluent was spearheaded by the bauxite/alumina companies operating in Jamaica, and they are the largest recyclers at the present time. The bauxite/alumina industry produces a waste product known locally as "red mud," which consists of over 70% water, enriched with caustic soda and organics.

The waste is thickened to 28% solids and sprayed on a sloping drying bed in a layer 8 to 10 cm thick. The liquid fraction is collected at the toe of the drying bed and is channeled via pipelines to a sealed holding pond. Pumps move the effluent from the holding pond back to the plant via a pipeline where it is recycled through the process. The system consists of:

1. Deep mud thickeners (conical vessels).
2. High pressure pumps and pipelines to the drying beds.
3. Drying beds, sealed to prevent infiltration of the effluent to the groundwater.
4. An effluent holding pond, also sealed to prevent infiltration of the effluent to the groundwater.
5. Recycling pumps and pipelines to the plant.

This technology is used at four bauxite/alumina plants in Jamaica. Efforts are under way to encourage other industries to follow suit and recycle process and waste waters.

Problems encountered in the operation and maintenance of the system include mechanical breakdowns of the pumps; ruptures of the pipelines, necessitating a total shutdown of the system; and heavy rains that overload the system, resulting in spillage to the environment. The bauxite/alumina companies, all being multinational corporations, have few problems in replacing parts or equipment, and generally maintain a large equipment inventory. Each bauxite company has a preventive maintenance program, which also reduces downtime.

The skills needed to operate the system are varied. Overall direction is provided by the senior production engineer. However, skill levels range from laborers, who turn valves on and off, to chemical engineers, who manage the system.

The private sector and the government are involved in the implementation of this technology and in certain facets of the operation. The bauxite/alumina companies provide the capital and the engineering designs, and construct the systems. The government, through several specialized agencies, reviews the engineering designs and grant the permits for construction to proceed. Part of the permitting process involves the conduct of an environmental impact assessment. After the permit is granted, construction of the systems is monitored by the government to ensure that design specifications are adhered to. The relationship between the public and private sectors is cooperative and complementary.

Initial capital costs vary and are dependent on the volume of work to be done in preparing the site, resettling persons living on or near the site, and making the necessary changes in the plant infrastructure. The minimum investment to date in any one system has been $50 million. Operation and maintenance costs are not available as this information is confidential and proprietary to the bauxite companies.

The system, as designed and operated, is very effective in reducing contamination of groundwater resources. Because it is completely sealed, it does not allow infiltration of liquid effluents, and recycling this fraction reduces the risk of contamination of groundwater resources from effluent disposal. The use of this system has reduced groundwater contamination in one area by 44% since 1985, as reported by the Water Resources Authority. Despite some disadvantages, due predominantly to the large land areas consumed by the drying beds and holding ponds, the application of this technology, in all cases, has proved to be advantageous.

The technology is suitable for application in areas where large tracts of non-agricultural land - *i.e.,* in excess of 200 ha - are available. In addition, the land should not be steeply sloped, and a supply of nondispersive clay should be available in close proximity to provide impermeable material for sealing the bottom and sides of the drying beds and holding ponds. The technology can be, and is being, adapted for other situations.

Use of this technology reduces the rate of freshwater withdrawal from aquifers; savings of 4 to 5 Mm^3/year of freshwater have been recorded. Recycling of process water reduces the volume of caustic soda solution needed, as the caustic soda is recycled with the effluent. The use of energy, to pump freshwater from depths greater than 100 m, is reduced, thereby saving on the import bill (foreign exchange) for oil.

Contamination of groundwater is reduced by removing and recycling the liquid fraction of the waste stream that is a risk to groundwater quality; likewise, the retention of a high percentage of the caustic soda in the thickened mud (solid fraction) and in the recycled process water makes this contaminant less available for migration to the groundwater. The bauxite/alumina companies are better able to meet the ISO 9000 and ISO 14000 certifications and thereby gain a competitive advantage in the market place. The decreased input costs reduce operational costs, resulting in higher profit margins for the companies and more tax revenue for the government, increasing both the level of investment in the country and the GDP. Better environmental management by the corporate sector results in fewer governmental regulations; other multinational corporations are likely to see such conditions as favorable and invest in Jamaica. The incidence of water pollution is reduced, increasing the availability of freshwater for domestic and irrigation uses and reducing the cost of water to citizens; this increases the standard of living and governmental popularity (Bond *et.al.*, 1996).

There is an increased risk of pollution of surface water resources, due to the large size of the holding ponds and the possibility of spillages. Technical problems within the plants may be experienced, reducing the level of production and affecting the volume of recycled effluent; hence, storage volumes can increase to the point where overflows occur, affecting the environment. The quality of effluent may vary significantly, affecting the degree of treatment provided by this technology and thus, potentially, the level of production at the plants. The technology is capital-intensive, not labour-intensive, and provides few spin-offs for nearby communities where unemployment may be high. As a result of the land-intensive nature of this technology, its implementation may result in the relocation of residents, disrupting their lives and causing great inconvenience; for farmers and other small businesspeople, a new location may be less suitable and/or create the need to seek other employment. Agricultural land may be lost in some cases, decreasing food production (Metcalf & Eddy, 1991).

This technology can be more effective if overflows and spills from the system are managed better. Design parameters, especially relating to the effects of rainfall/runoff and the rate at which the plants can accept recycled effluent to prevent negative environmental impacts, need to be better refined.

— — —

17

Biological Methods of Recycling

17.1 Introduction

Bioenergy is an array of energy produced by biomass (organic matter) including liquid, solid, and gaseous fuels, electricity, heat, steam, biochemicals and materials. Biofuel is any plant derived organic matter available on a renewable basis, including dedicated energy crops and trees, agricultural food and feed crops, agricultural crop wastes and residues, wood wastes and residues, aquatic plants, animal wastes, municipal wastes, and other waste materials. An organic matter such as wood, plants, residues from agriculture or forestry, and the organic component of municipal and industrial wastes that can now be used as an energy source. Today, many bioenergy resources are replenished through the cultivation of energy crops, such as fast-growing trees and grasses, called bioenergy feedstocks.

Resources of biomass are

— Herbaceous energy crops, which are perennials that are harvested annually after taking two to three years to reach full productivity (examples: switchgrass, miscanthus (also known as Elephant grass or e-grass), bamboo, sweet sorghum, tall fescue, kochia, wheatgrass..)

— Short-rotation woody crops, which are fast growing hardwood trees harvested within five to eight years after planting. (examples: hybrid poplar, hybrid willow, silver maple, eastern cottonwood, green ash, black walnut, sweetgum, and sycamore...)

— Industrial crops, which are being developed and grown to produce specific industrial chemicals or materials. (examples: kenaf and straws for fiber, castor for ricinoleic acid..)

— Agricultural Crops,which include the currently available commodity products and any newly developed component of future commodity crops that generally yield sugars, oils, and extractives and also can be used to produce plastics and other chemicals and products. (examples: cornstarch and corn oil; soybean oil and meal; wheat starch, other vegetable oils)

— Aquatic biomass resources (examples: algae, giant kelp, other seaweed, and marine microflora.)

— Agriculture crop residues, which are like primarily stalks and leaves, not harvested or removed from the fields in commercial use. (examples: corn stover (stalks, leaves, husks and cobs), wheat straw, and rice straw.)

— Forestry residues, which are not harvested or removed from logging sites in commercial hardwood and softwood stands as well as material resulting from forest management operations such as pre-commercial thinnings and removal of dead and dying trees.

— Municipal Wastes including residential, commercial, and institutional post-consumer wastes.(examples: waste paper, cardboard, wood waste and yard wastes)

— All processing of biomass yields byproducts and waste streams collectively called biomass processing residues, which are collected byproducts and waste streams from all processing of biomass. (examples: processing of wood for products or pulp produces sawdust and collection of bark, branches and leaves/needles.)

— Animal Wastes from farms and animal processing operations, which can be used to make many products, including energy.

Biofuels are various fuels made from biomass resources, including liquid fuels ethanol, methanol, biodiesel, Fischer-

Tropsch diesel, and gaseous fuels such as hydrogen and methane. Biofuels are primarily used to fuel vehicles, but can also fuel engines or fuel cells for electricity generation.

Biomass can be converted directly into liquid fuels.

Ethanol is made by converting the carbohydrate portion of biomass into sugar, which is then converted into ethanol in a fermentation process similar to brewing beer. Ethanol is the most widely used biofuel today mostly based on starch crops such as corn. It is mostly used as a fuel additive to cut down a vehicle's carbon monoxide and other smog-causing emissions. Ethanol produced from cellulosic biomass is currently being developed.

Biodiesel is produced through a process in which organically derived oils are combined with alcohol (ethanol or methanol) in the presence of a catalyst to form ethyl or methyl ester. The biomass- derived ethyl or methyl esters can be blended with conventional diesel fuel or used as a neat fuel (100% biodiesel). Biodiesel can be made from soybean or Canola (rapeseed) oils, animal fats, waste vegetable oils, or microalgae oils. It can be used as a diesel additive to reduce vehicle emissions or in its pure form to fuel a vehicle.

Biomass can be gasified to produce a synthesis gas composed primarily of hydrogen and carbon monoxide, also called syngas or biosyngas. Hydrogen can be recovered from this syngas, or it can be catalytically converted to methanol. It can also be converted using Fischer-Tropsch catalyst into a liquid stream with properties similar to diesel fuel, called Fischer-Tropsch diesel. However, all of these fuels can also be produced from natural gas using a similar process.

Gas can be produced from biomass for generating electricity. Gasification systems use high temperatures to convert biomass into a gas (a mixture of hydrogen, carbon monoxide, and methane). The gas fuels a turbine, which is very much like a jet engine, only it turns an electric generator instead of propelling a jet. The decay of biomass in landfills also produces a gas, methane, that can be burned in a boiler to produce steam for electricity generation or for industrial processes.

17.2 Conversion Processes to Produce Biofuels

17.2.1 Biochemical Conversion Processes

Enzymes and microorganisms are frequently used as biocatalysts to convert biomass or biomass derived compounds into desirable products. Cellulase and hemicellulase enzymes break down the carbohydrate fractions of biomass to five and six carbon sugars, a process known as hydrolysis. Yeast and bacteria ferment the sugars into products such as ethanol. Biotechnology advances are expected to lead to dramatic biochemical conversion improvements.

17.2.2 Photobiological Conversion Processes

Photobiological processes use the natural photosynthetic activity of organisms to produce biofuels directly from sunlight. For example, the photosynthetic activities of bacteria and green algae have been used to produce hydrogen from water and sunlight.

17.2.3 Thermochemical Conversion Processes

Heat energy and chemical catalysts are used to break down biomass into intermediate compounds or products. In gasification, biomass is heated in an oxygen-starved environment to produce a gas composed primarily of hydrogen and carbon monoxide. In pyrolysis, biomass is exposed to high temperatures in the absence of air, causing it to decompose. Solvents, acids and bases can be used to fractionate biomass into an array of products including sugars, cellulosic fibers and lignin.

Heat can be used to chemically convert biomass into a fuel oil, which can be burned to generate electricity. Biomass can also be burned directly to produce steam for electricity production or manufacturing processes. In a power plant, a turbine usually captures the steam, and a generator then converts it into electricity. In the lumber and paper industries, wood scraps are sometimes directly fed into boilers to produce steam for their manufacturing processes or to heat their buildings. Some coal-fired power plants use biomass as a supplementary energy source in high-efficiency boilers to significantly reduce emissions. All of today's capacity is based on mature, direct-combustion technology, which involves the burning of biomass with excess air, producing hot flue gases that are used to produce steam in the heat exchange sections of boilers. The steam is used to produce electricity in steam turbine generators.

Biobased Chemicals and Materials are commercial or industrial products derived from biomass feedstocks. Biobased products include green chemicals, renewable plastics, natural fibers, and natural structural materials. Many of these products can replace products and materials traditionally derived from petrochemicals, but new and improved processing technologies will be required.

Its products and applications are:

— ***Green Chemicals*** - Many organic commodity chemicals, fine chemicals, and chemical intermediates can be made from biomass resources. Commodity chemicals include solvents, fuel additives, lubricants, surfactants, adhesives, and inks. Major fine chemical groups include enzymes, nutraceuticals, and pharmaceuticals. Chemical intermediates include sugars, organic acids (such as levulinic acid), and other monomers or monomer precursors.

— ***Renewable Plastics*** - Plastics produced from biomass resources show great promise for replacing plastics derived from petrochemicals. General categories include plant-based degradable polymers, carbohydrate (cellulose, starch and chitin) polymers, and lignin polymers. Examples include starch esters, cellulose acetate blends, polylactide (PLA), polyhydroxybutyric acid (PHB), and thermoplastic proteins.

— ***Natural Fibers*** - Paper products, some textile products, and many types of rope, twine and string are all made from biomass fibers. Pulp and paper processes are being improved and new processes developed to use alternative feedstocks. New products are being developed based on natural fibers including insulation, and geotextiles for soil erosion control applications. These fibers are also being used to replace nonrenewable materials as fillers for many products.

— ***Natural Structural Materials*** - Many building products, such as engineered lumber and structural panels, are made primarily from wood. New composite structural materials are being made that incorporate biomass fibers as fillers with other organic (*e.g.* plastic) or inorganic (*e.g.* cement) components.

— ***Bioremediation*** - Bioremediation is the application of biological systems to contaminated soils and water to convert or remove the contaminants and thereby improve their quality or restore them to their original state. Enzymes, microorganisms, and plants are the major groups of bioremediation catalysts (Hammer, 1989).

New and improved biomass processing technologies are being developed to allow wider use of biomass resources to produce chemicals and materials. Major routes include chemical processing, bioprocessing, thermochemical processing, and mechanical processing. Integrated or hybrid processes may offer the best opportunities for commercial success. Examples of existing integrated processes include corn wet mills and some pulp mills. Also, the ability to separate chemicals, chemical intermediates, and materials from unique and complex processed biomass streams is essential to the commercial viability of these new technologies.

— — —

18

Chemical Methods of Recycling

18.1 Introduction

Recycling of industrial wastewater is not only environmentally beneficial, but it is typically more cost effective than conventional treatment and discharge. Through application of stream segregation and appropriate treatment technologies, high purity water is produced for continuous reuse where by metals are recovered and solid wastes reduced. Recycling of industrial effluent by chemical treatment includes many separation methods for getting pure waters. It is very essential to discuss about reverse osmosis, filtration, adsorption evaporation *etc.* This chapter includes the discussion about the methodology of chemical treatments.

18.2 Conventional Treatments

The oldest and most widely applied method of wastewater treatment involves the addition of chemicals and applications of aerators *etc.* to alter the make-up constituents of a waste. Although generally downsized, the process continues to play an important role in newer systems used today. Automated controls and advanced instrumentation have improved this technology in recent years. (Tomer *et.al.,* 1997)

18.3 Ion Exchange

Ion exchange is a process that removes dissolved ions from solution using synthetic resins to attract cations or ions, then releases (exchanges) counter-ions until resin is exhausted. As solution flows through a resin bed, ion exchange occurs. The process continues by regeneration or replacement of ions on the resin. Ion exchange is used in many industrial applications for various purposes.

- Improves the quality of incoming tap water.
- Purifies and recycles contaminated rinse water.
- Eliminates contamination prior to discharge.
- Extends the life of a process solution.

18.4 Membrane Separation

There are several membrane separation technologies, each characterized by different capabilities and operating specifications. Membrane types listed by pore size from largest to smallest. Membrane separation systems employ's a cross flow filtration process. The flow of influent or contaminated feed water is pumped through the system at a relatively high velocity perpendicular to the membrane surface. The cross flow helps to prevent a build up of rejected or filtered materials on the membrane surface.

18.4.1 Evaporation

Evaporation technology reduces liquid volumes by using heat and in some cases reduced pressures. Atmospheric evaporation is used to reduce the volume of solution by applying heat and allowing water to evaporate into air leaving behind the contaminants or concentrates. The evaporative process can be aided by atomizing sprays and forced air volumes that increase the surface area of the liquid requiring reduction. Depending upon the waste involved, some areas where strict air discharge requirements exist, permits must be obtained to use the technology. Options are available to condense and recover the evaporated water.

18.4.2 Vacuum Evaporation

Vacuum evaporation is a more advanced process than atmospheric evaporation used to reduce the volume of solution as well as recover water. Acting like a traditional still, the process involves boiling solution at a reduced heat, reducing the pressure of the solution below atmosphere (vacuum), collecting steam and condensing it as a purified solution while the constituent without water remains. Single, double, and multistage evaporators are available.

18.4.3 Filtration/Adsorption

Filtration is the process of removing suspended material (or solids) from a solution. Kinetico offers many methods of filtration. For industrial applications, pressure filtration is generally used. Contaminated or raw fluid is fed under pressure through a media bed (bag or cartridge) made of porous material. In media pressure filtration, backwashing (passing of water in the opposite direction of flow) is used to free the bed of captured contaminants.

18.4.4 Electrochemical

Electrowinning / Metal Recovery a type of electroplanting process where metals are plated onto electrodes from industrial wastewater. In an integrated wastewater treatment or recycling system, electrowinning is used to remove metals that have been accumulated on ion exchange resins, or metals present in process chemistry solutions that are being discarded.

The benefit of electrowinning is removal of a potentially hazardous metal from a waste stream and preventing it from becoming hazardous sludge. Operating costs can be decreased by reducing the volume, costs and liabilities associated with sludge disposal. Electrowinning is typically used to recover copper in printed circuit board manufacturing for acid copper plating, microtech dumps and cation exchange regenerations.

18.5 Automated Controls

Automating and monitoring operations is key to the application of newer integrated wastewater recycling and wastewater treatment systems. It has expertise including designing, programming and installing PLC controls, touch screen interface panels and remote monitoring. Specialists in electrical engineering and technical field service provide quick response for system adjustments and modifications when needed.

18.6 Membrane Filtration Treatment & EDI Systems

The problem of the water has been getting attentions all over the world. There are the problems like such as the access to the drinkable water, the contaminated river water problem, the industrial wastewater from the industries for the electrical products, medical products, or the foods and so forth.

18.6.1 Reverse Osmosis (RO) Water Filtration System

This system is the best accurate filtration of all effective similar systems. With this system, it is possible to dissolve substances like mineral and inorganic compounds, in addition, it allows even organic compounds whose molecular weight is about 100. The water molecular can easily get through the membrane in the system. This membrane is called semi permeable membrane. By putting pressure on the semipermeable membrane from the higher dense side, only the water molecular would go through, and rest of bigger molecular would remain. Using this fact, this system makes it possible to produce the pure water from the tap water, the well water, the seawater and the irrigation water.

1 The usage of the RO Water Filtration System

1. Transfer the well water into the drinkable water or the industrial water.
2. Produce the pure water from the industrial use water.
3. Recycle the waste water.
4. Pre-treatment of the ultra pure water.
5. Transfer the sea water and irrigational water into the drinkable water or the pure water.

2) The other membrane filtration systems

There are the other filtration systems with the different types of membranes, besides the RO Water Filtrations System.

MF Filtration system (MF membrane, microfiltration): the particles about 0.1μm - 1μm can be eliminated. *UF Filtration System (UF membrane, ultrafiltration):* the particles about 20Å - 1,000Å can be eliminated. MF *Filtration System (MF membrane, nanofiltration):* the particle about 1nm(10Å) can be eliminated.

The usage of the systems

1) High technological treatment of the upper water (elimination of the bacteria)
2) Recycling of the waste water
3) Producing of the water for industrial use from well water

3) Electro Deionization (EDI) System

Electro Deionization System, in place of the former ion-exchange resin tower, is an attractive alternative to mixed-bed or twin-bed into exchange for the ultrapure projects without regeneration chemicals. EDI system makes it possible to produce the ultrapure project, by observing the cation and the ion in the actual water into the ion-exchange membrane in the equipment. EDI system, combined with a RO system for pre-treatment, can produce 18 mega-ohms permeate. Because of the electric exchange, many regeneration chemicals are needed which can reduce the cost as well.

4) Pre-treatment & Post-treatment

In order to give full play of these equipment such as filtrations systems; RO, NF, UF, MF Membranes, and EDI System, for the ultrapure water production, the wastewater recycling system, the purification system, industrial water production and so forth.

18.7 Reverse Osmosis

18.7.1 Solarflow Operates in Remote Regions

The solarflow units, manufactured by solar energy systems which uses solar power to pump water from brackish sources below the surface and passes it through RO membranes, removing pathogens, metals and dissolved solids, with just 20% of the power of a standard RO unit. Each unit can produce 500 liters of water per day from a single 100 watt solar panel.

The solarflow is designed specifically for operation from solar panels, combining the solarflow RO unitwith a sun mill solar water pump, a sun tracer tracking array, solar panels and a purpose-built stand with storage tanks. The system can be erected wherever clean water is required as long as an acceptable water source is located nearby. Solarflow is completely automatic and designed for easy periodic maintenance.

In operation, the solar pump delivers pre-treated source water to a header tank on the RO system. Upto 4,500 liters are stored in the tank, which may be used for any non-potable purpose. Water from the header tank then is filtered once again, driven by the static head pressure combined with the positive displacement piston pump in the solarflow unit. The pump then forces the pre-filtered feed through spiral RO membranes housed in a corrosion proof cylinder. About 15% of pumped water is purified; the remaining water is used to flush the membrane constantly, minimizing foulant build-up and maintenance requirements.

The still-pressurized wastewater is used to pump more water through the system *via* an energy recovery system. This system makes the unit self-starting and self-regulating at all operational speeds from sunrise to sunset and also enables battery-free operation. Purified ready-for-use water is sent to a storage tank on the bottom level of the solarflow system. Since the TDS concentration of the wastewater is raised by only about 15%, the water may be used for non-potable purposes.

18.8 Water Purification Could Drive Economic Development

Recent studies indicate that investments in a nation's water sector can drive economic growth, improve health and reduce poverty. The cost of making such investments is within the reach of most developing regions and in some cases could be quite small. Funding as little as $4 to $7 per capita annually in countries such as Tanzania, Bangladesh, Cambodia, Ghana and Uganda could result in health, agricultural and industrial sector benefits ranging from $3 to $34 (in some cases as high as $60) for every dollar invested.

Benefits are dependent on the region and the technologies applied in water supply, sanitation and water resource management. Manufacturers of membrane equipment will most likely not see immediate widespread adoption of their advanced water and wastewater treatment processes by emerging nations. But, opportunities may exist in small portable systems capable of operating at remote locations, possibly those using alternative energy sources. In "Making Water a Part of Economic Development: The Economic Benefits of Improved Water Management & Services," a report developed jointly by the Stockholm International Water Institute and the World Health Organization, the authors noted that the GDPs of poor countries with access to improved water and sanitation average an annual growth rate of 3.7%, while those without adequate investment see GDP grow at only 0.1% annually.

Investing in water is also a good business. Improved water supply and sanitation contributes significantly to increased production and productivity within the various economic sectors. The report estimates that 322 million working days per year, and an annual global value of $750 million from working days are gained as a result of improved health. Better water and sanitation also create a competitive advantage for attracting business investment.

The report establishes an investment priority list: improve access to safe water supply, basic sanitation and hygiene, including household water management; protect the integrity of aquatic and water-related terrestrial ecosystems; and invest in water resource management including, where feasible, hydraulic infrastructures such as dams and irrigation schemes. Overall, the public and private investments demands for improved water supply and sanitation, and water resources management are considerable. But, broken down nationally, meeting such investment challenges by 2015 is clearly feasible generally small, the cost of alternative supply is high, and the underground water present beneath islands represents a suitable water source.

Two major barriers to renewable energy-powered infrastructures in remote areas have been high up-front capital costs and the difficulties ensuring maintenance of the system. Other remote RO systems are powered mostly by diesel. Solarflow is less expensive than diesel-powered systems on a price per liter basis and have none of the fossil fuel's impact on air pollution, climate change or maintenance problems. Besides solar energy's novel combination of solar power and water purification, the company has a unique business model: selling the treated water, not the means to produce it, a strategy that has not been tried before in the solar field.

18.8.1 Electrochemical Degassing Improves Economics of ED

An Australian chemist has discovered that degassing seawater prior to electrodialysis (ED) could improve the efficiency and economics of applying the process to desalination. Removing trace amounts of nitrogen and oxygen dramatically increases the water's ability to conduct electricity. Electrodialysis uses an electrical current and an arrangement of permeable membranes to separate sodium and chloride ions from seawater, leaving water suitable for drinking or irrigation. In previous work, which challenges basic thought regarding the properties of water, the chemist found he could mix oil and water by removing oxygen and nitrogen gas from the mixture. Removing traces of gas also had another, unexpected effect, increasing the water's electrical conductivity by a factor of 20. Pashley theorizes this is because the trace gases disturb the structure of the water, reducing electrical conductivity. Dissolved nitrogen had been assumed to have no influence on conductivity. But, the studies showing water molecules only form two strong bonds per molecule means that the effect of dissolved gas molecules might be quite dramatic in reducing water's conductivity. Recycling of industrial effluent by chemical treatments are discussed with details about RO plant, filtration evaporation.

— — —

19

Evapotranspiration

19.1 Introduction

The combination of two separate processes whereby water is lost on the one hand from the soil surface by evaporation and on the other hand from the tree by transpiration is referred to as evapotranspiration (ET).

19.2 Evaporation

Evaporation is the process whereby liquid water is converted into water vapour (vaporization) and removed from the evaporating surface (vapour removal). Water evaporates from a variety of surfaces, such as lakes, rivers, pavements, soils and wet vegetation. (Penman, 1963).

Energy is required to change the state of the molecules of water from liquid to vapour. Direct solar radiation and, to a lesser extent, the ambient temperature of the air provide this energy. The driving force to remove water vapour from the evaporating surface is the difference between the water vapour pressure at the evaporating surface and that of the surrounding atmosphere. As evaporation proceeds, the surrounding air becomes gradually saturated and the process will slow down and might stop if the wet air is not transferred to the atmosphere. The replacement of the saturated air with drier air depends greatly on wind speed. Hence, solar radiation, air temperature, air humidity and wind speed are climatological parameters to consider when assessing the evaporation process.

Where the evaporating surface is the soil surface, the degree of shading of the tree canopy and the amount of water available at the evaporating surface are other factors that affect the evaporation process. Frequent rains, irrigation and water transported upwards in a soil from a shallow water table wet the soil surface. Where the soil is able to supply water fast enough to satisfy the evaporation demand, the evaporation from the soil is determined only by the meteorological conditions. However, where the interval between rains and irrigation becomes large and the ability of the soil to conduct moisture to pear the surface is small, the water content in the topsoil drops and the soil surface dries out. Under these circumstances the limited availability of water exerts a controlling influence on soil evaporation. In the absence of any supply of water to the soil surface, evaporation decreases rapidly and may cease almost completely within a few days.

19.3 Transpiration

Transpiration consists of the vaporization of liquid water contained in plant tissues and the vapour removal to the atmosphere. Trees predominately lose their water through stomata. These are small openings on the plant leaf through which gases and water vapour pass (Fig 19.1). The water,

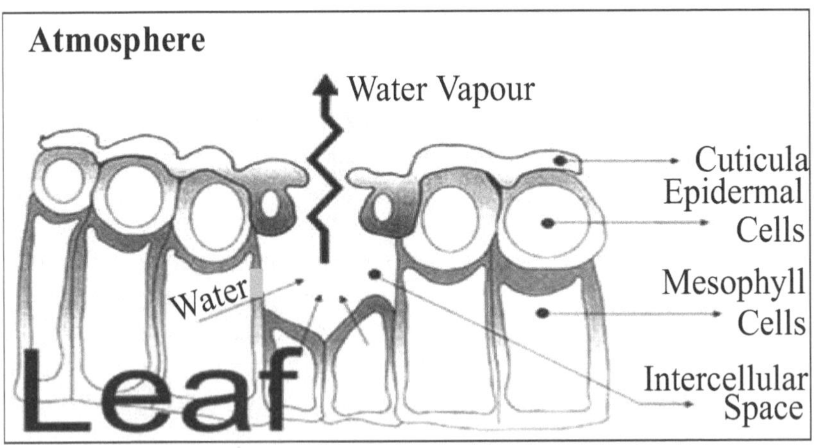

Figure 19.1: Structure of a Leaf Area with Transport of Water

together with some nutrients, is taken up by the roots and transported through the plant. The vaporization occurs within the leaf, namely in the intercellular spaces, and the vapour exchange with the atmosphere is controlled by the stomatal aperture. Nearly all water taken up is lost by transpiration and only a tiny fraction is used within the plant.

Transpiration, like direct evaporation, depends on the energy supply, vapour pressure gradient and wind. Hence, radiation, air temperature, air humidity and wind terms should be considered when assessing transpiration. The soil water content and the ability of the soil to conduct water to the roots also determine the transpiration rate, as do waterlogging and soil water salinity. The transpiration rate is also influenced by tree characteristics, environmental aspects and cultivation practices. Different kinds of plants may have different transpiration rates. Not only the type of tree, but also the tree development, environment and management should be considered when assessing transpiration.

19.4 Evapotranspiration (ET)

Evaporation and transpiration occur simultaneously and there is no easy way of distinguishing between the two processes. Apart from the water availability in the topsoil, the evaporation from a treeped soil is mainly determined by the fraction of the solar radiation reaching the soil surface. This fraction decreases over the growing period as the tree develops and the tree canopy shades more and more of the ground area. When the tree is small, water is predominately lost by soil evaporation, but once the tree is well developed and completely covers the soil, transpiration becomes the main process. In Figure 19.2 the partitioning of evapotranspiration into evaporation and transpiration is plotted in correspondence to leaf area per unit surface of soil below it. At sowing nearly 100% of ET comes from evaporation, while at full tree cover more than 90% of ET comes from transpiration. (Pereira, 1996).

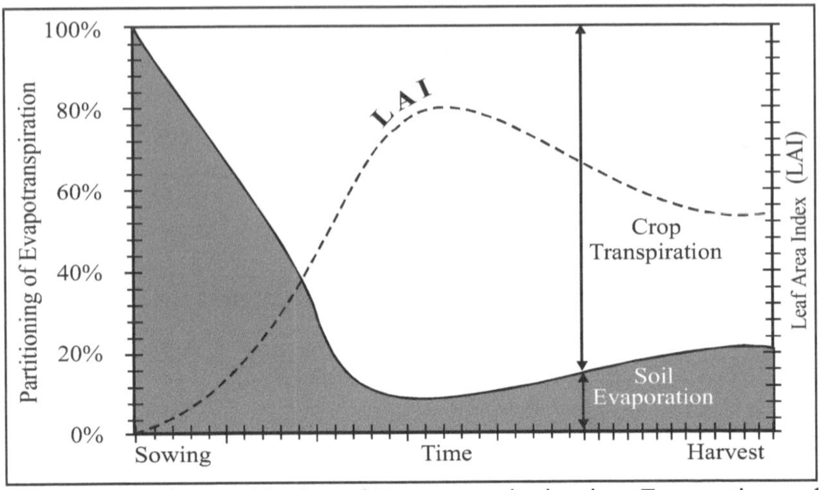

Figure 19.2: The Partitioning of Evapotranspiration into Evaporation and Transpiration

19.5 Factors affecting evapotranspiration

Weather parameters, tree characteristics, management and environmental aspects are factors affecting evaporation and transpiration.

19.5.1 Weather parameters

The principal weather parameters affecting evapotranspiration are radiation, air temperature, humidity and wind speed. Several procedures have been developed to assess the evaporation rate from these parameters. The evaporation power of the atmosphere is expressed by the reference tree evapotranspiration (ET_o). The reference tree evapotranspiration represents the evapotranspiration from a standardized vegetated surface.

19.5.2 Tree factors

The tree type, variety and development stage should be considered when assessing the evapotranspiration from trees grown in large, well-managed fields. Differences in resistance to transpiration, tree height, tree roughness, reflection, ground cover and tree rooting characteristics result in different ET levels in different types of trees under identical environmental conditions. Tree evapotranspiration under standard conditions (ET_c) refers to the evaporating demand from trees that are grown in large fields under optimum soil water, excellent management and environmental conditions, and achieve full production under the given climatic conditions.

19.5.3 Management and environmental conditions

Factors such as soil salinity, poor land fertility, limited application of fertilizers, the presence of hard or impenetrable soil horizons, the absence of control of diseases and pests and poor soil management may limit the tree development and reduce the evapotranspiration. Other factors to be considered when assessing ET are ground cover, plant density and the soil water content. The effect of soil water content on ET is conditioned primarily by the magnitude of the water deficit and the type of soil. On the other hand, too much water will result in waterlogging which might damage the root and limit root water uptake by inhibiting respiration.

When assessing the ET rate in industrial effluent irrigation, additional consideration should be given to the range of management practices that act on the climatic and tree factors affecting the ET process. Cultivation practices and the type of irrigation method can alter the microclimate, affect the tree characteristics or affect the wetting of the soil and tree surface. A windbreak reduces wind velocities and decreases the ET rate of the field directly beyond the barrier. The effect can be significant especially in windy, warm and dry conditions although evapotranspiration from the trees themselves may offset any reduction in the field. Soil evaporation in a young orchard, where trees are widely spaced, can be reduced by using a well-designed drip or trickle irrigation system. The drippers apply water directly to the soil near trees, thereby leaving the major part of the soil surface dry, and limiting the evaporation losses. The use of mulches, especially when the tree is small, is another way of substantially reducing soil evaporation. Anti-transpirants, such as stomata-closing, film-forming or reflecting material, reduce the water losses from the tree.

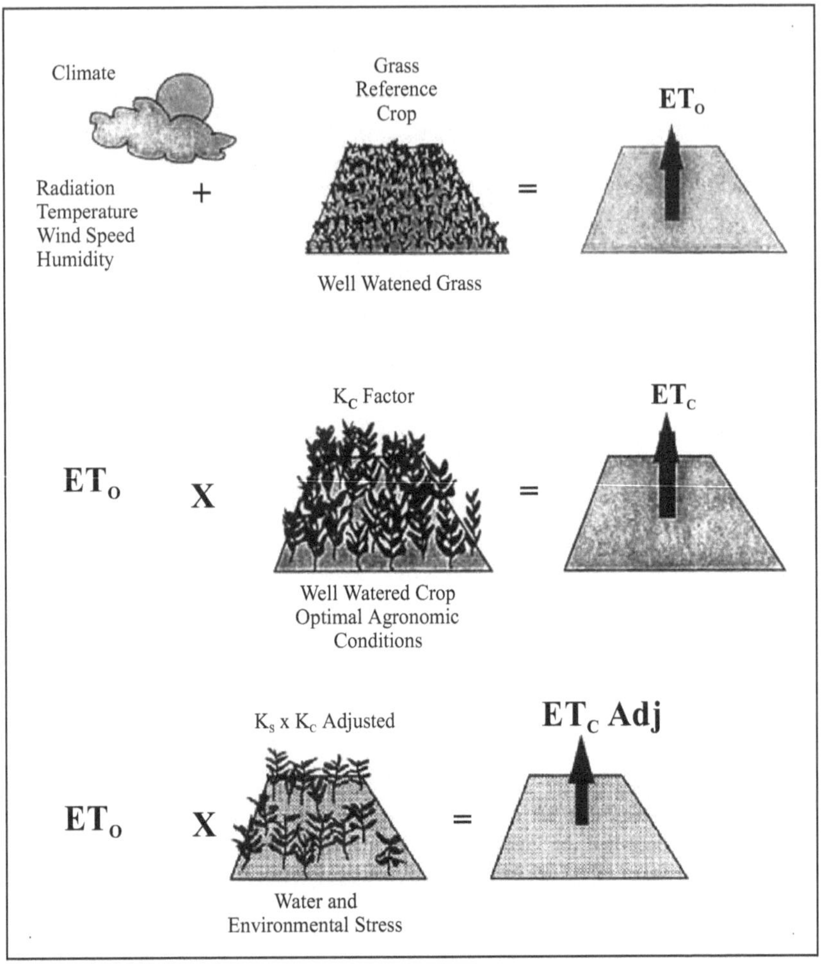

Figure 19.3: Reference (ET_o), Tree Evapotranspiration under Standard (ET_c) and Non-Standard Conditions ($ET_{c\,Adj}$)

Where field conditions differ from the standard conditions, correction factors are required to adjust ET_c. The adjustment reflects the effect on tree evapotranspiration of the environmental and management conditions in the field.

19.6 Evapotranspiration Concepts

Distinctions are made (Figure 19.3) between reference tree evapotranspiration (ET_o), tree evapotranspiration under standard conditions (ET_c) and tree evapotranspiration under non-standard conditions ($ET_{c\ adj}$). ET_o is a climatic parameter expressing the evaporation power of the atmosphere. ET_c refers to the evapotranspiration from excellently managed, large, well-watered fields that achieve full production under the given climatic conditions. Due to sub-optimal tree management and environmental constraints that affect tree growth and limit evapotranspiration, ET_c under non-standard conditions generally requires a correction. (Pereira *et.al.,* 1996).

19.6.1 Reference Tree Evapotranspiration (ET_o)

The evapotranspiration rate from a reference surface, not short of water, is called the reference tree evapotranspiration or reference evapotranspiration and is denoted as ET_o. The reference surface is a hypothetical grass reference tree with specific characteristics. The use of other denominations such as potential ET is strongly discouraged due to ambiguities in their definitions. (Allen *et.al.,* 1994a).

The concept of the reference evapotranspiration was introduced to study the evaporative demand of the atmosphere independently of tree type, tree development and management practices. As water is abundantly available at the reference evapotranspiring surface, soil factors do not affect ET. Relating ET to a specific surface provides a reference to which ET from other surfaces can be related. It obviates the need to define a separate ET level for each tree and stage of growth. ET_o values measured or calculated at different locations or in different seasons are comparable as they refer to the ET from the same reference surface.

The only factors affecting ET_o are climatic parameters. Consequently, ET_o is a climatic parameter and can be computed from weather data. ET_o expresses the evaporating power of the atmosphere at a specific location and time of the year and does not consider the tree characteristics and soil factors. The FAO Penman-Monteith method is recommended as the sole method for determining ET_o. The method has been selected because it closely approximates grass ET_o at the location evaluated, is physically based, and explicitly incorporates both physiological and aerodynamic parameters. Moreover, procedures have been developed for estimating missing climatic parameters.

Typical ranges for ET_o values for different agroclimatic regions are given in Table 19.1. These values are intended to familiarize inexperienced users with typical ranges, and are not intended for direct application.

19.7 Tree Evapotranspiration Under Standard Conditions (ET_c)

The tree evapotranspiration under standard conditions, denoted as ET_c, is the evapotranspiration from disease-free, well-fertilized trees, grown in large fields, under optimum soil water conditions, and achieving full production under the given climatic conditions.

Table 19.1: Average ET_o for different agroclimatic regions in mm/day

Regions	Mean daily temperature (°C)		
	Cool ~10°C	Moderate 20°C	Warm > 30°C
- Humid and sub-humid	2 - 3	3 - 5	5 - 7
- Arid and semi-arid	2 - 4	4 - 6	6 - 8
Temperate region			
- Humid and sub-humid	1 - 2	2 - 4	4 - 7
-Arid and semi-arid	1 - 3	4 - 7	6 - 9

The amount of water required to compensate the evapotranspiration loss from the treeped field is defined as tree water requirement. Although the values for tree evapotranspiration and tree water requirement are identical, tree water requirement refers to the amount of water that needs to be supplied, while tree evapotranspiration refers to the amount of water that is lost through evapotranspiration. The irrigation water requirement basically represents the difference between the tree water requirement and effective precipitation. The irrigation water requirement also includes additional water for leaching of salts and to compensate for non-uniformity of water application. (Perrier, 1985).

Tree evapotranspiration can be calculated from climatic data and by integrating directly the tree resistance, albedo and air resistance factors in the Penman-Monteith approach. As there is still a considerable lack of information for different trees, the Penman-Monteith method is used for the estimation of the standard reference tree to determine its evapotranspiration rate, *i.e.*, ET_o. Experimentally determined ratios of ET_c/ET_o, called tree coefficients (K_c), are used to relate ET_c to ET_o or $ET_c = K_c$ ET_o.

Differences in leaf anatomy, stomatal characteristics, aerodynamic properties and even albedo cause the tree evapotranspiration to differ from the reference tree evapotranspiration under the same climatic conditions. Due to variations in the tree characteristics throughout its growing season, K_c for a given tree changes from sowing till harvest.

19.8 Tree Evapotranspiration Under Non-standard Conditions ($ET_{c\ adj}$)

The tree evapotranspiration under non-standard conditions ($ET_{c\ adj}$) is the evapotranspiration from trees grown under management and environmental conditions that differ from the standard conditions. When cultivating trees in fields, the real tree evapotranspiration may deviate from ET_c due to non-optimal conditions such as the presence of pests and diseases, soil salinity, low soil fertility, water shortage or waterlogging. This may result in scanty plant growth, low plant density and may reduce the evapotranspiration rate below ET_c.

The tree evapotranspiration under non-standard conditions is calculated by using a water stress coefficient K_s and/or by adjusting K_c for all kinds of other stresses and environmental constraints on tree evapotranspiration.

19.9 Determining Evapotranspiration

19.9.1 ET Measurement

Evapotranspiration is not easy to measure. Specific devices and accurate measurements of various physical parameters or the soil water balance in lysimeters are required to determine evapotranspiration. The methods are often expensive, demanding in terms of accuracy of measurement and can only be fully exploited by well-trained research personnel. Although the methods are inappropriate for routine measurements, they remain important for the evaluation of ET estimates obtained by more indirect methods. (Rijtema, 1965).

19.9.2 Energy Balance and Microclimatological Methods

Evaporation of water requires relatively large amounts of energy, either in the form of sensible heat or radiant energy. Therefore the evapotranspiration process is governed by energy exchange at the vegetation surface and is limited by the amount of energy available. Because of this limitation, it is possible to predict the evapotranspiration rate by applying the principle of energy conservation. The energy arriving at the surface must equal the energy leaving the surface for the same time period.

All fluxes of energy should be considered when deriving an energy balance equation. The equation for an evaporating surface can be written as:

$$R_n - G - ET - H = 0 \qquad (1)$$

where R_n is the net radiation, H the sensible heat, G the soil heat flux and ET the latent heat flux. The various terms can be either positive or negative. Positive R_n supplies energy to the surface and positive G, ET and H remove energy from the surface.

In Equation 1 only vertical fluxes are considered and the net rate at which energy is being transferred horizontally, by advection, is ignored. Therefore the equation is to be applied to large, extensive surfaces of homogeneous vegetation only. The equation is restricted to the four components: R_n, ET, H and G.

Other energy terms, such as heat stored or released in the plant, or the energy used in metabolic activities, are not considered These terms account for only a small fraction of the daily net radiation and can be considered negligible when compared with the other four components.

The latent heat flux (ET) representing the evapotranspiration fraction can be derived from the energy balance equation if all other components are known. Net radiation (R_n) and soil heat fluxes (G) can be measured or estimated from climatic parameters. Measurements of the sensible heat (H) are however complex and cannot be easily obtained. H requires accurate measurement of temperature gradients above the surface. (Allen *et.al.,* 1994).

Another method of estimating evapotranspiration is the mass transfer method. This approach considers the vertical movement of small parcels of air (eddies) above a large homogeneous surface. The eddies transport material (water vapour) and energy (heat, momentum) from and towards the evaporating surface. By assuming steady state conditions and that the eddy transfer coefficients for water vapour are proportional to those for heat and momentum, the evapotranspiration rate can be computed from the vertical gradients of air temperature and water vapour via the Bowen ratio. Other direct measurement methods use gradients of wind speed and water vapour. These methods and other methods such as eddy covariance, require accurate measurement of vapour pressure, and air temperature or wind speed at different levels above the surface. Therefore, their application is restricted to primarily research situations.

19.9.3 Soil water balance

Evapotranspiration can also be determined by measuring the various components of the soil water balance. The method consists of assessing the incoming and outgoing water flux into the tree root zone over some time period. Irrigation (I) and rainfall (P) add water to the root zone. Part of I and P might be lost by surface runoff and by deep percolation (DP) that will eventually recharge the water table. Water might also be transported upward by capillary rise (CR) from a shallow water table towards the root zone or even transferred horizontally by subsurface flow in (SF_{in}) or out of (SF_{out}) the root zone. In many situations, however, except under conditions with large slopes, SF_{in} and SF_{out} are minor and can be ignored. Soil evaporation and tree transpiration deplete water from the root zone. If all fluxes other than evapotranspiration (ET) can be assessed, the evapotranspiration can be deduced from the change in soil water content (SW) over the time period:

$$ET = I + P - RO - DP + CR \pm SF \pm SW \qquad (2)$$

Some fluxes such as subsurface flow, deep percolation and capillary rise from a water table are difficult to assess and short time periods cannot be considered. The soil water balance method can usually only give ET estimates over long time periods of the order of week-long or ten-day periods.

19.9.4 Lysimeters

By isolating the tree root zone from its environment and controlling the processes that are difficult to measure, the different terms in the soil water balance equation can be determined with greater accuracy. This is done in lysimeters where the tree grows in isolated tanks filled with either disturbed or undisturbed soil. In precision weighing lysimeters, where the water loss is directly measured by the change of mass, evapotranspiration can be obtained with an accuracy of a few hundredths of a millimetre, and small time periods such as an hour can be considered. In non-weighing lysimeters the evapotranspiration for a given time period is determined by deducting the drainage water, collected at the bottom of the lysimeters, from the total water input.

A requirement of lysimeters is that the vegetation both inside and immediately outside of the lysimeter be perfectly matched (same height and leaf area index). This requirement has historically not been closely adhered to in a majority of lysimeter studies and has resulted in severely erroneous and unrepresentative ET_c and K_c data. As lysimeters are difficult and expensive to construct and as their operation and maintenance require special care, their use is limited to specific research purposes.

19.10 ET Computed from Meteorological Data

Owing to the difficulty of obtaining accurate field measurements, ET is commonly computed from weather data. A large number of empirical or semi-empirical equations have been developed for assessing tree or reference tree evapotranspiration from meteorological data. Some of the methods are only valid under specific climatic and agronomic conditions and cannot be applied under conditions different from those under which they were originally developed.

Numerous researchers have analysed the performance of the various calculation methods for different locations. As a result of an Expert Consultation held in May 1990, the FAO Penman-Monteith method is now recommended as the standard method for the definition and computation of the reference evapotranspiration, ET_o. The ET from tree surfaces under standard conditions is determined by tree coefficients (K_c) that relate ET_c to ET_o. The ET from tree surfaces under non-standard conditions is adjusted by a water stress coefficient (K_s) and/or by modifying the tree coefficient.

19.11 ET Estimated from Pan Evaporation

Evaporation from an open water surface provides an index of the integrated effect of radiation, air temperature, air humidity and wind on evapotranspiration. However, differences in the water and treeped surface produce significant differences in the water loss from an open water surface and the tree. The pan has proved its practical value and has been used successfully to estimate reference evapotranspiration by observing the evaporation loss from a water surface and applying empirical coefficients to relate pan evaporation to ET_o (Christiansen, 1968).

19.12 FAO Penman-Monteith Equation

This chapter introduces the user to the need to standardize one method to compute reference evapotranspiration (ET_o) from meteorological data. The FAO Penman-Monteith method is recommended as the sole ET_o method for determining reference evapotranspiration. The method, its derivation, the required meteorological data and the corresponding definition of the reference surface are described in this chapter. (Penman, 1948).

19.13 Need for a Standard ET_o Method

A large number of more or less empirical methods have been developed over the last 50 years by numerous scientists and specialists worldwide to estimate evapotranspiration from different climatic variables. Relationships were often subject to rigorous local calibrations and proved to have limited global validity. Testing the accuracy of the methods under a new set of conditions is laborious, time-consuming and costly, and yet evapotranspiration data are frequently needed at short notice for project planning or irrigation scheduling design. The Blaney-Criddle, radiation, modified Penman and pan evaporation methods. The modified Penman method was considered to offer the best results with minimum possible error in relation to a living grass reference tree. It is expected that the pan method would give acceptable estimates, depending on the location of the pan. The radiation method is suggested for areas where available climatic data include measured air temperature and sunshine, cloudiness and radiation, but not measured wind speed and air humidity. Finally, the proposed the use of the Blaney-Criddle method for areas where available climatic data cover air temperature data only.

These climatic methods to calculate ET_o are all calibrated for ten-day or monthly calculations, not for daily or hourly calculations. The Blaney-Criddle method is recommended for periods of one month or longer. For the pan method it is suggested that calculations should be done for periods of ten days or longer. Users have not always respected these conditions and calculations have often been done on daily time steps.

Advances in research and the more accurate assessment of tree water use have revealed weaknesses in the methodologies. Numerous researchers and scientists analysed the performance of the four methods for different locations. Although the results of such analyses can have been influenced by site or measurement conditions or by bias in weather data collection, it became evident that the proposed methods do not behave the same way in different locations around the world. Deviations from computed to observed values are often found to exceed ranges indicated by FAO. The modified Penman is frequently found to overestimate ET_o, even by up to 20% for low evaporative conditions. The other FAO recommended equations showed variable adherence to the reference tree evapotranspiration standard of grass.

To evaluate the performance of these and other estimation procedures under different climatological conditions, a major study was undertaken under the auspices of the Committee on Irrigation Water Requirements of the American Society of Civil Engineers (ASCE). The ASCE study analysed the performance of 20 different methods, using detailed procedures to assess the validity of the methods compared to a set of carefully screened lysimeter data from elevan locations with variable climatic conditions. The study proved very revealing and showed the widely varying performance of the methods under different climatic conditions. In a parallel study commissioned by the European Community, a consortium of European Research Institutes evaluated the performance of various evapotranspiration methods using data from different lysimeter studies in Europe. The comparative studies may be summarized as follows:

- The Penman methods may require local calibration of the wind function to achieve satisfactory results.
- The radiation methods show good results in humid climates where the aerodynamic term is relatively small, but performance in arid conditions is erratic and tends to underestimate evapotranspiration.

- Temperature methods remain empirical and require local calibration in order to achieve satisfactory results. A possible exception is the 1985 Hargreaves' method which has shown reasonable ET_o results with a global validity.
- Pan evapotranspiration methods clearly reflect the shortcomings of predicting tree evapotranspiration from open water evaporation. The methods are susceptible to the microclimatic conditions under which the pans are operating and the rigour of station maintenance. Their performance proves erratic.
- The relatively accurate and consistent performance of the Penman-Monteith approach in both arid and humid climates has been indicated in both the ASCE and European studies.

The analysis of the performance of the various calculation methods reveals the need for formulating a standard method for the computation of ET_o. The FAO Penman-Monteith method is recommended as the sole standard method. It is a method with strong likelihood of correctly predicting ET_o in a wide range of locations and climates and has provision for application in data-short situations. The use of older FAO or other reference ET methods is no longer encouraged.

19.14 Formulation of the Penman-Monteith Equation

19.14.1 Penman-Monteith Equation

In 1948, Penman combined the energy balance with the mass transfer method and derived an equation to compute the evaporation from an open water surface from standard climatological records of sunshine, temperature, humidity and wind speed. This so-called combination method was further developed by many researchers and extended to treeped surfaces by introducing resistance factors.

The resistance nomenclature distinguishes between aerodynamic resistance and surface resistance factors. The surface resistance parameters are often combined into one parameter, the 'bulk' surface resistance parameter which operates in series with the aerodynamic resistance. The surface resistance, r_s, describes the resistance of vapour flow through stomata openings, total leaf area and soil surface. The aerodynamic resistance, r_a, describes the resistance from the vegetation upward and involves friction from air flowing over vegetative surfaces. Although the exchange process in a vegetation layer is too complex to be fully described by the two resistance factors, good correlations can be obtained between measured and calculated evapotranspiration rates, especially for a uniform grass reference surface.

The Penman-Monteith form of the combination equation is:

$$\lambda ET = \frac{\Delta(R_n - G) + \rho_a c_p \frac{(e_s - e_a)}{r_a}}{\Delta + \gamma\left(1 + \frac{r_s}{r_a}\right)} \qquad (3)$$

where R_n is the net radiation, G is the soil heat flux, $(e_s - e_a)$ represents the vapour pressure deficit of the air, $_a$ is the mean air density at constant pressure, c_p is the specific heat of the air, represents the slope of the saturation vapour pressure temperature relationship, is the psychrometric constant, and r_s and r_a are the (bulk) surface and aerodynamic resistances.

The Penman-Monteith approach as formulated above includes all parameters that govern energy exchange and corresponding latent heat flux (evapotranspiration) from uniform expanses of vegetation. Most of the parameters are measured or can be readily calculated from weather data. The equation can be utilized for the direct calculation of any tree evapotranspiration as the surface and aerodynamic resistances are tree specific.

19.14.2 Aerodynamic Resistance (r_a)

The transfer of heat and water vapour from the evaporating surface into the air above the canopy is determined by the aerodynamic resistance:

$$r_a = \frac{\ln\left[\frac{z_m - d}{z_{om}}\right]\ln\left[\frac{z_h - d}{z_{oh}}\right]}{k^2 u_z} \quad (4)$$

where

r_a aerodynamic resistance [s m^{-1}],
z_m height of wind measurements [m],
z_h height of humidity measurements [m],
d zero plane displacement height [m],
z_{om} roughness length governing momentum transfer [m],
z_{oh} roughness length governing transfer of heat and vapour [m],
k von Karman's constant, 0.41 [-],
u_z wind speed at height z [m s^{-1}].

The equation is restricted for neutral stability conditions, *i.e.,* where temperature, atmospheric pressure, and wind velocity distributions follow nearly adiabatic conditions (no heat exchange). The application of the equation for short time periods (hourly or less) may require the inclusion of corrections for stability. However, when predicting ET_o in the well-watered reference surface, heat exchanged is small, and therefore stability correction is normally not required. (Monteith, 1973).

Many studies have explored the nature of the wind regime in plant canopies. Zero displacement heights and roughness lengths have to be considered when the surface is covered by vegetation. The factors depend upon the tree height and architecture. Several empirical equations for the estimate of d, z_{om} and z_{oh} have been developed.

19.14.3 (Bulk) Surface Resistance (r_s)

The 'bulk' surface resistance describes the resistance of vapour flow through the transpiring tree and evaporating soil surface. Where the vegetation does not completely cover the soil, the resistance factor should indeed include the effects of the evaporation from the soil surface. If the tree is not transpiring at a potential rate, the resistance depends also on the water status of the vegetation.

The Leaf Area Index (LAI), a dimensionless quantity, is the leaf area (upper side only) per unit area of soil below it. It is expressed as m² leaf area per m² ground area. The active LAI is the index of the leaf area that actively contributes to the surface heat and vapour transfer. It is generally the upper, sunlit portion of a dense canopy. The LAI values for various trees differ widely but values of 3-5 are common for many mature trees. For a given tree, green LAI changes throughout the season and normally reaches its maximum before or at flowering LAI further depends on the plant density and the tree variety.

The bulk stomatal resistance, r_l, is the average resistance of an individual leaf. This resistance is tree specific and differs among tree varieties and tree management. It usually increases as the tree ages and begins to ripen. There is, however, a lack of consolidated information on changes in r_l over time for the different trees. The information available in the literature on stomatal conductance or resistance is often oriented toward physiological or ecophysiological studies.

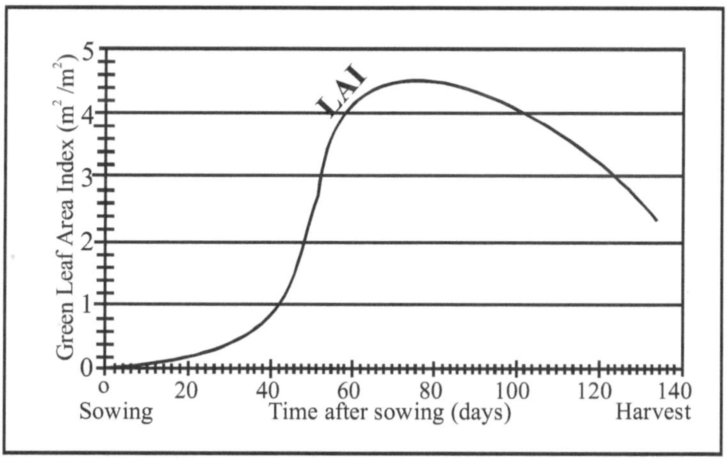

Figure 19.4: Typical Variation in the Active (Green) Leaf Area Index Over the Growing Season for a Maize Tree.

The stomatal resistance, r_l, is influenced by climate and by water availability. However, influences vary from one tree to another tree and different varieties can be affected differently. The resistance increases when the tree is water stressed and the soil water availability limits tree evapotranspiration. Some studies indicate that stomatal resistance is influenced to some extent by radiation intensity, temperature, and vapour pressure deficit.

19.14.4 Reference Surface

To obviate the need to define unique evaporation parameters for each tree and stage of growth, the concept of a reference surface was introduced. Evapotranspiration rates of the various trees are related to the evapotranspiration rate from the reference surface (ET_0) by means of tree coefficients.

In the past, an open water surface has been proposed as a reference surface. However, the differences in aerodynamic, vegetation control and radiation characteristics present a strong challenge in relating ET to measurements of free water evaporation. Relating ET_0 to a specific tree has the advantage of incorporating the biological and physical processes involved in ET from tree surfaces. (Monteith & Unsworth, 1990).

Grass, together with alfalfa, is a well-studied tree regarding its aerodynamic and surface characteristics and is accepted worldwide as a reference surface. Because the resistance to diffusion of vapour strongly depends on tree height, ground cover, LAI and soil moisture conditions, the characteristics of the reference tree should be well defined and fixed. Changes in tree height result in variations in the roughness and LAI. Consequently, the associated canopy and aerodynamic resistances will vary appreciably with time. Moreover, water stress and the degree of ground cover have an effect on the resistances and also on the albedo.

To avoid problems of local calibration which would require demanding and expensive studies, a hypothetical grass reference has been selected (Fig. 19.5). Difficulties with a living grass reference result from the fact that the grass variety and morphology can significantly affect the evapotranspiration rate, especially during peak water use. Large differences may exist between warm-season and cool-season grass types. Cool-season grasses have a lower degree of stomatal control and hence higher rates of evapotranspiration. It may be difficult to grow cool-season grasses in some arid, tropical climates.

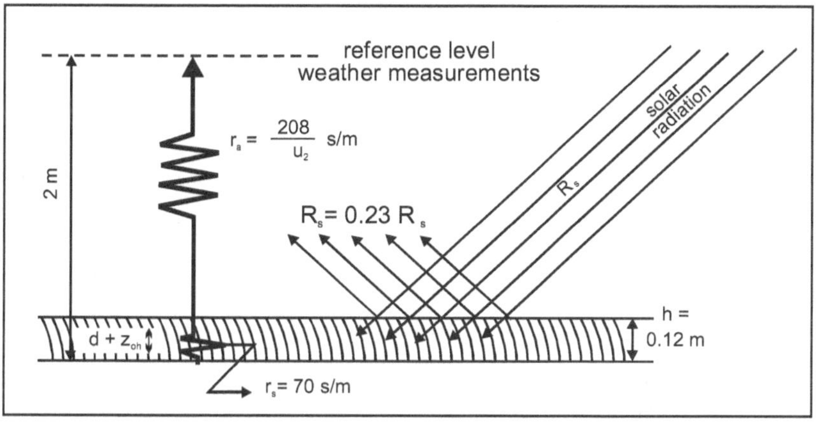

Figure 19.5: Characteristics of The Hypothetical Reference Tree

The FAO Expert Consultation on Revision of FAO Methodologies for Tree Water Requirements accepted the following unambiguous definition for the reference surface: "A hypothetical reference tree with an assumed tree height of 0.12 m, a fixed surface resistance of 70 s/m^{-1} and an albedo of 0.23."

The reference surface closely resembles an extensive surface of green grass of uniform height, actively growing, completely shading the ground and with adequate water. The requirements that the grass surface should be extensive and uniform result from the assumption that all fluxes are one-dimensional upwards.

The FAO Penman-Monteith method is selected as the method by which the evapotranspiration of this reference surface (ET_o) can be unambiguously determined, and as the method which provides consistent ET_o values in all regions and climates.

19.14.5 Equation

A consultation of experts and researchers are organized by FAO in May 1990, in collaboration with the International

Commission for Irrigation and Drainage and with the World Meteorological Organization, to review the FAO methodologies on tree water requirements and to advise on the revision and update of procedures.

The panel of experts recommended the adoption of the Penman-Monteith combination method as a new standard for reference evapotranspiration and advised on procedures for calculation of the various parameters. By defining the reference tree as a hypothetical tree with an assumed height of 0.12 m having a surface resistance of 70 s m^{-1} and an albedo of 0.23, closely resembling the evaporation of an extension surface of green grass of uniform height, actively growing and adequately watered, the FAO Penman-Monteith method was developed. The method overcomes shortcomings of the previous FAO Penman method and provides values more consistent with actual tree water use data worldwide.

From the original Penman-Monteith equation (Equation 3) and the equations of the aerodynamic (Equation 4) and surface resistance (Equation 5), the FAO Penman-Monteith method to estimate ET_o can be derived.

$$ET_o = \frac{0.408\Delta(R_n - G) + \gamma \frac{900}{T+273} u_2 (e_s - e_a)}{\Delta + \gamma(1 + 0.34u_2)} \quad (5)$$

where

ET_o reference evapotranspiration [mm day^{-1}],
R_n net radiation at the tree surface [MJ m^{-2} day^{-1}],
G soil heat flux density [MJ m^{-2} day^{-1}],
T mean daily air temperature at 2 m height [°C],
u_2 wind speed at 2 m height [m s^{-1}],
e_s saturation vapour pressure [kPa],
e_a actual vapour pressure [kPa],
$e_s - e_a$ saturation vapour pressure deficit [kPa],

The equation uses standard climatological records of solar radiation (sunshine), air temperature, humidity and wind speed. To ensure the integrity of computations, the weather measurements should be made at 2 m (or converted to that height) above an extensive surface of green grass, shading the ground and not short of water.

No weather-based evapotranspiration equation can be expected to predict evapotranspiration perfectly under every climatic situation due to simplification in formulation and errors in data measurement. It is probable that precision instruments under excellent environmental and biological management conditions will show the FAO Penman-Monteith equation to deviate at times from true measurements of grass ET_o. However, the Expert Consultation agreed to use the hypothetical reference definition of the FAO Penman-Monteith equation as the definition for grass ET_o when deriving and expressing tree coefficients.

It is important, when comparing the FAO Penman-Monteith equation to ET_o measurements, that the full Penman-Monteith equation (Equation 3) and associated equations for r_a and r_s (Equations 4 and 5) be used to enable accounting for variation in ET due to variation in height of the grass measured. Variations in measurement height can significantly change LAI, d and z_{om} and the corresponding ET_o measurement and predicted value. When evaluating results, it should be noted that local environmental and management factors, such as watering frequency, also affect ET_o observations.

The FAO Penman-Monteith equation is a close, simple representation of the physical and physiological factors governing the evapotranspiration process. By using the FAO Penman-Monteith definition for ET_o, one may calculate tree coefficients at research sites by relating the measured tree evapotranspiration (ET_c) with the calculated ET_o :

$$K_c = ET_c/ET_o \qquad (6)$$

In the tree coefficient approach, differences in the tree canopy and aerodynamic resistance relative to the hypothetical reference tree are accounted for within the tree coefficient. The K_c factor serves as an aggregation of the physical and physiological differences between trees and the reference definition.

19.14.6 Data

Apart from the site location, the FAO Penman-Monteith equation requires air temperature, humidity, radiation and wind speed data for daily, weekly, ten-day or monthly calculations. The computation of all data required for the calculation of the reference evapotranspiration is given in Chapter 3. It is important to verify the units in which the weather data are reported.

19.14.7 Location

Altitude above sea level (m) and latitude (degrees north or south) of the location should be specified. These data are needed to adjust some weather parameters for the local average value of atmospheric pressure (a function of the site elevation above mean sea level) and to compute extraterrestrial radiation (R_a) and, in some cases, daylight hours (N). In the calculation procedures for R_a and N, the latitude is expressed in radian.

A positive value is used for the northern hemisphere and a negative value for the southern hemisphere.

19.14.8 Temperature

The (average) daily maximum and minimum air temperatures in degrees Celsius (°C) are required. Where only (average) mean daily temperatures are available, the calculations can still be executed but some underestimation of ET_o will probably occur due to the non-linearity of the saturation vapour pressure - temperature relationship. Using mean air temperature instead of maximum and minimum air temperatures yields a lower saturation vapour pressure e_s, and hence a lower vapour pressure difference (e_s-e_a), and a lower reference evapotranspiration estimate.

19.14.9 Humidity

The (average) daily actual vapour pressure, e_a, in kilopascals (kPa) is required. The actual vapour pressure, where not available, can be derived from maximum and minimum relative humidity (%), psychrometric data (dry and wet bulb temperatures in °C) or dewpoint temperature (°C) according to the procedures.

19.14.10 Radiation

The (average) daily net radiation expressed in megajoules per square metre per day (MJ m^{-2} day^{-1}) is required. These data are not commonly available but can be derived from the (average) shortwave radiation measured with a pyranometer or from the (average) daily actual duration of bright sunshine (hours per day) measured with a (Campbell-Stokes) sunshine recorder.

19.14.11 Wind Speed

The (average) daily wind speed in metres per second (m s^{-1}) measured at 2 m above the ground level is required. It is important to verify the height at which wind speed is measured, as wind speeds measured at different heights above the soil surface differ. The calculation procedure to adjust wind speed to the standard height of 2 m is presented in Chapter 3.

19.14.12 Missing Climatic Data

Situations might occur where data for some weather variables are missing. The use of an alternative ET_0 calculation procedure, requiring only limited meteorological parameters, should generally be avoided. It is recommended that one calculate ET_0 using the standard FAO Penman-Monteith method after resolving the specific problem of the missing data. Differences between ET_0 values obtained with the FAO Penman-Monteith equation with, on the one hand, a limited data set and, on the other hand, a full data set, are expected to be smaller than or of similar magnitude to the differences resulting from the use of an alternative ET_0 equation.

Even where the data set contains only maximum and minimum air temperature it is still possible to obtain reasonable estimates of ten-day or monthly ET_0 with the FAO Penman-Monteith equation radiation data can be derived from the air temperature difference, or, along with wind speed and humidity data, can be imported from a nearby weather station.

Humidity data can also be estimated from daily minimum air temperature. After evaluating the validity of the use of data from another station, ten-day or monthly estimates of ET_0 can be calculated.

The procedures for estimating missing data should be validated at the regional level. This can be done for weather stations with full data sets by comparing ET_0 calculated with full and with limited data sets. The ratio should be close to one. Where the ratio deviates significantly from one, the ratio can be used as a correction factor for estimates made with the limited data set. Where the standard error of estimate exceeds 20% of the mean ET_0, a sensitivity analysis should be performed to determine causes (and limits) for the method utilized to import the missing data. A validation should be completed for each month and variable, for the monthly as well as for the daily estimates.

19.15 Meteorological Data

The methods for calculating evapotranspiration from meteorological data require various climatological and physical parameters. Some of the data are measured directly in weather stations. Other parameters are related to commonly measured data and can be derived with the help of a direct or empirical relationship. This chapter discusses the source, measurement and computation of all data required for the calculation of the reference evapotranspiration by means of the FAO Penman-Monteith method. Different examples illustrate the various calculation procedures. Appropriate procedures for estimating missing data are also provided.

19.15.1 Meteorological Factors Determining ET

The meteorological factors determining evapotranspiration are weather parameters which provide energy for vaporization and remove water vapour from the evaporating surface. The principal weather parameters to consider are explained ahead.

19.15.2 Solar Radiation

The evapotranspiration process is determined by the amount of energy available to vaporize water. Solar radiation is the largest energy source and is able to change large quantities of liquid water into water vapour. The potential amount of radiation that can reach the evaporating surface is determined by its location and time of the year. Due to differences in the position of the sun, the potential radiation differs at various latitudes and in different seasons. The actual solar radiation reaching the evaporating surface depends on the turbidity of the atmosphere and the presence of clouds which reflect and absorb major parts of the radiation. When assessing the effect of solar radiation on evapotranspiration, one should also bear in mind that not all available energy is used to vaporize water. Part of the solar energy is used to heat up the atmosphere and the soil profile.

19.15.3 Air Temperature

The solar radiation absorbed by the atmosphere and the heat emitted by the earth increase the air temperature. The sensible heat of the surrounding air transfers energy to the tree and exerts as such a controlling influence on the rate of evapotranspiration. In sunny, warm weather the loss of water by evapotranspiration is greater than in cloudy and cool weather (Fig. 19.6).

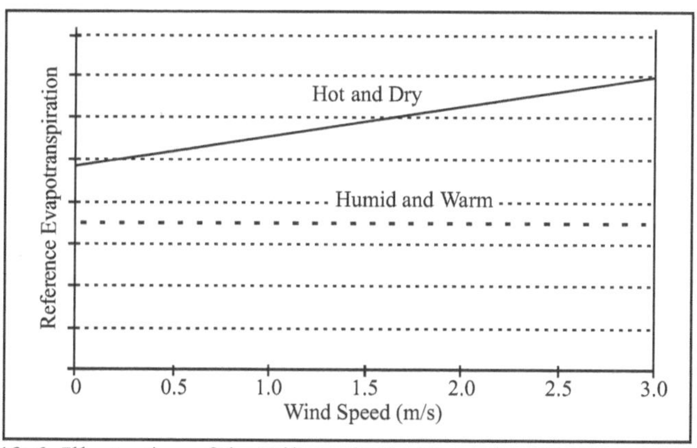

Figure 19.6: Illustration of the Effect of Wind Speed on Evapotranspiration in Hot-Dry and Humid-Warm Weather Conditions Air humidity

While the energy supply from the sun and surrounding air is the main driving force for the vaporization of water, the difference between the water vapour pressure at the evapotranspiring surface and the surrounding air is the determining factor for the vapour removal. Well-watered fields in hot dry arid regions consume large amounts of water due to the abundance of energy and the desiccating power of the atmosphere. In humid tropical regions, notwithstanding the high energy input, the high humidity of the air will reduce the evapotranspiration demand. In such an environment, the air is already close to saturation, so that less additional water can be stored and hence the evapotranspiration rate is lower than in arid regions.

19.15.4 Wind Speed

The process of vapour removal depends to a large extent on wind and air turbulence which transfers large quantities of air over the evaporating surface. When vaporizing water, the air above the evaporating surface becomes gradually saturated with water vapour. If this air is not continuously replaced with drier air, the driving force for water vapour removal and the evapotranspiration rate decreases.

The combined effect of climatic factors affecting evapotranspiration is illustrated in Figure 10 for two different climatic conditions. The evapotranspiration demand is high in hot dry weather due to the dryness of the air and the amount of energy available as direct solar radiation and latent heat. Under these circumstances, much water vapour can be stored in the air while wind may promote the transport of water allowing more water vapour to be taken up. On the other hand, under humid weather conditions, the high humidity of the air and the presence of clouds cause the evapotranspiration rate to be lower. The effect on evapotranspiration of increasing wind speeds for the two different climatic conditions has already been illustrated. The drier the atmosphere, the larger the effect on ET and the greater the slope of the curve. For humid conditions, the wind can only replace saturated air with slightly less saturated air and remove heat energy. Consequently, the wind speed affects the evapotranspiration rate to a far lesser extent than under arid conditions where small variations in wind speed may result in larger variations in the evapotranspiration rate.

19.15.5 Atmospheric Parameters

Several relationships are available to express climatic parameters. The effect of the principal weather parameters on evapotranspiration can be assessed with the help of these equations. Some of the relationships require parameters which express a specific characteristic of the atmosphere. Before studying the four principal weather parameters, some atmospheric parameters will be discussed. (Burnman & Pochop, 1994).

19.15.6 Atmospheric Pressure (P)

The atmospheric pressure, P, is the pressure exerted by the weight of the earth's atmosphere. Evaporation at high altitudes is promoted due to low atmospheric pressure as expressed in the psychrometric constant. The effect is, however, small and in the calculation procedures, the average value for a location is sufficient. A simplification of the ideal gas law, assuming 20°C for a standard atmosphere, can be employed to calculate P:

$$P = 101.3\left(\frac{293 - 0.0065z}{293}\right)^{5.26} \tag{7}$$

where

P atmospheric pressure [kPa],

z elevation above sea level [m],

19.15.7 Latent Heat of Vaporization (l)

The latent heat of vaporization, l, expresses the energy required to change a unit mass of water from liquid to water vapour in a constant pressure and constant temperature process. The value of the latent heat varies as a function of temperature. At a high temperature, less energy will be required than at lower temperatures. As l varies only slightly over normal temperature ranges a single value of 2.45 MJ kg^{-1} is taken in the simplification of the FAO Penman-Monteith equation. This is the latent heat for an air temperature of about 20°C.

19.15.8 Psychrometric Constant (g)

The psychrometric constant, g, is given by:

$$\gamma = \frac{c_p P}{\varepsilon \lambda} = 0.665 \times 10^{-3} P \tag{8}$$

where

g psychrometric constant [kPa $°C^{-1}$],
P atmospheric pressure [kPa],
l latent heat of vaporization, 2.45 [MJ kg^{-1}],
c_p specific heat at constant pressure, 1.013 10^{-3} [MJ kg^{-1} $°C^{-1}$],
e ratio molecular weight of water vapour/dry air = 0.622.

The specific heat at constant pressure is the amount of energy required to increase the temperature of a unit mass of air by one degree at constant pressure. Its value depends on the composition of the air, *i.e.,* on its humidity. For average atmospheric conditions a value c_p = 1.013 10^{-3} MJ kg^{-1} $°C^{-1}$ can be used. As an average atmospheric pressure is used for each location (Equation 7), the psychrometric constant is kept constant for each location. Values for the psychrometric constant as a function of altitude are given in Annex 2 (Table 2.2).

19.15.9 Air Temperature

Agrometeorology is concerned with the air temperature near the level of the tree canopy. In traditional and modem automatic weather stations the air temperature is measured inside shelters (Stevenson screens or ventilated radiation shields) placed in line with World Meteorological Organization (WMO) standards at 2 m above the ground. The shelters are designed to protect the instruments from direct exposure to solar heating. The louvered construction allows free air movement around the instruments. Air temperature is measured with thermometers, thermistors or thermocouples mounted in the shelter. Minimum and maximum thermometers record the minimum and maximum air temperature over a 24-hour period. Thermographs plot the instantaneous temperature over a day or week. Electronic weather stations often sample air temperature each minute and report hourly averages in addition to 24-hour maximum and minimum values.

Due to the non-linearity of humidity data required in the FAO Penman-Monteith equation, the vapour pressure for a certain period should be computed as the mean between the vapour pressure at the daily maximum and minimum air temperatures of that period. The daily maximum air temperature (T_{max}) and daily minimum air temperature (T_{min}) are, respectively, the maximum and minimum air temperature observed during the 24-hour period, beginning at midnight. T_{max} and T_{min} for longer periods such as weeks, 10-day's or months are obtained by dividing the sum of the respective daily values by the number of days in the period. The mean daily air temperature (T_{mean}) is only employed in the FAO Penman-Monteith equation to calculate the slope of the saturation vapour pressure curves (D) and the impact of mean air density (P_a) as the effect of temperature variations on the value of the climatic parameter is small in these cases. For standardization, T_{mean} for 24-hour periods is defined as the mean of the daily maximum (T_{max}) and minimum temperatures (T_{min}) rather than as the average of hourly temperature measurements.

$$T_{mean} = \frac{T_{max} - T_{min}}{2} \tag{9}$$

The temperature is given in degrees Celsius (°C) or Fahrenheit (°F). In some calculation procedures, temperature is required in Kelvin (K), which can be obtained by adding 273.16 to the temperature expressed in degrees Celsius (in practice K = °C + 273.16). The Kelvin and Celsius scale have the same scale interval.

19.16 Air Humidity

19.16.1 Concepts

The water content of the air can be expressed in several ways. In agrometeorology, vapour pressure, dewpoint temperature and relative humidity are common expressions to indicate air humidity.

19.16.2 Vapour Pressure

Water vapour is a gas and its pressure contributes to the total atmospheric pressure. The amount of water in the air is related directly to the partial pressure exerted by the water vapour in the air and is therefore a direct measure of the air water content.

In standard S. I. units, pressure is no longer expressed in centimetre of water, millimetre of mercury, bars, atmosphere, etc., but in pascals (Pa). Conversion factors between various units and Pa are given in Annex 1. As a pascal refers to a relatively small force (1 newton) applied on a relatively large surface (1 m^2), multiples of the basic unit are often used. In this handbook, vapour pressure is expressed in kilopascals (kPa = 1000 Pa).

When air is enclosed above an evaporating water surface, an equilibrium is reached between the water molecules escaping and returning to the water reservoir. At that moment, the air is said to be saturated since it cannot store any extra water molecules. The corresponding pressure is called the saturation vapour pressure [$e^\circ(T)$]. The number of water molecules that can be stored in the air depends on the temperature (T). The higher the air temperature, the higher the storage capacity, the higher its saturation vapour pressure.

As can be seen from Figure 19.7, the slope of the curve changes exponentially with temperature. At low temperatures, the slope is small and varies only slightly as the temperature rises. At high temperatures, the slope is large and small changes in T result in large changes in slope. The slope of the saturation vapour pressure curve, D, is an important parameter in describing vaporization and is required in the equations for calculating ET_o from climatic data.

The actual vapour pressure (e_a) is the vapour pressure exerted by the water in the air. When the air is not saturated, the actual vapour pressure will be lower than the saturation vapour pressure. The difference between the saturation and actual vapour pressure is called the vapour pressure deficit or saturation deficit and is an accurate indicator of the actual evaporative capacity of the air (Figure 19.8).

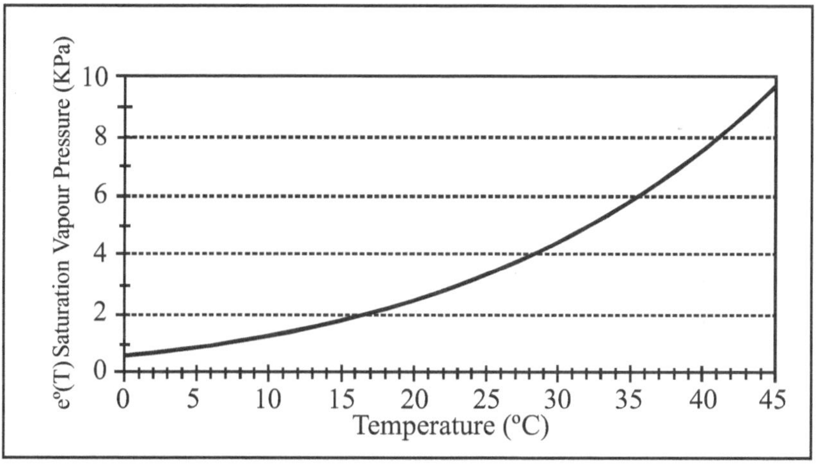

Figure 19.7: Saturation Vapour Pressure Shown as A Function of Temperature: E°(T) Curve

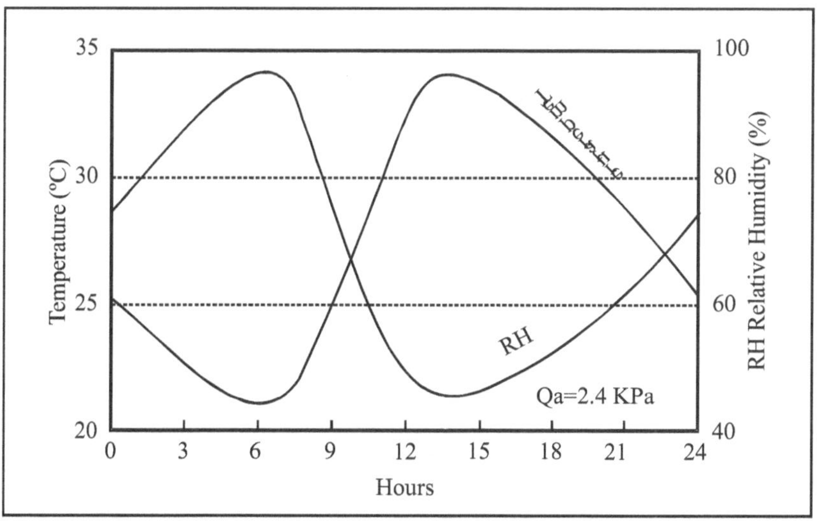

Figure 19.8: Variation of the Relative Humidity Over 24 Hours for a Constant Actual Vapour Pressure of 2.4 Kpa

19.16.3 Dewpoint Temperature

The dewpoint temperature is the temperature to which the air needs to be cooled to make the air saturated. The actual vapour pressure of the air is the saturation vapour pressure at the dewpoint temperature, The drier the air, the larger the difference between the air temperature and dewpoint temperature.

19.16.4 Relative Humidity

The relative humidity (RH) expresses the degree of saturation of the air as a ratio of the actual (e_a) to the saturation ($e°(T)$) vapour pressure at the same temperature (T):

$$RH = 100 \frac{e_a}{e°(T)} \tag{10}$$

Relative humidity is the ratio between the amount of water the ambient air actually holds and the amount it could hold at the same temperature. It is dimensionless and is commonly given as a percentage. Although the actual vapour pressure might be relatively constant throughout the day, the relative humidity fluctuates between a maximum near sunrise and a minimum around early afternoon. The variation of the relative humidity is the result of the fact that the saturation vapour pressure is determined by the air temperature. As the temperature changes during the day, the relative humidity also changes substantially.

19.16.5 Measurement

It is not possible to directly measure the actual vapour pressure. The vapour pressure is commonly derived from relative humidity or dewpoint temperature.

Relative humidity is measured directly with hygrometers. The measurement is based on the nature of some material such as hair, which changes its length in response to changes in air humidity, or using a capacitance plate, where the electric capacitance changes with RH. Vapour pressure can be measured indirectly with psychrometers which measure the temperature difference between two thermometers, the so-called dry and wet bulb thermometers. The dry bulb thermometer measures the temperature of the air. The bulb of the wet bulb thermometer is covered with a constantly saturated wick. Evaporation of water from the wick, requiring energy, lowers the temperature of the thermometer. The drier the air, the larger the evaporative cooling and the larger the temperature drop. The difference between the dry and wet bulb temperatures is called the wet bulb depression and is a measure of the air humidity.

The dewpoint temperature is measured with dewpoint meters. The underlying principle of some types of apparatus is the cooling of the ambient air until dew formation occurs. The corresponding temperature is the dewpoint temperature.

Relative humidity and dewpoint temperature data are notoriously plagued by measurement errors. Measurement error is common for both older hygrothermograph types of instruments and for the more modem electronic instruments. Great care should be made to assess the accuracy and integrity of RH and dewpoint data. The user is encouraged to always compare computed dewpoint temperatures to daily minimum air temperatures. Frequently, it is better to utilize a dewpoint temperature that is predicted from daily minimum air temperature, rather than to use unreliable relative humidity measurements.

19.16.6 Mean Saturation Vapour Pressure (e_s)

As saturation vapour pressure is related to air temperature, it can be calculated from the air temperature. The relationship is expressed by:

$$e^{\circ}(T) = 0.6108 \exp\left[\frac{17.27T}{T + 237.3}\right] \quad (11)$$

where

$e^{\circ}(T)$ saturation vapour pressure at the air temperature T [kPa],

T air temperature [°C],

exp[..] 2.7183 (base of natural logarithm) raised to the power [..].

Due to the non-linearity of the above equation, the mean saturation vapour pressure for a day, week, decade or month should be computed as the mean between the saturation vapour pressure at the mean daily maximum and minimum air temperatures for that period:

$$e_s = \frac{e^\circ(T_{max}) + e^\circ(T_{min})}{2} \quad (12)$$

Using mean air temperature instead of daily minimum and maximum temperatures results in lower estimates for the mean saturation vapour pressure. The corresponding vapour pressure deficit (a parameter expressing the evaporating power of the atmosphere) will also be smaller and the result will be some underestimation of the reference tree evapotranspiration. Therefore, the mean saturation vapour pressure should be calculated as the mean between the saturation vapour pressure at both the daily maximum and minimum air temperature.

19.16.7 Slope of Saturation Vapour Pressure Curve (D)

For the calculation of evapotranspiration, the slope of the relationship between saturation vapour pressure and temperature, D, is required. The slope of the curve at a given temperature is given by.

$$\Delta = \frac{4098\left[0.6108\exp\left(\frac{17.27T}{T+237.3}\right)\right]}{(T+237.3)^2} \quad (13)$$

where

D slope of saturation vapour pressure curve at air temperature T [kPa °C^{-1}]:

T air temperature [°C]:

exp[..] 2.7183 (base of natural logarithm) raised to the power [..].

In the FAO Penman-Monteith equation, where D occurs in the numerator and denominator, the slope of the vapour pressure curve is calculated using mean air temperature (Equation 9).

19.16.8 Actual Vapour Pressure (e_a) Derived from Dewpoint Temperature

As the dewpoint temperature is the temperature to which the air needs to be cooled to make the air saturated, the actual vapour pressure (e_a) is the saturation vapour pressure at the dewpoint temperature (T_{dew}) [°C], or:

$$e_a = e°(T_{dew}) = 0.6108 \exp\left[\frac{17.27\, T_{dew}}{T_{dew} + 237.3}\right] \quad (14)$$

19.16.9 *Actual Vapour Pressure (e_a) Derived from Psychrometric Data*

The actual vapour pressure can be determined from the difference between the dry and wet bulb temperatures, the so-called wet bulb depression. The relationship is expressed by the following equation:

$$e_a = e° (T_{wet}) - g_{psy} (T_{dry} - T_{wet}) \quad (15)$$

where

e_a actual vapour pressure [kPa],

$e°(T_{wet})$ saturation vapour pressure at wet bulb temperature [kPa],

g_{psy} psychrometric constant of the instrument [kPa °C^{-1}],

T_{dry}-T_{wet} wet bulb depression, with T_{dry} the dry bulb and T_{wet} the wet bulb temperature [°C].

The psychrometric constant of the instrument is given by:

$$g_{psy} = a_{psy} P \quad (16)$$

where a_{psy} is a coefficient depending on the type of ventilation of the wet bulb [°C^{-1}], and P is the atmospheric pressure [kPa]. The coefficient a_{psy} depends mainly on the design of the psychrometer and rate of ventilation around the wet bulb. The following values are used:

a_{psy}	= 0.000662	for ventilated (Asmann type) psychrometers, with an air movement of some 5 m/s,
	0.000800	for natural ventilated psychrometers (about 1 m/s),
	0.001200	for non-ventilated psychrometers installed indoors.

19.16.10 Actual Vapour Pressure (e_a) Derived from Relative Humidity Data

The actual vapour pressure can also be calculated from the relative humidity. Depending on the availability of the humidity data, different equations should be used.

For RH_{max} and RH_{min}:

$$e_a = \frac{e^\circ(T_{min})\frac{RH_{max}}{100} + e^\circ(T_{max})\frac{RH_{min}}{100}}{2} \quad (17)$$

where

e_a actual vapour pressure [kPa],

$e^\circ(T_{min})$ saturation vapour pressure at daily minimum temperature [kPa],

$e^\circ(T_{max})$ saturation vapour pressure at daily maximum temperature [kPa],

RH_{max} maximum relative humidity [%],

RH_{min} minimum relative humidity [%].

For periods of a week, ten days or a month, RH_{max} and RH_{min} are obtained by dividing the sum of the daily values by the number of days in that period.

For RH_{max}:

When using equipment where errors in estimating RH_{min} can be large, or when RH data integrity are in doubt, then one should use only RH_{max}:

$$e_a = e^\circ(T_{min})\frac{RH_{max}}{100} \quad (18)$$

For RH_{mean}:

In the absence of RH_{max} and RH_{min}, another equation can be used to estimate e_a:

$$e_a = \frac{RH_{mean}}{100}\left[\frac{e^\circ(T_{max}) + e^\circ(Tmin)}{2}\right] \quad (19)$$

where RH_{mean} is the mean relative humidity, defined as the average between RH_{max} and RH_{min}. However, Equation 19 is less desirable than are Equations 17 or 18.

19.17 Vapour Pressure Deficit (e_s - e_a)

The vapour pressure deficit is the difference between the saturation (e_s) and actual vapour pressure (e_a) for a given time period. For time periods such as a week, ten days or a month e_s is computed from Equation 12 using the T_{max} and T_{min} averaged over the time period and similarly the e_a is computed with one of the equations 4 to 19, using average measurements over the period. As stated above, using mean air temperature and not T_{max} and T_{min} in Equation 12 results in a lower estimate of e_s, thus in a lower vapour pressure deficit and hence an underestimation of the ET_o. When desired, e_s and e_a for long time periods cal also be calculated as averages of values computed for each day of the period.

19.17.1 Radiation

The radiation striking a surface perpendicular to the sun's rays at the top of the earth's atmosphere, called the solar constant, is about 0.082 MJ m^{-2} min^{-1}. The local intensity of radiation is, however, determined by the angle between the direction of the sun's rays and the normal to the surface of the atmosphere. This angle will change during the day and will be different at different latitudes and in different seasons. The solar radiation received at the top of the earth's atmosphere on a horizontal surface is called the extraterrestrial (solar) radiation, R_a.

If the sun is directly overhead, the angle of incidence is zero and the extraterrestrial radiation is 0.0820 MJ m^{-2} min^{-1}. As seasons change, the position of the sun, the length of the day and, hence, R_a change as well. Extraterrestrial radiation is thus a function of latitude, date and time of day. Daily values of R_a throughout the year for different latitudes are plotted in figure 19.9.

19.17.2 Solar or Shortwave Radiation (R_s)

As the radiation penetrates the atmosphere, some of the radiation is scattered, reflected or absorbed by the atmospheric gases, clouds and dust. The amount of radiation reaching a horizontal plane is known as the solar radiation, R_s. Because the sun emits energy by means of electromagnetic waves characterized by short wavelengths, solar radiation is also referred to as shortwave radiation.

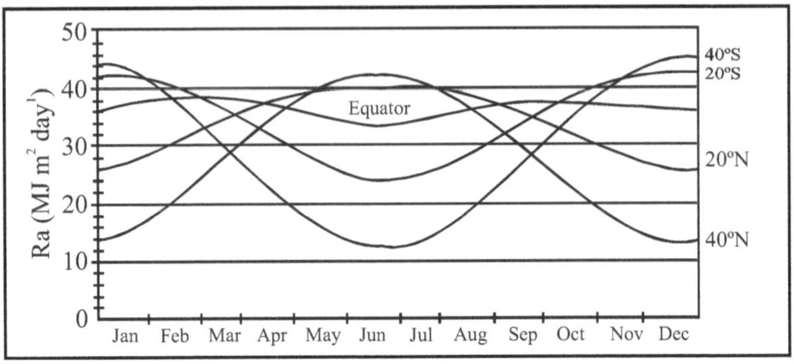

Figure 19.9: Annual Variation in Extraterrestrial Radiation (R_a) at The Equator, 20 and 40° North and South

For a cloudless day, R_s is roughly 75% of extraterrestrial radiation. On a cloudy day, the radiation is scattered in the atmosphere, but even with extremely dense cloud cover, about 25% of the extraterrestrial radiation may still reach the earth's surface mainly as diffuse sky radiation. Solar radiation is also known as global radiation, meaning that it is the sum of direct shortwave radiation from the sun and diffuse sky radiation from all upward angles.

19.17.3 Relative Shortwave Radiation (R_s/R_{so})

The relative shortwave radiation is the ratio of the solar radiation (R_s) to the clear-sky solar radiation (R_{so}). R_s is the solar radiation that actually reaches the earth's surface in a given period, while R_{so} is the solar radiation that would reach the same surface during the same period but under cloudless conditions.

The relative shortwave radiation is a way to express the cloudiness of the atmosphere; the cloudier the sky the smaller the ratio. The ratio varies between about 0.33 (dense cloud cover) and 1 (clear sky). In the absence of a direct measurement of R_n, the relative shortwave radiation is used in the computation of the net longwave radiation. (Figure 19.10).

19.17.4 Relative Sunshine Duration (n/N)

The relative sunshine duration is another ratio that expresses the cloudiness of the atmosphere. It is the ratio of the actual duration of sunshine, n, to the maximum possible duration of sunshine or daylight hours N. In the absence of any clouds, the actual duration of sunshine is equal to the daylight hours (n = N) and the ratio is one, while on cloudy days n and consequently the ratio may be zero. In the absence of a direct measurement of R_s, the relative sunshine duration, n/N, is often used to derive solar radiation from extraterrestrial radiation.

As with extraterrestrial radiation, the day length N depends on the position of the sun and is hence a function of latitude and date. Daily values of N throughout the year for different latitudes are plotted in Figure 19.10.

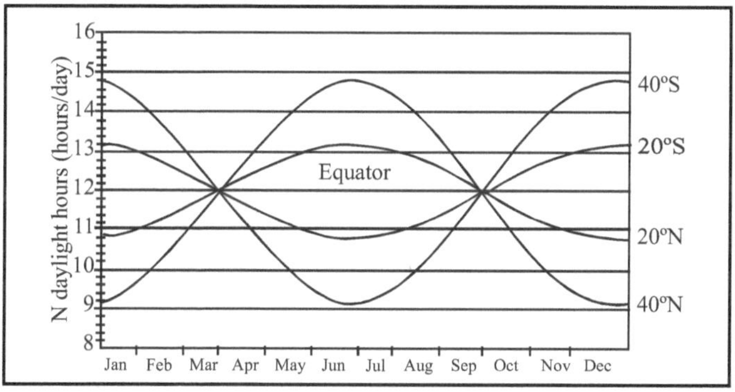

Figure 19.10: Annual Variation of the Daylight Hours (N) at The Equator, 20 and 40° North and South

19.17.5 Albedo (a) and Net Solar Radiation (R_{ns})

A considerable amount of solar radiation reaching the earth's surface is reflected. The fraction, a, of the solar radiation reflected by the surface is known as the albedo. The albedo is highly variable for different surfaces and for the angle of incidence or slope of the ground surface. It may be as large as 0.95 for freshly fallen snow and as small as 0.05 for a wet bare soil. A green vegetation cover has an albedo of about 0.20-0.25. For the green grass reference tree, a is assumed to have a value of 0.23.

The net solar radiation, R_{ns}, is the fraction of the solar radiation R_s that is not reflected from the surface. Its value is $(1-a)R_s$.

19.17.6 Net Longwave Radiation (R_{nl})

The solar radiation absorbed by the earth is converted to heat energy. By several processes, including emission of radiation, the earth loses this energy. The earth, which is at a much lower temperature than the sun, emits radiative energy with wavelengths longer than those from the sun. Therefore, the terrestrial radiation is referred to as longwave radiation. The emitted longwave radiation ($R_{l,up}$) is absorbed by the atmosphere or is lost into space. The longwave radiation received by the atmosphere ($R_{l,\ down}$) increases its temperature and, as a consequence, the atmosphere radiates energy of its own. Part of the radiation finds it way back to the earth's surface. Consequently, the earth's surface both emits and receives longwave radiation. The difference between outgoing and incoming longwave radiation is called the net longwave radiation, R_{nl}. As the outgoing longwave radiation is almost always greater than me incoming longwave radiation, R_{nl} represents an energy loss.

19.17.7 Net Radiation (R_n)

The net radiation, R_n, is the difference between incoming and outgoing radiation of both short and long wavelengths. It is the balance between the energy absorbed, reflected and emitted by the earth's surface or the difference between the incoming net shortwave (R_{ns}) and the net outgoing longwave (R_{nl}) radiation. R_n is normally positive during the daytime and negative during the nighttime. The total daily value for R_n is almost always positive over a period of 24 hours, except in extreme conditions at high latitudes.

19.17.8 Soil Heat Flux (G)

In making estimates of evapotranspiration, all terms of the energy balance (Equation 1) should be considered. The soil heat flux, G, is the energy that is utilized in heating the soil. G is positive when the soil is warming and negative when the soil is cooling. Although the soil heat flux is small compared to R_n and may often be ignored, the amount of energy gained or lost by the soil in this process should theoretically be subtracted or added to R_n when estimating evapotranspiration.

The standard unit used in this book to express energy received on a unit surface per unit time is megajoules per square metre per day (MJ m^{-2} day^{-1}). In meteorological bulletins other units might be used or radiation might even be expressed in units no longer accepted as standard S. I. units, such as calories cm^{-2} day^{-1}.

In the FAO Penman-Monteith equation (Equation 6), radiation expressed in MJ m^{-2} day^{-1} is converted (Box 8) to equivalent evaporation in mm day^{-1} by using a conversion factor equal to the inverse of the latent heat of vaporization.

$$(1/l = 0.408)\text{: equivalent evaporation [mm day}^{-1}] = 0.408 \times \text{Radiation [MJ m}^{-2}\text{ day}^{-1}] \quad (20)$$

Common units used to express energy received on a unit surface per unit time, and conversion factors are summarized in Table 19.2.

Table 19.2: Conversion Factors for Radiation

	Multiplier to obtain energy received on a unit surface per unit time equivalent evaporation				
	MJ m^{-2} day^{-1}	J cm^{-2} day^{-1}	cal cm^{-2} day^{-1}	W m^{-2}	mm day^{-1}
1 MJ m^{-2} day^{-1}	1	100	23.9	11.6	0.408
1 cal cm^{-2} day^{-1}	4.1868 10^{-2}	4.1868	1	0.485	0.0171
1 W m^{-2}	0.0864	8,64	2.06	1	0.035
1 mm day^{-1}	2.45	245	58.5	28.4	1

Solar radiation can be measured with pyranometers, radiometers or solarimeters. The instruments contain a sensor installed on a horizontal surface that measures the intensity of the total solar radiation, *i.e.*, both direct and diffuse radiation from cloudy conditions. The sensor is often protected and kept in a dry atmosphere by a glass dome that should be regularly wiped clean.

Net longwave and net shortwave radiation can be measured by recording the difference in output between sensors facing upward and downward. In a net radiometer, the glass domes are replaced by polyethylene domes that have a transmission range for both shortwave and longwave radiation.

Where pyranometers are not available, solar radiation is usually estimated from the duration of bright sunshine. The actual duration of sunshine, n, is measured with a Campbell-Stokes sunshine recorder. This instrument records periods of bright sunshine by using a glass globe that acts as a lens. The sun rays are concentrated at a focal point that burns a hole in a specially treated card mounted concentrically with the sphere. The movement of the sun changes the focal point throughout the day and a trace is drawn on the card. If the sun is obscured, the trace is interrupted. The hours of bright sunshine are indicated by the lengths of the line segments.

The quantity of heat conducted into the soil, G, can be measured with systems of soil heat flux plates and thermocouples or thermisters.

19.18 Extraterrestrial Radiation for Daily Periods (R_a)

The extraterrestrial radiation, R_a, for each day of the year and for different latitudes can be estimated from the solar constant, the solar declination and the time of the year by:

$$R_a = \frac{24(60)}{\pi} G_{sc} d_r [\omega_s \sin(\varphi)\sin(\delta) + \cos(\varphi)\cos(\delta)\sin(\omega_s)] \qquad (21)$$

where

R_a extraterrestrial radiation [MJ m^{-2} day^{-1}],
G_{sc} solar constant = 0.0820 MJ m^{-2} min^{-1},
d_r inverse relative distance Earth-Sun (Equation 23),
w_s sunset hour angle (Equation 25 or 26) [rad],
j latitude [rad] (Equation 22),
d solar decimation (Equation 24) [rad].

R_a is expressed in the above equation in MJ m^{-2} day^{-1}. The corresponding equivalent evaporation in mm day^{-1} is obtained by multiplying R_a by 0.408 (Equation 20). The latitude, j, expressed in radians is positive for the northern hemisphere and negative for the southern hemisphere. The conversion from decimal degrees to radians is given by:

$$[\text{Radians}] = \frac{\pi}{180}[\text{decimaldegrees}] \tag{22}$$

The inverse relative distance Earth-Sun, d_r, and the solar declination, d, are given bv:

$$d_r = 1 + 0.033\cos\left(\frac{2\pi}{365}J\right) \tag{23}$$

$$\delta = 0.409\sin\left(\frac{2\pi}{365}J - 1.39\right) \tag{24}$$

where J is the number of the day in the year between 1 (1 January) and 365 or 366 (31 December). Values for J for all days of the year and an equation for estimating J are given in Annex 2 (Table 2.5).

The sunset hour angle, w_s, is given by:

$$w_s = \arccos\,[-\tan(j)\tan(d)] \tag{25}$$

As the arccos function is not available in all computer languages, the sunset hour angle can also be computed using the arctan function:

where

$$X = 1 - [\tan(j)]^2[\tan(d)]^2 \tag{26}$$

$$X = 0.00001 \text{ if } X \pounds 0 \tag{27}$$

Values for R_a for different latitudes are given in Annex 2 (Table 2.6). These values represent R_a on the 15th day of each month. These values deviate from values that are averaged over each day of the month by less than 1% for all latitudes during non-frozen periods and are included for simplicity of calculation. These values deviate slightly from the values in the Smithsonian tables. For the winter months in latitudes greater than 55° (N or S), the equations for R_a have limited validity. Reference should be made to the Smithsonian tables to assess possible deviations.

19.19 Extraterrestrial Radiation for Hourly or Shorter Periods (R_a)

For hourly or shorter periods the solar time angle at the beginning and end of the period should be considered when calculating R_a:

$$R_a = \frac{12(60)}{\pi} G_{sc} d_r [(\omega_2 - \omega_1)\sin(\varphi)\sin(\delta) + \cos(\varphi)\cos(\delta)(\sin(\omega_2) - \sin(\omega_1))] \quad (28)$$

where

R_a extraterrestrial radiation in the hour (or shorter) period [MJ m^{-2} $hour^{-1}$],

G_{sc} solar constant = 0.0820 MJ m^{-2} min^{-1},

d_r inverse relative distance Earth-Sun (Equation 23),

d solar declination [rad] (Equation 24),

j latitude [rad] (Equation 22),

w_1 solar time angle at beginning of period [rad] (Equation 29),

w_2 solar time angle at end of period [rad] (Equation 30).

The solar time angles at the beginning and end of the period are given by:

$$\omega_1 = \omega - \frac{\pi t_1}{24} \quad (29)$$

$$\omega_2 = \omega + \frac{\pi t_1}{24} \quad (30)$$

where

w solar time angle at midpoint of hourly or shorter period [rad],

t_1 length of the calculation period [hour]: *i.e.,* 1 for hourly period or 0.5 for a 30-minute period.

The solar time angle at midpoint of the period is:

$$\omega = \frac{\pi}{12}[(t + 0.06667(L_z - L_m) + S_c) - 12] \quad (31)$$

where

t standard clock time at the midpoint of the period [hour]. For example for a period between 14.00 and 15.00 hours, t = 14.5,

L_z longitude of the centre of the local time zone [degrees west of Greenwich]. For example, L_z = 75, 90, 105 and 120° for the Eastern, Central, Rocky Mountain and Pacific time zones (United States) and L_z = 0° for Greenwich, 330° for Cairo (Egypt), and 255° for Bangkok (Thailand),

L_m longitude of the measurement site [degrees west of Greenwich],

S_c seasonal correction for solar time [hour].

Of course, $w < -w_s$ or $w > w_s$ from Equation 31 indicates that the sun is below the horizon so that, by definition, R_a is zero.

The seasonal correction for solar time is:

$S_c = 0.1645 \sin(2\,b) - 0.1255 \cos(b) - 0.025 \sin(b)$ (32)

$$b = \frac{2\pi(J - 81)}{364} \quad (33)$$

where J is the number of the day in the year.

19.19.1 Daylight Hours (N)

The daylight hours, N, are given by:

$$N = \frac{24}{\pi}\omega_s \quad (34)$$

where w_s is the sunset hour angle in radians given by Equation 25 or 26. Mean values for N (15th day of each month) for different latitudes are given in Annex 2, Table 2.7.

19.19.2 Solar Radiation (R_s)

If the solar radiation, R_s, is not measured, it can be calculated with the Angstrom formula which relates solar radiation to extraterrestrial radiation and relative sunshine duration:

$$R_s = \left(a_s + b_s \frac{n}{N}\right) R_a \quad (35)$$

where

R_s solar or shortwave radiation [MJ m^{-2} day^{-1}],

n actual duration of sunshine [hour],

N maximum possible duration of sunshine or daylight hours [hour],
n/N relative sunshine duration [-],
R_a extraterrestrial radiation [MJ m^{-2} day^{-1}],
a_s regression constant, expressing the fraction of extraterrestrial radiation reaching the earth on overcast days (n = 0),
a_s+b_s fraction of extraterrestrial radiation reaching the earth on clear days (n = N).

R_s is expressed in the above equation in MJ m^{-2} day^{-1}. The corresponding equivalent evaporation in mm day^{-1} is obtained by multiplying R_s by 0.408 (Equation 20). Depending on atmospheric conditions (humidity, dust) and solar declination (latitude and month), the Angstrom values a_s and b_s will vary. Where no actual solar radiation data are available and no calibration has been carried out for improved a_s and b_s parameters, the values a_s = 0.25 and b_s = 0.50 are recommended.

The extraterrestrial radiation, R_a, and the daylight hours or maximum possible duration of sunshine, N, are given by Equations 21 and 34. Values for R_a and N for different latitudes are also listed in Annex 2 (Tables 2.6 and 2.7). The actual duration of sunshine, n, is recorded with a Campbell Stokes sunshine recorder.

19.19.3 Clear-sky Solar Radiation (R_{so})

The calculation of the clear-sky radiation, R_{so}, when n = N, is required for computing net longwave radiation.

For near sea level or when calibrated values for a_s and b_s are available:

$$R_{so} = (a_s+b_s)R_a \tag{36}$$

where

R_{so} clear-sky solar radiation [MJ m^{-2} day^{-1}],

a_s+b_s fraction of extraterrestrial radiation reaching the earth on clear-sky days (n = N).

When calibrated values for a_s and b_s are not available:

$$R_{so} = (0.75 + 2\ 10^{-5}z)R_a \tag{37}$$

where

z station elevation above sea level [m].

Other more complex estimates for R_{so}, which include turbidity and water vapour effects have been discussed in previous chapters.

19.19.4 Net Solar or Net Shortwave Radiation (R_{ns})

The net shortwave radiation resulting from the balance between incoming and reflected solar radiation is given by:

$$R_{ns} = (1\text{-}a)R_s \tag{38}$$

where

R_{ns} net solar or shortwave radiation [MJ m^{-2} day^{-1}],
a albedo or canopy reflection coefficient, which is 0.23 for the hypothetical grass reference tree [dimensionless],
R_s the incoming solar radiation [MJ m^{-2} day^{-1}].
R_{ns} is expressed in the above equation in MJ m^{-2} day^{-1}.

19.19.5 Net Longwave Radiation (R_{nl})

The rate of longwave energy emission is proportional to the absolute temperature of the surface raised to the fourth power. This relation is expressed quantitatively by the Stefan-Boltzmann law. The net energy flux leaving the earth's surface is, however, less than that emitted and given by the Stefan-Boltzmann law due to the absorption and downward radiation from the sky. Water vapour, clouds, carbon dioxide and dust are absorbers and emitters of longwave radiation. Their concentrations should be known when assessing the net outgoing flux. As humidity and cloudiness play an important role, the Stefan-Boltzmann law is corrected by these two factors when estimating - the net outgoing flux of longwave radiation. It is thereby assumed that the concentrations of the other absorbers are constant:

$$R_{nl} = \sigma\left[\frac{T_{max K^4} + T_{min K^4}}{2}\right]\left(0.34 - 0.14\sqrt{e_a}\right)\left(1.35\frac{R_s}{R_{so}} - 0.35\right) \tag{39}$$

where

R_{nl} net outgoing longwave radiation [MJ m^{-2} day^{-1}],

s Stefan-Boltzmann constant [4.903 10^{-9} MJ K^{-4} m^{-2} day^{-1}],

$T_{max, K}$ maximum absolute temperature during the 24-hour period [K = °C + 273.16],

$T_{min, K}$ minimum absolute temperature during the 24-hour period [K = °C + 273.16],

e_a actual vapour pressure [kPa],

R_s/R_{so} relative shortwave radiation (limited to £ 1.0),

R_s measured or calculated. (Equation 35) solar radiation [MJ m^{-2} day^{-1}],

R_{so} calculated (Equation 36 or 37) clear-sky radiation [MJ m^{-2} day^{-1}].

An average of the maximum air temperature to the fourth power and the minimum air temperature to the fourth power is commonly used in the Stefan-Boltzmann equation for 24-hour time steps. The term (0.34-0.14Ö e_a) expresses the correction for air humidity, and will be smaller if the humidity increases. The effect of cloudiness is expressed by (1.35 R_s/R_{so} - 0.35). The term becomes smaller if the cloudiness increases and hence R_s decreases. The smaller the correction terms, the smaller the net outgoing flux of longwave radiation. Note that the R_s/R_{so} term in Equation 39 must be limited so that R_s/R_{so} £ 1.0.

Where measurements of incoming and outgoing short and longwave radiation during bright sunny and overcast hours are available, calibration of the coefficients in Equation 39 can be carried out.

19.19.6 Net Radiation (R_n)

The net radiation (R_n) is the difference between the incoming net shortwave radiation (R_{ns}) and the outgoing net longwave radiation (R_{nl}):

$$R_n = R_{ns} - R_{nl} \tag{40}$$

19.19.7 Soil Heat Flux (G)

Complex models are available to describe soil heat flux. Because soil heat flux is small compared to R_n, particularly when the surface is covered by vegetation and calculation time steps are 24 hours or longer, a simple calculation procedure is presented here for long time steps, based on the idea that the soil temperature follows air temperature:

$$G = c_s \frac{T_i - T_{i-1}}{\Delta t} \Delta z \qquad (41)$$

where

G soil heat flux [MJ m^{-2} day^{-1}],
C_s soil heat capacity [MJ m^{-3} °C^{-1}],
T_i air temperature at time i [°C],
T_{i-1} air temperature at time i-1 [°C],
D t length of time interval [day],
D z effective soil depth [m].

As the soil temperature lags air temperature, the average temperature for a period should be considered when assessing me daily soil heat flux, i.e., D t should exceed one day. The depth of penetration of the temperature wave is determined by the length of the time interval. The effective soil depth, D z, is only 0.10-0.20 m for a time interval of one or a few days but might be 2 m or more for monthly periods. The soil heat capacity is related to its mineral composition and water content. (Jensen, *et.al.*, 1990)

19.19.8 For Day and Ten-day Periods

As the magnitude of the day or ten-day soil heat flux beneath the grass reference surface is relatively small, it may be ignored and thus:

$$G_{day} \gg 0 \qquad (42)$$

19.19.9 For Monthly Periods

When assuming a constant soil heat capacity of 2.1 MJ m^{-3} °C^{-1} and an appropriate soil depth, Equation 41 can be used to derive G for monthly periods:

$$G_{month,\,i} = 0.07\,(T_{month,\,i+1} - T_{month,\,i-1}) \qquad (43)$$

or, if $T_{month,\,i+1}$ is unknown:

$$G_{month,\,i} = 0.14\,(T_{month,\,i} - T_{month,\,i-1}) \qquad (44)$$

where

$T_{month,\,i}$ mean air temperature of month i [°C],

$T_{month,\,i-1}$ mean air temperature of previous month [°C],

$T_{month,\,i+1}$ mean air temperature of next month [°C].

19.19.10 For Hourly or Shorter Periods

For hourly (or shorter) calculations, G beneath a dense cover of grass does not correlate well with air temperature. Hourly G can be approximated during daylight periods as:

$$G_{hr} = 0.1\,R_n \qquad (45)$$

and during nighttime periods as:

$$G_{hr} = 0.5\,R_n \qquad (46)$$

Where the soil is warming, the soil heat flux G is positive. The amount of energy required for this process is subtracted from R_n when estimating evapotranspiration.

19.19.11 Wind Speed

Wind is characterized by its direction and velocity. Wind direction refers to the direction from which the wind is blowing. For the computation of evapotranspiration, wind speed is the relevant variable. As wind speed at a given location varies with time, it is necessary to express it as an average over a given time interval. Wind speed is given in metres per second (m/s^{-1}) or kilometres per day (km/day^{-1}).

Wind speed is measured with anemometers. The anemometers commonly used in weather stations are composed of cups or propellers which are turned by the force of the wind. By counting the number of revolutions over a given time period, the average wind speed over the measuring period is computed.

19.19.12 Wind Profile Relationship

Wind speeds measured at different heights above the soil surface are different. Surface friction tends to slow down wind passing over it. Wind speed is slowest at the surface and increases with height. For this reason anemometers are placed at a chosen standard height, *i.e.*, 10 m in meteorology and 2 or 3 m in agrometeorology. For the calculation of evapotranspiration, wind speed measured at 2 m above the surface is required. To adjust wind speed data obtained from instruments placed at elevations other than the standard height of 2 m, a logarithmic wind speed profile may be used for measurements above a short grassed surface:

$$u_2 = u_z \frac{4.87}{\ln(67.8z - 5.42)} \tag{47}$$

where

u_2 wind speed at 2 m above ground surface [m s^{-1}],

u_z measured wind speed at z m above ground surface [m s^{-1}],

z height of measurement above ground surface [m].

The corresponding multipliers or conversion factors are given in Figure 19.11.

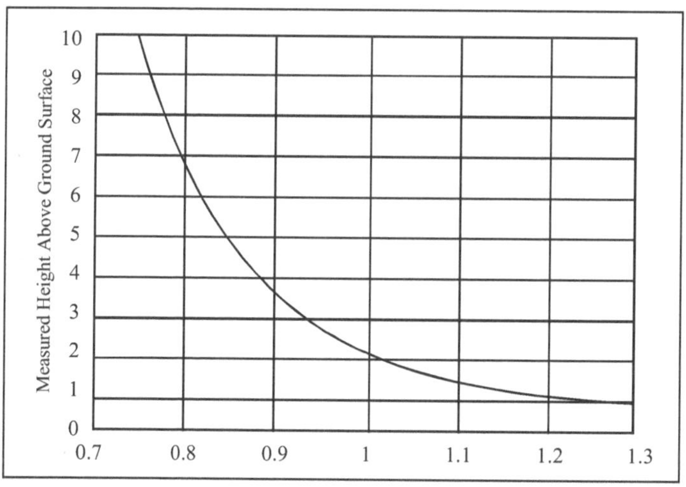

Figure 19.11: Conversion Factor to Convert Wind Speed Measured at a Certain Height Above Ground Level to Wind Speed at The Standard Height (2 M)

19.19.13 Determination of ET_o

The calculation procedure consists of the following steps:

1. Derivation of some climatic parameters from the daily maximum (T_{max}) and minimum (T_{min}) air temperature, altitude (z) and mean wind speed (u_2).
2. Calculation of the vapour pressure deficit (e_s - e_a). The saturation vapour pressure (e_s) is derived from T_{max} and T_{min}, while the actual vapour pressure (e_a) can be derived from the dewpoint temperature (T_{dew}), from maximum (RH_{max}) and minimum (RH_{min}) relative humidity, from the maximum (RH_{max}), or from mean relative humidity (RH_{mean}).
3. Determination of the net radiation (R_n) as the difference between the net shortwave radiation (R_{ns}) and the net longwave radiation (R_{nl}). In the calculation sheet, the effect of soil heat flux (G) is ignored for daily calculations as the magnitude of the flux in this case is relatively small. The net radiation, expressed in MJ m^{-2} day^{-1}, is converted to mm/day (equivalent evaporation) in the FAO Penman-Monteith equation by using 0.408 as the conversion factor within the equation.
4. ET_o is obtained by combining the results of the previous steps.

19.19.14 Computerized Calculations

Calculations of the reference tree evapotranspiration ET_o are often computerized. The calculation procedures of all data required for the calculation of ET_o by means of the FAO Penman-Monteith equation. Typical sequences in which the calculations can be executed are given in the calculation sheets. The procedures presented in vapour pressure deficit, extraterrestrial radiation and daylight hours, net radiation and ET_ocan be used when developing a spreadsheet or computer program to calculate ET_o. Many software packages already use the FAO Penman-Monteith equation to assess the reference evapotranspiration.

19.19.15 ET_o Calculated with Different Time Steps

The selection of the time step with which ET_o is calculated depends on the purpose of the calculation, the accuracy required and the time step of the climatic data available.

Notwithstanding the non-linearity in the Penman-Monteith equation and some weather parameter methods, mean ten-day or monthly weather data can be used to compute the mean ten-day or monthly values for the reference evapotranspiration. The value of the reference evapotranspiration calculated with mean monthly weather data is indeed very similar to the average of the daily ET_o values calculated with daily average weather data for that month.

The meteorological data consist of:

- Air temperature: Ten-day or monthly average daily maximum (T_{max}) and average daily minimum temperature (T_{min}).
- Air humidity: Ten-day or monthly average of the daily actual vapour pressure (e_a) derived from psychrometric, dewpoint or relative humidity data.
- Wind speed: Ten-day or monthly average of daily wind speed data measured at 2 m height (u_2).
- Radiation: Ten-day or monthly average of daily net radiation (R_n) computed from the mean ten-day or monthly measured shortwave radiation or from actual duration of daily sunshine hours (n). The extraterrestrial radiation (R_a) and daylight hours (N) for a specific day of the month can be computed using Equations 21 and 34.

When the soil is warming (spring) or cooling (autumn), the soil heat flux (G) for monthly periods may become significant relative to the mean monthly R_n. In these cases G cannot be ignored and its value should be determined from the mean monthly air temperatures of the previous and next month.

Calculation of ET_o with the Penman-Monteith equation on 24-hour time scales will generally provide accurate results. The required meteorological data consist of:

- Air temperature: Maximum (T_{max}) and minimum (T_{min}) daily air temperatures.
- Air humidity: Mean daily actual vapour pressure (e_a) derived from psychrometric, dewpoint temperature or relative humidity data.
- Wind speed: Daily average for 24 hours of wind speed measured at 2 m height (u_2).
- Radiation: Net radiation (R_n) measured or computed from solar and longwave radiation or from the actual duration of sunshine (n). The extraterrestrial radiation (R_a) and daylight hours (N) for a specific day of the month should be computed using Equations 21 and 34. As the magnitude of daily soil heat flux (G) beneath the reference grass surface is relatively small, it may be ignored for 24-hour time steps. In areas where substantial changes in wind speed, dewpoint or cloudiness occur during the day, calculation of the ET_o equation using hourly time steps is generally better than using 24-hour calculation time steps. Such weather changes can cause 24-hour means to misrepresent evaporative power of the environment during parts of the day and may introduce error into the calculations. However, under most conditions, application of the FAO Penman-Monteith equation with 24-hour data produces accurate results.

With the advent of electronic, automated weather stations, weather data are increasingly reported for hourly or shorter periods. Therefore, in situations where calculations are computerized, the FAO Penman-Monteith equation can be applied on an hourly basis with good results. When applying the FAO Penman-Monteith equation on an hourly or shorter time scale, the equation and some of the procedures for calculating meteorological data should be adjusted for the smaller time step. The FAO Penman-Monteith equation for hourly time steps is:

$$ET_o = \frac{0.408\Delta(R_n - G) + \gamma \frac{37}{T_{hr} + 273} u_2 (e^\circ(T_{hr}) - e_a)}{\Delta + \gamma(1 + 0.34 u_2)} \quad (48)$$

where

ET_o reference evapotranspiration [mm $hour^{-1}$],
R_n net radiation at the grass surface [MJ m^{-2} $hour^{-1}$] (Equation 40),
G soil heat flux density [MJ m^{-2} $hour^{-1}$] (Equations 45 and 46),
T_{hr} mean hourly air temperature [°C],
saturation slope vapour pressure curve at T_{hr} [kPa $°C^{-1}$] (Equation 13),
psychrometric constant [kPa $°C^{-1}$] (Equation 8),
$e^\circ(T_{hr})$ saturation vapour pressure at air temperature T_{hr} kPa] (Equation 11),
e_a average hourly actual vapour pressure [kPa] (Equation 4),
u_2 average hourly wind speed [m s^{-1}].

Given relative humidity measurements, the actual vapour pressure is determined as:

$$e_a = e^\circ(T_{hr}) \frac{RH_{hr}}{100} \quad (49)$$

where

e_a average hourly actual vapour pressure [kPa],

$e^\circ(T_{hr})$ saturation vapour pressure at air temperature T_{hr} [kPa] (Equation 11),

RH_{hr} average hourly relative humidity [%].

The net radiation is the difference between the net shortwave radiation (R_{ns}) and the net longwave radiation (R_{nl}) at the hourly time steps.

Since the ratio R_s/R_{so} is used to represent cloud cover, when calculating R_{nl} for hourly periods during the nighttime, the ratio R_s/R_{so} can be set equal to the R_s/R_{so} calculated for a time period occurring 2-3 hours before sunset, before the sun angle becomes small. This will generally serve as a good approximation of cloudiness occurring during the subsequent nighttime. The hourly period that is 2 to 3 hours before sunset can be identified during computation of R_a as the period.

Soil heat flux is important for hourly calculations. Equations 45 and 46 can be used to derive G for the hourly periods.

The required meteorological data consist of:
Air temperature: mean hourly temperature (T_{hr}).
Air humidity: average hourly relative humidity (RH_{hr}).
Wind speed: average hourly wind speed data measured t 2 m height (u_2).
Radiation: total hourly solar (R_s) or net radiation (R_n).

Because of the need for standardization, the constants in Equation 48 presume a constant surface resistance (r_s) of 70 s/m during all periods. This constant resistance may cause some underprediction of hourly ET_o during some daytime periods when actual r_s may be somewhat lower. The constant resistance may cause some overprediction of hourly ET_o during evening periods when actual r_s may be somewhat higher. However, when the calculations of hourly ET_o from Equation 48 are summed over 24 hour periods to produce an equivalent 24-hour ET_o, the hourly differences tend to compensate one another and the results are generally equivalent to calculations of ET_o made on a 24-hour time step. Precise estimates of ET_o for specific hourly periods may require the use of aerodynamic stability functions and functions for modifying the value for r_s based on levels of radiation, humidity and temperature.

19.20 Introduction to Tree Evapotranspiration (ET_c)

This chapter outlines the tree coefficient approach for calculating the tree evapotranspiration under standard conditions (ET_c). The standard conditions refer to trees grown in large fields under excellent agronomic and soil water conditions. The tree evapotranspiration differs distinctly from the reference evapotranspiration (ET_o) as the ground cover, canopy properties and aerodynamic resistance of the tree are different from grass. The effects of characteristics that distinguish field trees from grass are integrated into the tree coefficient (K_c). In the tree coefficient approach, tree evapotranspiration is calculated by multiplying ET_o by K_c.

Differences in evaporation and transpiration between field trees and the reference grass surface can be integrated in a single tree coefficient (K_c) or separated into two coefficients: a basal tree (K_{cb}) and a soil evaporation coefficient (K_e):

$$K_c = K_{cb} + K_e \qquad (49)$$

The approach to follow should be selected as a function of the purpose of the calculation, the accuracy required and the data available.

19.21 Direct Calculation

The evapotranspiration rate from a treeped surface can be directly measured by the mass transfer or the energy balance method. It can also be derived from studies of the soil water balance determined from treeped fields or from lysimeters.

Tree evapotranspiration can also be derived from meteorological and tree data by means of the Penman-Monteith equation (Eq. 3). By adjusting the albedo and the aerodynamic and canopy surface resistances to the growing characteristics of the specific tree, the evapotranspiration rate can be directly estimated. The albedo and resistances are, however, difficult to estimate accurately as they may vary continually during the growing season as climatic conditions change, as the tree develops, and with wetness of the soil surface. The canopy resistance will further be influenced by the soil water availability, and it increases strongly if the tree is subjected to water stress.

The reference evapotranspiration concept has been gaining significant acceptance by the engineers and scientists throughout the world since its introduction. Specific equations and standardized procedures are being recommended for reference evapotranspiration estimates. The International Commission for Irrigation and Drainage (ICID) and the Food and Agriculture Organization of the United Nations (FAO)

Expert Consultation on Revision of FAO Methodologies for Tree Water Requirements recommended that the Food and Agriculture Organization of the United Nations Paper No. 56 Penman-Monteith equation (FAO56-PM) be used as the standard method to estimate ET_0. This equation has been increasingly gaining acceptance and used throughout the world for reference evapotranspiration estimations. It is recommended that the grass-reference evapotranspiration concept be used for irrigation scheduling and water management, hydrologic studies, and drainage researches in Florida in order to establish a common and standard ground between the growers/farmers and their advisors and between the researchers.

— — —

20

Zero Waste

20.1 Introduction

High levels of energy and materials consumption in industrial countries are the driving force behind the decline in virtually all major life support systems on Planet Earth. Over the last decade an increasing number of scientists and other thoughtful people have come to conclude that modern levels of materials and energy consumption are having a destabilizing influence on the world's ecosystems.

Energy consumption contributes directly to climate change by adding carbon-based molecules to the atmosphere in excess of naturally occurring amounts. Carbon molecules, primarily carbon dioxide from burning petroleum products, trap radiant heat and keep it from escaping from the Earth's atmosphere. The resulting warming of the air is changing our global climate.

Materials consumption contributes indirectly to climate change because it requires energy to mine, extract, harvest, process, and transport raw materials, and more energy to manufacture, transport and, after use, dispose of products.

All the materials used in products, only 1% is used in products 'durable' enough to still be in use six months later, according to industrial ecologist Robert Ayres. This wasteful consumption of materials wreaks havoc on our land, water resources and their ecosystems. What's seldom appreciated is that it also wreaks havoc on our atmosphere and contributes to climate change. Waste prevention and recycling are critical to stopping climate change.

A growing international Zero Waste Movement is calling for radical resource efficiency and eliminating rather than managing waste strategies that have major benefits for slowing climate change. There are zero emission cars and zero accident worksites; Zero Waste is a goal for how we should responsibly manage materials and the energy required to make them. Zero Waste is a 'whole system' approach to resource management that maximizes recycling, minimizes waste, reduces consumption and ensures that products are made to be recycled, repaired or recycled back into nature or the marketplace Zero Waste systems including waste prevention and recycling reduce greenhouse gases by saving energy :

- Especially by reducing energy consumption associated with extracting, processing and transporting 'virgin' raw materials manufacturing with recycled materials uses less energy overall compared with manufacturing using virgin materials;
- Increasing carbon uptake by forests (recycled paper, for example, leaves more trees standing so they can breathe in our carbon dioxide); and
- Reducing and eventually eliminating the need for landfills (which release methane) and incinerators (which waste energy relative to recycling and reuse).

20.2 Recycling, Waste Prevention and Product Redesign: Saves Energy

Wasting materials causes massive amounts of energy to be used to extract and manufacture natural resource replacement materials. Reducing material use through waste prevention and increasing material efficiency through product redesign have the greatest beneficial impact on climate change. Recycling adds further to greenhouse gas savings by reducing the need for energy-intensive resource extraction. (Bastian & Ryan, 1986)

The U.S. Environmental Protection Agency estimates that by cutting the amount of waste we generate back to 1990 levels, we could reduce greenhouse gas emissions by 11.6 million metric tons of carbon equivalent (MTCE), the basic unit of measure for greenhouse gases. Increasing our national recycling rate from its low level to high levels would reduce greenhouse gas emissions by 9.8 million MTCE, compared to land filling the same material. Together, these levels of waste prevention and recycling would slash emissions of more amounts equal to the average annual emissions from the electricity consumption of roughly 11 million households. Manufacturing using recycled rather than virgin material saves substantial energy in virtually every case.

– Net carbon emissions are four to five times lower when materials are produced from recycled steel, copper, glass, and paper. They are 40 times lower for aluminum.

Making a ton of aluminum cans from its virgin source, bauxite, uses 229 British thermal units (BTUS). In contrast, producing cans from recycled aluminum uses only 8 Btus per ton, an energy

– Savings of 96% despite this, 45 billion aluminum beer and soft drink cans were wasted in the U.S. in 1998.
– Likewise, extracting and processing petroleum into common plastic containers (No. 1 'PET' and No. 2 'HDPE') takes four to eight times more energy than making plastics from recycled plastics. Yet the recycling rate for these plastic containers was only 20.2% in 1998.

Of course, energy conservation is just one of the environmental benefits attained by eliminating waste, increasing material efficiency and manufacturing products from recycled rather than virgin materials. As noted by Jeffrey Morris, virgin materials extraction (including drilling, digging, cutting, refining, smelting, and pulping) also: "(1) releases chemical substances, carbon dioxide, waste heat and processing refuse into air and water and onto land; (2) impairs the health of people exposed to polluting chemical releases; (3) dislocates and

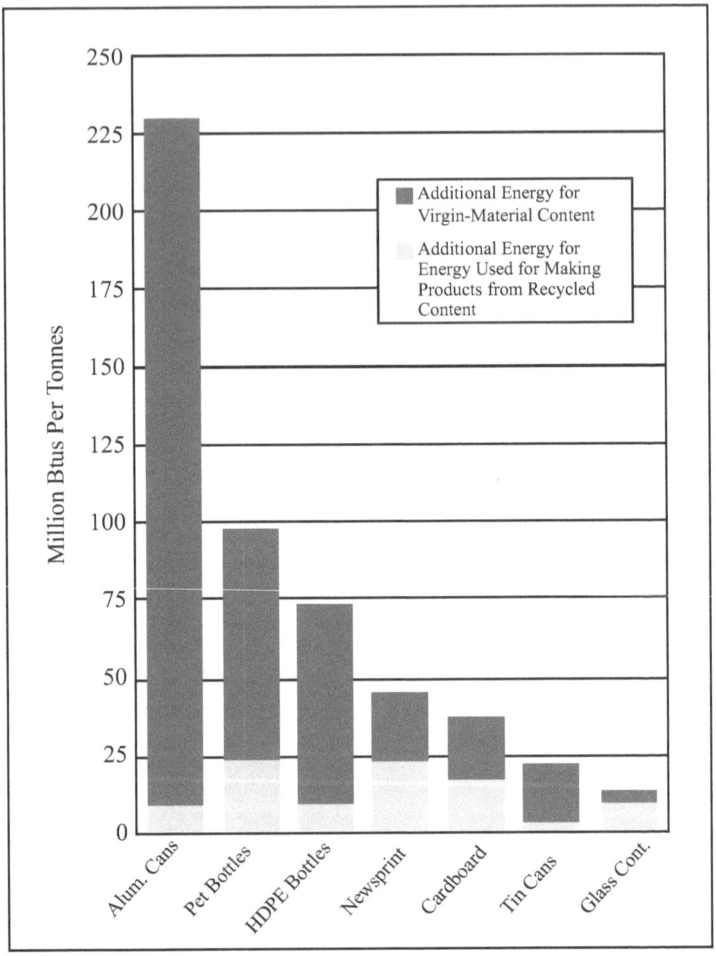

Figure 20.1: Energy vergin versus recycled content products

destroys habitat for a wide variety of non-human creatures and organisms; (4) diminishes productivity in natural resource industries that depend on healthy species and ecosystems; (5) impairs ecological functions and biological diversity in ecosystems; and (6) alters the sights, sounds, smells and feelings humans enjoyed in many previously pristine, natural places. Such consequences create an important difference between recycled material- and virgin material-based systems that is not adequately captured by life-cycle inventories.

20.3 Recycling, Reducing Paper and Wood Use: Saves Forests

Recycling a ton of paper saves about 24 trees, which absorb 250 pounds of carbon dioxide from the air each year, reducing the global greenhouse effect. Trees take carbon from the atmosphere and store it in their tissues for long periods.

In India, the amount of forest land (33 % of total land surface area) has remained fairly constant during the last several decades. Intensive tree farming practices and regeneration of previously cleared forest areas (particularly in the East) have offset tree harvesting and urban sprawl into forested area, resulting in an annual net uptake (*i.e.*, sequestration) of carbon.

While the net increase in tree biomass in India is good news for climate change, it is not necessarily good news for biodiversity or other aspects of environmental quality. That's because the dominant trend in forestry today is harvesting by clear-cutting and conversion of ecologically complex forests to single-species, single-aged tree farms. E.O. Wilson, a Harvard biologist and Pulitzer Prize winner, estimates that a pine plantation contains 90 to 95 % fewer species than the forest that preceded it. (Perttu, 1993)

More importantly, waste prevention and recycling reduce greenhouse gases by saving trees that take up carbon dioxide. Protecting and restoring diverse forests requires addressing the staggering waste of forest products considering the fact that :

- India sends more paper to landfills and incinerators than all of other countries even uses, despite its being the world's developing countries.
- While the timber industry touts advances in paper recycling, unsustainable paper wasting rates are seldom mentioned: 58.3% of all paper and paperboard is dumped in the landfill or burned in incinerators.
- Paper and wood account for almost half of all waste that goes to landfills and incinerators. Forest products (paper and wood) constitute 38.3% by weight of 'municipal solid

waste' and 51.9 % by weight of all products (*i.e.*, excluding food scraps and yard trimmings) sent to municipal waste facilities.

- Wasted paper alone constitutes 48% of the greenhouse gases emitted during the production of products that wind up in a ton of 'municipal waste' sent to landfill, and 64% of commonly diverted waste.

20.4 Reducing Landfilling and Incineration cuts Methane: Saves Energy

Landfills and incinerators contribute to global climate change by destroying resources, causing more new resources to extracted. We mixed 156 million tons of used products and packaging together in 1997, called it trash, and buried or burned it. Then we extracted from the environment billions of tons of virgin materials to make new products and packaging to replace those we wasted.

We should not just look at weight diverted as a measure of system performance, but rather prioritize recovering for reuse and recycling the materials that otherwise would waste so much if they had to be replaced by products made from scratch from natural resources. For example, some complain, "Why all the talk about soft drink containers when they are only 2 per cent of the waste stream?" Well, aluminum cans only comprise 1.4 % of the entire waste stream by weight, but they contribute ten times as much — 14 % — of the emissions embodied in a ton of divertible waste sent to landfill. Likewise, as the graph above shows, plastic containers take large amounts of energy to manufacture.

20.5 Landfills and Methane

Landfills are the top human-caused source of methane: 36% of human caused methane releases come from our municipal solid waste landfills, according to the U.S. Environmental Protection Agency. Organic materials [derived from living (USEPA, 1997) organisms] produce methane in landfills when they decompose without oxygen, under tons of garbage.

Methane gas is a potent greenhouse gas, 21 times more effective at trapping heat in the atmosphere than carbon dioxide. A ton of municipal solid waste landfilled produces 123 pounds of methane.

Some landfills operators try to recover methane. This is a voluntary effort at all but the largest landfills. According to one expert, "60% is about the best recovery of methane being reported, and most landfills that collect methane recover somewhere around 40%." In 1996, only 14 % of landfill methane was captured (most landfill methane is flared on site, some is used to produce energy).

20.6 Landfills *Vs.* Composting

Current 'state of the art' landfill design aims to entomb garbage and keep it dry forever. Many engineers, and even U.S. EPA, acknowledge that this is impossible, that all landfills will eventually leak and pollute groundwater. Recently, new systems are being developed, called 'bioreactors,' to try to capture methane more effectively. By recirculating leachate (garbage juice) and adding water, decomposition rates can be increased, making methane recovery more economical. This also compacts garbage, further increasing the value of remaining landfill space.

From the limited perspective of managing waste, this may seem reasonable. But from a Zero Waste perspective of managing resources, bioreactors make little sense. Over 62 % of what gets buried in municipal landfills is readily recyclable or compostable organics, including paper, wood, yard trimmings and food scraps (USEPA, 1992). Organic material is needed to replenish our depleted, eroding and artificially-fertilized soils.

Yet when paper, wood, yard trimmings and food scraps are mixed with the myriad toxic products in household and industrial waste, they become too contaminated to apply to soils. The rational solution is to separate clean organics at the source and compost them into soil amendments.

When done properly, both centralized and backyard composting generally result in no net greenhouse emissions, according to USEPA. Somewhat like trees, application of yard trimmings compost to degraded agricultural land results in carbon storage.

20.7 Incineration *v/s* Recycling

One might think that burning garbage for energy production would ameliorate global climate change by reducing the need to burn other fuels. There are two serious problems with this notion.

First, any gains in energy are outweighed by the production of toxic emissions and toxic ash, even in 'state-of-the-art' incinerators. Incinerator emissions of acid gases, mercury, dioxins and furans have led to widespread protests in North America, Japan and continental Europe, forcing the closure of plants and the abandonment of plans for new ones. In the U.S., 248 new municipal incinerators have been blocked and the number still in operation has fallen from 170 in 1991 to 119 in 1998. In 1997, 17 % of U.S. municipal discards was burned (in a relatively few states), 55 % was landfilled and 28 % was recycled.

Second, the energy produced by burning garbage is only a quarter of the energy saved by recycling. Recycling used resources has energy impacts, but they are much less than burning those materials. Richard Denison of Environmental Defense examined detailed life-cycle studies and concluded.

- When all activities entailing energy use are tallied, MSW [municipal solid waste] incineration results in only 28% of the net reduction in energy use realized through residential MSW recycling (Stewart *et.al.*, 1986).
- Within the waste management system itself, recycling uses somewhat more energy than the other options; system-wide, however, recycling uses the least energy by a large margin.
- From a system-wide view, recycled production plus recycling collection uses the least energy, considerably less than virgin production plus incineration. This difference

is due to the substantial reduction in energy use associated with manufacturing processes that use recycled materials relative to those that use virgin materials.

– Transportation energy required to ship processed recyclable materials to market (*i.e.* points of remanufacture) is quite modest, amounting to at most a few % of manufacturing energy.

20.8 Take Action: Getting to Zero

Implementation of Zero Waste resource management systems is arguably one of the most important steps to the sustainability of the earth's atmosphere and ecosystems. Zero Waste confronts the whole idea of endless consumption without needing to say so, by enabling even those who are locked into the system to challenge their own behavior in a positive way without immediately threatening it.

The Grass Roots Recycling Network (GRRN) has been spearheading the North American arm of a growing international movement that promotes Zero Waste as essential to reversing current unsustainable resource practices and policies. GRRN is building effective coalitions and partnerships for Zero Waste policies based on government, corporate and individual accountability for waste.

GRRN has identified the following outcomes as essential to move us towards a Zero Waste society: (a) Extended Producer Responsibility for Waste; (b) Consumer Action Against Wasteful Corporations; (c) Deposit Programs; (d) Jobs Through Reuse and Recycling; (e) Incentives for Reducing Trash; (f) Full-Cost Accounting and Life-Cycle Analysis; (g) Minimum Recycled Content; (h) Ending Subsidies for Extracting Virgin Resources; (i) Shifting Taxes from 'Goods' to 'Bads'; (j) National Resource Policy; and (k) Campaign Finance Reform.

Recognizing that the implementation of Zero Waste is a long-term, ambitious goal, a key component to our outreach is to educate other organizations whose work/mission might not be readily identifiable as impacted by Zero Waste. Practical strategies and actions can be taken by all sectors of society in all institutions.

Recycling technology leads to zero waste generation and minimize the global worming. It is essential to make awareness on zero waste generation and recycling in national , regional as well as upto the local and village level.

— — —

21

Case Studies

21.1 Introduction

The industrial revolution, which began in the early 18th century in some countries of Europe, set in motion new forces in the environment and greatly changed the pattern of social life. Rapid industrialization and urbanization subsequently brought many changes in the environment and ecosystem. India also witnessed a phenomenon of industrial growth in the post independent era. Progress in the industrial development in Tamil Nadu during recent past is appreciable. New industries developed, existing industries expanded and new technologies are introduced.

In India, the past decades have witnessed population explosion and increase in per capita consumption of food and consumer goods. These have led to the proportionate increase in the domestic and industrial wastes. The waste is continuously increasing at an alarming rate. By the end of this century, India's population is likely to increase from the present level of 700 million to about billion. Similarly the per capita consumption of food has been estimated to increase by 40% resulting in double production and disposal of industrial and domestic wastes (Manivanan, 2004).

Apart from the quantitative increase there will be also a qualitative change in the waste product, which are likely to contain greater amount of oil, toxic chemicals, detergents and dyes. A large number of these compounds are non-degradable and are cumulative, thus rendering the toxic products. Certain group of plants like algae and bacteria are selective in their functions and can executive certain toxic chemicals and heavy metals. The microorganism communities are helping in effective recycling of industrial effluents.

The government is taking serious efforts to keep the production of toxic substances under strict control at production centers. It carefully watches the efforts that are made to discharge the toxic waste from industries within the permissible limits and usages of toxic chemicals within the prescribed limits. The majority of rural population being uneducated is prone to excessive use of water which has become pollutant. The pollutant ultimately is drained into the natural aquatic environment, the rivers and the oceans. A part of these wastes are recycled and they again enter the food chain and cause detrimental effects to human health. Thus in nature, long and short term chain reactions are continuously in progress and these are required to be understood. Even when the best available yardsticks are applied to conserve the environment. It is a stupendous task to enforce these regulations.

In addition to production of more waste the coming years will see a qualitative change in the composition of waste. These wastes are likely to contain greater amount of toxic chemicals, detergents, non-degradable products based on hydrocarbons, and its derivatives. Large amount of wastes which are non degradable and cumulative in nature produce a series of new and complex problems. Therefore, alternative methods should develop for treatment and disposal of cumulative and non-degradable chemicals and pollutants.

21.2 Textile Industries

Industrial effluents are normally considered as toxicants due to the presence of organic and inorganic compounds, acids, alkalis and suspended solids. Such untreated effluents when discharged in to the environment, destroy the ecological niches of living organisms and disturb the fragile ecosystem. One of the most important waste water from the point of view of water pollution in our country is textile waste water. There are more than 670 textile industries in our country processing about 3960 meters of cloth every day. These industries are located mainly in Gujarat, Maharashtra, Delhi, Karnataka and Tamil Nadu (Fig. 21.1).

Figure 21.1: Location Plan of Textile Industries In India

These industries consume large amount of fresh water for their various processes such as sizing, desizing, bleaching, mercerizing dyeing and printing. These processes need large quantity of fresh water during their operations and release large volume of wastewater containing different types of toxic pollutants. It is estimated that 12.65 liters of water is required for processing one meter of cloth, which results in about 20 to 30ppm of biological oxygen demand.

It is only in the recent years these textile industries are becoming aware of the problem of wastewater treatment and disposal and have shown good response towards the challenging problems of pollution abatement.

In textile industries, raw cotton is corded, spun, spooled and wrapped, sized, drawn and woven into cloth before being sent to the finishing unit. No water borne diseases complained in the sequence of operations since all are mechanical processes, except sizing. The major wet process in the textile industries are described below.

Sizing

The warp is sized using strength and abrasive resistance to withstand the stress and strain in the process of weaving. There is practically no effluent from sizing section as such except for the spill over and washing during weekends.

Desizing

Before fabric is taken for wet processing like merceri-zation, bleaching, dyeing it is made properly absorbent. The sized cloth reformed to 'Gray gouels' contains sizing ingredients deposited on the warp yarn. It is necessary that the size is removed by one of the methods available. Enzymes desizing is a widely adapted method in Indian textile industries. Enzymes acts on starch to produce easily washable compounds of low molecular weight. Alkaline scoring also helps in desizing processes.

Bleaching

The bleaching process is necessary wherever fabrics are to be given a full white finish or where they are to be dyed in specific shades. In this process the natural colouring matter in the material is removed by the use of oxidizing chemicals. Thus in this section more quantity of effluent released.

Mercerization

The fabric is treated with strong caustic soda solution (230 to 260 g/litre). The cloth is washed by a counter current system to recover the soda. The process of mercerization improves the strength, elasticity, lusture and dye affinity.

Dyeing

Dyeing is necessary to improve the aesthetic and functional values of the fabric. Khaki dyeing is carried out by depositing inside the textile complex salts of iron and chromium depending upon the quantity of salts of iron and chromium used. Various shades of khaki can be produced. Fabrics are first impregnated with the solution of ferrous sulphates and basic chromic sulphates. It is then passed through a strong solution of caustic soda to precipitate iron and chromium salts as hydroxides. After proper ageing in a steaming chamber, the khaki shade is developed.

Sources of Wastewater

There is practically no effluent from sizing process such as except spill over and washing during weekends. The gray goods are desized to allow further wet processing and kiered to remove natural impurities. Large quantities of effluent are discharged from the desizing process. Bleaching process also discharges moderate amount of wastewater. During screen-printing, after fixing of the print, the fats and unfixed dyestuff and thickening materials are removed. This process also release wastewater.

Quantities of Wastewater

The quantity of waste water discharged by the textile industries are highly variable from one to another depending upon the fresh water usage and the average production of the cloth per day. Generally, one meter of cloth to be produced requires 12.65 liters of fresh water. The wastewater generated for this one meter of cloth 20-30 ppm of biological oxygen demand.

Treatment of Textile Industrial Effluent

As a first step, it is necessary to neutralize the effluent, screening of impurities such as fibrous materials and solid materials followed by addition of alum and ferrous sulphates reduces the biological oxygen demand and chemical oxygen demand values to arrive 50% and 80% respectively. The textile industrial effluent, after chemical treatment, can be treated by any one of the biological treatments for further purification. In this case, treatment with aeration tank is considered more suitable. (Band *et.al.,* 1995)

Disposal of untreated or partially treated effluents of various industries is one of the major environmental problem in our country. There is an urgent need to study, assess, evaluate and understand the effect of different industrial effluents on various ecosystems. Erode is a place known for several industries in Tamil Nadu. Generally the untreated and partially treated effluents are discharged into river Kaveri, Bhavani and their tributaries. Erode, one of the most important industrial cities of Tamil Nadu, has a large number of industries like sugar factories, pulp and paper, distillery units, tanneries refined oil mills, dyeing units. Hence an attempt is made to assess the impact of different industries effluent on growth performances of certain forest species and to evaluate the recycling capability of the forest tree species. (Manivanan, 2004)

21.3 *Acacia Ferruginea*

The above ground height at an interval of 20 days up to period of one year is monitored on the trial plot at Vellalar College for Women, Erode. The data indicated that the maximum above ground height in treated effluent up to a period of 80 days, from 100 days to 140 days in well water, from 160 to 180 days in treated effluent, from 200 to 360 days in well water (Fig.21.2 and 21.3).

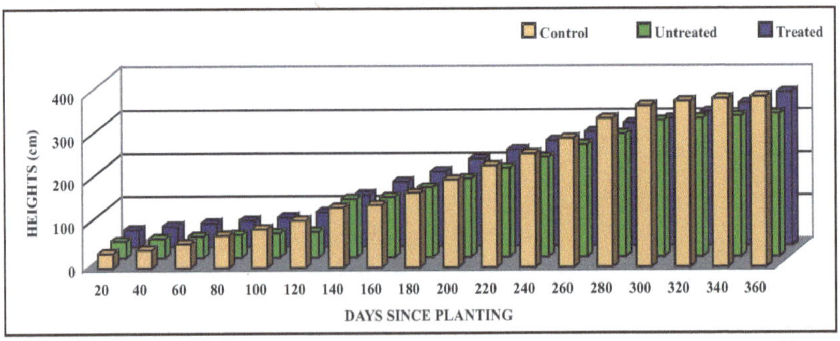

Figure 21.2: Above ground height values for control, treated, raw effluent for *Acacia Ferruginea.*

The basal diameters was indicated in well water up to 80 days. From 100 days to 180 days, the increase was in raw effluent and from 200 to 240 days it was in treated effluent. Later maximum diameter was found in well water and finally at 360 days in treated effluent irrigated seedlings (Fig.21.3)

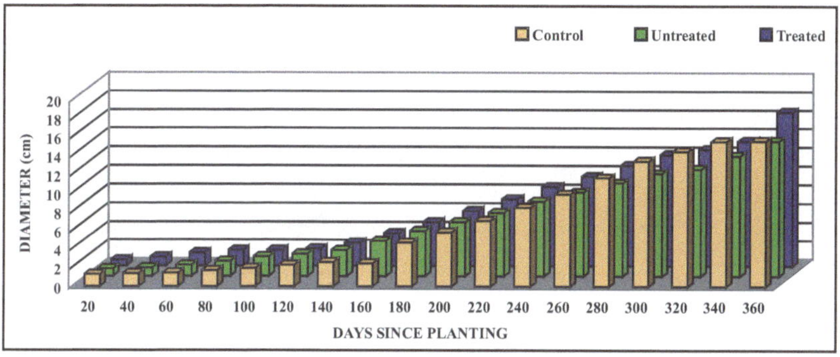

Figure 21.3: Basal diameter (cm) for control, treated, raw textile effluent for *Acacia ferruginea.*

The fresh weight, dry weight and moisture content of leaves, stems and roots are monitored for control, treated and untreated textile effluent. The tables 21.1,21.2, 21.3, 21.4 depicts higher fresh weight values in well water irrigation and decreased fresh weight was found in raw effluent irrigation. The enhanced dry weight was also recorded in well water-irrigated seedlings.

Figure 21.4: Industrial effluent irrigation for *Acacia Ferruginea*

Thus it is clear that the well water irrigated seedlings showed higher values for fresh weight, dry weight and moisture content of leaves, stem and roots. The data on top dry weight showed maximum in well water irrigation (Table 21.5). The leaf weight ratio, stem weight ratio and root weight ratio are calculated. The leaf weight ratio and stem weight ratio were maximum in well water irrigation but root weight ratio was in treated effluent due to the presence of materials. (Table 21.6)

Table 21.1: Fresh Weight(gm), Dry Weight(gm) and Water Content (gm) after 3rd Month

Sr. No.	Treatments	Leaves			Stem			Root			Total		
		FW	DW	WC	FW	DW	WC	FW	DW	WC	FW	DW	WC
1.	Control	150	25	125	178	46	132	63	27	36	391	98	293
2.	Untreated	38	21	17	65	22	43	45	18	27	148	61	87
3.	Treated	48	17	31	40	28	12	40	18	22	128	63	65

Table 21.2: Fresh Weight(gm), Dry Weight(gm) and Water Content (gm) after 6th Month

Sr. No.	Treatments	Leaves			Stem			Root			Total		
		FW	DW	WC	FW	DW	WC	FW	DW	WC	FW	DW	WC
1.	Control	300	52	248	350	95	255	120	50	70	770	197	573
2.	Untreated	80	20	60	120	40	80	90	30	60	290	90	200
3.	Treated	90	30	60	90	50	40	90	40	50	270	110	160

Table 21.3: Fresh Weight(gm), Dry Weight(gm) and Water Content (gm) After 9th Month

Sr. No.	Treatments	Leaves			Stem			Root			Total		
		FW	DW	WC	FW	DW	WC	FW	DW	WC	FW	DW	WC
1.	Control	450	79	401	540	139	401	193	88	105	1213	306	907
2.	Untreated	136	45	91	190	70	120	140	52	88	466	167	299
3.	Treated	145	53	92	130	92	38	145	62	83	420	207	213

Table 21.4: Fresh Weight(gm), Dry Weight(gm) and Water Content (gm) after 12th Month

Sr. No.	Treatments	Leaves			Stem			Root			Total		
		FW	DW	WC	FW	DW	WC	FW	DW	WC	FW	DW	WC
1.	Control	780	110	670	720	190	530	270	125	150	1770	425	1345
2.	Untreated	190	76	114	240	95	145	190	84	106	620	255	365
3.	Treated	190	84	106	184	133	51	195	84	111	569	301	268

Table 21.5: Top Dry Weight (gm) for the Period of One Year

Sr. No.	Treatments	3rd month	6th month	9th month	12th month
1.	Control	71	147	218	300
2.	Untreated	43	60	115	171
3.	Treated	45	80	145	217

Table 21.6: Leaf Weight Ratio, Stem Weight Ratio and Root Weight Ratio of *Acacia Ferruginea.*

Sr. No.	Weights	TREATMENTS								
		Control			Untreated			Treated		
		LWR	SWR	RWR	LWR	SWR	RWR	LWR	SWR	RWR
1.	Fresh Weight	38.96	45.46	15.58	27.59	41.38	31.03	38.7	29.05	32.25
2.	Dry Weight	26.39	48.22	25.39	22.22	44.44	33.34	36.36	36.36	27.28
3.	Moisture Content	43.28	44.50	12.22	30.00	40.00	30.00	44.44	11.12	44.44

Indices

Sturdiness quotient and volume index were also calculated and presented in figure numbers 21.5 and 21.6 respectively. Table 21.7 showed quality index for control, untreated and treated irrigated seedling. Sturdiness quotient was high in well water and low in treated effluent. The highest volume index was found to be in well water and lowest in raw effluent.

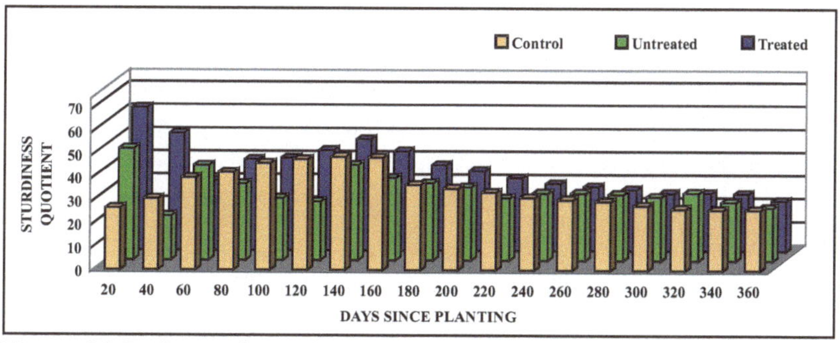

Figure 21.5: Comparison of sturdiness quotient for various treatments

Table 21.7: Comparison of quality index for various months

Sr. No.	Treatments	3rd month	6th month	9th month	12th month
1.	Control	2.02	4.97	9.53	15.32
2.	Untreated	2.10	2.55	5.44	10.54
3.	Treated	1.48	2.83	7.22	12.94

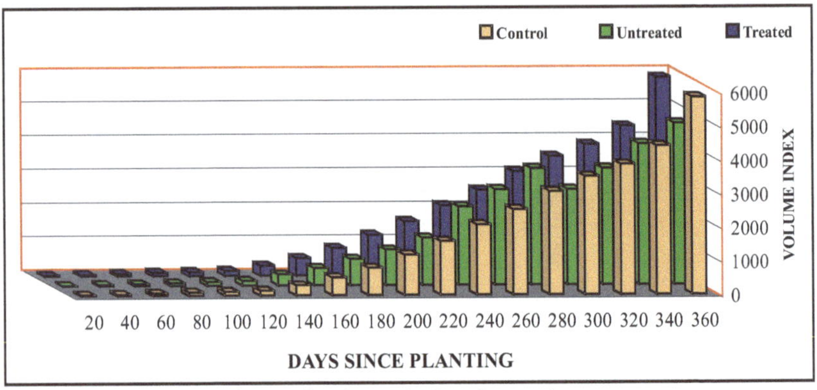

Figure 21.6: Comparison of volume index for various treatments

Quality index was observed to be high in untreated effluent and low in treated effluent for after third month. After six month, the highest value found to be in well water and lowest in untreated effluent. The highest value was observed in well water and lowest in untreated for nine-month period. The over all observation is found to be in well water-irrigated seedling. *Acacia ferruginea* plant is not suitable for recycling of textile effluent either untreated or treated effluent. (Manivanan, 2004)

21.4 *Delonix Regia*

The above ground height at an interval of 20 days up to period of one year is monitored on the trial plot at Vellalar College for Women, Erode. The data indicated that maximum above ground height in treated effluent up to a period of 360 days in well water (Fig.21.7).

The basal diameters was indicated in untreated effluent up to 40 days. From 60 days to 360 days, the increase was in treated effluent irrigated seedlings (Fig.21.8).

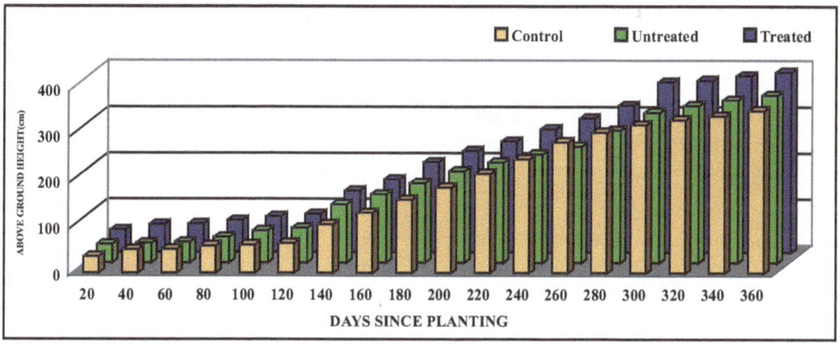

Figure 21.7: Above ground height values for control, treated, raw effluent for *Delonix Regia.*

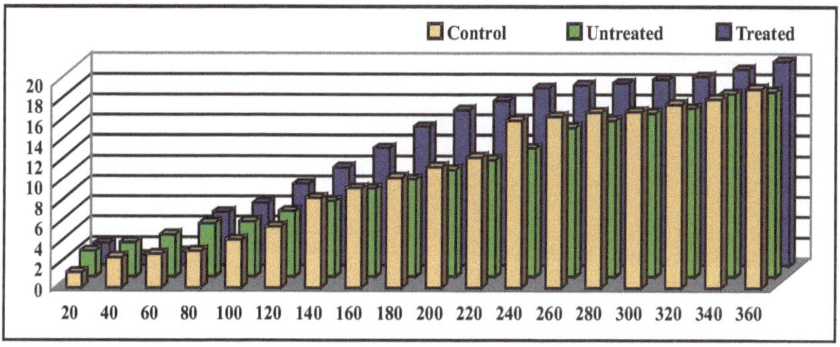

Figure 21.8: Basal diameter (cm) for control, treated, raw textile effluent for *Delonix Regia.*

The fresh weight, dry weight and moisture content of leaves, stems and roots are monitored for control, treated and untreated textile effluent. The tables 21.8, 21.9, 21.10 and 21.11 depicts higher fresh weight values in well water irrigation and decreased fresh weight was found in raw effluent irrigation. The

Table 21.8: Fresh weight (gm), dry weight (gm) and water content (gm) after 3rd month.

Sr. No.	Treatments	Leaves			Stem			Root			Total		
		FW	DW	WC	FW	DW	WC	FW	DW	WC	FW	DW	WC
1.	Control	875	190	685	390	195	195	360	60	300	1625	445	1180
2.	Untreated	700	170	530	450	165	285	370	50	320	1520	385	1135
3.	Treated	640	180	460	360	220	140	330	80	250	1330	480	850

enhanced dry weight was also recorded in well water-irrigated seedlings.

Table 21.9: Fresh weight (gm), dry weight (gm) and water content (gm) after 6th month.

Sr. No.	Treatments	Leaves			Stem			Root			Total		
		FW	DW	WC	FW	DW	WC	FW	DW	WC	FW	DW	WC
1.	Control	1760	390	1370	800	390	410	700	100	600	3260	880	2380
2.	Untreated	1260	300	960	850	310	440	750	110	640	2760	720	2040
3.	Treated	1250	370	885	710	420	290	650	190	460	2610	980	160

Table 21.10: Fresh weight (gm), dry weight (gm) and water content (gm) after 9th month.

Sr. No.	Treatments	Leaves			Stem			Root			Total		
		FW	DW	WC	FW	DW	WC	FW	DW	WC	FW	DW	WC
1.	Control	2635	610	2025	1280	510	770	1170	180	990	5085	1300	3785
2.	Untreated	2260	650	1610	1350	400	950	1020	122	848	4630	1222	3408
3.	Treated	2150	680	1470	1150	610	540	1010	260	750	4310	1550	2760

Table 21.11: Fresh weight (gm), dry weight (gm) and water content (gm) after 12th month.

Sr. No.	Treatments	Leaves			Stem			Root			Total		
		FW	DW	WC	FW	DW	WC	FW	DW	WC	FW	DW	WC
1.	Control	3710	910	2800	2550	1115	1435	1530	340	1190	7790	2365	5425
2.	Untreated	3390	890	2500	2150	850	1300	1610	240	1370	7150	1980	5170
3.	Treated	3800	1150	2650	3150	1210	1940	1720	480	1240	8640	2840	5830

Thus it is clear that the treated effluent irrigated seedlings showed higher values for fresh weight, dry weight and moisture content of leaves, stem and roots. The data on top dry weight showed maximum in well water irrigation (Table 21.12). The leaf weight ratio, stem weight ratio and root weight ratio are calculated. The leaf weight ratio and stem weight ratio were maximum in well water irrigation but root weight ratio was in treated effluent due to the presence of materials. (Table 21.13)

Table 21.12: Top dry weight (gm) for the period of one year.

Sr. No.	Treatment	3rd month	6th month	9th month	12th month
1.	Control	385	780	1120	2025
2.	Untreated	335	610	1050	1740
3.	Treated	400	790	1290	2360

Table 21.13: Leaf weight ratio, stem weight ratio and root weight ratio of *Delonix Regia.*

Sr. No.	Weights	TREATMENTS								
		Control			Untreated			Treated		
		LWR	SWR	RWR	LWR	SWR	RWR	LWR	SWR	RWR
1.	Fresh Weight	47.90	27.20	24.90	44.06	29.72	26.22	53.98	24.54	21.48
2.	Dry Weight	37.75	42.87	19.38	41.67	43.07	15.28	44.31	44.31	11.38
3.	Moisture Content	54.12	17.73	28.15	47.06	21.51	31.37	57.56	17.23	25.21

Indices

Sturdiness quotient and volume index were also calculated and presented in figure numbers 21.9 and 21.10 respectively. Table 21.21 shows quality index for control, untreated and treated irrigated seedling. Sturdiness quotient was high in well water and low in treated effluent. The highest volume index was found to be in well water and lowest in raw effluent (Manivanan, 2004).

Quality index was observed to be high in untreated effluent and low in treated effluent for after third month. After six month,

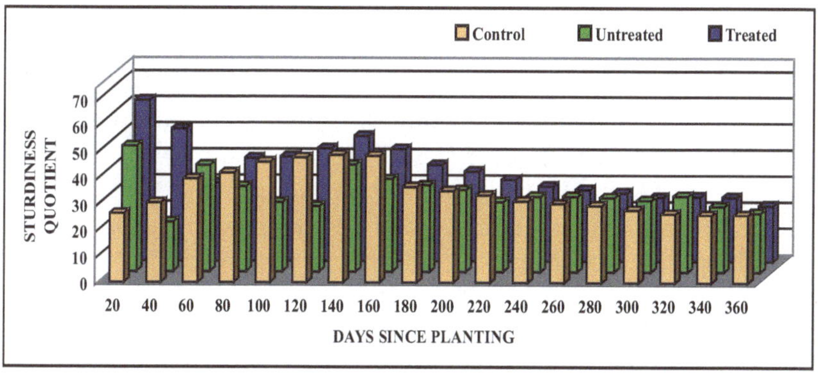

Figure 21.9: Comparison of sturdiness quotient for various treatments

the highest value found to be in well water and lowest in untreated effluent. The highest value was observed in well water and lowest in untreated for nine-month period. The over all observation is found to be in well water-irrigated seedling. Acacia ferruginea plant is not suitable for recycling of textile effluent either untreated or treated effluent (Table 21.14)

Table 21.14: Comparison of quality index for various months.

Sr. No.	Treatments	3rd month	6th month	9th month	12th month
1.	Control	22.82	39.15	54.26	98.46
2.	Untreated	19.67	30.55	49.12	72.58
3.	Treated	27.18	52.92	60.55	116.78

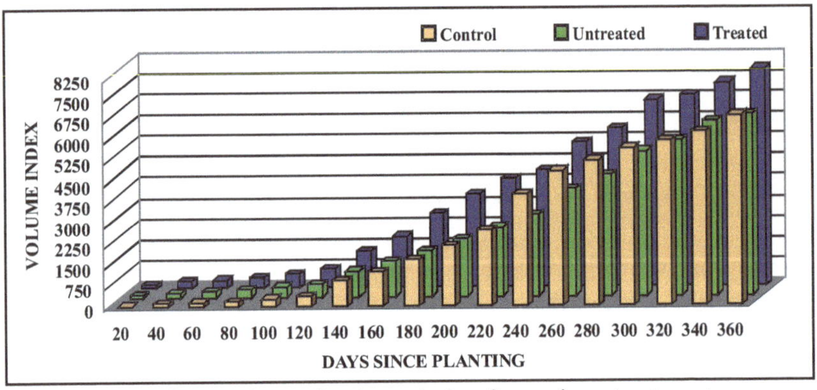

Figure 21.10: Comparison of volume index for various treatments

21.5 *Tamarindus Indica*

The above ground height at an interval of 20 days up to period of one year is monitored on the trial plot at Vellalar College for Women, Erode. The data indicated that maximum above ground height in treated effluent up to a period of 360 days in well water (Fig.21.12 and Photo 21.13).

The basal diameters was indicated in untreated effluent up to 40 days. From 60 days to 360 days, the increase was in treated effluent irrigated seedlings (Fig.21.12).

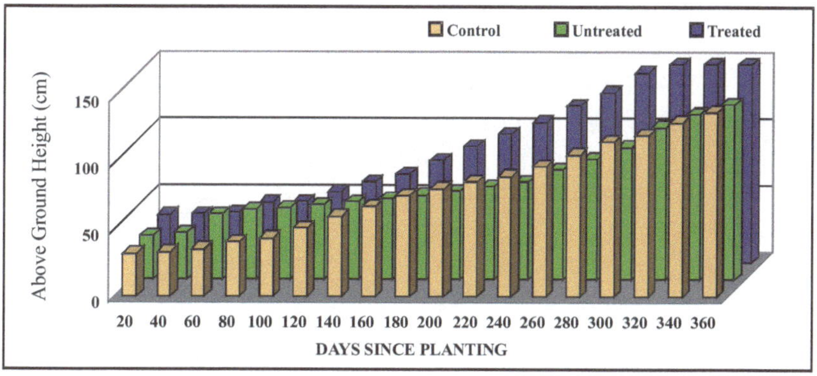

Figure 21.11: Above ground height values for control, treated, raw effluent for *Tamarindus Indica.*

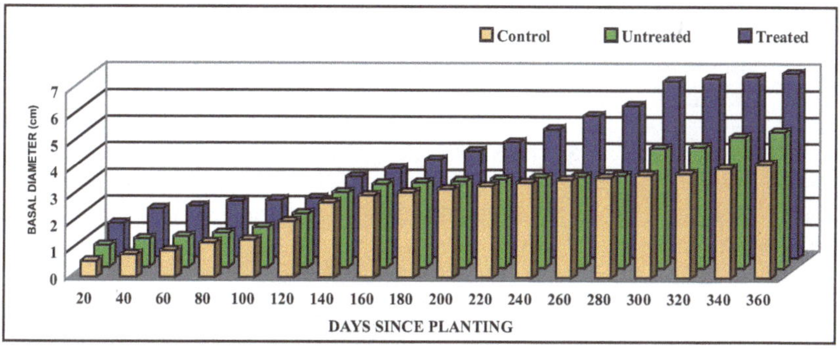

Figure 21.12: Basal diameter (cm) for control, treated, raw textile effluent for *Tamarindus Indica.*

Figure 21.13: Industrial effluent irrigation for *Tamarindus Indica.*

The fresh weight, dry weight and moisture content of leaves, stems and roots are monitored for control, treated and untreated textile effluent. The tables 21.15,21.16, 21.17 and 21.18 depicts higher fresh weight values in well water irrigation and decreased fresh weight was found in raw effluent irrigation. The enhanced dry weight was also recorded in well water-irrigated seedlings.

Table 21.15: Fresh weight (gm), dry weight (gm) and water content (gm) after 3rd month.

Sr. No.	Treatments	Leaves			Stem			Root			Total		
		FW	DW	WC	FW	DW	WC	FW	DW	WC	FW	DW	WC
1.	Control	40	17	28	54	18	30	32	22	11	126	57	69
2.	Untreated	23	09	16	20	17	06	19	08	06	62	34	28
3.	Treated	29	18	12	24	19	03	26	17	10	79	54	25

Table 21.16: Fresh weight (gm), dry weight (gm) and water content (gm) after 6th month.

Sr. No.	Treatments	Leaves			Stem			Root			Total		
		FW	DW	WC	FW	DW	WC	FW	DW	WC	FW	DW	WC
1.	Control	90	30	60	110	40	70	60	50	10	260	120	140
2.	Untreated	50	20	30	40	30	10	40	20	20	130	70	60
3.	Treated	40	20	45	40	5	50	30	15	155	110	45	45

Table 21.17: Fresh weight (gm), dry weight (gm) and water content (gm) after 9th month.

Sr. No.	Treatments	Leaves			Stem			Root			Total		
		FW	DW	WC	FW	DW	WC	FW	DW	WC	FW	DW	WC
1.	Control	140	52	88	167	58	109	105	74	31	412	184	228
2.	Untreated	82	33	49	70	52	18	75	34	41	227	119	108
3.	Treated	94	61	33	84	64	20	84	49	35	262	174	88

Table 21.18: Fresh weight (gm), dry weight (gm) and water content (gm) after 12th month.

Sr. No.	Treatments	Leaves			Stem			Root			Total		
		FW	DW	WC	FW	DW	WC	FW	DW	WC	FW	DW	WC
1.	Control	190	72	118	225	82	143	145	98	47	560	252	308
2.	Untreated	110	45	65	104	74	30	116	62	54	330	181	149
3.	Treated	135	82	53	115	85	30	110	78	32	360	245	115

Thus it is clear that the treated effluent irrigated seedlings showed higher values for fresh weight, dry weight and moisture content of leaves, stem and roots. The data on top dry weight showed maximum in well water irrigation (Table 21.19). The leaf weight ratio, stem weight ratio and root weight ratio are calculated. The leaf weight ratio and stem weight ratio were maximum in well water irrigation but root weight ratio was in treated effluent due to the presence of materials. (Table 21.20)

Table 21.19: Top dry weight (gm) for the period of one year.

S. No.	Treatment	3rd month	6th month	9th month	12th month
1.	Control	35	70	110	154
2.	Untreated	26	50	85	119
3.	Treated	37	80	125	167

Table 21.20: Leaf weight ratio, stem weight ratio and root weight ratio of *Delonix Regia.*

S. No.	Weights	TREATMENTS								
		Control			Untreated			Treated		
		LWR	SWR	RWR	LWR	SWR	RWR	LWR	SWR	RWR
1.	Fresh Weight	34.61	42.30	23.09	38.48	30.76	30.76	38.70	29.05	32.25
2.	Dry Weight	47.05	23.52	29.43	28.57	43.40	28.57	36.36	36.36	27.28
3.	Moisture Content	42.85	50.00	7.15	50.00	16.67	33.33	50.00	12.50	37.50

Indices

Sturdiness quotient and volume index were also calculated and presented in figure numbers 21.14 and 21.15 respectively. Table 21.21 showed quality index for control, untreated and treated irrigated seedling. Sturdiness quotient was high in well water and low in treated effluent. The highest volume index was found to be in well water and lowest in raw effluent.

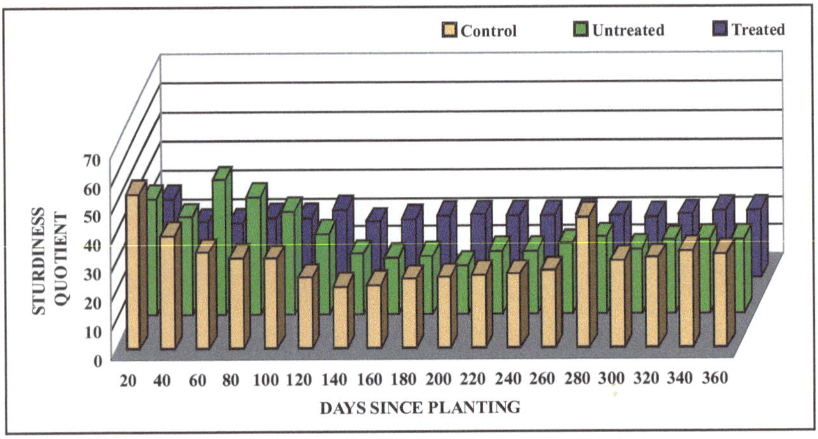

Figure 21.14: Comparison of sturdiness quotient for various treatments.

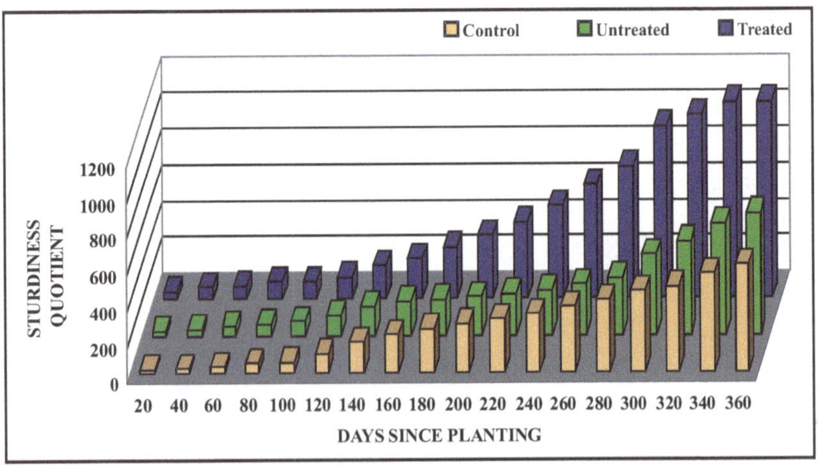

Figure 21.15: Comparison of volume index for various treatments.

Table 21.21: Comparison of quality index for various months.

S. No.	Treatments	3rd month	6th month	9th month	12th month
1.	Control	1.73	4.73	6.14	7.33
2.	Untreated	0.87	3.08	4.10	6.51
3.	Treated	2.28	4.63	9.49	116.78

Quality index was observed to be high in untreated effluent and low in treated effluent for after third month. After six month, the highest value found to be in well water and lowest in untreated effluent. The highest value was observed in well water and lowest in untreated for nine-month period. The over all observation is found to be in well water-irrigated seedling. *Acacia ferruginea* plant is not suitable for recycling of textile effluent either untreated or treated effluent.

Rapid industrialization and urbanization lead to the generation of large volumes of wastewater, the treatment and disposal of which can cause considerable problems. About 13153 million gallons of wastewater is released every day from various urban and rural centers in India (Vimal & Talashikar, 1985). Land application of wastewater through an age old practice is being given a higher preference since it provides scope for exploiting the reuse potential of waste water.

Disposal of secondary treated wastewater on to land is frequently a desirable alternative to direct disposal into surface water (Bower & Chaney, 1974 and Ditri, 1977). The soil, water and the vegetation act as wastewater living filter. In recent years a number of wastewater irrigation projects are proposed to utilize forest ecosystems for nutritional recycling and ground water recharge. Land treatment of wastewater is a biological treatment method. The present study aims at recycling textile wastewater by land application and assessing the manorial value of the effluent on certain forest trees.

Identifying forest trees species adapted to the moisture and nutrient regimen provided by the wastewater irrigation is a pre-request. The tree species evaluated in this study for wastewater recycling suitability are *Acacia ferruginea, Delonix regia* and

Tamarindus indica. Field experiments were conducted with well water, treated and untreated effluent irrigation. Various phyto-sociological parameters such as above ground height, basal diameter, fresh weight, dry weight and moisture content of leaves, stem and root, top dry weight, leaf weight ratio, stem weight ratio and root weight ratio, sturdiness quotient, volume index and quality index were determined.

The physico-chemical analysis of the untreated and treated effluent revealed an alkaline pH 8-8.5 due to high carbonate and bicarbonate when compared to BIS standard. The values of other parameters are not much significant. The study also indicated negligible chemical difference between untreated and treated effluent. Treatment has slightly reduced certain parameters like pH, electrical conductivity, calcium and bicarbonate. An increase was reported after treatment in zinc, copper and lead due to the application of urea and copper sulphates in the raw effluent for chemical treatment in the industry.

Growth increments were measured by above ground height and basal diameter. In *Acacia ferruginea,* the maximum above ground height was reported in well water irrigation but in *Delonix regia* and *Tamarindus indica* was treated effluent irrigation. Increased basal diameter may be positively correlated with treated effluent irrigation in *Delonix regia* and *Tamarindus indica* but negative trend is shown *Acacia ferruginea* as well water irrigation produced maximum basal diameter. Thus the present study above ground height and basal diameter were found to be increased by treated effluent irrigation in *Delonix regia* and *Tamarindus indica* by well water irrigation in *Acacia ferruginea.*

Fresh weight, dry weight and moisture content of leaves, stem and root are indices of over all growth performance. The present study shows enhanced values for fresh weight, dry weight and moisture content of leaves in *Acacia ferruginea* seedlings irrigated with well water. In *Delonix regia* up to a period of 6 months increased values were obtained in well water irrigation but after 6 months same results continued for fresh weight and moisture content while dry weight was high in treated effluent irrigation. *Tamarindus indica* showed high values for fresh weight and moisture content in well water irrigation but dry weight was high in treated effluent irrigation.

With reference to the fresh weight, dry weight and moisture content of stem in *Acacia ferruginea* well water irrigation enhanced in values but in *Delonix regia* untreated and treated effluent irrigated seedlings produced significant values. In *Tamarindus indica* well water irrigation increased the fresh weight and moisture content of stem but dry weight increased in well water irrigation upto 6 month, after that treated effluent irrigation showed higher values.

Regarding the fresh weight, dry weight and moisture content of root, in *Acacia ferruginea* and *Tamarindus indica* seedlings irrigated with well water showed maximum values. The moisture content of roots in *Tamarindus indica* was increased by untreated effluent irrigation. In support of the present observation increased root dry weight was recorded in vigna radiate (Neelam, 1986) treated with distillery effluent, *Arachis hypogea* (Swaminathan *et. al*, 1990) treated with glucose factory effluent.

The results obtained for top dry weight depicts high values in *Acacia ferruginea* seedlings irrigated with well water but treated effluent irrigation enhanced the top dry weight in *Delonix regia* and *Tamarindus indica.*

Growth performance was also assessed by leaf weight ratio, stem weight ratio and root weight ratio. In *Acacia ferruginea,* the results of leaf weight ratio indicated maximum in well water irrigation for fresh weight and in treated effluent for dry weight and moisture content. In *Delonix regia,* fresh and dry weight were enhanced by treated effluent and moisture content by well water. The treated effluent irrigation increased fresh weight and moisture content while well water increased dry weight in *Tamarindus indica.*

Relating the results of stem weight ratio with irrigation, it is understood that in *Acacia ferruginea* well water irrigation had a good support on fresh weight, dry weight and moisture content. In *Delonix regia* untreated effluent irrigation promoted fresh weight and moisture content while treated effluent the dry weight. Well water irrigation increased fresh weight and moisture content and untreated effluent irrigation dry weight in *Tamarindus indica.*

Correlating root weight ratio and irrigation, treated effluent irrigation produced good results for fresh weight, dry weight and moisture content in *Acacia ferruginea,* fresh weight and moisture content in *Tamarindus indica,* untreated effluent irrigation the fresh weight and moisture content in *Delonix regia,* well water the dry weight in *Tamarindus indica* and *Delonix regia* (Manivanan & Das, 2002).

Sturdiness quotient, volume index and quality index are the three important indices used to asses the out plantation programme in forestry. These indices are used in the present study to monitor the plantation success of selected trees. Low sturdiness quotient, high volume index and high quality index are indications of best plantation programmes (Kumaran *et. al.,* 1996). In the present study low sturdiness quotient was o btained with untreated and treated effluent in *Acacia ferruginea, Delonix regia* and *Tamarindus indica.* In *Acacia ferruginea* high volume index and high quality index are obtained in well water irrigation. But effluent irrigated seedlings showed high quality index and volume index in *Delonix regia* and *Tamarindus indica.*

Effect of distillery waste on the seedling growth in rice was assessed and it was found that effluent after dilution produced good results (Behera & Misra, 1981). In *Arachis hypogea* seed germination and seedling development was favoured by dyeing factory effluent on dilution (Swaminathan & Vaidheeswaran, 1991). Using paper mill effluent an increase of height and collar diameter in *Eucalyptus camaldulenis, pongamia pinnata, Acacia auriculformis. Leucaena leuocephala* and *Dentrocalamus strictus* have been reported by Neelay Dhondized (1985). The present study shows enhanced growth performance in *Delonix regia* and *Tamarindus indica.*

Studies on sewage irrigated Teak (*Tectona grandis*) plantation has revealed that irrigation boosts growth oarameters such as diameter, volume index and basal area. Experiments were conducted to assess the early growth response of 5 forest tree species (*Tectona grandis, Bambusa* sp. *Leucaena leucocaphala, Gmalina arborea ciselpinnae ciperia*) to sewage application. The results showed that waste had favourable effect on the germination and early seedling growth (Chakrabarti & Nashikar, 1994; Joshi &Farooqui,1991; Gogate *et.al.*,1995). In a case study of tea plantations irrigated with sewage it was observed that growth in terms of height and girth was significanltly higher than the growth from plots irrigated with ordinary water (Dakshindas *et. al.*, 1995). Though textile effluent is used in the present study, it is linearly related with the above report on Teak, as *Delonix regia* and *Tamarindus indica* showed boosted response in all the parameters undertaken. *Acacia ferruginea* in the present study shows negative correlation as well water irrigation indicated good results on most of the parameters.

The better growth performance may be related to increased water holding capacity of the soil when irrigated with effluent due to the presence of dissolved and suspended solids. Similar observations on increase of water holding capacity by addition of paper mill effluent (Rajannan & Oblisami, 1979), distillery effluent (Manonmani, *et. al.* 1990) Steel mill effluent (Archana & Naik, 1992) had also been reported. The enhanced growth in *Delonix regia* and *Tamarindus indica* observed during observation suggests that these trees were able to utilize the minerals ansd nutrients of the effluent. It is also inferred from the present experiment that *Acacia ferruginea* is chemically satisfied with well water irrigation.

Swaminathan *et. al* (1992) have reported that when the viscose factory effluent was added to the soil for irrigation purpose the effluent decreased the hygroscopic moisture and water holding capacity and increases potassium and sodium content of soil thereby making the soil unfit for plant growth. This is negatively correlated with the present study as no negative effect is recorded. However this statement requires long term study for clarification.

Several species and hybrids of Populus seem to be ideally suited for effluent irrigation sites(Cole 1978). Other trees that have responded favourably to irrigation during their seedling stage include *Fraxinus pennsylvanica, Pinus strobes, Pinus resinosa, Pinus nigra, Pinus rigida* (Soper & Kardos,1973; Neary *et. al.*, 1975 ; Cole & Schiess, 1978; Cooley). Pinus radiate and a number of Eucalyptus species have been successfully grown by utilization of the wastewater (Cromer, 1980; Edgar & Stewart, 1978).

Species performance for wastewater irrigation was evaluated in 9 forest trees and eastern cotton wood was found to be superior in over all performance and was recommended for wastewater irrigation programme. A study undertaken by Central Soil Salinity Research Institute, Karnal (Anon,1990) had shown that forestry crops such as *Eucalyptus tereticornis, Leucaena leucocephala* and *Populus* can be grown successfully using untreated sewage.

Short rotation forests consisting of various Salis species were found to be suitable as vegetation filters with regard to the removal of nutrients from municipal sewage, sludge and wastewater (Perttu, 1993)

Trees were grouped into 2 sub groups as species not requiring soil amelioration tolerant to textile effluent water and species requiring soil amelioration therefore less tolerant to effluent water. *Eucalyptus camaldulensis, Acacia nilotica, azadirca indica and Prosopis cineraria* belong to the first group and *Colophospermum mopane, Acacia tortilis, Prosopis juliflora* and *Hardwickia pinnata* belong to the second group (Aggarwal *et. al,* 1994)

The present chapter assesses the species performance for textile wastewater irrigation using three multipurpose forest trees such as *Acacia ferruginea, Delonix regia* and *Tamarindus indica*. *Delonix regia* and *Tamarindus indica* are found to be superior in overall performance hence recommended for textile effluent irrigation programme. Indications from the studies, that textile effluent causes no damage to the forest trees, in certain cases showed increased growth performances.

— — —

Bibliography

Aggarwal R.K., Praveen Kumar, Harsh. L.N. & Sharma B.M.: 'Effect of effluents of textile industry on the growth of tree species and soil properties in an arid environment'. *Indian Forester* 120(1): 40-47.

Allen R.G., Smith, M., Perrier, A., and Pereira, L.S.: An update for the definition of reference evapotranspiration. *JCID Bulletin*, 32(2). 1-34, 1994.

Anon: Sweage water utilisation through foresty brochure, Pub: Central Soil Salinity Res. Institute, ICAR, Karnal 1-15, 1990.

APHA: Standard Methods for the Examination of Water and Wastewater, 19th ed. American Public Health Association, Washington, D.C. 1995.

Arachana S. & Naik M.L.: Effects of Steel mill effluent irrigation on physico chemical characteristics of Kanhar Soil. *Jr. Ind. Poll. Cont.* (7) 11-16: 1992.

Bastian, R.K., and J.A. Ryan: Design and management of succcessful land application systems. 217-234 pp. *In Proceedings, Utilization treatment and disposal of waste on land*. Soil Science Society of America, Madison, Wisconsin. 1986.

Behera B.K. & Misra B.N.: "Analysis of the effect of Industrial effluent on growth and development of rice seedlings" *Environmental Research*, 28(10): 10-19. 1981.

Bond WJ, Polglase PJ, Smith CJ, Falkiner RA, Myers BJ, and Theiveyanathan S.: Effluent irrigation: Implications for groundwater. In : Groundwater and the Community, Muray Darling Workshop, 11-13 September, Wagga, Australia, NSW, Australia, Aust. *Geol. Surv. Org., Record* 61: 40-44, 1995.

Bond WJ, Polglase PJ, Smith CJ, Falkiner RA, Myers BJ, and Theiveyanathan S: Impact of effluent irrigation on groundwater.

In *1st Int. Conf. Contaminants and the Soil Environment*. Extended Abstracts, Adelaide, 259-260, 1996.

Bower H & Chaney R.L.: Land Treatment - II water quality and economics aspects of the flushing meadours Projects, *Jr. Wat. Pollut. Control Fedn.* 46(5): 844-859, 1974.

Burman, R. and Pochop. L.O.: *Evaporation, Evapotranspiration and Climatic Data.* Elsevier Science B.V., Amsterdam. 1994.

Central Pollution Control Board: *Documents on Ground Water Quality Critical Areas.* GOI, New Delhi. 1994.

Central Pollution Control Board: *Implementation Status of the Pollution Control Programme in Major Polluting Industries.* Ministry of Environment and Forestry, New Delhi. 1995.

Central Pollution Control Board: Report on Tank Irrigation in India Ministry of Environment and Forestry, New Delhi. 2000.

Central Pollution Control Board: A Report on MINARS GOI New Delhi. 1999.

Centre for Monitoring Indian Economy: *Indian Agricultural Sector: A Compendium of Statistics* 1995.

Centre for Monitoring Indian Economy: Basic Statistics, States. 1994.

Central Water Commission: *Water Demand in India.* 1993.

Central Water Commission: *Availability* of *Water in India.* 1997.

Chitale, M. A. Population and Water Resources of India In *The Inevitable Billion Plus: Science, Population and Development, An Exploration of Inter connectivity and Action Possibilities in India, Umesh Communications.* Pune. 111-117 pp. Edited by Vasant Gowariker 1992.

Chakrabarti C & Nashikar V.J.: *"Forest tree fertilization with sewage Bioresource Technology"* 50:85-187. 1994.

Christiansen, J. E.: Pan evaporation and evapotranspiration from climatic data. *J. Irrig. and Drain. Div.*, 94: 243-265, 1968.

Cole, D.W & Schiess P.: Renovation of wastewater and response of forest ecosystems. The pack forest study. In: *Proc. State of Knowledge in land treatment of wastewater,* H.L. Mckim U.S. Army cold regions Research and Engineering laboratory, Hanover New Hampshire (2): 323-331. 1978.

Cooly, J. H.: "Growing trees on effluent irrigation sites with sand soil in the upper Midwest", *Technical Report Date*, EPA, Chicago. 127-135. 1981.

Cromer: Irrigation of radiata pine with wastewater. A review of the potential for tree growth and water renovation. *Aust. Forestry* 43 (2):87-100. 1980

Czabator. F.J.: 'Germination Value' and index combining speed and completeness of pine seed germination. *Forest Science*. 8: 386-396. 1962.

Dakshindas. S.D., Faroqui .U.M & Joshi V.S: Use of sewage as fertilizer in teak plantations - A case studies, *Proce. IV thjregional meeting of silviculturists. and research workers of central regions*. 26-28. 1995.

Ditri: 'Vegetation management for land treatment of municipal waste water. *Report Institute of Water Research*, EastLansing, Chicago. 1977.

Edgar J.G & Stewart H.T.L: Wastewater disposal and reclamation using Eucalyptus and other trees. *Inst. Assoc. on water pollution research paper* 12: 11, Melbourne, Australia. 1978.

Environmental Protection Agency. World Bank Standard, Pub: EPA. 1972.

Fernandez. B.P: Water quality of beach water in wastewater recycling project report. *Water Resources Authority*, Kingston, Jamaica. 2004.

Forest Survey of India, *The State of Forests Report*. Ministry of Environment and Forestry. Government of India. 1987.

Gogate, M.G, Farooqui. V.M & Joshi ,V.S: Sewage water as potential fir the tree growth - A study on teak (Tectona grandis) Plantation . *Indian Forester:* 472-481 1995.

Hammer, D. A. (ed.): Constructed Wetlands for Wastewater Treatment: Municipal, Industrial.and Agricultural. Lewis Publishers, Chelsea. MI. : 831. 1989.

Hammer. D.A. and R.K. Bastian: Wetlands ecosystems : Natural water purifiers. 5-20 pp. In *Constructed wetlands for wastewater treatment.* Lewis publishers, Chelsea, Michigan 1989.

House, C.H: Engineered Environments: Mimicking Nature to Clean Our Waters. Waterwise. N. C. Sea Grant College Program. 3, (1). 1995.

House, C. H., S.W. Broome and M. T. Hoover: Constructed Upland-Wetland wastewater treatment system efficacy, 346-354 pp. *In: Proceedings of the Sixth National Symposium on Individual and Small Community Sewage Systems.* Held in Chicago, Illinois on December 16-17, 1991. American Society of Agricultural Engineers, St. Josephs. Michigan. 1991.

Joshi, V.S & Farooqui V.M.: Irrigated teak plantation in Maharastra - A case study International Teak Symposium: Thiruvanantahpuram, Kerala. 1991.

Jensen, M. E., Burman, R. D., and Alien, R. G. (ed): *Evapotranspiration and Irrigation Water Requirements.* ASCE Manuals and Reports on Engineering Practices: New York, NY, No. 70: 360. 1990.

Kumaran. K.: Selection of specio-genotypes in neem for high growth oil and azadiractin. Ph.D thesis. TNAU, Mettupalayam. 1991.

Kiunaran. K. C. Surendran and M.Palani: Effect of presowing treatments on germination and seedling growth in neem (*Azadiracta indica* A. Juss) *Indian Jr. of Forest* : 87 - 88. 1996.

Manivanan R. and S.K. Das: Phytoremidiation of textile effluent by forest trees *(Acacia ferruginea* and *Delonix regia Indian Jr. Environ & Ecoplan*, 6(2):213-218. 2002.

Manivanan R.: Recycling of raw and treated textile effluent by forest tree species *viz. Acacia ferruginea and Delonix regia.* Environmental Biotechnology/edited by Arvind Kumar.

Manonmani K., Chitrarasu., and K. Swaminathan: Effect of alcohol and chemical industry effluent on physico- chemical and biological properties of soil. *Poll Res*, 9: 95-105. 1990.

Metcalf and Eddy. Inc Wastewater Engineering: Treatment, Disposal and Reuse. McGraw Hill, New York, 815 1991.

Ministry of Agriculture 1996-97: *Land use statistics at a Glance*, GOI. 2000.

Ministry of Agriculture: *Agricultural Statistics at a Glance.* Government of India, New Delhi. 1995.

Ministry of Food and Agriculture: *A Report on National Forest Policy* GOI, New Delhi. 1952.

Ministry of Health and Family Welfare: CBHI, *Health Information of India*, 1991. GOI, New Delhi. 1992.

Ministry of Industry: 1994. Handbook of Industrial Statistics. Office of Economic Advisor, New Delhi. 1993

Ministry of Water Resources: Status of water resources in India. GOI, New Delhi 2003.

Monteith, J. L.: Principles of Environmental Physics. Edward Arnold, London. 1973.

Monteith, J. L. and Unsworth, M. H.: Principles of Environmental Physics, 2nd ed. Edward Arnold, London. 1990.

Neary D.G, Schneicker.G and D.P. White: Boron toxicity in red pine following municipal waste water irrigation, *Soil Sci.Soc. Amer. Proc.* 39:981-982. 1975.

Neelay V.R. and Dhondized L.P.: Observation on the possibility of using industrial effluent water for raising forest plantation. *Jr. Trop.For.* 2: 131-139. 1985.

Neelam S.R.: Effect of distillaryeffluent on the growth behaviour nitrogen content and nitrogen uptake of vigna radiata L, *Jr. Indian. Bot. Soc.* 65: 93. 1986.

Odum E.L: Basic Ecology Holt- Saunders Intl. Ed. Japan 1983.

Patrik. R.: The role of aquatic pplants in aquatic ecosystems in Biological Control of Water Pollution (Eds: Jourbier . J and Pierson Jr., R.W): 53-59. 1976.

Perttu K.L.: Biomass production and nutrient removal from municipal waste using willow vegetations filters, *Jr. of Sus. For.* 1(3): 57-70. 1993.

Pescod M. B.: Wastewater treatment and use in Agriculture, irrigation and drainage paper 47, Food and Agriculture Organisations of the United Nations. 1992.

Planning Commission: 1st Five Year Plan. GOI, New Delhi. 1951.

Planning Commission: 8th Five Year Plan. GOI. New Delhi. 1992.

Planning Commission: 9th Five Year Plan. GOI. New Delhi. 1997.

Penman. H. L.: Natural evaporation from open water, bare soil and grass: *Proc. Roy. Soc. London*, A193, 120-146. 1948.

Penman, H. L.: *Vegetation and Hydrology*. Tech. Comm. No. 53, Commonwealth Bureau of Soils. Harpenden, England. 125. 1963.

Pereira, L. S.. Perrier, A. Alien, R. G. and Alves: I. Evapotranspiration: Review of concepts and future trends. *J. Irrig. and Drain.*, ASCE25. 1996.

Rayol Commision on Environmental Pollution. Environmental Report 1992.

Registrar General. Government of India. Census of India, 1991. New Delhi. 1991.

Rajannan, G & Oblisami: G. Effect of distillery effluent on soil and crop plants: *Indian . Jr . Environ.Health.* 1: 173-177. 1979.

Ramakrishnana: Biostatistics , Pub: Saras Publication, New Delhi. 1995,

Rijtema, P. E.: Analysis of actual evapotranspiration. *Agric. Res. Rep. No. 69*, Centre for Agric. Publ. and Doc. Wageningen. 1965.

Sooper, W.E & Kardos. L.T.: Vegetation response to irrigation with treated municipal wastewater. In: *Recycling treated municipal wastewater and sludge through forest and cropland* W.E. Scooper & L.T. Kardos, (eds). The Pennsylvania State University Press. University Park, Pennsylvania, 16802: 271-294. 1973.

Stewart. H.T.L., E.Allender, P.Sandell, and P.Kube: Irrigation of tree plantations with recycled water in Australia: Research developments and case studies. Pages 431-441 In Cole, D.W., C.L.Henry, and W.L.Nutter (Eds). The forest alternative for treatment and utilization of municipal and industrial wastes. University of Washington Press: Seattle, Washington. 1986.

Swaminathan, K, Arjunan. J and Gurusamy, R.: Effect of glucose factory effluents on seed germination and seedling development of groundnut. In : *Proce. of 10 th Session of AEB and symposium on Environ. Impact on Biosystems* : 81-87. 1990.

Swaminathan, K. & Vaitheeswaran P.: Effect of dyeing factory effluent on seed germination and seeding development of groundnut (*Arachis hypogea*), *Jr. Enviro, Biol.*, 12(4): 353-358. 1991.

Swaminathan, K, Manonmani K & Sarojini: Studies on the toxicity of South India Viscose factory effluent on groundnut (*Arachis hypogea*), *Jr.Enviro, Biol.*, 13(4): 253-260. 1992.

Tata Energy Research Institute (TERI), *TERI Energy Database and Directory Yearbook (TEDDY)*, 1996-96. New Delhi. 2001.

Tomer MD. Schipper LA, Knowles SF. Rijkse WC, McMahon SD, Thron A, Charleson: A land-based system for wastewater treatment at Whakarewarewa Forest New Zealand: Characterisation of soil, plant, groundwater, and wetland components. *New Zealand Forest Research Institute Ltd. Bulletin 199,* Rotorua 1997.

United Nations Food and Agriculture Organization: Forestry Statistics: Looking for Tomorrow. FAO, Rome 1993.

USEPA: Cincinnati. Ohio. USA. 1983. Vimal. O.P & Talashilkar, Recycling of sewage waste in agriculture prospects and problems, *J.Sci, Ind, Res,* 14: 126-142. 1985.

USEPA: Proceses Design Manual: Guideline for Water Recycling Cincinnati, Ohio, (Report No. EPA-625/ R-92-004) USEPA, 1988. Design Manual: Constructed Wetlands and Aquatic Plant Systems for Municipal Wastewater Treatment. EPA/625/1-88/022. U.S. Environmental Protection Agency, Office of Research and Development, Washington, DC: 83. 1992.

U.S. Environmental Protection Agency: Inventory of U.S. Greenhouse Gas Emissions and Sinks: 1990 - 1997, (EPA 236-R-99-003) 1999.

U.S. Environmental Protection Agency: Sample preservation, pp.xv-xx. In Methods for Chemical Analysis of Water and Wastes. EPA-600/4-79-020.

Wildlife Institute of India: Biodiversity and Its Conservation in India. Dehradun. 1993.

World Bank: *India's Environment*. 1996.

World Resources Institute: *World Resources,* 1994/95.

— — —

Index

A

B

C

D

U

V

W

XYZ

— — —

Kolibri 360 GmbH
Ferdinand-Jühlke-Straße 7
99095 Erfurt, Deutschland
produktsicherheit@kolibri360.de